Persia: An Archaeological Guide

Persia:
An Archaeological Guide

SYLVIA A. MATHESON

FABER AND FABER LIMITED
London · Boston

First published in 1972
by Faber and Faber Limited
3 Queen Square, London WC1
Second edition, revised, 1976
Reprinted 1979
Printed in Great Britain
by Ebenezer Baylis and Son Limited
The Trinity Press, Worcester, and London
All rights reserved

ISBN 0 571 04888 9

Contents

Illustrations

FIGURES

*1

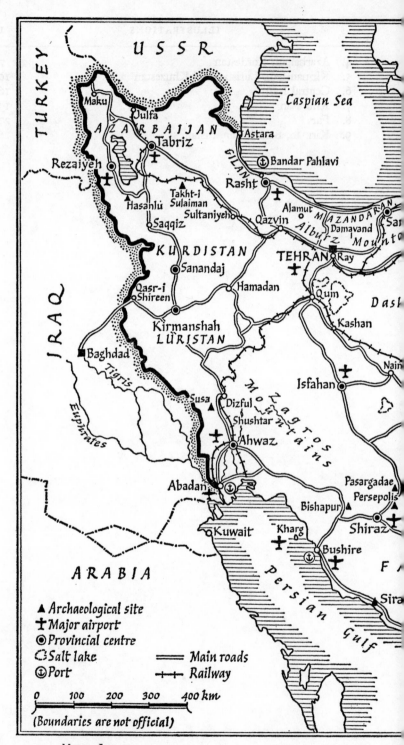

USSR

TURKEY

Caspian Sea

Maku

Julfa

AZARBAIJAN

Astara

GILAN

Bandar Pahlavi

Tabriz

Rezaiyeh

Rasht

Hasanlu

Takht-i
Sulaiman

Sultaniyeho

Alamut

MAZANDARAN

Damavand

Saqqiz

Qazvin

Sar

Alburz Mounta

KURDISTAN

TEHRAN

Ray

Sanandaj

Hamadan

Qum

Dash

Qasr-i
Shireen

Kashan

Kirmanshah

LURISTAN

IRAQ

Zagros

Baghdad

Tigris

Susa

Dizful

Mountains

Nain

Shushtar

Isfahan

Euphrates

Ahwaz

Abadan

Pasargadae

Persepolis

Bishapur

Shiraz

Kuwait

Kharg

ARABIA

Bushire

F

Persian

Sira

▲ Archaeological site
✝ Major airport
◎ Provincial centre
☾ Salt lake
⚓ Port

Main roads

+++ Railway

Gulf

0   100   200   300   400 km

(Boundaries are not official)

Map 1. Iran

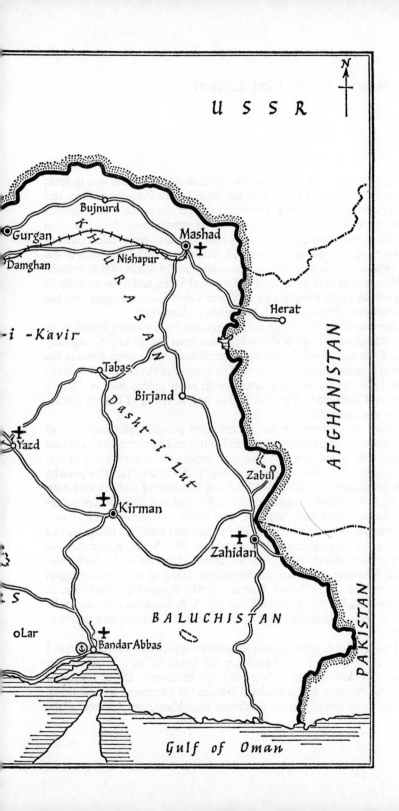

Foreword to the First Edition

There are said to be something like 250,000 archaeological sites in Iran; there are almost a thousand in the plain before Persepolis alone, and more are constantly being discovered all over the country. It is obvious that in a volume this size one cannot even mention more than a fraction of the sites by name, and the policy therefore has been to select those of greatest significance or where there is still something for the visitor to see.

Most archaeological sites are mentioned in the works of that redoubtable explorer and archaeologist, Sir Aurel Stein, and more recently in the Bibliography compiled by Professor Louis Vanden Berghe who has himself contributed so much to Iranian archaeology.

Because of the size of the country and the extraordinary wealth of its monuments, the scope of this volume has been limited to covering early sites from the known beginnings of prehistoric settlements down to the effective end of Saljuq rule, in the first quarter of the thirteenth century A.D. Later monuments are described in other guides such as Nagel's *Iran* and Hachette's *The Middle East* and in these, of course, further maps can be found.

I have endeavoured to include the latest possible information on all excavations currently in progress and to this end have received assistance from so many quarters that it is, alas, impossible to name every individual here. I must, however, acknowledge publicly the courtesy shown by His Excellency Mr. Mehrdad Pahlbod, Minister of Culture and Arts, to whose organization (particularly in Mashad and Shiraz) I am indebted for assistance with transport. The Director-General of the Iranian Archaeological Service, Mr. A. Pourmand, and members of the Service have given ungrudging help and advice: Mr. S. M. Khorramabadi, Deputy Director-General, Mr. A. Hakemi, Director of the Archaeological Museum, Professor E. Negahban, Head of the Archaeological Department of the Tehran University, Mr. Kambakhsh Fard, Mr. Z. Rahmatian, Dr. M. Y. Kiyani and Mr. A. A. Sarfaraz, have especially added their help to that of all the excavation Directors now active in Iran.

I cannot fail to mention also the active support and encouragement I have received from His Excellency Sir Denis Wright, formerly Her Majesty's Ambassador to Iran, and His Excellency Dr. Manouchehr Eqbal, Chairman of the National Iranian Oil Company, who with Mr. C. A. E. O'Brien, former Chairman and Managing Director of the

Iranian Oil Operating Companies, made possible several tours of Khuzestan and Kharg Island; His Excellency Dr. Ghazzem Rezai, formerly Director-General of the Iranian National Tourist Organization, and his former Deputy Director, Dr. Reza Sadoughi, were equally kind in providing information and enabling me on occasion to camp out in Tourist Inns which had not been completed at the time of my visits.

The Directors and staff of the archaeological missions permanently in Tehran have been more than generous with their time, information and material, in particular, Professor H. Luschey and Professor W. Kleiss of the German Archaeological Institute, who provided a number of original illustrations, Professor Roman Ghirshman, doyen of foreign archaeologists in Iran and for over thirty years Director of the French Archaeological Mission; the present Director, Mr. Jean Perrot, and Mr. Audran Labrousse who drew the plan of Susa; Professor Giuseppe Tucci, President of IsMEO in Rome, and Dr. Maurizio Tosi, Director of the current excavations in Sistan; and Dr. William Sumner of the American Institute of Iranian Studies, who has given valuable assistance with the bibliography. I would also thank Mrs. Helen Potamianos for so kindly checking a number of last-minute queries.

Most of all, however, I am indebted to Mr. David Stronach, Director of the British Institute of Persian Studies, to whom I have constantly referred and without whose guidance and frequent collaboration I could never have undertaken this task. Together with Mr. Robert Hillenbrand, a Fellow of the B.I.P.S., and Dr. Klaus Schippmann, Mr. Stronach has read the entire manuscript.

Other members of the British Institute have also assisted in many ways, particularly Miss Romayne Dawney who has drawn most of the maps, Mr. Antony Hutt, former Assistant Director, whose researches into early minarets in Iran have enabled me to include some hitherto unpublished material which he has kindly made available to me, and Dr. Georgina Herrmann, Joint Editor of *Iran*, for further information on bas-reliefs.

The late Professor Arthur Upham Pope before his death in 1969 generously gave me permission to make use of material from his *Persian Architecture*, while Professor Richard Frye, who succeeded him as Director of the Asia Institute in Shiraz, has allowed me to use his genealogical tables and informative historical maps.

Professor Robert H. Dyson, Jr., Professor Edith Porada and Professor Louis Vanden Berghe are among the many others whose names are mentioned in the text and who have so kindly allowed me to use much of their published material.

The final responsibility for any errors, of course, remains entirely my own.

Foreword to the Second Edition

Less than eighteen months had elapsed since the publication of this Guide, when I was asked to prepare a revised second edition, but even in that short period, tremendous changes have taken place in Iran. Hotel accommodation and air and land communications throughout the country have been greatly expanded, entirely new roads often superseding old ones; continuing developments in existing archaeological excavations, and many newly discovered sites have in some cases completely changed existing theories.

Some sections such as Siraf, Ganj Dareh and Chogha Mish have been rewritten, others, such as Susa and Persepolis, expanded, while entirely new excavations at Shahdad, Sagzabad and elsewhere, appear in the appendix and are indicated in the text by an asterisk*. Many new plans and photographs will, I hope, make this edition even more useful to the visitor interested in archaeology. However, with the rapid progress being made in Iran it is almost certain that even further changes will have taken place by the time this is in the reader's hands, and I cannot urge too strongly that routes and accommodation should be checked in Tehran before leaving for any extended journey. The Ministry of Information and Tourism, and the various archaeological institutions listed, should be able to give the latest information.

So much archaeological work is taking place in Iran that there are inevitably some sites of little visual impact omitted from the Guide and my apologies are due to those whose work has not been mentioned. A subscription to *Iran*, the annual publication of the British Institute of Persian Studies, will help keep readers informed of the work of Iranian and International archaeologists, while similar publications of the French, German and Italian Institutes give further invaluable information in those languages.

In 1974, the Archaeological Service of Iran was reorganized into four separate departments under the general direction of Dr. Firouz Bagherzadeh, and the official title of these are as follows:

The Iranian Centre for Archaeological Research.
The National Centre for Research on Anthropology and Folklore.
General Administration for the Protection of Monuments and Sites.
General Direction of Museums.

For the sake of brevity in the text, the first-named is generally referred to as the Iranian Archaeological Service.

The Archaeological Museum in Tehran will be completely re-organized when the current structural alterations are complete, and the whole of the original Museum building will be devoted to pre-Islamic material. Islamic exhibits will be displayed in the newer building next door. It has therefore not been feasible to change the descriptions of the arrangement of exhibits, but it is hoped that in due course the Museum itself will publish a guide in a European language.

The Iranian National Tourist Organization (I.N.T.O.), has also changed its title, and is now the Ministry of Information and Tourism; again, for brevity in the text, it is usually referred to as the Tourist Organization. The Iranian Oil Operating Companies (I.O.O.C.), has been renamed the Oil Service Company of Iran (Private), shortened to O.S.C.O. I am indebted to all the above organizations for their continuing interest.

With very few exceptions I have visited every site personally, often several times, and in preparing this new edition I am happy to acknowledge the ungrudging and invaluable assistance and co-operation given me by the archaeological institutes and directors of excavations both in Tehran and abroad, and by many fellow enthusiasts who have kindly brought changed travel conditions to my attention. However, be warned that extensive town planning throughout Iran is resulting in constant alterations both in street plans and even names, while restaurants are particularly liable to change in quality. Although I have suggested certain hotels in small provincial towns, this does not mean they are necessarily of a high standard, but only that they are the best available, which is often fairly primitive.

As elsewhere in the world, prices are rising rapidly and though I have updated (to 1974) those quoted in the text they should be taken only as a guide.

As in the case of many other authors, I too have had the dubious honour of having my work reproduced in Tehran in a cheap photocopied edition from which many pages are usually missing, and also translated into Persian, both without permission or payment. It is hoped that a new Iranian law relating to copyright and passed in 1974 will offer effective protection for this and future works.

Tehran, 1975.

Notes on Travel

Iran is about three times the size of France and offers almost every conceivable kind of scenery and climatic conditions. Generally speaking the best season to visit is autumn. Summer can be extremely torrid in the south, with considerable humidity on the Persian Gulf and by the shores of the Caspian Sea in the north. Spring brings floods, particularly in Azarbaijan, while winter lingers for some time in areas like Azarbaijan and Khurasan, snow and blizzards often cutting communications completely. In the south the winter weather is pleasant. One should, whenever possible, avoid visiting Iran during the movable religious festivals of Ramadan and Muharram, and exercise discretion both in dress and times of visiting mosques, preferably not on Fridays or during services (11 a.m.–12.30 p.m. and about 5.30–6 p.m.).

Communications have improved tremendously in recent years and new roads and air routes are being opened all the time. But there are still many areas of particular interest to archaeologists where travel requires considerable advance organization. Anyone contemplating journeys off the normal routes is strongly advised to seek up-to-date information from the helpful Ministry of Information and Tourism offices found in all major towns, or at the local Ministry of Culture and Arts offices.

There is a lack of reliable detailed touring maps of Iran but one can manage most trips with the use of both the official map published by the Tourist Organization and another produced by the Oil Service Company of Iran. In addition, a series of good maps with detailed physical features but not all the roads, is published by D Survey of War Office and Air Ministry, 1962, and obtainable from Edward Stanford Ltd., 12 Long Acre, London, WC2E 9OP. There is also a very good set of four maps covering the whole country in some detail, prepared by the Plan Organization for the Imperial Government of Iran at the National Cartographic Center, published in 1968 and obtainable from the N.C.C. office, P.O.B. 1844, Mehrabad, Tehran, price 50 rials each but sold only in sets; postage extra.

Accommodation in Tehran and other big cities varies from *de luxe* hotels of international standard, like the Royal Tehran Hilton, to modest pensions. Travel agents can supply full details. In smaller towns there are only unpretentious, inexpensive hotels where beds are often three or four to a room, and the plumbing leaves much to be desired.

Although chai khanehs (tea houses) in larger villages sometimes have arrangements for travellers using their own bedding on wooden platforms in communal rooms, there is often no public accommodation at all. Camping in isolated areas is inadvisable, unless in a large, well-organized party.

The Government Tourist Accommodation Corporation (T.A.C.), however, has already built a large number of Tourist Inns providing a standard type of clean, modern and reasonably priced but limited accommodation usually with quite reasonable restaurants. Several Tourist Camps, with large Continental-type tents, proper beds and washing and cooking facilities, have also been opened and these, together with the Tourist Inns already available, are listed separately (p. 22).

Popular holiday places such as Shiraz, Isfahan, and the Caspian resorts, during special festivities such as the Iranian New Year (mid-March to the end of March) or the International Festival of Arts in Shiraz (August-September), are usually fully booked for months in advance.

Travel on the limited rail network is comfortable; the Company hires bedding for first- and second-class passengers for 50 rials, and restaurant cars are attached to most lines. Long-distance buses are less expensive and usually quicker, with reliable timetables. The leading companies are listed separately (p. 21). Local buses are more antiquated and tend to start only when full.

Iranair, the national airline, serves an increasing number of towns at moderate charge, and private cars may be hired from many firms including the international companies, Hertz and Avis. The many travel agencies in existence can arrange guided tours.

Taxis within city limits are cheap, in Tehran charging by meter, in other cities usually making a fixed charge for any distance, 10 rials or even less. There are also Service Taxis (Keriyehs) carrying passengers on designated routes at fixed low prices. Some knowledge of Persian is an advantage and recognition of the Persian numerals advisable since taximeters show the charges in Persian characters.

The Persian language is written in a modified version of the Arabic alphabet and a number of phrase books and grammars are now on sale.

Most large towns have a Government handicraft shop (Tehran has two), with a constantly changing variety of handicrafts from all parts of the country, made under Government supervision. Picturesque Zurkhanehs (where gymnasts in colourful kneebreeches perform traditional exercises with unusual equipment, reminders of the Arab invasion) are also found in many towns. The most sophisticated are probably those in Tehran, including the Zurkhaneh Jafari in Kh. Varzesh, with performances open to the public daily (except Fridays), at about 5.30 p.m.

Most prices quoted in the text applied at the time of writing (1975) and should therefore serve only as a rough guide. The 1975 rate of exchange is 66 rials = $1; 146 rials = £1. 10 rials = 1 touman and prices are often quoted in toumans. Notes start at 20 rials (2 toumans).

Larger towns have reliable chemists, usually one or more of them open for 24 hours and selling recognized patent medicines. Doctors, dentists and hospitals are good but very expensive.

Outside Tehran and the major cities where the big hotels and many restaurants serve an international cuisine, food and drink lacks variety. The standard meal is chelo-kebab—cooked rice (some of the best in the world comes from Iran) and barbecued lamb or chicken, with soft drinks and tea without milk as the standard accompaniment, together with ab-dough, a refreshing mixture of mast (yoghourt) and mineral water.

With few exceptions one can buy alcoholic drinks, imported and local whiskies, brandies, etc. (the imported brands are very expensive); local vodkas, especially the best varieties, are excellent, and there are some very drinkable, inexpensive local wines.

There is a large variety of superb fruit, melons, vegetables, etc. The fish from the Caspian and the enormous prawns from the Persian Gulf are outstanding. Confectioners offer a splendid selection of tempting pastries, biscuits, chocolates and sweetmeats.

In Tehran there are several supermarkets where practically all necessities and delicacies can be purchased. Western-style bread is called 'Nan-i Feranghi' but there are many different, very delicious types of Iranian unleavened bread which can be seen at bakers' shops in every town, and usually cost about 5 rials per large piece. They are especially tasty when still warm. Iran's speciality, caviar, is a Government monopoly and should be purchased only at authorized stores. The current official price for half a kilo of best quality caviar is 2,500 rials.

Shops, including covered bazaars, usually open about 8 a.m. until about 1 p.m. and again from about 3.30 to 7 or 8 p.m. Almost all of them close on Fridays, the Muslim holy day; the weekend is Thursday and Friday. Museums in most towns are closed on Mondays. Remember, it is strictly forbidden to take any archaeological material out of the country without a permit.

An unusual combination of unofficial museum and Persian restaurant is the Ab-Anbar in Kh. Cyrus, Tehran, included on Ministry of Information and Tourism city tours. Finally one should mention the spectacular Shahyad monument just outside Tehran's Mehrabad airport, built for the 25th Centennial Celebrations in 1971. The basement houses an interesting light and sound display of Iranian history and a small museum exhibiting some fine archaeological pieces.

Useful Addresses

The American Institute of Iranian Studies, 9 Khiaban-i Moshtaq.

The Austrian Cultural Office, 276 Khiaban Villa.

The British Institute of Persian Studies, Kh. Kurosh-e Kabir, Gulhak. Tel. 264901.

The French Cultural Institute, Heshmat Dowleh.

The German Archaeological Institute, (D.A.I.), Kouche 32, Khiaban Vozara, Abbasabad.

The Institute of Archaeology of Tehran University, 3188 Upper Khiaban Pahlavi (Corner of Khiaban Pesian).

The Italian Cultural Institute, 11 Kouche Hartef, Khiaban Hafiz.

The Japanese Institute for West Asian Studies, 20 Kouche Panahi, Khiaban Villa, Shumali.

The Ministry of Information and Tourism,
head office, 174 Boulevard Elizabeth.
This also has information counters in all airports, and offices in most large towns and at the border posts of Khosravi, Bazargan, Zahidan and Tayabad.

For tourist information in London, consult the Ministry of Tourism representative at the Imperial Iranian Embassy, 16 Prince's Gate, London, SW7 1PX (Tel. 01-937-5225); in Paris the Ministry representative at the Maison de l'Iran, 65 Champs-Elysées, Paris 8 (Tel. 2256290); in U.S.A., 630 Fifth Avenue, New York, N.Y. 10020; in West Germany, 6 Frankfurt Main, Grosse Bockenheimer Str. 32, and elsewhere abroad, the appropriate Imperial Iranian Embassy.

The British Council Library,
main branch, 38 and 58 Khiaban Ferdowsi.
Branches also in Isfahan, Mashad, Shiraz and Tabriz.

Major long-distance auto-bus services include T.B.T. (which also goes to Munich), 164 Kh. Fisherabad, and Levantour, Maidan-i Ferdowsi.

T.A.C. (Tourist Accommodation Corporation) accommodation, 1974.
12 Khiaban Ghadesi, Boulevard Elizabeth.
Reservations, Tel. 636299, 636612, 638683.

TOURIST CAMPS
Bandar Pahlavi, Chalus, Isfahan, Mashad, Persepolis, Shiraz, Tabriz,
Tehran, Zahidan.

T.A.C. HOTELS
Cyrus (Shiraz)
Darius (Persepolis)
Shemshak (Alburz Mountains)

TOURIST INNS

Ardabil	Lahijan	Rafsanjan
Astara	Mahabad	Rezaiyeh
Bam	Maku	Sari
Behbehan	Malayer	Semnan
Birjand	Marand	Shahabad-Gharb
Bushehr	Mianeh	Shahreza
Chahbahar	Mirjaveh	Shahrud
Darab	Nain	Shemshak
Estahbanat	Natanz	Shiraz
Fasa	Niriz	Shush (Susa)
Gunabad	Nishapur	Shushtar
Ilam	Nosratabad	Sirjan
Jahrom	Qaen	Tabas
Khoi	Qasr-i Shireen	Tabriz
Khonsar	Qazvin	Tayabad
Khorramabad	Quchan	Zahidan

(Others are under construction.)

Historical Survey

Iran, which today is about three times as large as France, takes its name from the Aryans, an Indo-European nomadic people originally from Central Asia, who in several migrations entered the high plateau in the second millennium B.C. It was the Greeks who applied the name of Persia to the land, taking it from Persis or Fars, the south-western province which was the homeland of the Achaemenians. Scholars are apt to think of the present country as Persia and of Iran as being the much larger territory of the past, which included part of the Caucasus, Central Asia, Afghanistan and Iraq, all of which were Iranian or partly Iranian in language and culture.

Some of the most ancient open settlements in the world have been found in Iran, dating from 8000 B.C. or earlier, but little is known of the origins of their inhabitants. Later civilizations such as the Akkadians, the Urartians in north-western Iran, and the Elamites in Khuzestan, have left monumental traces of their cities and conquests, often depicted in vivid bas-reliefs carved into the cliffs overlooking the country's ancient highways, and in written records.

The history of Iran, however, properly begins with the rise of the Medes in the western and northern parts of the Plateau from at least the eighth century B.C. onwards. The royal houses of the Medes and the Persians, both of Indo-European stock, were united when the daughter of the Median King Astyages married Cambyses I, son of Cyrus I, king of Fars. Cyrus II (The Great), the offspring of this marriage, defeated his grandfather, Astyages, in battle c. 550 B.C., re-affirmed the fortunes of the Achaemenian dynasty and established his new empire with capitals in at least Pasargadae (Fars), Babylon and Ecbatana, present-day Hamadan.

The later Achaemenians combined the worship of Ahura Mazda, 'the wise lord' of the prophet Zoroaster, with the worship of Mithras and that of Anahita, goddess of water and fertility.

Cyrus, whose conquests ranged from Central Asia to the Mediterranean, treated his vanquished enemies with a generosity and tolerance remarkable for his time. It was he who liberated the Jewish exiles in Babylon and restored Jerusalem to them. His successors, particularly Darius the Great and his son Xerxes (who defeated the Spartans at

Thermopylae and incurred the lasting hatred of the Greeks by burning the Acropolis in Athens), continued the expansion of the empire which included many of the Greek islands; it reached north to the banks of the Danube, south to Egypt and Ethiopia, and north and east to Afghanistan and India. The most outstanding monument of the Achaemenians existing today is the magnificent ceremonial city of Persepolis, near Shiraz, built by paid, not slave labour as was the custom among other nations at the time.

The Achaemenians influenced the protocol and arts of the Indian Maurya dynasty under Asoka; they were the first to achieve Iranian unity and a fusion of peoples and culture; they developed agriculture, particularly the underground irrigation system of qanuts, encouraged the arts and sciences, especially astronomy, established a precise system of weights and measures and coinage, including private banks with current accounts, cheques, loans, deposits and capital investments; and they developed a magnificent system of roads as well as a merchant navy.

It was Alexander of Macedon who defeated the last of the Achaemenians, Darius III Codamanus, in 331–30 B.C., and burnt Persepolis, some say in revenge for the destruction of the Acropolis. Alexander, who married Darius' daughter, died only a few years later and his empire was divided between his generals, Seleucus I ultimately winning Iran and founding the Hellenistic dynasty of the Seleucids, with a new capital at Ctesiphon on the Tigris. Greek settlements and temples were established in Iran but the dynasty was soon challenged by the Arsacid Parthians, an Iranian people from the north-east, who first achieved a measure of permanent control of the Iranian plateau c. 238 B.C.

During their nearly 500 years of power, the Parthians clashed with the Romans in the west and with nomadic Scythian tribes—the Sacas— from Chinese Turkestan in the east, but established trade with countries as far apart as China and Italy. Pahlavi became the national language, and these once nomadic horsemen introduced many features of knighthood and chivalry to the west, including jousting and coats of arms. Their most notable contribution to architecture was the invention of the 'ivan', a vaulted hall open on the fourth side.

The last of the Parthians, Artabanus V, fell in battle in A.D. 224 with a vassal, Ardashir I, ruler of Fars and Kirman, who claimed descent from the Achaemenians. Ardashir founded the great dynasty of the Sassanians during whose 400-year rule the country became wealthier than ever before, with an efficient administration in which heavy taxes supported a social welfare system including state hospitals, schools and colleges.

Town planning, irrigation and industrialization were carried out on a lavish scale; the empire was expanded; Ardashir and his son Shahpur I defeated Roman emperors such as Valerian, Philip the Arab and Gordian III, carrying many to captivity with thousands of prisoners. When Shahpur was crowned in A.D. 242 he inherited an empire stretching from the Euphrates to Merv and the Punjab, including Herat and Sistan. The cult of Mithras was probably taken to the west by released Roman prisoners.

Many of the Sassanian victories are commemorated in huge bas-reliefs, mostly in the province of Fars. Christian communities were established in Iran, but the official religion was that of Zoroaster. The magnificence and ceremonial of Sassanian court life influenced the later European courts, while the excellence of Sassanian architecture, sculpture, textiles and metal work left an unmistakable and lasting impression on the culture of the west.

Most vital of all, perhaps, the Sassanian empire formed a protective barrier between the ruthless nomadic tribes of Central Asia and western civilization.

The Sassanians succumbed to the invasion of the Umayyad Caliphs, desert Arabs who brought with them a new, austere religion, that of Islam, when they invaded Iran and defeated Yazdigird III in the years after 637 A.D. Pockets of Sassanian resistance were to remain around the southern shores of the Caspian Sea for some further 200 years and the old Pahlavi script was still in use as late as the eleventh century. Even to-day there is still a minority section of the population which follows the old Zoroastrian faith although many Iranians left Iran for India, where they founded the important Parsee community; the majority however, adopted the new faith of Islam.

(Today most Iranian Muslims follow the Shi'ite sect of Islam, supporting the claim of Ali, cousin and son-in-law to the Prophet Mohammad, as successor to the founder of the religion.)

Iranian customs and dress however, were to become fashionable in the courts of the Abbasid Caliphs who established the Shi'ite supremacy in the middle of the eighth century A.D. and who remained in power for over 500 years. During this time many local dynasties still ruled various small kingdoms in Iran and among the most important of these were the Buyids (or Dailamites) who rose to power in northern Iran in the tenth century, and the Ghaznavids who ruled from the east at the same period. Between c. A.D. 1040 and 1055 both dynasties were defeated by the Saljuqs, a Turkish-speaking tribe of Irano-Turkish stock established in Turkistan.

The Saljuqs established an empire which extended from China to Syria and from the River Oxus to Arabia, and were responsible for some notable architectural monuments. Their tomb towers were particularly striking, and like their mosques and colleges were remarkable for their elaborate, ornamental brickwork and stucco decoration. During this period too, the arts, including literature, astronomy, ceramics, the sciences and medicine, all flourished. Saljuq power, however, effectively came to an end with the first Mongol invasion from the east, under Chinghis Khan in A.D. 1218. A second Mongol invasion took place between 1251 and 1256 when Chinghis Khan's grandson, Hulagu, destroyed the power of the notorious Assassin sect in their mountain fortresses in north and eastern Iran, together with that of the Caliphate in Baghdad. They left such devastation behind them that many of Iran's great, historic cities were virtually wiped from the face of the earth although afterwards the Mongols themselves constructed some of the outstanding religious monuments found in Iran today.

In the fourteenth century, Tamurlane, another conqueror from Central Asia, put an end to Mongol rule and established the Timurid dynasty under which, for a time, literature and the arts were once again to flower.

The rise of the Turkoman Qara Qoyunlu tribes in the west in the first half of the fifteenth century, followed by that of the Ottoman Turks, resulted in much confusion and rivalry which was only finally resolved when the spectacular Safavids came to power with the advent of Shah Ismail who was crowned in 1501. Of the Safavid dynasty the remarkable sixteenth century ruler Shah Abbas the Great is best known to the west. He not only consolidated his kingdom, suppressing rebellions and recovering territories lost by his predecessors, but he built many hundreds of kilometres of roads with fine bridges and caravanserais. Besides improving communications, he beautified his splendid cities with mosques, bazaars, schools and parks, encouraged a renaissance of all the arts and attracted craftsmen, merchants and ambassadors from all parts of the world to his brilliant court.

After Shah Abbas's death the country was plunged into a series of wars once more, with the Uzbegs and Afghans in the east and with Russia and Turkey in the north and west. The last of the Safavids died in 1722 and a new conqueror, Nadir Quli, a brilliant military commander from a nomadic Khurasan family, seized power and was crowned in 1736. His assassination in 1747 was followed by a struggle for power from which Karim Khan, a chieftain of the Kurdish Zand tribe, emerged triumphant, making his capital at Shiraz. He died in 1779 and after a few years Agha Mohammad, leader of the powerful Qajar tribe, was proclaimed Shah in 1787.

The Qajars ruled Iran until 1925, a period during which a constitutional revolution led to the establishment of a House of Deputies in 1906. In 1909 the despotic Mohammad Ali Shah abdicated, and in

World War I, although Iran was neutral she was nevertheless entered by foreign armies, contributing to the disintegration of the country which was already crushed by corruption and heavy taxes. The last of the Qajars, Ahmad Shah, was formally deposed in 1925 and the following year the brilliant Commander-in-Chief, General Reza Khan, former Commander of the famous Persian Cossack Brigade, was crowned in Tehran, taking the ancient name of Pahlavi for his new dynasty.

Reza Shah, the Great, as he was justly called, virtually reshaped the nation's existence and in less than twenty years laid the foundations for a new stability and an unprecedented progress in every field of life. Economy was revived, notably with the exploitation of the immensely rich southern oil fields; roads and railway systems were inaugurated, hospitals and schools were built, and the emancipation of women was initiated by the example set by the Shah's own queen and daughters.

In 1941, the Shah abdicated in favour of his eldest son, Mohammed Reza Pahlavi, who declared his intention of ruling as a constitutional monarch on democratic lines. It was not until 1967 however, when he felt that a coronation ceremony was finally justified, that the Shahanshah, on whom the nation had bestowed the title Arya Mehr, 'Light (or Sun) of the Aryans', was crowned, together with his Queen, Empress Farah. The Shahanshah has undoubtedly given a personal lead in the tremendous strides taken by his country during his reign. Following his proclamation of the 'White Revolution', the Shahanshah Arya Mehr began in 1951 to distribute his personal lands among his peasant farmer tenants. He followed this over the years with a twelve-point plan which included the formation of various specialist corps in which young men and women spend a period of national service giving a primary education to illiterate villagers, teaching elementary hygiene, new methods of agriculture and small construction projects among many educational schemes, while newly graduated doctors and dentists manning mobile health clinics in remote areas, have vastly improved the general standard of the nation's health.

There is still much to be achieved in spite of the many other reforms that have been introduced, but the steady rise in the national income and standard of living is itself an impressive witness to progress in what is surely one of the most stable and forward-looking of all Middle East countries today.

Glossary

AB-ANBAR Underground water reservoir.

ABBASIDS Arab Caliphs of Baghdad (A.D. 750–1258).

ACHAEMENIANS Persian royal dynasty whose name derives from Achaemenes, first of the line, c. 700 B.C.

AHRIMAN Power of evil and darkness, twin to Ahura Mazda, the good spirit, with whom he is constantly at war.

AHURA MAZDA 'The Wise Lord', the 'great' god of the Achaemenians and creator of the physical world. The incarnation of goodness, and supreme deity; in the Zoroastrian religion, often represented as a human figure in profile rising from a winged ring.

AKKAD The city-state of Akkad, founded by Sargon, whose dynasty ruled Mesopotamia from 2470 to 2285 B.C.

AMBULATORY Passageway around a chamber.

ANAHITA 'The Immaculate', goddess of the waters and fertility and associated with warfare. Possibly partly identifiable with the Elamite-Babylonian goddess Nana, and with Artemis, Greek goddess of the moon and protectress of women.

ANATHYROSIS Technique of joining two stone surfaces.

ANNUBANINI King of the Lullubi, third millennium B.C., in the northern Zagros range.

ANSHAN The name given to an ancient city and country located in southern Iran east of Elam. The name disappears c. 500 B.C.

ANTHROPOMORPHIC In human form, applied here usually to pottery.

APADANA Large audience hall in Achaemenian palaces.

ARAMAIC A tongue indigenous to Syria and Phoenicia that became the lingua franca of the Achaemenian Empire.

ARSACIDS A name often given to members of the Parthian dynasty, c. 250 B.C.–A.D. 224, founded by Arsaces.

ASTODAN (Ossuary) Container or cavity in which were placed the defleshed bones of the dead, particularly Zoroastrians.

ATESHGAH, ATESHGADEH or ATESHKADEH Fire temple sheltering the sacred fire of the Zoroastrian religion, and entered only by priests.

AVESTA See Zend-Avesta.

BAD-GIR Wind tower, conducting a breeze to lower chambers in domestic or public buildings, mainly found in the hot central and southern regions of Iran.

BARREL VAULT Semicircular vault.

BARSOM Bundle of twigs tied together symbolizing vegetal life in Zoroastrian ceremonies; small metal sticks are used today.

BUYIDS Islamic dynasty of Persian descent, also known as Dailamites from their place of origin in the Alburz mountains south of the Caspian Sea. They controlled western Iran and Mesopotamia (c. A.D. 932–1056).

CELLA Inner sanctuary.

CHADOR Ankle-length veil worn by Iranian women, particularly when visiting shrines and mosques.

CHAHAR TAQ (Literally 'Four arches') Open-sided pavilion with four pillars supporting a domed roof. The sacred fire used in Zoroastrian ceremonies in the Sassanian period was displayed to the public in this building.

CHAI KHANEH Tea house.

CHALCOLITHIC Final phase of the Neolithic period or the phase of human development following the Neolithic. (See Neolithic.)

CUNEIFORM Wedge-shaped writing used in ancient Assyria, Persia, etc.

DAKHME Also known as 'Tower of Silence', usually a high wall on a hill top, inside which are exposed the corpses of Zoroastrians, a practice now giving place to conventional burial.

DIACONICON Chamber on the right of the altar in Orthodox churches, where the deacons' robes are kept and sometimes the Eucharist and Church treasure.

ELAM Ancient kingdom in what is now south-western Iran, including the plain of Susiana and the Bakhtiari Mountains. Conquered by Assurbanipal the Assyrian, c. 640 B.C.

ELAMITES A people of Asianic or 'Zagro-Elamite' origin thought by some to belong to the Caucasian peoples.

ELYMAIS The 'Eulaios' of the Greeks, a name given to Elam in Achaemenian Persia and also to an ill-defined kingdom of the Seleucid and Parthian period, in the mountains and valleys to the east of the River Karun.

GRIFFIN A composite monster with the features of an eagle and a lion.

GUTI A mountain tribe of Asianic or 'Zagro-Elamite' origin, in the central zone of the Zagros. They invaded Mesopotamia at the close of the third millennium B.C., putting an end to the Akkadian dynasty.

HAMAM Bath house.

HAOMA (Homa) Juice extracted from the leaves of the Ephedra plant and used in Zoroastrian religious ceremonies.

HEGIRA Islamic era reckoned from A.D. 622, date of the Prophet Mahommed's flight from Mecca to Medina.

HERAKLES (Hercules) Hero and god of Greek mythology and identified in Iran with Verethragna, later Bahram, a national hero; epitome of victory in battle.

ḤUSSEINIYEH A stage for the performance of religious plays presented during the Muslim mourning period of Muharram; usually an open platform with an enclosed courtyard attached to or near a mosque.

IBEX Mountain goat with long, curved and ridged horns.

IMAMZADEH Muslim shrine, usually the mausoleum of a descendant of one of the twelve Imams venerated by Shi'ite Muslims.

INANNA-ISHTAR The Sumerian goddess Inanna, patron goddess of Uruk, associated with fertility was also equated with the Akkadian Ishtar, goddess of procreation and battle and the principal astral deity.

INSHUSHINAK Supreme god in the Elamite pantheon to whom the ziggurat of Choga Zanbil, in present-day Khuzestan, was dedicated.

IVAN (or Iwan) Barrel-vaulted hall whose fourth side was open onto a courtyard.

JEMDAT NASR Mound in Iraq, c. 3100–2900 B.C., with characteristic polychrome pottery, wheel-turned with geometrical decorations of black, red or brown.

KASSITES An Asianic or 'Zagro-Elamite' people of the central Zagros area (present-day Luristan). They conquered Babylonia and retained power there from the sixteenth to the twelfth century B.C.

KHANEGAH Darvish monastery.

KHIABAN (Kh.) Avenue.

KORYMBOS The topknot of curls worn by Sassanian kings, usually wrapped in a light gauzy silk.

KOUCHE Street.

KUFIC Angular form of Islamic calligraphy used extensively in the first five centuries of Islam. There are eight different types of Kufic but all are distinguished by the accentuated vertical strokes.

KUSHANS A people of Iranian origin who ruled from the first to the third century A.D. over a vast empire, including Afghanistan, part of India and parts of Russian and Chinese Turkestan.

LULLUBI A mountain people of Asianic or 'Zagro-Elamite' stock, occupying a region in the northern Zagros range extending to Lake Rezaiyeh or further north.

MADRASSEH Theological college usually attached to a mosque.

MAIDAN Public square or plaza.

MASJID Mosque.

MASSAGETAE Confederation of nomadic hordes east of the Caspian, known to the ancient Greeks.

MAST Yoghourt.

MEDIA Ancient kingdom of western Iran whose capital was Ecbatana (present-day Hamadan).

MIHRAB The niche in the qibla wall of a mosque, facing Mecca, and to which the faithful face when praying. Often elaborately decorated.

MINARET (Minar) Literally 'tower', from which the call to prayer is made, and either attached to, or close by, a mosque.

MINBAR Pulpit, of wood or stone.

MITANNIANS People of Indo-European origin whose kingdom, Mitannia, was on the Euphrates in the second millennium B.C.

MITHRAS Persian god of light and the sun, of contracts, justice, prosperity and victory, and one of the three judges of the souls of the dead. Particularly prominent in the Mithraic cult brought by Roman soldiers to Europe.

MOUFFLON Wild sheep with large, almost circular horns.

MUD BRICK Bricks of sun-dried mud.

MUHARRAM Muslim month regarded as a period of mourning by the Shi'a sect, in commemoration of the martyrdom of Hussein at the battle of Kerbala.

MUSALLA An open-air oratory.

NAKHL Wooden structure seen in central Iran, carried in processions during Muharram.

NAMEH Writing, epistle or book.

NARAM-SIN King of the Akkadian dynasty, c. 2300 B.C., son of Sargon of Akkad.

NASKHI A cursive form of Arabic (Islamic) calligraphy, which gradually replaced Kufic from the eleventh century onward.

NEOLITHIC A stage of human development, after the Old Stone Age or Palaeolithic, and before the Chalcolithic when metal began to be used.

NESTORIAN Follower of the heretical doctrine of Nestorius, c. A.D. 380–440, who saw two complete persons in Christ, human and divine.

ORMUZD, ORMIZD Later form of the name of Ahura Mazda.

OSSUARY See Astodan.

PAHLAVI Language of ancient Persia under the Sassanians.

PALAEOLITHIC Period marked by the use of primitive stone implements.

PANNEAU Mantel.

PARNI (Parthians) Nomadic tribe of Iranian origin, one of whose chieftains, Arsaces, founded the Parthian dynasty.

PARTHIA Province of Iran south-east of the Caspian Sea. The name was applied to the whole of Iran during the reign of the Parthian dynasty.

PISÉ (Mud Brick) Mud mixed with straw or grass and moulded into shape by hand to form a wall of superimposed courses, each of which is allowed to dry before the next is positioned. A method of building houses still in use today.

PODIUM Projecting base, pedestal or raised platform.

POL Bridge.

PROTOME Foreparts of an animal, represented in art.

QALEH Castle.

2

QIBLA (Kibla) The main wall of a mosque facing the direction of Mecca, in which the mihrab is placed.

RADIO-CARBON DATING (C. 14) A method of dating organic material based on carbon-14, a naturally active carbon isotope which is absorbed by all living organisms during life and disintegrates at a known rate after death.

RHYTON A drinking vessel in the form of a horn or animal's head or the entire animal, provided with single or double spouts for drinking purposes.

SAKAS (Sacas) Scythian tribe of Chinese Turkestan who, with the Yueh-chi, conquered the Graeco-Bactrian kingdom c. 130 B.C.

SCYTHIANS Nomads of Iranian origin who migrated to western Asia from south Russia, probably by way of the Caucasus. In the seventh century B.C. they invaded Iran and among their tribes were mercenaries who served in the Median and Assyrian armies.

SQUINCH A section of vaulted masonry bridging an angle of a rectangular room, often used to create a circular base for a dome.

STEATITE A kind of soapstone.

STELAE Upright stone slabs, usually inscribed, marking graves or victories.

STUCCO Carved or moulded plaster often painted and used as an ornamental and protective covering for mud-brick walls, widely used by the Parthians and Sassanians. The design must be blocked out and carved before the plaster sets. The art form reached its peak in the Saljuq and Mongol periods.

SUSIANA The modern province of Khuzestan in south-west Iran, and a major province in the Achaemenian empire. Before the Persians arrived, Susiana was the centre of the Elamite Kingdom.

TAKIEH Grandstand from which religious (Muslim) processions and plays are watched.

TAL, TELL, TEPE Artificial mound formed by the accumulation of man-made debris, most often the foundations and collapsed walls of successive mud-brick structures.

TAZIYA Religious passion play depicting episodes from the life of the martyred Hussein, performed during the mourning period of Muharram.

THERIOMORPHIC Made in animal form, usually applied here to pottery.

TORUS Lowest portion of base of column.

UBAID (El), or OBEID Period prior to Uruk, Neolithic in origin.

UNTASH GAL Elamite king, thirteenth century B.C. who built Choga Zanbil, the immense ziggurat in Khuzestan.

URARTU Powerful kingdom flourishing between the ninth and sixth centuries B.C., around Lake Van in Turkey to Lake Rezaiyeh in Iran. Absorbed in the sixth century B.C. by Media.

URMIA Old name for Lake Rezaiyeh in Azarbaijan, western Iran.

URUK The 'Erech' of the Bible, present-day Warka in Iraq, with monumental architecture of *c.* 3400 to 3100 B.C. and early picture writing of *c.* 3200 B.C.

YAKCHAWL Traditional ice store.

YURT Circular tent of skins or felt spread over a wicker frame, common in Turkestan.

ZEND-AVESTA Collection of the sacred books of Zoroastrianism.

ZIGGURAT Mesopotamian name for a staged temple composed of multiple tiers and resembling an artificial mountain. The Biblical Tower of Babel was a ziggurat. The largest known example today is that of Choga Zanbil in Khuzestan, Iran.

ZOOMORPHIC In the shape of an animal, here referring to pottery.

ZOROASTER (Zarathustra) Prophet and founder of the Zoroastrian religion, a reformed version of Mazdaean religion, and believed to have lived and taught in the seventh century B.C. His teachings are known as the Avesta. Ahura Mazda is the highest divine power; the three main beliefs are 'Good thoughts, good words, good deeds'. The Parsees of India are followers of this religion.

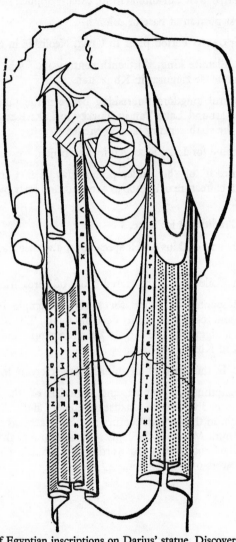

Position of Egyptian inscriptions on Darius' statue. Discovered at Susa, 1972; now in Tehran Archaeological Museum.
(*By courtesy of Délégation Archéologique Française en Iran from* Journal Asiatique, *Paris, 1972*)

1 · Tehran and Environs

Tehran, which only became the capital of Iran with the advent of the Qajar dynasty at the end of the eighteenth century, has been generally regarded as having nothing of archaeological or historic interest. It is true there are no monuments of any great age in the city, but during the course of building operations quite a number of prehistoric sites have been discovered in and around the capital which indicate that it has attracted settlers for some thousands of years.

Among other sites recently excavated is an important Iron Age cemetery dating from c. 1200 to 800 B.C., at Gheytariyeh, just to the east of the old Shemiran Road, in the north-east of Tehran. The Iranian Archaeological Service under the direction of Mr. Kambakhsh Fard and Mr. Zabihollah Rahmatian excavated the site from 1968 to 1969. Here in some 15,000 square metres of land, about 350 Early Iron Age graves were discovered. The dead were interred in earth pits, usually lying on their sides with their legs and arms strongly flexed. Handsome red and grey burnished pottery vessels accompanied each burial, often disposed in clusters near the head and the feet. Other characteristic finds from the cemetery included bronze weapons, jewellery of both gold and bronze and tiny wooden sculptures of men, women and animals.

In keeping with the new burial customs introduced during the course of the second millennium by the Indo-European invaders of Iran, the cemetery proved to be extra-mural—lying outside the limits of any local settlement.

What should not be missed in Tehran today is the Archaeological Museum (Muzeh Iran Bostan), on the corner of Khiaban-i Sepah and Khiaban-i Ghavam Sultaneh, housed in a building constructed after the Sassanian style, planned by André Godard the distinguished French architect who from 1931 to 1960 was Director of the Iranian Archaeological Service. The high ivan entrance leads into wide galleries built around two central patios. With slight changes in summer and winter hours, the Museum is open daily except Mondays, 9 a.m.–12 a.m. and 3 p.m.–6 p.m. (Fridays, mornings only). A small charge is made for admission but photography without flash or tripod is allowed, free of charge. (See p. 16, Foreword to the Second Edition.)

A new building directly adjoining the Museum was opened in 1968

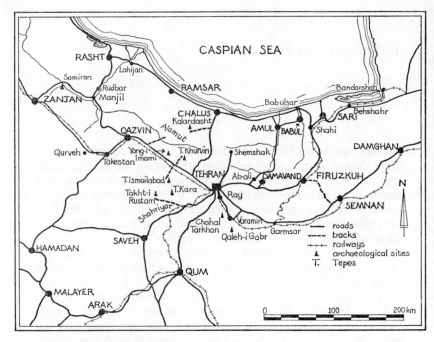

Map 2. Tehran and Environs

to house the Fifth International Congress of Iranian Art and Archaeology and is now used for the storage of archaeological finds and for special exhibitions and conferences.

In the main Museum, the collections have been arranged with the earliest objects on the right and one is automatically directed to make the tour from right to left. The excellent Museum library is in the extreme right-hand corner and stairs on both sides of the entrance lead to the upper galleries with their Islamic exhibits.

Not all the showcases are numbered and those that are display their numbers on small tickets inside the cases, usually with added descriptions in French. The arrangement is not in strict numerical order. Beginning with the exhibits placed down the centre of the galleries, the first case is on the immediate left on entering the Museum and contains Mesolithic flints, burins, flakes and cores, some from Tepe Sarab (p. 130). No. 2 is on the immediate right and is exclusively confined to Tepe Sialk (p. 170); exhibits include the small bone handle of a flint knife carved into a standing male figure with arms crossed, the earliest known such effigy, *c.* 4200 B.C.

Turning right, into the alcove by the stairs, one comes to case No. 3

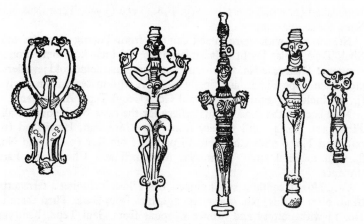

Fig. 1. Luristan bronzes; standards or idols. Twelfth and seventh centuries B.C.
From 'Bronzes. Iran-Luristan Caucasus' by Louis Vanden Berghe
and Rene Joffroy, *Le Bronze Industriel*, Rene Loisean et Cie 1973.
(*By courtesy of Professor L. Vanden Berghe.*)

against the wall which contains pottery from Kara Tepe, Shahriar
(p. 60), fourth millennium B.C., and standing on a pedestal, an enormous red bowl with black decoration from Ismailabad (p. 60). In the
corner right under the stairs is another large red vessel on a pottery
base, from Sialk. The door to the library is in this corner.

At the head of the Eastern gallery, an unnumbered case contains
seals of many types, mainly from Susa (p. 147) and Luristan (p. 107),
and including the famous cylinder seal of Darius the Great.

Continuing now with the cases in the middle of the gallery, next is
No. 7 with Tall-i Bakun (p. 235) pottery of fourth millennium date,
and between this and the next case is a cast of the famous Hammurabi
stele, a copy of the original which was discovered at Susa and is now in
the Louvre Museum, on which is engraved the legal code of Hammurabi, *c.* 1750 B.C.

Next, case No. 10 with more pottery from Susa, figurines and other
small finds, and then No. 12A with material from Tepe Giyan (p. 116)
and Kalar Dasht near Chalus. Opposite the short connecting corridor
between the two patios stands a terracotta bull, restored by Madame
Ghirshman, one of a pair that was found guarding a gateway of the
ziggurat of Choga Zanbil (p. 144), *c.* 1250 B.C., with a dedicatory inscription on its back in which the King of Susa and Anshan, King Untash
Gal, pays tribute to the god Inshushinak.

The large case next to this contains objects from Shah Tepe (p. 67),

Ismailabad (p. 60), Tepe Hissar (p. 196), Tepe Giyan, Tepe Sialk and Susa, for comparison.

Next is 21A with more mixed exhibits from Tureng Tepe (p. 67), Shah Tepe, Kalar Dasht (Mazandaran) (p. 72) including some bronze weapons. Then case No. 24 with pottery, weapons, some gold jewellery, etc., from Tepe Hissar, and finally No. 26A with material from Ziwiye (p. 96) including gold earrings, and Gok (Geoy) Tepe, Azarbaijan.

Now back to the head of this gallery for the cases by the outer wall. First, case No. 4, with pottery from Tepe Musallan, Ismailabad (p. 60); next No. 6 with Chesmeh Ali pottery from Ray (p. 48) and No. 8, with material from Taimuran, Moushaki and Chogan in Fars province.

Case No. 11 contains small objects from Susa including a terracotta head. Next to this, No. 9 also has figurines from Susa. Then there is No. 13 with pottery and bronze weapons from Ganj Tepe, Khurvin (p. 60), and No. 14 with material from Choga Zanbil; above this, on the wall, are tiles with projecting knobs, some bearing Elamite script, and a sample of reed matting.

After this there are No. 20 with objects from Tepe Hissar, and an unnumbered case containing some of the dramatic anthropomorphic pottery from Marlik (p. 73), weapons, and bronze figurines. No. 23 has more material from Ziwiye including some alabaster and bronze, and the next, unnumbered case contains Hasanlu material including some gold jewellery and figurines. Finally comes another case, No. 25, with more pottery from Hasanlu, and nearby Solduz.

Along the inner courtyard walls are a number of large pottery vessels from Sialk, two stone sockets for barring a door, from Choga Zanbil, and a bronze wheel rim from Susa.

On the corner of the connecting passage, a remarkably Chinese-looking lion from Susa is to be seen, and opposite it, a great pottery vessel, also from Susa. In the corridor itself are three unnumbered cases, all containing material from Luristan (third to first millennium B.C.); the first case displays various weapons of bronze, the second an assortment of weapons, finials and a small bronze figurine, as well as some terracotta objects. The third case has a number of small objects including bracelets, bits, pins and mirrors.

Returning to the East wing, one finds more pottery vessels and a burial vessel along the inner wall and finally a single trilingual foundation tablet from Persepolis (p. 225).

On the northern wall at the end, is a bas-relief taken from the Treasury at Persepolis (sixth century B.C.), showing Darius the Great on his throne, with his son, Crown Prince Xerxes, standing immediately behind him, and in front, beyond two small incense burners, a Median

official, probably the 'Chiliarch' in charge of the Treasury, and also
Commander of the Army, holding his hand before his mouth in a gesture of respect. Other Achaemenian reliefs and inscribed stones are
placed around these walls.

In the centre of this corridor, one sees first the gold foundation tablet
of Darius I, with a trilingual inscription in Old Persian, Neo-Babylonian
and Neo-Elamite (often out on exhibition), discovered underneath the
Apadana at Persepolis (p. 228). Then comes an excellent scale model of
Persepolis itself, followed by two cases set back to back—No. 28 with a
silver Achaemenian foundation tablet from Hamadan (p. 109), and some
gold jewellery, and No. 30, with small gold objects from Pasargadae,
Persepolis and Hamadan. Case No. 31 contains one of the finest bronzes
from Persepolis, that of three prowling lions which served to form part
of the base for a tall candelabrum.

Against the wall, glazed bricks from the walls of Achaemenian palaces
in Susa and Persepolis include an archer from the royal bodyguard and
a pair of human-headed winged creatures over which floats the winged
symbol of the Zoroastrian deity, Ahura Mazda. By the stairs sits a
polished black stone guardian mastiff combining the characteristics of
both sexes, found in the Apadana at Persepolis.

Other Achaemenian exhibits from Persepolis include a huge human-
headed capital standing against a small staircase ornamented with bas-
reliefs of the royal bodyguard and vassals bearing gifts; the portal of a
door, showing the king grappling with a monster, is also from Persepolis, as are the polished black stone foundation tablets of Xerxes on a
stand against the outer wall, being the Daiva inscriptions in which he
attacks the cult of the Daivas and praises the worship of Ahura
Mazda.[159]

Continuing now down the middle of the Western gallery, one comes
to an unnumbered case containing various objects from Susa including
some gold objects and some coloured plaster (one piece showing a
man's head), and, usually out on exhibition elsewhere, a lapis-lazuli
head of an Achaemenian prince, generally believed to portray Xerxes I.

Case No. 35, next, contains alabaster, stone and other Achaemenian
period vessels from Persepolis, and No. 37, Parthian objects from Susa
and Nihavand (p. 115). Case No. 38 has Parthian objects from Susa
and opposite these, in the centre of the connecting corridor, is the huge
bronze statue of a Parthian Prince, from Shami (p. 163), probably
first century A.D. The body was most likely cast on the spot, the head,
slightly too small in proportion, was probably cast elsewhere.

Continuing down the centre of the West wing, case No. 39 contains

[159] All superior numerals like this refer to the numbered entries in the
Bibliography on pp. 326–35.

2*

other objects and fragments of bronze statues including the mask
sometimes attributed to Antiochus IV, from Shami; an unnumbered
case has Sassanian pottery and finally No. 44, silver dishes, vases and
some glass and terracotta objects all from the Caspian area.

Along the outer wall, beginning next to the tablets of Xerxes, are a
broken capital from Persepolis, then small objects, including some
alabaster duck-shaped weights, from Susa and Persepolis (case No. 33),
and still further Achaemenian objects in Nos. 34 and 36.

Examples of stucco are shown on the walls and portions of columns
between the windows and the next showcase, No. 40, which contains
Seleucid and Parthian beads, mother-of-pearl and terracotta figurines
from Susa. No. 41 contains figurines from Khuzestan and Fars and
No. 43, replicas of Sassanian-style silver dishes now in the Hermitage,
Leningrad.

A stucco capital found near Taq-i Bustan, Kirmanshah (p. 130),
stands in the middle of the end gallery, and other examples of stucco
from Damghan, Chahal Tarkhan, etc. (p. 49) are shown on the walls,
while the small mosaics on the end wall come from the Palace of
Shahpur I at Bishapur (p. 238). Under these, case No. 45 contains pieces
of stucco, terracotta, ivories and bronzes from Susa, all of the Sassanian
period. A small case to the left of this, No. 5C, exhibits a series of coins
from the reign of Darius down to recent times.

Along the inner wall, starting from the North, are various pieces of
Achaemenian statuary, and on the corner of the central gallery, a stone
memorial with a Greek inscription, found at Nihavand; this is all that
remains of a Seleucid temple which Antiochus III dedicated to his wife
Laodicea in 193 B.C. Around the corner are several terracotta heads
from Kirmanshah, possibly Dinavar (p. 126), including heads of a satyr
and of Silenus, originally attached to basins.

On the opposite corner of this gallery is a shallow relief on limestone
found at Susa, depicting King Artabanus V handing the ring of office to
Khwasak, satrap of Susa, with an inscription in Pahlavi, dated September 14th, A.D. 215.

Continuing along the inner side of the Western gallery, one sees first
a marble head of a woman wearing a crown bearing the name of the
sculptor, 'Antiochus, the son of Dryas'. Found at Susa, it is believed to
be either a goddess, the Spirit of Susa, or Queen Musa, the Roman slave
presented to Phraates IV, who became his queen and later married her
own son, Phraates V, in the first century A.D.

There are then several stone reliefs, mainly of Parthian figures,
Parthian 'slipper' coffins and a Greek-style torso found at Susa.

Going now to the upper floor by the stairs near the Bishapur Mosaics,
turn right for an exhibit of early Islamic Korans (ninth to tenth cen-

Fig. 2. Persepolis. Reconstruction of central part of eastern Apadana stairway
façade with original relief panel showing audience scene of King
Darius. (From 'Studies and Restorations at Persepolis and other
sites of Fars' by Anne Britt Tilia.)
(By courtesy of IsMEO, Rome. 1972)

tury A.D.) in cases Nos. 46 and 47. In the centre of the gallery, Nos.
48, 49 and 50 contain a varied collection of ninth and tenth century
ceramics including bowls from both Nishapur (p. 199) and Susa (p.
147).

In front of these cases is a large bronze vessel, probably tenth
century A.D. from a mosque where it would have contained drinking
water. The jars standing by the windows are probably ninth to tenth
century, the same period as the painted plaster on the rear wall between
the Korans.

In the corner by the stairs is a room, opened on request, displaying
the famous Safavid collection of china and porcelain from Ardabil
(p. 78) together with some beautiful carpets.

The galleries are now divided into bays. The first of these, on the
east side, contains on the rear wall, protected by glass, what is claimed
to be the oldest known Islamic painting, a ninth century fresco from
Nishapur (p. 197) depicting a prince hunting with a falcon. An artist's
attempt to reconstruct the original is seen on the right. Above and
around are some splendid examples of stucco of the same period and
also from Nishapur. The unnumbered case in the front of the bay contains ninth to tenth century splashed ware, and case No. 52 by the side
wall, silver gilt objects and some painted plaster, all from Nishapur.
In one corner remnants of paint can be seen on the bust of a man, found
at Ray (p. 46) probably eleventh century, and the tenth century
carved wooden doors come from Qum (p. 167).

The next bay contains two glass showcases set into the back wall:
the first, unnumbered, shows silver from Azarbaijan, the second, No.
55, eleventh to twelfth century glass from Gurgan (p. 66). A stucco
mihrab from a Saljuq imamzadeh near Isfahan is set between these and

dates from the first half of the twelfth century A.D., while the round metal bowl in the centre of the bay is Saljuq, eleventh century, like the round stucco medallion on the side wall which depicts a king surrounded by his court.

On the opposite side wall is a small carved wooden 'window' with a Kufic inscription. The stucco squinches are from a Saljuq building at Ray, together with good stucco panels and the eleventh century carved wooden doors from the province of Fars. Splashed ware and wood carving can be seen in the unnumbered case in the front of the bay.

In the bay facing the short passage between the two patios, another large metal bowl of the twelfth century stands in the centre and a thirteenth to fourteenth century lustre glaze tile mihrab from Qum takes the place of honour in the middle of the rear wall. Glass cases in this wall contain eleventh to thirteenth century ceramics in case No. 57, and twelfth to thirteenth century metalware in No. 58. There are more ceramics in the unnumbered cases by the side walls and in the space between this bay and the corridor case No. 64 contains a variety of coins from the seventh to thirteenth centuries A.D.

On one corner of the inner, patio wall is an inscribed twelfth century tombstone and on the other, a delicately-wrought bronze incense burner of the same date.

The fourth bay on the east side displays mainly thirteenth to fourteenth century material including, in case No. 68, a lovely thirteenth century enamelled glass lamp from a mosque, some fourteenth century Korans in an unnumbered case next to this, and an early fourteenth century mihrab from an imamzadeh at Ushtarjan near Isfahan; then glazed lustre tiles from Saveh, of the fourteenth century, in No. 72, and twelfth to thirteenth century bronzes in No. 73 in the front of the bay. The carved wooden doors under glass bear the name of their maker and date from the thirteenth to fourteenth century. By the inner, patio wall are two bronze pestle and mortar sets of the same period.

In the short passage between the two wings of the gallery are five cases. In the centre, No. 62, with tenth to thirteenth century glassware; next No. 63, with thirteenth century ceramics including lustre glaze, and thirteenth century pottery from Ray and other sites in No. 64 (the second case of that number). By the northern wall is No. 66 with eleventh to twelfth century Saljuq silver jewellery, small bronze objects of the thirteenth century and a Koran of the period, while No. 65 displays a charming miniature mihrab in turquoise from Hamadan (p. 109) and two thirteenth century Korans. The remaining bays are all devoted to the fourteenth century and later.

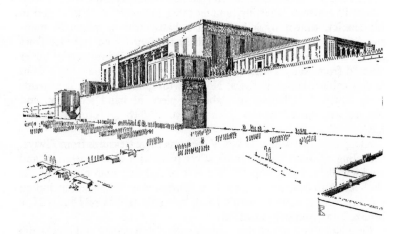

Fig. 3. Persepolis. Reconstruction of west façade by F. Krefter.
(*By courtesy of Professor H. Luschey*)

The pick of all the Museum's treasures, however, are closely guarded in the 'Treasure Room', in the south-west corner by the staircase. It is normally open from 9 a.m. till noon on Saturday, Sunday, Tuesday and Wednesday. The exhibits begin in chronological order from the left. Case No. I contains fifteenth to eighth century B.C. bronzes from Luristan, and No. II has gold objects as well as bronzes of the same period. Then comes a Greek marble torso found at Persepolis, and case No. III with some of the Marlik (p. 73) gold objects including the small statuette of a king and the bowl with projecting rams' heads. Next to this an unnumbered case with gold and silver objects from Gilan including the Amlash districts (p. 71), a pottery vessel on wheels, in the shape of a humped bull with spouted mouth, some long-handled spoons, and from Hasanlu (p. 91) a delicate small bowl of lapis-lazuli supported by a hand carved on its reverse side, decorated with a golden lion's head and presumably intended for burning tallow.

Gold earrings and gold and silver vases are also in this case.

In the middle of the end wall, an unnumbered case contains some of the most magnificent of all the Museum's treasures; they include the powerful golden vessel from Marlik[123] with its projecting bulls' heads worked in repoussé; from Kalar Dasht (p. 72) a gold dagger and a bowl with the heads of lionesses made separately and riveted onto the relief of the bodies; the famous crushed gold bowl from Hasanlu, with its vivid scenes in registers, showing, among other incidents, a weather god in his chariot, drawn by a bull, and a battle with a mountain monster.[38,42,130] Here too is the exquisitely fashioned gold bracelet from Ziwiye[130] (p. 96) with its lions' heads, and the controversial silver tankard from Marv Dasht (p. 212) believed to be Elamite.[93] In front of this cabinet are two others, No. 12 with gold and silver ornaments from Ziwiye[70] including an elaborate piece of hand jewellery, and No. 14 with carved ivories from Ziwiye (eighth to seventh century B.C.).

Along the third wall, case No. V contains more treasures from Ziwiye, including a bronze horse's head, silver plate with gold decoration, and gold jewellery. Next, No. VI, is a case of Achaemenian objects of the sixth and fifth centuries B.C. all from Kordestan or Hamadan, including a delicate little silver leopard's head, two gold tablets of Darius II, a bronze bowl, and gold bracelets.

Case No. VII is also Achaemenian with a gold dagger and bowl from Hamadan and a little silver statuette of a mountain goat, a gold rhyton and silver vases from Hamadan and gold earrings, bracelets and a silver spoon from the Garden Pavilion at Pasargadae[159] (p. 214) in the front right-hand corner.

No. VIII contains Parthian and Sassanian exhibits from the second century B.C. to fourth century A.D. and includes silver dishes—one portraying the 'Parthian shot'—a bronze plaque, and glass, mainly from the Caspian area.

Two cases on the wall by the door contain (No. IX) Sassanian silver dishes, a silver spoon and fork and gold jewellery of the later Sassanian period, and (No. X) Islamic period bronze plates, an astrolabe from Isfahan and gold and silver jewellery from Gurgan and Ray.

The case in front of these, No. 13, contains gold jewellery from Dailaman[46,47] in Gilan (p. 71), and bronze and lapis-lazuli objects, including Parthian and Sassanian material.

Since going to press, exhibits in the Museum have been re-arranged. Future plans include the transfer of Islamic exhibits to the new building next door.

There are a number of monuments and prehistoric sites that can be visited on a day's trip from Tehran.

Shahr Ray (ancient Rhages), some 12 km. from the heart of the capital is now virtually a suburb. It was probably the site of a small Achaemenian town visited by Alexander the Great in 330 B.C. during his pursuit of the last Achaemenian king, Darius III Codamanus. (Traditionally it was to Rhages that the Apocryphal character, Tobias, with his companions the archangel Raphael and a small dog, came to collect a debt after stopping at Ecbatana (Hamadan) where he married his cousin.)

We know that Seleucus Nicator, the first of the Seleucid dynasty, rebuilt the town about 300 B.C., calling it Europos, after his birthplace in Macedonia. A century later the Parthians captured and fortified it, building temples there, and it became the spring residence of the Parthian kings, described by Isidore of Charax as the 'greatest city in Media'. The Sassanians occupied it until the Arab conquest in A.D. 637 and under the Abbasids, in the eighth century, it was known as Mohammadiyeh.

Harun al-Rashid was born here in A.D. 763 while his father was rebuilding the city. In the tenth century it was known as Ray, and although captured by Mahmud of Ghazni in 1029, it became a flourishing Saljuq capital by the mid eleventh century when it was described as 'the most beautiful city of all the East with the exception of Baghdad'. Its pottery industry flourished at this time—and, indeed, down to 1220 when the Mongols destroyed the town completely. Ghazan Khan ordered its reconstruction, but this was never carried out, since the survivors of the Mongol massacre had already fled to settle down in Varamin and Tehran.

Shahr Ray is reached from the south of Tehran, following the signs from Khiaban-i (Avenue) Sepah, or else via a new route that begins near the south end of Khiaban-i Hafiz.

Avoid visiting Ray during religious festivals since one of its greatest attractions for Muslim pilgrims is the sacred shrine of Shah Abdul Azim, distinguished from afar by its golden dome and tall minarets, and seen right at the end of the road from Tehran. Here are buried Husain, great-grandson of the second Imam Hassan, Taher, a descendant of the fourth Imam, and Hamzeh, brother of the eighth Imam, Reza. Non-Muslims are strictly forbidden to enter even the outer courtyard, but the nineteenth century dome and minarets can be seen from the pleasant gardens surrounding the modern mausoleum of Reza Shah the Great, founder of the Pahlavi dynasty (d. 1945). Entry is by special permit from the police and women are expected to wear a head-scarf.

Before the shrines are reached, however, a signposted turning to the left brings you to old Ray, and driving along the short road you can see, on the right, the roofless upper walls of a fluted Saljuq tomb-tower. The next turning to the right, also signposted, takes you to a wall (right) where a door leads into the garden in which the tower stands. A small charge is made for admission.

The tower, which is empty and is incorrectly known as Tughril Beg's tower, is thought to date from A.D. 1139 and probably originally had a conical roof.

Between the tower and the nearby cliffs is the spring called Cheshmeh Ali, reached through a series of narrow lanes. Here, where thousands of pounds' worth of rugs and carpets are washed with detergents and spread to dry on the cliffs, is the heart of the ancient town. A mound on the right, separated from the cliffs by a dirt road, marks the spot where Erich Schmidt[140] directed his excavations in 1934 and 1936, on behalf of the Boston Museum of Fine Art, and the University Museum. The work revealed a particularly striking artistic tradition in the earliest fourth millennium levels. Chesmeh Ali pottery is distinctively fine with a reddish-orange colouring, often polished and coated with a slip, and with sophisticated black and dark brown decoration. The site was suddenly abandoned in the third millennium for some centuries, probably again inhabited at the end of the second millennium B.C. and later used by Parthians and Sassanians. Traces of Parthian walls can be seen on the south spur in the centre of the excavations. A temple probably dating from the beginning of the Christian era was found in the deep square hole which was the area of the main test dig.

On the face of the cliff overlooking the spring, is a nineteenth century Qajar bas-relief, but the top of the cliff is fringed with remains of early Islamic mud-brick city walls, and from here some idea can be gained of the defensive system of the old city.

Further east, right by the mountains, and half hidden by clouds of dust and smoke from the cement and brick factories on their very edge, are the other remnants of Ray's historic past. The so-called Nagareh Khaneh or 'Kettle-drum House' excavated by Schmidt, and a nearby tomb-tower, are of either Buyid (ninth to tenth century) or Saljuq date. Both are reached by taking the turning east signposted to Aminabad, after crossing the railway bridge on the Tehran-Ray road. This links up with the old road and, less than a kilometre along, a hill stands out on the left, at the foot of which a factory abuts onto the terrace supporting the foundations of the massive Nagareh Khaneh. Judging from the size of these the original tower[140] may have been as large and high as the Gunbad-i Qabus (p. 69) and it is thought to have been used as a burial ground for the Buyid royal family. Fragments of silk fabric and stucco decoration were found in the debris and outer rooms; an enclosing wall and a later tower can still be seen here.

From here, a rough and fairly steep path following the line of original rock-cut steps leads up to Yazid's tower, named after the Caliph who ruled between A.D. 683 and 690. This tomb-tower is said to have contained the graves of two Buyid princes but is now empty, the floor of the main chamber having been destroyed, probably by treasure-seekers. The roof too has collapsed but some interesting brickwork decorates the cornices.

On this same hill the Zoroastrian community used to expose their dead in the traditional Dakhme or Tower of Silence, demolished in the early years of this century.

The Shrine of Bibi Shahrbanu,[11] reached by the right-hand (easterly) fork of the track to the rear of Yazid's tower, is said to house the remains of the daughter of the last Sassanian king, Yazdigird III. According to an unfounded tradition she married the Iman Husain, grandson of the Prophet Mohammad. The shrine may only be visited by women (wearing an ankle-length veil or chador) or by Sayyids, descendants of the Prophet through the male line; the oldest parts of the shrine containing the tomb enclosed within a grille, may date from the tenth century A.D., but the dome and main structure are comparatively recent, having been extended by the Safavids and the Qajars.

The road at the foot of the shrine follows the line of hills south-east until the junction of the old Mashad road, where a chai khaneh and petrol station stand close together. A turn to the left will take you back now to Tehran, but if you drive right for about one kilometre you will see a track going into the hills on the left. From the main road you can just see the top of a square brick structure known as the Zendan-i Harun (Harun's Prison), which Lockhart[111] believes might be eighth century A.D. It is thought to have been used as a maximum security prison in Buyid times; others think it might have been a Sassanian fire temple.

From Ray one can continue south-east to Varamin, some 45 km. from Tehran, passing a number of prehistoric and Sassanian mounds on either side of the road. About 10 km. from Ray, a mound just off the road to the right is crowned with the restored remains of a very large Sassanian monument called Tepe Mil. A track leaves the road and takes you right to the tepe which itself must have been an important prehistoric site, while the imposing Sassanian structure appears to have been a residential complex with many only partly excavated rooms.

The mound is littered with sherds of various periods, and the wide arches of the what some supposed to be a fire temple, frame a distant view of the flare from Tehran's modern oil refinery at Ray. The palace is built on a massive scale with a four-pillared porch and flat ceiling; on the east side are windows and the remains of corridors and several chambers can be seen on its various levels, with fallen pillars and capitals, some still with stucco decoration, lying on the ground below the main building.

Nearer Varamin itself, just past Farahabad village, at Chahal Tarkhan,

are more Sassanian ruins, on the right of the road. These are the remains
of a Sassanian citadel and small hunting lodge, probably of one of the
later Sassanian princes, where many beautiful stuccos depicting Bahram
V Gur, the great hunter, were discovered. Some of these are in the
Tehran Museum. The citadel, of which quite substantial walls remain,
stands on the crown of a pudding-basin shaped mound close to the
road, while the 'palace' or lodge, with its massive round columns, was
excavated a few hundred metres to the north of the citadel. The whole
area is covered with mounds from prehistoric to Islamic periods and
much still remains to be scientifically excavated.

Varamin itself is a charming little town which owes its growth to the
flight of refugees from Ray at the time of the Mongol invasion, and
although it contains a well-preserved tomb-tower (A.D. 1289), a very
beautiful fourteenth century Friday Mosque and many charming
shrines, none is earlier than the Mongol period.

Beyond Varamin, about 2½ km. to the north-east, are the remains of
a great (one km. square) walled enclosure known as the Qaleh-Gabr,
which Professor Luschey believes was an early Islamic fortification but
others think more probably a Sassanian 'paradeisos' in which game was
enclosed for the royal hunt.

Several interesting places off the main road west from Tehran can
be visited in one day. Among the most distant is a very early Saljuq
mosque in the village of Qurveh, about a 2½–3 hour drive from Tehran
along the fast motorway to Karaj (one touman toll) and on to Qazvin.
About a third of the way along, the road passes through the village of
Hasht Gerd. On the north side, among other shops and cafés, is Arsen's,
a restaurant and wine shop owned by an elderly Armenian who makes
his own excellent wines, not sold elsewhere. The restaurant offers a
limited menu of veal, kebabs and dolmas and is especially attractive
at the end of a day's outing. (Restaurant temporarily closed in
1974.)

It is possible to avoid going through the town by taking the left fork
along the old road which takes you past one of two surviving Qajar
town gates, restored in recent years.

Continue straight ahead over all crossings and for the final few
hundred metres on a roughish patch of road, to join the main Qazvin-
Hamadan road. Turn left and drive on to Takestan (about 33 km.), a
village that seems to consist mainly of chai khanehs catering for bus-
loads of travellers to Hamadan and Tabriz. Drive straight through and
past a large petrol station on the right, part of a complex of extraordinary
buildings resembling some industrial exhibition but which in fact
comprise a motel offering not only public toilets but a pleasant little
snack-bar, coffee shop and restaurant, the Sham Shop, serving steaks,

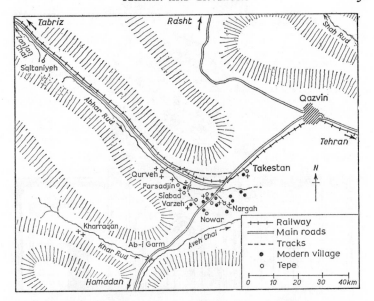

Fig. 4. Sketch plan showing location of Qurveh and Takestan.
(*By courtesy of Professor W. Kleiss*)

chicken Kievsky, omelettes, Persian dishes and alcoholic drinks at reasonable prices.

Just beyond this the road forks right for Zanjan and Tabriz (straight ahead for Hamadan and Kirmanshah), and about 26 km. down the Zanjan road, turn left down a narrow dirt track by the first of a strung-out line of three chai khanehs. A yellow signpost in Persian indicates the village of Qurveh less than a kilometre away, half hidden in a hollow, but the strikingly Sassanian-like brick dome of its Mosque, in the middle of the village, can be seen from the road if you are on the look-out. This dome has been likened by Dr. Mostafavi[119] to that of the Sarvistan Palace (p. 259), while the interior has been compared by Professor Wolfram Kleiss of the German Archaeological Institute, Tehran (in conversation with the author), to that of the Masjid-i Jumeh at Gulpaigan (p. 188). (See *Archaeologische Mitteilungen aus Iran*, 4, 1971.)

The narrow lanes lead into the fascinating village whose mud-brick houses, terraced up the steep gorge of the rushing Abhar Rud, blend into their surroundings. Drive across the bridge and park in a little open space beyond, then walk up one of several short steep lanes to your right, which bring you out in front of the Saljuq mosque.

This is quite plain externally, with a prayer hall at the side, and a

0　1　2　3　4　5 m

Fig. 5. Qurveh. Masjid-i Jumeh. Section of dome.
(*By courtesy of Professor W. Kleiss*)

faded painted inscription below the zone of transition in the dome, dating it to A.D. 1022–3. Other inscriptions give a date of A.D. 1179 for the restoration of the dome. The mihrab, which Hillenbrand dates to the eleventh century, has traces of the original blue and red paint in the stucco, but has been badly damaged and there have been Mongol additions to the original stucco. The plan of the square domed chamber flanked by plain barrel-vaulted chambers is not unlike that of the Sar-i Kucha Mosque at Muhammadiyya (p. 176), and it is worth using binoculars to study the painted and stucco decoration round the squinches and base of the high dome. Some of the large bricks used in the lower part of the dome chamber may be Sassanian while the very thick walls at the base suggest the original dome was lower and that this building was converted from a Chahar Taq. (See: 'Saljug Monuments in Iran' by D. Hillenbrand. *Oriental Art*, Spring 1972, and W. Kleiss, *Archaeologische Mitteilungen aus Iran*, Neue Folge Band 5, Berlin, 1972.)

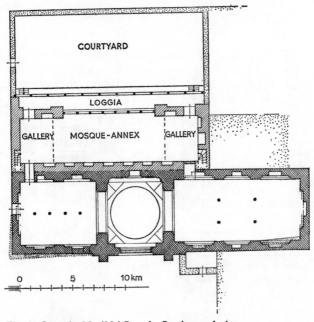

Fig. 6. Qurveh. Masjid-i Jumeh. Section and plan.
(*By courtesy of Professor W. Kleiss*)

From Qurveh, drive back to Qazvin, stopping at Takestan for another Saljuq monument, the Pir Mausoleum. As you drive towards Tehran, entering Takestan, the old road to Zanjan is on the left, and opposite it, between two chai khanehs, another dirt road goes to the right (east), crossing the railway line. Continue along here, passing a new Red Lion and Sun clinic on the left, as far as a cross-roads with small shops on either side. Turn right, and follow the lane as it winds through an irregularly shaped open space, crossing this diagonally to continue a few more metres to the edge of a dried-up river bed, on the opposite bank of which you can see the Imamzadeh.[92, 102]

The floor level is now below the present ground level and one steps down to enter the door, the key to which is kept nearby—there is always somebody whom one can ask for this. The building faces north-west so afternoon is best for photographing the interesting façade of this little-known eleventh century building which has been restored. Trilobed arches flank the door and there is also a section of brick pattern in the rear wall.

The interior dome and squinches are decorated with carved stucco

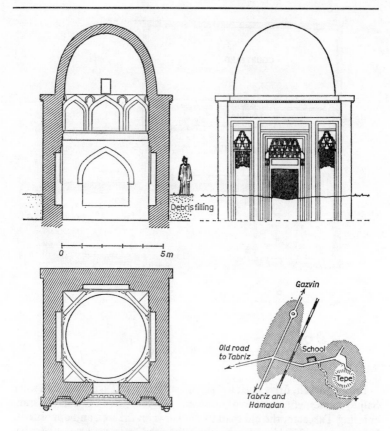

Fig. 7. Takestan. Sketch plan of site, section and plan of Mausoleum of
Pir-i Takestan. (*By courtesy of Professor W. Kleiss*)

insets similar to those in the Masjid-i Jumeh at Qurveh, with small
swastikas set in the arms of the crosses.

It is worth while spending at least half a day in Qazvin which still has
a welcome old-fashioned air about it. It is said to have been founded by
Shahpur I who called it Shad-i Shahpur (The Joy of Shahpur). It was
often ravaged by the Dailamites, an aggressive mountain tribe living in
the Alburz mountains north of Qazvin; captured by the Arabs in A.D.
644 the city was later fortified as a base against the Dailamite raids.
Harun al-Rashid's elder brother built a suburb called Medinah Musa
here, and about A.D. 809 Harun al-Rashid himself stayed in the city
on his way to Khurasan. After the Dailamites were converted to Islam,

Qazvin came under attack from the Assassins who took over many of the Dailamite strongholds and whose headquarters at the end of the eleventh century were in the famous Alamut fortress, north-west of Qazvin (p. 57). Raided by the Mongols in 1220, Qazvin was again sacked by them in 1256 when Hulagu Khan captured Alamut. Here, in Qazvin, Hamadullah Mostowfi, the historian and geographer, was born and died in the fourteenth century; his restored tomb-tower with its turquoise tiled, conical roof, lies to the east of the Ali Qapu, almost all that is left of the capital of the Safavid Shah Tahmasp (1524–1576).

Only two monuments remain from the Saljuq period, the most outstanding of which is the early twelfth century Madrasseh-i Haidarieh. Today it is entirely hidden behind high walls in the eastern quarter of the town, and one must ask the way; locally it is often known as the 'Ateshkadeh' (fire temple). Approaching it from the main street Khiaban Shah-Pahlavi, take a left turn down Faroukhi, just east of the Sabz-i Maidan. About the third main turning right then links through narrow streets with the Khiaban-i Sepah near the Ali Qapu, but before you reach this, set back on the left in a small open space is the entrance to the Dabirestan-i Rahnameh, a school that now occupies part of the old Madrasseh attached to the Haidarieh.

It looks rather drab and disappointing until you examine it closely, seeing the characteristics of a Sassanian fire temple with a square room covered by a dome, and one of the loveliest Saljuq stucco mihrabs, still with traces of blue paint. Pope[129] describes the stucco frieze as having 'perhaps the finest Kufic in all Persia . . . its deep corner squinches, formed by high pointed arches, are echoed in the decorative arched panels surrounding the upper wall.'

The brick vaulting and exotic floral stucco patterns are extraordinarily rich, and one of the first examples of small glazed elements can be seen here.

From the Haidarieh one can continue westwards to the Khiaban-i Sepah to see the other legacy of the Saljuqs, part of the splendid four-ivan Masjid-i Jumeh. A small open space with gardens lies before the entrance of the mosque, which stands on the west side of Sepah. The main part of the building is Safavid and Qajar but behind the south ivan lies the Saljuq prayer hall and sanctuary (A.D. 1109 to 1115), covered with a large dome, one of the two largest Saljuq domes in Iran, having the same diameter as the Masjid-i Jumeh in Isfahan, over 15 m. It was built in the reign of Muhammad, Malik Shah's son, on the site of a pre-Islamic building, probably also a Sassanian fire temple.

Originally the qibla wall was almost entirely covered by 'the largest mihrab in Islam', now disappeared; its workmanship must have been comparable with that of the contemporary Haidarieh and the Alavian tomb-tower in Hamadan (p. 111).

A double inscription frieze encircling the chamber bears an upper inscription in Kufic and a lower one in Naskhi, both white against a blue ground of vines and tendrils, again, to quote Pope, 'for sheer loveliness perhaps not equalled in Islam'. Ornamental loops of outset brick with sweeping curves decorate the walls. (Now being restored.)

In the Sabz-i Maidan a charming little Safavid pavilion is the only reminder (with the Ali Qapu gateway which is now the entrance to Police H.Q.) of Shah Tahmasp's palace. An upper floor and balcony was added in Qajar times, and the whole is a small museum, not open on Fridays. It houses a collection of prehistoric pottery, painted and carved wooden panels, Safavid tiles and paintings, stained glass, curtained palanquins and clothing, in a series of small vaulted rooms from the walls and ceilings of which layers of whitewash have recently been removed to reveal some engaging and very early Safavid murals.

As you leave the little museum, turn to your left and left again down Paigambaneh, the street that runs into Khiaban-i Sepah, and you'll find the old-fashioned but pleasant Grand Hotel, entered between a row of small shops. The chelo kebab here is good, and until the opening of the Tourist Inn, the Grand was the only recommended place for an overnight stay. Less sophisticated than the Inn, but clean and with a restaurant on the ground floor, is the Hotel Sa'di, in Kh. Sa'adi, (north), a crossing with Kh. Pahlavi. (*Sagzabad and Zagheh.)

From Qazvin one can reach the Assassin (formerly Dailamite) stronghold of Alamut and the shortest time in which the trip can comfortably be made is two days and a night, camping or taking sleeping bags and food. Beginning in summer 1974, Iran Safaris and Gulf Travel (Phone: Tehran 858271-5) jointly inaugurated inclusive escorted trips to Alamut, for 4,500 rials (August 1974) per person. This includes road transport to and from Tehran, mules for the final assault, overnight camping and food; parties leave on Thursday morning, returning Friday evening, during July and August only.

However, with your own transport, perhaps the loveliest time to try this is in May or autumn when the mountain route is lined with wild roses or russet autumnal tints. The longer but better route is by a good dirt road which goes north off the main Qazvin-Karaj road, just outside Qazvin itself. This is a regular country bus route, via Fanifin along the banks of the Shah Rud to Moallem Kelayeh and on to Shahrak and Shutur Khan on the Alamut river. From here a turn up the tributary leads to Gazur Khan, where you hire mules (about 150-200 rials a day, plus food for the mule), or climb some 800 m. to the base of the Alamut rock. From here the final climb takes about another hour.

It is sometimes possible to find hospitality with the headman (Katkhoda) of Gazur Khan village, naturally recompensing him.

A shorter, more spectacular route from the main Qazvin-Karaj road requires the use of a Land-Rover, taking a dirt road north (about 21 km. east of Qazvin) over the Chala Pass. But this route, particularly over the Chala Pass, has deteriorated so badly since the longer road to Qazvin was improved, that it is not recommended at all.

Alamut ('Eagle's Nest') is only one of many Assassin strongholds in the Alburz and other mountain ranges of Iran[110,152] and recent intensive studies include those by a Japanese team, led by Professor M. Honda of Hokaidu University, and Peter Willey.[183a, 183b] The original Alamut castle was built c. A.D. 860–861, probably by religious refugees from the Abbasid caliphs. It was about A.D. 1090 when Hassan al-Sabbah, 'The Old Man of the Mountains' as Marco Polo called him, founder of an offshoot of the ninth century Ismaili sect, captured the castle and made extensive alterations, rebuilding the greater part. (Hassan al-Sabbah was born in Ray in 1040 and died in 1124; he is believed to have been buried in the Sanjideh Mosque in Kh. Darwaza-i Ray, east of Kh. Rahahan in Qazvin. This small, square building was possibly built on the site of a fire temple and restored in Safavid times.) His practice of encouraging recruits by giving them hashish, then transporting them to a valley near Alamut to awake in enchanting gardens with handmaidens waiting on them (the recruits thought this was 'Paradise'), is believed by many to have given Hassan's followers the name of Assassins, but Willey believes the name derives from 'assas' or 'mission', implying that they were followers of Hassan's religious mission.

Willey also contends that their political assassinations, which made them so notorious, have been over-emphasized and their contribution to art, their deep religious devotion and their sophisticated irrigation and defence systems, have been overlooked or minimized.

Alamut was probably rebuilt again in the Safavid period and used as a royal prison in the seventeenth and eighteenth centuries. It is not just a fortress but a complex of fortified living quarters, mosques, gardens, domestic and work rooms, stables, underground chambers, wells and irrigation channels. Today the ground is strewn with typical light green turquoise or yellow ochre glazed pottery with geometrical patterns.

The great rocky outcrop is surrounded by higher mountains with magnificent views across the deep ravines and through the gaps in the hills. It was Hulagu Khan, the Mongol, who captured and destroyed the castle in A.D. 1256.

Among the several other Assassin castles near Alamut is the famous one of Maymoun Diz, just above the village of Shams Kilaya, to the north-west, reached by retracing the path back along the Alamut to Shahrak, and then turning north up a track to Shams Kilaya, from which there is a very steep and difficult climb to the summit of the great sandstone rock. Originally Maymoun Diz was a fortified garrison, castle and royal palace complex but it was utterly destroyed by Hulagu Khan.

Best preserved of all in this area, is the castle at Lammassar at the extreme west of the valley, 4 km. north of the village of Shahristan Bala, and on the top of a hill on the left bank of a little tributary of the Shahrud.

However, if you are interested in the Dailamites and Assassins, but not too anxious to attempt the rather arduous climbs that Alamut and Maymoun Diz involve, it is possible, in a long day from Tehran, to visit Samiran (sometimes also called Darband). This was the capital of one of the Dailamite princes, west of the Shahbanu Farah dam at Manjil, and has a castle that was captured by the Assassins.

From Qazvin, take the main highway to the north-west via Aghababa (30 km.) where the one-time H.Q. of Reza Shah Pahlavi has been turned into a museum. From Tehran to the dam is 256 km., crossing the Kuhin Pass which in winter is often blocked with snow. The main highway continues through tunnels along the east bank of the Sefid Rud river, but cross the dam itself, taking the dirt road that bears slightly left, and follow the north bank of the lake formed by the dam—the old course of the Qizil Uzun River. Continue for about 20 km. during which only two habitations are passed, a small farm and a chai khaneh, and about here you can see the castle for the first time, away to the left at the end of the lake. At 20 km. a rough track goes off to the left at an angle, and unless you have four-wheel drive you can continue only a short distance along this track before parking the vehicle and walking about 2 km., to the edge of a small plateau. From here you look down upon the remains of Samiran, which command the exit of a 2 km. long gorge. The walk is easy going down, but bare of shade, stony and in summer very hot. This site was first noted by Sir Henry Rawlinson in 1838 and, a few years later, by Dr. J. C. Häntzsche.

At least five tenth century mausolea in various conditions, and a tenth century castle on a superb site, are here, almost certainly built by the Dailamites then captured by the Assassins at the end of the eleventh century and for long occupied by them. If further work does prove the tomb-towers to be tenth century, we may look on them as the ancestors of the Kharraqan tomb-towers (p. 107).

The ruins of the old town extend for more than a kilometre along the river to the north-west and included a tower (now disappeared) with a double spiral staircase, examined by Peter Willey[183] in 1960 before the dam and lake were created. From the small approach plateau one looks down on a mosque-shrine of uncertain date, the silhouette of the castle magnificently situated on a spur to the left, and a well-preserved octagonal tomb-tower standing on a rocky hill separated from the plateau by the river which, even in June, is waist-deep, though not very wide. As the summer continues, the river shrinks to a trickle.

Other remains lie dotted around the area, and it is best to begin with the castle which is in fact no more than a shell, very Norman in appearance. Its brick towers and curtain walls with traces of decorative bands of inlaid brick pattern, crown a spur of land almost touching the further bank of the lake. There is nothing standing inside the walls and the best view of the castle is from the mainland, so the rather steep climb up to it is only worth while for the specialist.

The morning light is best for a dramatic photograph, from this point, of the major mausoleum some 500 metres to the north-west; on a ridge opposite the castle, there is another tomb-tower, which although roofless still has part of a stucco inscription on its exterior walls, and a third tower between the mosque and the castle, with some traces of stucco patterns of acanthus leaves, etc. round the interior base of the fallen dome. Between this tower and the mosque is a small semi-underground mausoleum of later date on the edge of the extensive graveyard, and the ground-plan of yet another tomb-tower has been traced by Mr. Robert Hillenbrand, east of this.

To reach the remaining two towers, one has to venture across a patch of deep, sticky red mud and wade the river, while the climb to the major mausoleum itself is inclined to be taxing for all but the very active. The tower itself is built around a jutting rock which forms part of its floor. A well-preserved staircase winds inside one of the semi-engaged buttress pillars on the west, with interesting vaulting and remains of wooden lintels over the entrance.

Round the base of the dome, inside (the brick dome itself being almost completely destroyed), a plastered decoration of arches with various profiles appears, while in the walls are many of the typical funnel-shaped scaffolding holes.

At the northern foot of this hill, on another low mound, are the remains of a fifth small, octagonal tower which appears to have been built on the same pattern, in miniature, as the others.

From Qazvin, the road back to Tehran passes close to several sites of archaeological interest, but where there is now little or nothing to be seen. These include Yang-i Imami, on the north of the road, some 33 km. west of Karaj; it has not been dug but some Median and many early Islamic sherds have been found on the surface. A restored Imamzadeh and an unusually charming Safavid caravanserai (now a gendarmerie post where photography is forbidden) are grouped around the mound.

Two kilometres further east on the outskirts of the village of Ramshahr, a side road crosses the main road from north to south. A sign, pointing north, indicates Vilian, and some 15 km. along this road (very muddy in winter and spring), 1 km. to the north of the village of Khurvin, is the prominent towering hill of Ganj Tepe (Treasure Hill) and the neighbouring Siah Tepe (Black Hill), which is a prolongation of Mount Alburz. These two mounds form the necropolis of Khurvin; and a number of Iron Age (c. 1300–800 B.C.) tombs were found here during two brief excavations by Iranian archaeologists in 1949, and by a Belgian mission in 1954.

For details of these and other nearby sites see Professor L. Vanden Berghe's reports,[175, 177] and Yolande Maleki's article.[113]

Many objects found here show associations with Chesmeh Ali (p. 48) and even more closely with Kara Tepe to the south-east of Ismailabad, and about 36 km. south-west of Tehran, in the Shahriar plain. Kara Tepe was occupied only in prehistoric times and was excavated by T. Burton Brown of Manchester University[16] in 1957, when links with Sialk II and Chesmeh Ali IA (p. 48) were found, from c. 5000–4500 B.C.

A prehistoric sewer skirting the mound drains the waters towards the outer slope, a rare feature of neolithic communities. Fine quality red pottery with black designs, hand-shaped, some stone weapons and clay ovens of exceptionally good design were among the many discoveries here. Other sites with similar black-painted red ware in this plain include Muhammad Abad near the Qum road about 50 km. from Tehran, and Kaleh Dasht near Saveh.

The remains of two Sassanian fire altars can also be seen in the course of a pleasant excursion from Tehran to the Shahriar area, starting down the Saveh road for about 44 km. to Kenargard village. Here take a dirt road to the right (west), through the large village of Asilabad, passing many tepes among the grassy meadows and orchards. Just outside Asilabad a blue sign for the Bank-e Saaderat (in Persian) points along the track to Doguin (or Jagheen—the villagers here are Turki-speaking and not always easy to understand), and then Deh Bocheh from where you can see the sugar-loaf hill of Takht-i Rustam, standing out at the end of a spur of low hills to the south (about 15 km. from Asilabad). Because of the constantly changing course of irrigation channels it is necessary to pick one's way or take a villager as guide, but in summer the trip may be done by ordinary car.

The track runs right by the foot of Takht-e Rustam and continues on to the Karaj road. Noted by Herzfeld[89] in 1926 and by Maxime Siroux[144b] the three platforms are built into a steep hill. The first, a huge block of masonry some 7·25 m. above the soil in the north corner, is pitted with the holes of treasure-seekers and has the remains of a vaulted, stone-built structure with steps leading down to chambers below ground, as well as a small mortared stone building with a dome only 2·38 m. from the ground in the interior. A steeper climb up the shaly cliff takes one to the top of the spur on which are two more terraces superimposed, and believed by Siroux to have supported Sassanian fire altars tended by the priests and watched from the lower terrace by the public.

Some 12 km. to the west is a similar but less important monument called Takht-i Kaikaus, consisting of a stone platform at the summit of a hill, and a so-called Chahar Taq (fire temple) at the foot, of which only low walls remain.

Another day's excursion is to the village of Damavand 60 km. east of Tehran on a good asphalt road, leaving by the Ab-Ali road from Shah-naz Square in the east of the capital.

About 10 km. from Tehran, a secondary road goes left (west) to Ushan, a small village on an old caravan route. Some 36 km. along this road is the village of Shahrestanek and a difficult climb of 800 m. above the village brings one to a Sassanian fire temple called the Qaleh-i Dukhtar, described in detail by Maxime Siroux.[144c]

Avoid the Ab Ali road at weekends and holidays, especially when the mountains are still snow-covered, for Tehranis flock in their hundreds to the ski slopes at Ab Ali. At Rudahen, about 42 km. from Tehran, turn right at a signposted (Persian) road in the village along the old Firuzkuh road, and about 17 km. further a left fork takes you into Damavand village, another popular weekend resort with many pictur-esque shrines and tomb-towers.

Damavand is almost at the junction of three ancient provinces, Mazandaran, Qumis and Jibal, and in the tenth century was renowned for its fertile fields and vineyards. On the right of the square a new Masjid-i Jumeh has replaced a splendid Saljuq mosque which had Timurid, Safavid and Qajar additions and was still in use until a well-meaning local philanthropist demolished it about 1958, to replace it with something more up-to-date.

The authorities heard of this only in time to save the lower part of two of the massive columns, now in the centre of the enclosed prayer hall, and the Saljuq brick minaret at the south-east corner of the complex.

Leave the mosque by the carved wooden doors near the minaret and cross the river at the back, by the small footbridge. It is also possible to drive along the back of the mosque to a small open space and park the car. Follow the lane up the hill on the further side of the river until it opens out into a small square, on the left-hand side of which the lane continues; after a few paces, a steeper, narrow footpath leads off to the left, at the top of which is an eleventh century tomb-tower locally ascribed to Sheikh Shibli, which has been described in detail by David Stronach and T. Cuyler Young Jr.[162]

This beautiful tower, 9·89 m. high, with rounded buttresses at each corner, has been restored. Its octagonal dome is sharply angled at the top and each side of the tower, which has a distinct batter, displays a vertical set of three rectangular panels, each with a variety of designs, all in brick. There may have been an inscription over the entrance façade in a now-damaged horizontal panel. Inside, the circular chamber has a rectangular vaulted basement and Mr. Stronach sees a number of links with the architecture of the tenth century tomb of the Samanids at Bukhara and with the brickwork of the early eleventh century mausoleum of Arslan Jadhib at Sangbast (p. 200), among others. However, a late eleventh century date is attributed to the Shibli tower, on the strength of the latest parallels.

According to local tradition the tower, or an earlier one on the same site, was built for Abu Bakr Dulaf Djahdar al-Shibli, a Sunni mystic born in Baghdad in A.D. 861 who was a deputy governor of Damavand up to A.D. 901 when he returned to Baghdad where he died and was buried in A.D. 945.

There are at least seven tomb-towers in Damavand and its immediate vicinity, but most are later in date. From the Shibli tower one can see, down in the town itself, the strikingly tent-like form of the Imamzadeh Abdullah Davud just off the lane continuing south from the back of the Masjid-i Jumeh. At the very end of the same lane is another, higher tomb-tower, that of Abdullah Khalilah, brother of Davud, dated to the end of the thirteenth or early fourteenth century, while if you turn right on leaving the back of the mosque, and walk to the end of the path, crossing another bridge at the end, there is, on the immediate right of the bridge by the river bank, the small Imamzadeh of Shams ed Din, set inside a shady courtyard and said to date from the early thirteenth century.

Not far from the Imamzadeh Abdullah Davud, on the left of the lane leading to Abdullah Khalilah, are two small, plain Imamzadehs reached through a door in a garden wall, both in the same patch of land, and known as the Haft Tan and Hasht Tan, each containing a single large tomb, one said to contain seven bodies, the other eight, of martyrs murdered at some date as unknown as that of the tombs themselves.

2 · The Caspian: Mazandaran and Gilan

There are four highways from Tehran to the Caspian (not counting an easterly road branching off from Shahrud to Shah-pasand), and a fifth is planned.

The rich valleys and wooded hills of the Alburz mountains, between Tehran and the Caspian Sea, attract heavy rainfall and in summer are apt to be humid and cloudy. Invaders from Central Asia made good use of the natural passes, many tribes settling in the lush upland valleys where some of the most remarkable archaeological discoveries have been made.

MAZANDARAN

One of the loveliest of the Caspian highways is that from Tehran to Gurgan, via Firuzkuh, just over 407 km. by road (one can also travel by a spectacular railway route). Leaving Tehran by the Damavand road (p. 61) it is 137 km. to Firuzkuh where there may have been a Sassanian Paradeisos (an enclosed royal hunting ground); here a right turn over the railway line will take you to the old Khurasan road to Mashad (p. 49), but keeping to the left you drive through some entrancing mountain scenery along what was also an old caravan road to the Caspian. At Zirab (204 km.), a small town on both sides of the road, you can divert to see two early tomb-towers, those of Lajim (A.D. 1022-3) and Resget (A.D. 1009), the latter near Pol-i Safid.

Two roads go from Zirab to the east. One, running north-east, reaches Lajim after 29 km., and here can be seen the lovely circular tower with its ovoid roof still intact. Known locally as the Imamzadeh Abdullah, it is in reality the tomb-tower of Shahriyar b. al-'Abbas b. Shahriyar, and bears a Pahlavi inscription as well as an Arabic one, proof of the long-lasting influence of the Sassanians in this area. From here one can walk (about four hours) to Resget, or return to Zirab and take a south-easterly road for some 25 km. The Resget tower is also circular and according to its inscription is that of Hormizdyar b. Maskara[66c] (?), or Nusyar ibn Maskara.(*Resget.)

A smaller, undated tower can be seen on the north of the Resget road, not far from Zirab, at a place known as Lamsar of Savadkuh.

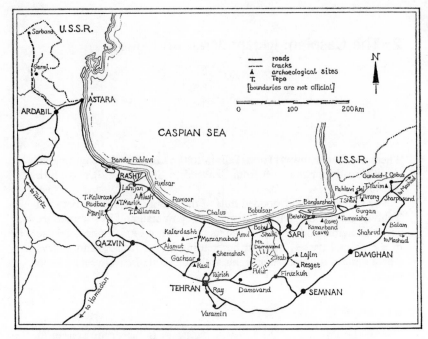

Map 3. The Caspian: Gilan, Mazandaran

Continuing north along the main road, there are glimpses of the lovely cone of Mount Damavand; the road passes through Shahi and then bears north-east for Sari. The town itself is thought to have been founded by the Sassanians, and when it was the capital of pre-Mongol Tabaristan (present-day Mazandaran province) it was called Sariyeh. It was the last part of Iran to be converted to Islam (four fire temples are said to have been in use here as late as the eighteenth century). The Tahirid dynasty moved the capital to nearby Amul in the ninth century. Devastated by Mongols at the beginning of the thirteenth century, Sari was rebuilt but again destroyed by Tamurlane in the fourteenth century.

There are a number of tomb-towers in and around Sari but none is older than the fourteenth century. Market day here is on Saturday, and the thatched, wooden houses with wide verandahs, often built on stilts, are typical of the Caspian and very reminiscent of the fertile mud hill tracts of Assam and Burma, particularly since this is a rice and tobacco-growing area.

For an overnight stop there are small local hotels and the Tourist Motel in Sari; alternatively, one can make a diversion of about 40 km. to the coast, turning north-west from Shahi to the little market town of

Babul (market day, Wednesday mornings) and on from there to Babul-sar and the Pahlavi Foundation's large Casino Hotel. Accommodation is not cheap, however (about 950 rials); much less expensive, clean and acceptable small hotels can be found in Shahi and Babul—at the Papoli in Babul, a room with three beds, armchairs and table, washbasin, etc., costs 200 rials each, with breakfast of eggs, bread, butter and coffee for 20 rials, served in the room (1970).

Returning to Shahi, continue along the fine, fast asphalt road north-east through Sari and on towards Gurgan—non-stop from Babul the drive takes about 2 hours, but there are many interesting sites in the district, the Gurgan plain being one of the richest areas for prehistoric mounds in the Near East.

About 3 km. west of Behshahr in the limestone cliffs to the south of the road, across some cotton fields, are the caves[24] dug by Dr. Carleton S. Coon of the University of Pennsylvania, in 1950. To reach them make for the village of Turujan, about 200 metres from the road, where the Ghar-i Kamarband or 'Belt Cave', whose entrance can be seen from the main road, looks across to the Caspian which was probably much nearer when the cave was occupied about 9500 B.C. There are two prehistoric mounds on the north of the main road, to help fix the location.

Both the Kamarband and the nearby Hotu cave, excavated by Dr. Coon, produced mesolithic and neolithic occupations, including the skeleton of a 12-year-old girl whose bones were painted with red ochre and interred after defleshing, her head upside down between her thighs.

Neolithic painted pottery similar to that found at Anau[25] in Russian Turkistan was found in the Hotu cave, where occupation levels, like those of Kamarband, were about 5 m. deep.

Carbon-14 tests gave a range of c. 9910 B.C. to c. A.D. 730 for the Hotu material, while the Kamarband Cave included what Coon then described as the oldest ceramic neolithic material so far found in the world, indicating that possibly the Caspian shores may have been the homeland of the neolithic peoples, some of whom moved westwards into Northern Europe. By 9500 B.C., the clay at the bottom of the cave had dried out sufficiently to be occupied by mesolithic seal hunters. Quarrying in this area has already damaged or threatened many caves and there is no saying how long Coon's caves may remain in existence.

Behshahr was formerly known as Ashraf, and on a hill overlooking its western approaches is the Safiabad palace, first built in the Safavid period, added to by Reza Shah and now used as a metereological station. Beyond Behshahr are more interesting caves dug by Dr. C. B. M. McBurney of the University of Cambridge in 1964.[114] About 1½ km. out of Behshahr, a small track to the south leads directly to the village of Ali Tappeh, at the eastern end of the ridge, in which there are

3

two caves. Closest to the village, one cave can be seen from the main road on an exposed limestone scar and this contained material dating to *c*. 12000 to 10000 B.C.

Dr. McBurney also excavated a cave south of Gunbad-i Qabus where tests of flints and similar material showed they originated from at least 40000 B.C. and possibly as far back as 60000 to 65000 B.C., being used by hunters of rhinoceros, wild horses and bears.

About 40 km. east of Behshahr, between Gaz and Kurdkuy, the road cuts through the walls that once stretched from the mountains south of the road, and the ninth century A.D. city of Tamis or Tammisha, to the Caspian, and were built as a protection against the raids of Turkoman tribes from Central Asia. The city's fortifications were partly Sassanian (probably A.D. 531–579, in the reign of Khusraw Anushirvan), and it was the capital of a local dynasty, with a cathedral mosque and a citadel, until the Mongol invasion in A.D. 1220. The remains are some 6 km. south of the new main road, between the villages of Sarkalata and Karkandeh and near the foot of the mountains. Dr. A. D. H. Bivar and Dr. G. Fehervari excavated the site in 1964 and today it is known locally as Kharabshahr, or 'the ruined city'.[9]

From the main road the long wall to the sea is now seen only as a series of low, grass-covered banks with a track along the top in places where the remains are between 2 and 2·50 m. wide. Saljuq sherds were found in the remains of a brick tower from lower levels, while terracotta figurines and other sherds probably date from the first to the fourth century A.D. The citadel was early Islamic and possibly built in A.D. 838 by Sarkhastan, Governor of Sari.

There is an early eleventh century tomb-tower, begun in A.D. 1016 by Abu Ja'far Muhammad b. Wandarin of the Bawand family, at Radkan West (not to be confused with the Radkan tomb-tower near Mashad). It was completed in A.D. 1020 and lies about 16 km. south of Kurdkuy near a village also called Radkan, and can be reached in a day's march or by horse, from the village of Sarkalata—arrangements should be made through the military authorities at Gurgan.

The Hotel Miami in the main square of Gurgan, in spite of rather garish lighting and decoration, offers comfortable rooms, some with European bathrooms, and a restaurant on the ground floor—reasonable prices and food. Originally called Astarabad ('City of Mules'), Gurgan is thought to have been founded about A.D. 720 by the Arabs, shortly after their conquest of Tabaristan. The town has a strikingly Turkoman air, its streets filled with Mongolian-featured men and women in colourful Turkoman dress. Behind the main street, on the north side, just before reaching the Miami Hotel, a tomb-tower, the Imamzadeh-i Nur (probably fourteenth century but possibly with Saljuq brickwork), lies near the Masjid-i Jumeh whose brick minaret may also be Saljuq.

On Thursday mornings, a Yamut Turkoman market is held from about 7–9 a.m. at the village of Pahlavi Dej, some 18 km. along a dirt road north from the main square of Gurgan. Turkoman yurts are occasionally seen in the plain, although many tribespeople now also live in permanent housing. Sturdy, small horses, carpets, karakol hats and tribal jewellery are offered for sale. A similar market is held on Monday mornings at Bandar Shah on the Caspian Sea.

Shah Tepe,[3] one of the first prehistoric mounds to be excavated in the Gurgan plain, lies about 10 km. north-west of Gurgan. Little can be seen of excavated structures although the Turkoman village at the base of the mound again provides an element of local colour.

Beyond Pahlavi Dej the so-called 'Alexander's Wall'—Sad-i Iskandar-or Qizil Alang (the 'Red Wall')—is about 20 km. north, across a flat plain in which there are dangerous quicksands. Here, so close to the frontier of the U.S.S.R., a police permit is required.

The wall was probably built by the Sassanian King Anushirvan in the sixth century A.D., as a defence against Central Asian tribes, and it stretched from about 5 km. east of the Caspian (which has since receded from the end of the wall) for more than 100 km. eastwards. It was reinforced by forts every 6 km. or so, but for centuries the wall has been robbed of bricks so that now it is reduced to little more than a low embankment some 5 m. wide and, in places, with several parallel ramparts.

As you continue along the road from Gurgan to Shah-pasand, the largest and perhaps most important of all prehistoric sites in the area, that of Tureng Tepe, Bronze Age capital of the district, can be seen about 17 km. from Gurgan and some nine km. on the north of the road, to be reached by a rough car track. There is a modern village at the foot of the mound overlooking a small lake, often dry in summer.

This huge, reddish-coloured mound was first excavated in 1931 by F. R. Wulsin,[186] on behalf of the University Museum. In 1960, Professor Jean Deshayes of the Universities of Lyon and Paris, and Mr. David Stronach, Director of the British Institute of Persian Studies in Tehran, explored various archaeological sites in the area, and subsequently Professor Deshayes began excavations.[32, 33, 34, 35] Islamic, Sassanian and Parthian structures were found on the upper levels, including a massive Sassanian building with thick walls, long corridors and elaborate terracotta drainage systems. This complex had often been rebuilt but finally destroyed by a tremendous fire in the later Sassanian period.

Remains of Achaemenian or possibly late Median buildings were found below these.

The lowest layers, unspoilt by an underground water level that halted the very deepest work, revealed sun-dried bricks of Bronze Age buildings mixed with small sherds of a very ancient pottery probably dating back to the sixth millennium B.C. From the early centuries of the third millennium B.C. a smooth grey ware, found on all the Gurgan Plain sites, was characteristic. Tureng Tepe was on the great highway from Central Asia to Mesopotamia and the vast number of lapis-lazuli beads that are found here are clear evidence of lively trade.[25]

Local peasants discovered the so-called 'Treasure of Astarabad' at this site, offering it to the then Shah in 1841, and it is believed to have come from the low mounded area of Bronze Age date making up the site which is spread in a circle round a small lake.

There were five main periods identified at Tureng Tepe, dating from about the sixth millennium B.C. down to Sassanian times, the richest epoch being Period III, c. 2800 to 1700 B.C., when the same kind of rhomboidal lapis-lazuli beads were found here as in the royal tombs of Ur, in Mesopotamia.

Soon after 2000 B.C. most Turkoman Steppe sites were deserted, but Tureng Tepe was occupied until about 1700 or 1600 B.C., by which time the local inhabitants—no doubt already dominated by Iranian invaders from the north—were producing new shapes in wheel-thrown grey pottery. Many of these last shapes anticipate those found from the mid-second millennium onwards in north-west Iran, at Khurvin (p. 60), Sialk (p. 170), Giyan (p. 116) and Hasanlu (p. 91). Recent studies of this ware have been connected with the movements of the Iranians who up till now were believed to have entered Iran through the north-west Caucasian passes about the ninth century B.C. Now it is thought likely that the earliest of the newcomers had already settled in the west as early as the second half of the second millennium, and from the fact that they appear to have adopted north-eastern pottery forms most of them at least probably entered Iran from this direction.[165]

Following the end of the Bronze Age settlement, there appears to have been a gap of some 1,000 years before the site was probably reoccupied in the Median period. An Achaemenian terrace of red baked bricks suggests a religious monument; following a Seleucid and Parthian occupation, the Sassanians built a series of impressive structures within fortified, buttressed walls. An eighth century A.D. fire temple was also erected on the summit of the mound before the site was destroyed by the Mongols. (*Iran*, Vols. XI, 1973 & XII, 1974.)

From Gurgan north-east to Shah-pasand is about 77 km. and here the asphalted highway continues east to Mashad, while another road branches south through the mountains to Bistam and Shahrud (p. 197).

In Shah-pasand there is a reasonable hotel, the Kurosh, and a few good shops for Turkoman saddle bags and rugs. A new road to the north takes you a further 20 km. to Gunbad-i Qabus where, of the small provincial hotels, the Sepid is probably the best. About 9 km. from Shah-pasand, a rough track to the west leads across fields to the pre-historic Yarim Tepe ('half tepe' since it is cut by the old road to Gonbad-i Qabus), excavated by Mr. David Stronach in 1960 and 1962.

This tepe, which stands 20 m. high and which was deeply cut by the river at its base, dates back to the early chalcolithic period, c. 5000 B.C. Following a gap in occupation, the mound was continuously in use from the late chalcolithic period, c. 3200 to 2800 B.C., down to c. 1800 B.C., when the site was abandoned, possibly with a hint of destruction.[25,26] Round about 1100 B.C. an Iron Age people occupied the site which continued to be inhabited until the late Parthian period, c. A.D. 200. The sequence revealed here shows many parallels with that emerging at Tureng Tepe (p. 67) to the west.

Gunbad-i Qabus (formerly known as Jurjan when it was the capital of the province) is a mainly Turkoman town whose claim to fame lies in the immense brick tomb-tower some 63 m. high and looking, even before some recent restoration at the summit, remarkably modern.

This unique great fluted shaft, with its conical roof, stands on a flattened mound and can be seen, like some gigantic pencil pointing to the sky, from very far away. Its intact inscription records that it was built by a local Ziyarid prince, Qabus ibn Vashmgir (or Shams al Ma'ali Qabus), in A.D. 1006. Qabus died in 1012 and his body is said to have been suspended at the top of the tower, which has no staircase, in a glass coffin on which the rays of the rising sun fell through a little opening on the east side of the roof.

The only decoration, apart from the ten dignified brick flanges, is in two bands of brick inscription on the exterior of the tower. These read, 'In the name of God the Merciful, the Compassionate: This is the lofty palace of the Amir Shams al-Ma'ali, the Amir, son of the Amir Qabus, son of Vashmgir. He ordered it to be built during his lifetime, year 399 lunar and year 375 solar.'

In 1899, Russians sank a shaft in the floor of the tower to a depth of some 12 m. searching for signs of a buried coffin, but found nothing other than a continuation of the deep foundations.

The old city of Jurjan lay about 4 km. west of the present-day town and was probably in ruins by the time of the Saljuq conquest. It was rebuilt by the grandson of Malik Shah in the twelfth century and later captured by the Mongols (Tamur built a palace there in A.D. 1393). The remains of a citadel, and several mounds covering other ruins, are divided by the Gurgan river, with the larger section on the south bank, behind the Imamzadeh Yahya. Here Dr. M. Y. Kiyani of the Iranian

Archaeological Service has been excavating since 1971, finding Samanid wells and storage pits, then paved Saljuq streets, large residential buildings, a haman and workshops with furnaces and pottery kilns. Much pottery from early Islamic to Mongol periods, including terra-cotta figurines, as well as gold coins, have been recovered. (See *Iran*, Vol. XI, 1973.)

Working now from east to west and taking the remaining highways across the Alburz to the Caspian in turn, the Haraz route is the shortest (175 km.) from Tehran. Like all these mountain roads, however, it is subject to avalanches and violent blizzards in winter, while during summer weekends and holidays it is often packed with holiday traffic as well as heavy vehicles.

From Tehran leave on the Damavand–Firuzkuh road past the ski resort of Ab Ali, off to the right, where there are several hotels and mineral springs, and an hotel and restaurant at the ski slopes themselves.

Ahead is the peak of Damavand volcano (5,629 m.), the highest peak in Iran, which can be easily climbed starting from the village of Rehneh just past the little town of Pulur.

Not far from here, Pulur is a good place for a coffee stop. Twenty-four km. further north a stone castle perches on the rocks across the river Haraz, on the right, blending into the generally brown land-scape. It is early medieval or possibly even Sassanian, and to reach it you must drive on as far as a bridge about a kilometre north of Rahneh and then turn back down the other side of the river.

The main road comes out of the mountains into terraced rice fields in a wide plain, and on down to Amul, capital of Tabaristan in the ninth century A.D., under the Tahirid dynasty, and at that time, with a port on the mouth of the Haraz, on the Caspian.

Famous in Saljuq times for its glazed pottery and glass, Amul lost its importance after the Mongol invasions of the thirteenth and fourteenth centuries.

It is a pleasant small town with a reasonable hotel, the Amul (400 rials single room and bath), by the river, and several interesting monu-ments including the fine Safavid Mashad Mir Buzurg built by Shah Abbas I on the site of a tenth to eleventh century shrine destroyed by Tamurlane. The unusual little Masjid-i Imam Ascari stands in a court-yard of orange trees, and close to this, three charming tomb-towers scattered in a meadow—but all are of the Mongol period or later.

Wander round the back streets by the Mashad Mir Burzurg to see the distinctive traditional Mazandaran houses with their sloping roofs, wide verandahs, stained-glass windows and cypress-tree and other decorative patterns painted on the outer walls.

From Amul one can drive to Babul, Sari and on to Gurgan, or to

Babulsar, and then, turning west, continue along the coast to Astara on the Soviet frontier. The route is scenically interesting, the paddy fields giving way to tea gardens in Gilan province; the local costumes, particularly those of the Gilan women, the thickly wooded hills to the south, where bears, wolves and other wild animals still roam, and the many summer resorts with numerous motels—usually quite expensive—and summer camps have made this a popular vacation area. The Imperial family have several summer homes along this coast, including one that is next to the fashionable Pahlavi Foundation's Grand Hotel at Ramsar. (The pleasant, clean little Pension Sahel, at the foot of the hill on which the Grand is built, offers rooms with two or three beds and wash-basin for 100 rials per head, a reasonable restaurant and car park.)

Ponies and cattle wander indiscriminately along the Caspian roads and can be a hazard, especially at dusk. The climate in this whole area is usually humid and rainfalls are frequent but it is an exceptionally green and attractive region. There are one or two shrines on the road, notably an unusually roofed Safavid mausoleum near Lahijan, the Sheikhaneh-bar, with a pagoda-type roof which can just be seen among the trees on the hills to the left of the road, before reaching Lahijan itself. Among the tombs in this shrine is that of the thirteenth century Sheikh Zahed Gilani, spiritual guide to Sheikh Safi al-Din, ancestor of the Safavid dynasty.

In the high valleys among the mountains to the south of Lahijan, Japanese archaeologists made a number of discoveries in the Dailaman region east of the Sefid Rud. It is a difficult area to reach, taking at least two days by mule or on foot from Lahijan. The Tokyo University expedition worked here from 1960 for several seasons, being particularly interested in the Partho-Sassanian tombs and their relationship to the T'ang and Sui dynasties in China and the Tomb and Nara periods of Japan.

Bronze Age and Partho-Sassanian tombs were found, certain of the later burials possibly being Achaemenian. Pit burials and shaft graves were found at Hassani Mahale,[151] east of Dailaman village, with lead and glass bowls, bronze mirrors and animal figurines among the furnishings. Two or more corpses were in the graves and the possibility exists that these represent the self-immolation of chieftains and their attendants. Other sites in the same area revealed pit and urn burials and, besides jewellery, pottery, etc., some armour typical of the Scytho-Sarmatians from eastern Russia, Siberia and north Mongolia.

Almost all the sites had previously been illegally dug (many antiques on sale in Tehran shops come from this region and are usually collectively designated as Amlash, the name of a district south of Langarud, near Lahijan, and generally dated to the first millennium B.C.).

Anthropological studies revealed that the area had been occupied in prehistoric times by a Mediterranean type and, by the mid second millennium B.C., was overrun by races from the north. By the tenth century B.C. these invaders had formed a kingdom and made large cists for their dead. Tombs for the common people of the old Mediterranean type were still in use and were found especially at Noruzmahale,[47] north-east of Dailaman, on top of a hill, and at Khoramrud, 2 km. east of a stream running near the possibly Achaemenid or Parthian site of Ghalekuti,[46] north-west of Kuhpas village, where there are catacombs similar to those found in southern Russia.

The main highway continues on to Rasht, Bandar Pahlavi and Astara on the Soviet frontier.

Taking the Chalus route, which rivals the Firuzkuh road in its magnificent scenery, one starts off from Tehran westwards to Karaj, a twenty minutes' drive along the freeway. At the roundabout in Karaj, turn right along the signposted road to the Amir Kabir Dam, which is a favourite summer outing for Tehranis. There is a water-ski club at the Dam, some 25 km. along the road, after which the highway twists and turns through an increasing number of tunnels and along spectacular precipices overlooking deep, wooded gorges.

About 100 km. from Tehran the road passes the village of Kasil, on the left of the valley, while on the right of the road, at the foot of the mountains, is a restored, early Mongol or possibly late Saljuq tomb-tower. Another 10 km. on, the road goes through the coal-mining town of Gach-i Sar with a small hotel on the left of the main road.

Next comes the 1200-m.-long tunnel of Kendvan which brings you out on the Caspian slopes of the mountains, and to Valiabad, about 140 km. from Tehran, where, on the right of the road, the late Reza Shah the Great built a small pavilion beside a waterfall.

The entire route is full of breathtakingly lovely panoramas. At 176 km., in the small town of Marzanabad, a fairly good road which is signposted goes left for some 24 km. to Kalar Dasht where, during excavations for a royal residence, in 1934, the famous Kalar Dasht treasure was found. It is now in the Tehran Museum. In underground chambers workmen found skeletons and funerary offerings of gold and bronze.

This road continues through forests and fertile valleys to the Alam Kuh and the Takht-i Sulaiman (not to be confused with the archaeological site of the same name, in Azarbaijan) peaks attracting many climbers. About 22 km. from Marzanabad is a Government Tourist complex and 5 km. further on is Chalus with several small hotels including the Chalus and smaller Kian. West of Chalus along the coast at Namak-abru, a luxury hotel with golf course and marina was scheduled to open in 1975.

GILAN

Last of the great highways across the Alburz mountains is the Rasht road (343 km. from Tehran), which offers most to the archaeologist. This highway is reached by continuing on from Karaj along to Qazvin, over the Kuhin pass and past the Shahbanu Farah Dam at Manjil (256 km.).

For the Caspian, however, keep on the east side of the river Sefid and about 9 km. from the dam you will reach Rudbar. Some 10 km. north of Rudbar, a turn east into the mountains for about 4 km. reaches the lovely valley of the Gohar Rud, dominated by the snow-capped peak of Mount Dolfak (2,705 metres), and here are five major, culturally related archaeological sites. There is also a new route from Rudbar bridge.

One of the most important recent discoveries in this valley has been that of the second to first millennium B.C. royal necropolis of Marlik,[123] dug by Professor Ezzatullah Negahban for the Iranian Archaeological Service in 1961 and 1962. (Other important sites here include Zeynab Bejar, Dura Bejar, Pileh Qal'eh and, close to Marlik, Jazim Kul.)

Marlik, locally known as Cheragh 'Ali Tepe, has the appearance of a natural hill, its crown being 135 m. long and 80 m. wide and covered with olive trees. But when Professor Negahban excavated it he discovered the burial mound of a vanished civilization whose existence had never even been suspected, and with priceless treasures including beautifully worked gold and silver vessels, now in the Tehran Museum.

Like many other tepes in these valleys, Marlik had been looted by antique hunters and illegal diggers. Some fifty-three roughly constructed tomb chambers were excavated, some with altars for funerary offerings, and hearths, occupying the single archaeological layer where the dead had been buried over a period of two to three centuries. The tombs were of four types, the first consisting of large, irregularly shaped rooms averaging 5 m. × 3 m., whose funerary furnishings of bronze weapons appeared to be those of the tombs of warriors or warrior kings.

The second type was smaller and rectangular, probably housing queens and royal princes, with delicate ornaments, gold jewellery and bronze and terracotta figurines. The third type was roughly 3 m. square, more carefully constructed than the others, but with fewer funerary objects and probably belonging to the earlier as yet undeveloped period of the Marlik culture. The last type, about 1 m. × 2 m., contained the remains of horses and was constructed of boulders, usually adjoining the tombs of their presumed owners. Bronze horse-bits

3*

and loops found here indicate the sacrifice of a horse that was to provide its dead owner with a mount in the next life.

The inscription on one of two cylinder seals was probably contemporary with the mid Assyrian period, 1250–883 B.C., while a comparative study of other objects seems to Professor Negahban to show that the Marlik culture influenced the craftsmen whose works were found in Sialk Cemetery B (p. 171), Ziwiye (p. 96), Hasanlu (p. 91), Kalar Dasht (p. 72), Khurvin (p. 60) and several Luristan and Caucasian sites. Such Assyrian motifs as the Tree of Life, winged bulls and griffins, and mountain goats eating the leaves of the Tree of Life, are all used on Marlik vessels. Marlik potters and goldsmiths were part of an artistic school that influenced an area embracing northern, western and central Iran and the art of Urartu, and the Neo-Assyrian, Median and Achaemenid arts. Behind this culture was the strong political power of Marlik which can be associated with the arrival of new Indo-European elements. Probably with the beginning of the first millennium B.C. Marlik began to decline, its people driven by pressure from western states to the central Iranian plateau, where they left their cultural evidence. Like other sites in the area, Marlik today is overgrown and has little to show the visitor.

Not far off, the site of another necropolis was found, at Kaluraz, where Mr. Ali Hakemi of the Iranian Archaeological Service carried out excavations in 1967. (See *Asia Institute Bulletin*, No. 3, 1973.)

The village of old Rostamabad lies on the west bank of the Sefid Rud about 15 km. north of Rudbar—the river can usually be crossed at this point. 1 km. west of the village is Gandjapar which is just on the north of the track going westwards, following the north bank of the river Kaluraz flowing into the Sefid Rud. Here was a centre for a people whose precise identity is again a matter for speculation.

This area—one possibly described in the Avesta as 'the fourteenth land, Varena, the best of them all'—lay between Urartu, Media and Scythia, the cross roads between great trade routes and therefore open to many influences.

This little-known Bronze Age civilization developed during the first half of the first millennium B.C. and preliminary excavations revealed the stone foundations of several wooden buildings and nearby tombs on both banks of the Kaluraz. One type of tomb was eliptical, being hollowed out of rock, the second type square, made of stone. The dead, including horses, were laid in a north-to-south direction, facing the sun and surrounded by rich funerary offerings. Two remarkable vases, one of gold and the other of gold and silver, with animals in high relief, together with necklaces and earrings in gold, are among the outstanding objects found here, and can now be seen in the Tehran Museum. Here in Kaluraz can also be seen similarities with pottery from Azarbaijan, Kordestan and Luristan, while Mr. Hakemi sees Urartu, Saca and Median influence in the metalwork.[77]

There must be many more as yet unknown sites hidden in the valleys in these wooded mountains.

The main highway on the east bank of the river continues on to Rasht where there is a reasonable hotel, the Iran, in the main square, and from thence on to the coast and the caviar centre of Bandar Pahlavi. Here there is the Grand Hotel Ghazeuan which charges the same as the Iran in Rasht (500 rials for a double room, some with private bath). On the outskirts, facing the sea, the newer Pahlavi Foundation Hotel offers first-class accommodation, and there is also a Tourist Camp.

The road continues to follow the Caspian northwards for another 152 km. to the frontier town of Astara, and Bronze Age sites of the second and first millennium B.C. have been found west of this road in the strip of land between the sea and the mountains, known as Talish. There is a small Government Tourist Inn by the sea at Astara.

From Astara one can drive to Ardabil (p. 78) only 70 odd km. west, but the road, through hilly, wooded country has deteriorated, and it may be better to reach Ardabil by the longer road from Tabriz.

In the area known as Germi, about 120 km. on a good road north-east of Ardabil, in the spur of land that juts into the U.S.S.R., Mr. Kambakhsh Fard of the Iranian Archaeological Service has carried out recent excavations, discovering literally hundreds of Parthian burials in urns and in stone graves. Many of the urns were closed with stones inscribed with the swastika sign and other emblems. One of them contained a body still wrapped in material in faded colours of blue, orange, brown and cream and which embodied the Greek key border pattern, the swastika and a checkered design.

Attractive pottery, beads, spindle whorls, coins, bracelets and other finds all helped to date the necropolis at about A.D. 50–70 in the reign of the Parthian King Gotarzes or Vologazes I.

3 · Azarbaijan, Kordestan

'The plains and mountain valleys of north-west Iran are littered with the skeletons of ancient cities. They lie, great mounds of deserted earth, like sleeping turtles upon the landscape. Each contains the secret of its own life and death. Collectively they constitute a monument to the pride and energy of their builders, a testament to their fate.'

This description by Professor Robert H. Dyson, Jr.,[38] is so accurate and vivid a picture of Azarbaijan that it cannot be bettered. For many thousands of years invaders of various nationalities have entered Iran by the natural highways and mountain passes in the west and north, some to conquer and withdraw, others to settle and themselves become part of the rich fabric of the country.

Even today the main highway from Europe to the Far East follows the old caravan route through Azarbaijan, passing via Tabriz, the provincial capital, to Tehran some 640 km. to the east.

There are daily flights to Tabriz and a good long-distance bus service by T.B.T., Levantour and others, as well as a daily train service which takes about sixteen hours.

The road goes through Qazvin (p. 54), Takestan (p. 53) and then to Zanjan, passing the turning for Qurveh (p. 51). After about 1½ hours' drive from Qazvin, some 160 km., one can see the astonishing egg-shaped dome of the Mausoleum of Oljeitu, rising above the rooftops of the little hamlet of Sultaniyeh about 8 km. to the left of the road. The access track to the Mausoleum has now been improved. Although this building is later than the Saljuq period limiting this guide, it cannot be ignored. Described by Pope as 'one of Persia's supreme architectural achievements',[129] it was built by Oljeitu in what was to have been the imperial capital of Sultaniyeh, at the beginning of the fourteenth century. A Mongol tomb-tower and Khanegah are also in the village and the traveller is strongly recommended to visit the Mausoleum whose impact cannot really be experienced from afar. Its dome has been described by Godard as being 'perfectly conceived and constructed'.[71] Italian experts are still restoring the building (1975) and permission to enter must be obtained from the Ministry of Art and Culture.

About 37 km. further along the main highway the town of Zanjan offers good overnight accommodation at a Pahlavi Foundation hotel, the

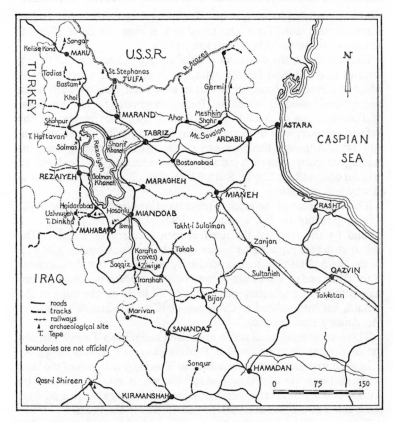

Map 4. Azarbaijan, Kordestan

Bimeh-Iran (double room and bath 550 rials) just off the main square; there are also several smaller hotels in the main street.

Zanjan was an important town during the Sassanian era but, like other towns along this route, was devastated during the Mongol invasion.

The remains of many Safavid and later caravanserais can be seen along the road, and just before Mianeh a very beautiful but ruined late fifteenth century bridge still spans part of the Qizul Uzun river.

Mianeh is a fairly large town, important, from Sassanian times until attacked by Mongols. (*Qaleh-i Zohak.) Back on the main Tabriz road, at Bostanabad, about 57 km. from Siah Chaman, a road goes to the right, to Ardabil, about 157 km. to the north-east. The mountain road is extremely picturesque but, like most of the roads of Azarbaijan, is not recommended for winter travel as it is swept by fierce blizzards and snow storms and often completely blocked.

Kuh-i Savalan, the dominant peak of eastern Azarbaijan (4,811 m.), features in the ancient Iranian epics, and is one of the many places in which the Prophet Zoroaster is said to have been born. Ardabil itself, said to be of Sassanian foundation, is justly celebrated for the very beautiful mausoleum of Sheikh Ishaq Safi al-Din, the founder of the Safavid dynasty, who lived and died in the city, being buried there in A.D. 1334. Although there are one or two other interesting sites, including an early sixteenth century mausoleum that has replaced an original one built for Sheikh Safi's father, the only Saljuq monument is in very poor condition.

This is the base of the brick minaret standing alone by the side of the ruined, possibly twelfth century or Mongol, Masjid-i Jumeh, on a mound by the river on the north-eastern outskirts of Ardabil. The Saljuq structure replaced an earlier cathedral mosque built c. A.D. 950. Of the Saljuq building there is practically nothing left but the remnants of the dome and exterior walls around which a modern mosque has been constructed. The minaret, which stands by itself on the edge of the mound, has been related to the group of Kirman minarets studied by Mr. Antony Hutt (p. 266).

There are several small hotels in Ardabil including a Tourist Inn and the simple but clean Aria in Kh. Pahlavi, (200 rials double, 1974).

In good weather one can drive back to Tabriz by the longer (269 km.) northern route via Meshkin Shahr;[75] the whole area is occupied by Turki-speaking Shahsavan nomadic tribes. The village boasts a Mongol tomb tower and a Sassanian inscription outside to the south.

Tabriz itself is surrounded by mountains which provide good skiing during its severe and often long winters, and although according to tradition it was founded in Sassanian times or even earlier, it was more probably founded after the Arab conquest, some say by the wife of Harun al-Rashid in A.D. 791, and was certainly a flourishing centre in Saljuq times. Often devastated by severe earthquakes, Tabriz today is the second largest city in Iran, but surprisingly little remains of its early glories.

There is a large Government Tourist Motel by the railway station, and a pleasant, efficient Government Tourist Camp on the shores of the Shahgoli Lake, set in attractive public gardens, but apt to be noisy on holidays. This is to the south-east of the University. In addition, a number of reasonable hotels in the centre of the town include the Asia, over the cinema of the same name in Kh. Shahpur, with an excellent restaurant serving European and Persian food, and, in nearby Kh.

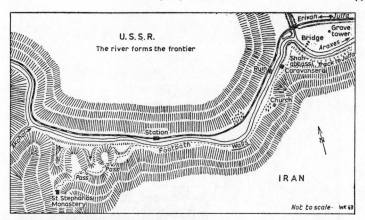

Fig. 8. Map showing route to St. Stephanos.
(*By courtesy of Professor W. Kleiss*)

Pahlavi, the Metropol. Among the even less expensive hotels are the Grand Hotel, and the Hotel Now, in Kucheh Pahlavi, and the noisy but clean and cheap Kayhan, by the side of the Paymah bus station. The newer International Hotel has costly air-conditioned accommodation.

Tabriz has a slightly old-fashioned, early nineteenth century atmosphere with a distinct Russian flavour. Its covered bazaars, offering splendid rugs and furs, especially fox pelts, lie mainly along Kh. Pahlavi. Skilled Armenian silversmiths—who will make jewellery and other articles to your design almost overnight—and numerous confectioners who cook a special type of gaz (nougat) each add to the city's attractions.

The Il-Khanid Mongol dynasty made Tabriz their capital, and the main intellectual centre of their empire. The Turkomen who followed, built the restored fifteenth century Masjid-i Kabud (or Blue Mosque) with its dazzling faience tilework and delicate marble dado with Naskhi inscriptions. The adjoining Azarbaijan Museum is also well worth a visit. The key to the Mosque, still under restoration (1974) is held in the museum.

Another small museum of specialist interest is attached to the old Armenian Church of St. Mary in the vicinity of the bazaar. The building was noted by Marco Polo in A.D. 1294, and possibly some of the original walls and vaulting still remain behind the altar. A varied range of exhibits includes the carved wooden doors taken from the Church of St. Thaddeus (p. 86).

The outstanding building dominating the Tabriz skyline is the massive qibla wall of the so-called Arg, built as the Masjid-i Ali Shah. Characterized by splendid plain brickwork this single fragment is now

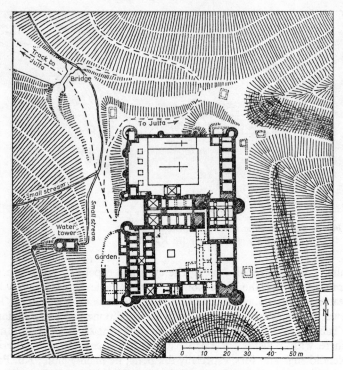

Fig. 9. Ground plan of the cloisters, St. Stephanos.
(*By courtesy of Professor W. Kleiss*)

all that remains of the extraordinarily lavish mosque of gold and marble that was erected by Oljeitu's vizier in the early fourteenth century.

The Masjid-i Jumeh in the fifteenth century covered bazaar is of eleventh century Saljuq origin but has often been restored and rebuilt.

Some 38 km. north-west of Tabriz, at Mujumbar, a tiny tenth century Armenian church and chapel are still maintained and reached by a track off the old road to Marand,[102] where there is a Tourist Inn. (*Mujumbar.)

The road from Tabriz to the Turkish border is a new, well-built highway passing through interesting country to Marand, 71 km., where the Masjid-i Jumeh, although of Saljuq origins, was rebuilt in the fourteenth century. The interior has a fine stucco mihrab.

From Marand the railway from Tabriz continues north to the border town of Julfa on the Soviet frontier. By road it is about 66 km.

Near here is the magnificent early Armenian Monastery Church of St. Stephanos, isolated among the mountains on the right bank of the

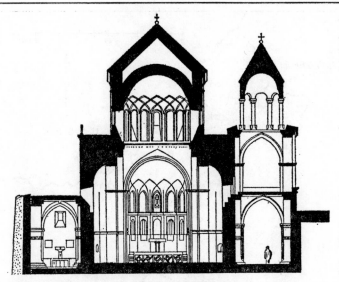

Fig. 10. Section of St. Stephanos, north-south.
(*By courtesy of Professor W. Kleiss*)

River Araxes which forms the frontier. For the necessary military permit apply to the Gendarmerie at Shah Abbasi, 11 km. w. of Julfa; no photography is allowed *en route* and foreigners must have an escort. Drive west for 45–60 mins. (instead of the three hour walk or mule ride formerly necessary).

The monastery is said to have been founded by St. Bartholomew the Apostle, probably in the year A.D. 62. The present sanctuary building is attributed to King Ashot of Armenia (crowned A.D. 885–6), although the major part of the strongly fortified building with its fluted dome in red and white stone, its stalactite portal and other Islamic-influenced tile decoration, stems from the sixteenth century.[101]

From Marand the main highway to Europe goes on to the Turkish frontier at Bazargan, passing through the little town of Maku, 22 km. east of the frontier. Here the houses cling to both sides of a steep gorge through which runs the main highway, forming the main street of Maku. On the western edge of the town the Government's Maku Inn offers comfortable accommodation (550 rials for rooms with two beds and bathroom), and a good restaurant. Smaller provincial hotels charge about 150 rials per bed, and one, Hotel Hafiz, is conveniently located near the Mihan Tour bus stop.

From Maku one can reach several interesting sites surveyed or excavated by Professor Kleiss. Among these is the Urartian site of Sangar[100]

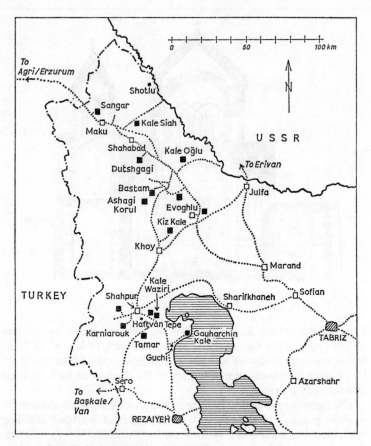

Fig. 11. Map of Urartian sites in Azarbaijan.
(*By courtesy of Professor W. Kleiss*)

about 9 km. west of Maku, along the main highway, and some 2 km. along a track to the north. The Urartians, a powerful people whose kingdom was centred around Lake Van in Turkey, have recently been found to have ruled much of western Azarbaijan from the late ninth to the seventh century B.C. There appears to have been a close relationship between the Urartians and the Armenians; some authorities believe the two races either intermarried or even that the Armenians are direct descendants of the Urartians.

At Sangar there is a terraced Urartian fortress of the eighth century B.C. with a rock-cut chamber and an impressive staircase of thirty steps carved out of the solid rock.

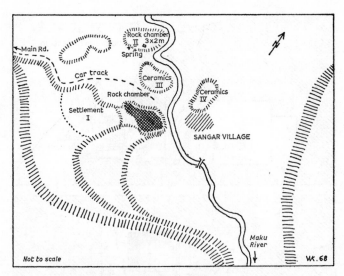

Fig. 12. Sketch map of route to Sangar.
(*By courtesy of Professor W. Kleiss*)

The scanty remains of a tenth century A.D. church (just one corner) called Kelise Kand or Arab Dizeh,[102] are sited 37 km. west of Maku, turning left on the last and only road in that direction (south) before reaching the frontier. The German team has identified some 50 Urartian sites in Azarbaijan. They include Kale Siah,[100] near the Soviet frontier, typified by its red polished ware; and Sufi,[102] a site with a striking 'chessboard' town plan, that lies east of Shahabad, about 45 km. east of Maku on the main highway, and 3 km. along a track running south from the main road.[6]

Driving back from Maku on the highway there are two sites of outstanding interest, that of Bastam, the most important Urartian site so far discovered in Iran, and the scene of regular excavations by Dr. Kleiss since 1968, and the famous Armenian church of St. Thaddeus or Tadios, in the heart of the mountains west of Bastam.

To reach Bastam, return for 72 km. from Maku, then just before a new road leading north to the Araxes Barrage, take a gravel road to the south, close to the village of Qaraziadin. This is the old road to Khuy (Khoi) that also brings you to the well-defined side road that leads westwards to Kara Kelise (Tadios) and on to Siah Cheshme. For Bastam, however, continue southwards for 2 km. until you see what appear to be two parallel diagonal lines of a natural rock outcrop on a steep hill 3 km. off to the right. These are in fact two of the solid

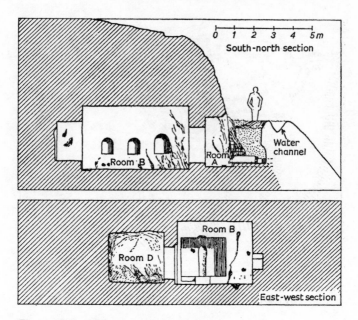

Fig. 13. Caves of Sangar, eighth century B.C.
(*By courtesy of Professor W. Kleiss*)

defensive walls of the Urartian fortress—each best photographed in the
early morning light.

At the time of writing the German Archaeological Institute is still
actively engaged in excavating the site during the summer months. The
camp of the expedition can be seen at the foot of the cliff. To the east
stretches the Urartian settlement, where in 1970 finds included a small
piece of gold decorated with six leaves, which could have been part of
the appliquéd decoration on the foot of a bronze chair, to judge from
examples found elsewhere. Between this and the camp are the massive
remains of the fortress with the great North gateway and its two flanking
towers and buttressed walls of stone, 5 m. high. Mud-brick walls were
originally constructed on top of these. An eighth century B.C. hall, whose
roof was supported by 14 columns, stands by the side of the gate.

The site of a square tower-temple measuring 14 × 14 m. was discovered near the summit of the cliff behind the settlement together
with fragments of a medieval period Armenian fortress and village,
including worked blocks of black stone of the same type as that found
at nearby Tadios, with Armenian crosses marked on them. A fragment
of an Urartian inscription was also found here in 1970, while other work

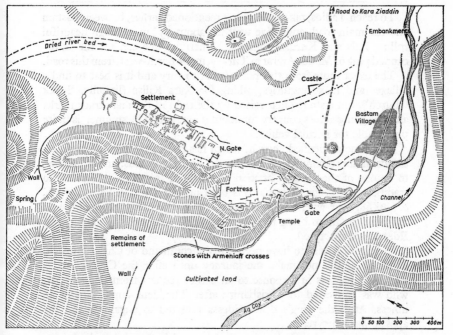

Fig. 14. Sketch plan of Bastam.
(*By courtesy of Professor W. Kleiss*)

that season saw the complete excavation of the South gate, with a columned hall close by, a small palace north of the Urartian village and the massive stone foundations of the inner fortification walls which still retained some of their original mud-brick construction above.

It should be added that a particularly unpleasant type of large spider conceals itself in webbed tunnels among the rocks around Bastam, emerging during rains to seek shelter in tents and houses.

From the crest of the fortified hill one looks down on the Aq Chai river and the old Khuy road winding through the hills to the south.

This site has been identified with the important Urartian city of Ruza-Urutur founded by King Rusa II, son of Arguishti, between 685 and 645 B.C., according to an inscription found in 1910 embedded in the walls of a house in Maku, and now in the Tehran Museum. The huge fortress, larger than any Urartian fortress so far discovered in Iran or outside, with the exception of two major ones at the Urartian capital by Lake Van, measures some 850 × 400 m. The town itself covers an area of 600 × 300 m. and, like the fortress, has already yielded a rich range of typical Urartian red polished ware.[100] (*Bastam.)

To reach Tadios, take the turning mentioned earlier, between Bastam and the main road, and drive west for about 45 km. through beautiful rolling hills and Kurdish villages. Sometimes one can see the snow-capped peak of Mount Ararat in Turkey, to the north-west, from this road.

The exact route from this point is apt to vary and it is best to find a villager and make inquiries, asking for Kara Kilise (literally, 'Black Church'), but a stone pillar raised by the right of the main track marks another going across country for about 7 km. which in summer is quite practicable for normal vehicles.

The famous fortified church, which has been restored several times, stands on a promontory surrounded by high, wild hills, and is claimed to be one of the oldest Christian churches in existence. According to tradition, the original church was built on the site of a pagan temple, c. A.D. 68, near where St. Thaddeus, son or brother of St. James, and the first apostle to bring the gospel to what was then the kingdom of Edessa, was martyred.

Thaddeus is said to have been sent by command of Christ Himself, although he did not make the journey until after the Crucifixion, c. A.D. 35. This was in response to an earlier request from King Abgar, who was converted to Christianity after Thaddeus cured him of an illness. After the king's death Edessa reverted to paganism and the apostle was martyred.

Most of the original church was destroyed in an earthquake in A.D. 1319, and the oldest part today is the rear portion, with the altar, baptistry and conical black and white striped stone dome, probably dating from about the tenth century A.D. The grave of the saint is believed to lie in the niche to the right of the altar. The newer portion of the church, in light golden stone with many decorative reliefs, was built in the seventeenth century, after the church was enlarged about the end of the fourteenth century, and restored in the nineteenth. An inscription in the church refers to the fourteenth century earthquake that created so much damage.

There are fifteen rooms on the north side of the courtyard surrounding the church, and nine on the east, while from the high ground on the north, which is reached by a flight of steps in the corner of the courtyard, one can see the monastery buildings, including kitchens, a flour mill and a carved wooden pole that forms part of an oil press.[102]

Once a year the church comes to life on the Feast of St. Thaddeus, about the middle of July, when services are held during a three days' festival attended by Armenian pilgrims from all parts of the world. Sometimes there are 7,000–8,000 people camping out in the meadows surrounding the church, when folk dances and songs are interspersed with solemn religious processions.

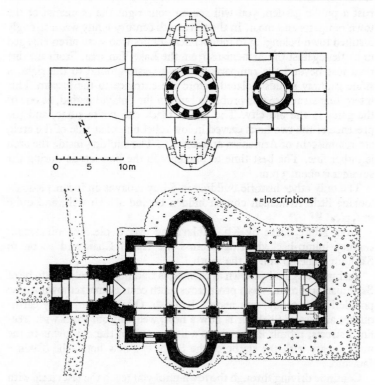

Fig. 15. Ground plan of St. Thaddeus showing position of inscriptions; the original small church is the extreme eastern portion.
(*By courtesy of Professor W. Kleiss*)

There are three small Armenian chapels perched on the hills around the main cathedral, the two best preserved being on the hills across a stream to the north of the church.

Take a picnic meal on this trip for there are no chai khanehs and only one or two small, isolated farm buildings.

The old road continuing south past Bastam for some 50 km. to Khuy can be traversed by car but it may prove more comfortable to return to the main Maku-Tabriz road, continue east for a few km. before reaching the fast new highway and then turn right, to Khuy, about 30 km. from the turning.

You come into the town by a petrol station and here a right turn takes you into the main centre. The Government Tourist Inn is situated along here, but if you bear left along a dirt road over a small bridge and past a public garden, you will see on your right the remnants of the town ramparts and moat. In the thirteenth century Khuy was a strongly fortified town belonging to independent Emirs who were often engaged in battles against the Armenians from the Lake Van area. From the dirt road just beyond the ramparts, across a waste-ground to the right, a stone gateway stands isolated before the entrance to the bazaar. This interesting structure was probably built in the Safavid period, as one of the gates to the old city. The use of black and white stone, and the presence of the two lions carved in low relief on either side of the arch, are reminiscent of Armenian architecture. The vaulting inside the arch is rather fine. The best time to photograph the lion façade during the summer is about 3 p.m.

The only other historic building in Khuy today is an inconspicuous-looking little Armenian church hidden behind a high wall, and quite untypical.[102]

From Khuy, leave by Kh. Pahlavi and over a pleasant nineteenth century hump-backed bridge across the Aland Chai, and so on to Shahpur some 40 km. to the south.

Shahpur, originally known as Selmas, is traditionally believed to be of Sassanian origin and was a prosperous tenth century market town whose population, as today, was mainly Kurdish. Often destroyed by earthquakes and wars, Shahpur is now a neat, well-laid-out town with tree-lined streets, rebuilt in the 1930s a little south of the old town. In the main square with the statue of the Shah, is a new hotel, the Takht-e Jamshid.

Continue driving through the town until you reach the last circle with a petrol station on the corner. Here you turn right on to a dirt road, and take the first turning left for about 4 km. to the village of Haftavan. On a corner on the right of the road, is an early thirteenth century Armenian church,[102] restored, and the roofless shell of what was once an Opera House built about 30 years ago. In the grounds surrounding these is the local school which in the season houses the British archaeological team, directed by Mr. Charles Burney of the University of Manchester, that has been excavating the major prehistoric site of Haftavan tepe since 1968.

To reach the site return to the filling station and continue on by the side of the garage on what is the main road to Rezaiyeh. A short distance along this road a dirt track takes off to the right, winding between garbage dumps and into the open fields which are cut by irrigation ditches and streams and much marshland. The large white mound can be seen from the main road, and the track to the tepe has been considerably improved since work here began.

This is one of the largest sites in north-western Iran with a long history of settlement dating back to the fourth millennium B.C. or earlier. The mound, which is also known as Butan Tepe, Toban Tepe and Tam Tepe, is some 550 × 400 m. in area and about 27 m. high. It was partially dug in the 1930s. Early Sassanian walls surrounded the town.

The highest part of the main mound was occupied by an Urartian citadel, probably destroyed by Sargon II (714 B.C.) or by the Cimmerians. In the early sixth century B.C. came a brief Median occupation, followed by Achaemenian and Parthian stone structures and pavements; finally early Sassanian graves were dug into the summit of the citadel.

The site was probably only partially occupied in the second millennium B.C. after a long, earlier occupation, the citadel being built on an Early Bronze Age mound. At the foot of the north-east slope of the mound, hard by a spring which doubtless supplied the earlier communities, both buildings and Early Bronze II pottery have been found dating from c. 2000 B.C.

Probably the tenth and ninth centuries B.C. saw Haftavan as a large town whose importance continued under the Urartians.[14]

In the cliffs west-south-west of Haftavan are more Urartian remains including a rock-cut tomb known as Karmiarukh or Karniyarik,[100] while rock chambers, terraces and rock-cut stairs can be seen on the west of the mountain, on top of which is a medieval fortress.

About 15 km. west of Shahpur are two Urartian terraces and a staircase at Qale Waseri,[100] while others include Qazun Basi, south of Shahpur on the shore of the lake with Sassanian and Armenian remains, and Zangir Qale, a pre-Urartian site later used by the Urartians.[136] There are many Urartian inscriptions too, in various places around the lake.

Continuing along the main road to Rezaiyeh for about 14 km. you come to Sarmas, Savus or Salmas, south-east of Shahpur, where the cliffs on either side of the wide valley begin to draw together. You must have keen eyesight to notice the early Sassanian bas-relief near the bottom of the cliff known as Pir Chavus, which stands to the left of the road, facing north-west. The relief probably depicts Ardashir I and the Crown Prince, Shahpur (I), receiving the homage of the Armenians after Ardashir's victory over them. To see this relief properly you must drive left onto a track running along the base of the cliffs. A medieval fortress and the Urartian site of Qale Waseri[100] are also situated on this cliff. The relief as observed in 1974 has a painted border.

The distance from Shahpur to Rezaiyeh is just over 100 km. along a road that winds through the hills giving glimpses of the blue lake. The lake itself, however, is so full of mineral salts that fish and vegetable life are non-existent.

The town of Rezaiyeh lies about 21 km. from the lake and was probably founded before the Christian era. Captured by the Arabs about the middle of the seventh century A.D., it was strongly fortified against the Armenians, and then came under the Saljuqs until it was destroyed and rebuilt by the Mongols. Today there is a strong Christian minority of Chaldeans, Nestorians and Armenians, many owning vineyards in the surrounding countryside.

There are a number of small provincial hotels in Rezaiyeh and a large Government Tourist Inn. The clean, but small, Park Hotel on Kh. Pahlavi, opposite the narrow entrance to the bazaar, leading to the Masjid-i Jumeh, offers reasonable accommodation, 300 rials for a double room, good food in the restaurant, and a small shady courtyard. On the same street, the Niagara when visited in 1973 had some double rooms with private shower for 450 rials.

There is an air service several times weekly from Tabriz, and buses run to the port of Golman Khaneh on the lake, from which a twice weekly boat service connects with Sharif Khaneh on the eastern shore, where there is a railway station on the Tehran-Tabriz line.

Two Saljuq monuments are now the principal objects of interest in the city. One is the restored tomb-tower known as the Seh Gunbad, A.D. 1180, with some fine stucco and stalactite decoration; this is built on a piece of wasteland on the south-western outskirts of the town. The other is the Saljuq Masjid-i Jumeh reached through the lively vegetable market north-west of Kh. Farah. The dome chamber of the mosque is built on the square lines of a Sassanian Chahar Taq and may well be on the site of a fire temple. It certainly replaced an earlier mosque. The wealth of detail and the exquisite craftsmanship of the stucco mihrab, dated 1277, and thus the first major architectural enterprise after the Mongol invasion, as well as the delicate yet bold Kufic inscription and decoration round the base of the huge dome, should not be missed.

There is a small, new museum in Kh. Band at the southern extremity of the town, close to the fragmentary remains of what may once have been a citadel mound.

Legend has it that one of the Three Wise Men who journeyed to Bethlehem is buried in the Christian church of St. Mary's, just off Pahlavi. The latter is a modern building erected on much older foundations, and Muslim pilgrims come here to light candles at the tomb which they hold in great respect.

Rezaiyeh mast (yoghurt) and the fruits and sweetmeats made from fresh fruit, are all particularly good.

From Rezaiyeh the road continues south, passing a number of archaeological sites; among them Geoy (or Gok) Tepe, just outside Rezaiyeh[15] on the left of the road after crossing the river. (*Kordlar Tepe.)

The road now passes through delightful country and through several Chaldean Christian villages surrounded by vineyards. After some 35 km. the lake again appears in view on the left. Just where the road runs closest to the southern end of the lake, the hamlet of Haidarabad stands at a junction. One branch of the road continues straight on, soon leaving the lake to cross some barren hills. It is a roughish road but represents the main one to Mahabad and on to Miandoab. The better surfaced road bends to the right towards the town of Naqadeh, some 20 km. to the south. Follow this road for about 13 km.; it rises to the top of some low hills from which can be seen a small lake and on the southern side of this a cluster of trees that hide the mound of Hasanlu, situated on a natural cross-roads.

A dirt track to the left some km. further on the road, where a signpost in Persian points to a bank in the village, leads directly to the trees and the mound, with the village of Hasanlu at its foot among the trees, about 3 km. from the main road.

Professor Robert H. Dyson, Jr., has been directing the archaeological work here on behalf of the University Museum of Pennsylvania University since 1957, the work also being sponsored by the Metropolitan Museum of Art since 1959. Hasanlu, which dominates the northern Solduz Valley, was one of those thriving local citadels of the Early Iron Age which were often attacked and devastated by Assyrian, Urartian and other armies, and was one of the two or three fortified citadels defending the western approaches to a kingdom so far unidentified, south of the lake. Today it is still one of the most impressive of archaeological sites, its great walls with their bastions, its streets and major public buildings all helping to bring the past to life in a vivid fashion.

Some 25 m. high, the central citadel mound is 200 m. in diameter with a lower, outer town mound of about 600 m. diameter. Sir Aurel Stein[156] made test excavations in the northern outer town area and at the base of the citadel in 1936, and further excavations were carried out in 1947 and 1949 by the Archaeological Service of Iran, directed by Mr. M. Rad and Mr. A. Hakemi, chiefly in the cemetery area of the Outer Town.

Then came the long-term American project,[38,39] the main objective of which is the exploration of the little-known period corresponding to the arrival of the Medes and the Persians in the first half of the first millennium B.C.

The excavations indicate that from the sixth to the third millennium B.C. a prehistoric settlement formed the core of the Central Mound, around the base of which grew up the later Outer Town. Later in the tenth century B.C. the Central Mound was fortified as a citadel and much of the outer mound came to be used as a cemetery. The citadel

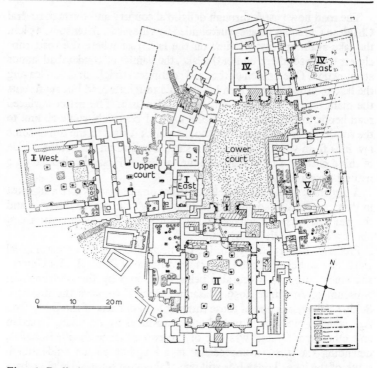

Fig. 16. Preliminary sketch plan of excavated buildings, Hasanlu, 1972.
(*By courtesy of Professor R. H. Dyson, University Museum, University of Pennsylvania*)

was built over existing ruins, its pavements of large slabs of limestone or sandstone brought from hills some 30 km. away. On these foundations rose superstructures of sun-dried mud-brick set in mud mortar, supporting houses of two or three storeys with framed windows and arched doorways. Some of the interior walls were decorated with glazed tiles, either representing imports or copies of the standard type of tile found in the Assyrian royal palaces.

The richest architectural remains at Hasanlu come from this citadel of Period IV, much of the plan of which still stands intact today. The main approach appears to have been up the west slope along twin roads to an enclosed area. Entrance to the central area was through a small gate on the east, now largely destroyed by the massive Urartian fortification wall.

After crossing a central area paved with small cobblestones, the contemporary visitor would have mounted a grand stairway to an Upper

Court faced by two monumental buildings—or he could have passed through a gate into a stone-paved Lower Court, on the right of which stood the imposing mass of Building II, believed to have been a temple or a palace.

Three tall stone stelae stood at the entrance of this last structure, a deep portico supported by wooden pillars that also sheltered a mud-brick bench covered with stone. This portico led through wooden doors into an anteroom with a bench along two walls, a small hearth for the cold winter nights, and a washroom with a stone-paved floor and sunken drain and a hearth on the left. Steps on the right led to the upper floor.

A second doorway with a pivoted wooden door led into the main hall, 18 × 24 m. in area, with four rows of poplar wood pillars over 7 m. high, each half a metre in diameter, standing on stone slabs covered with plaster. Round the walls were set mud-brick benches coated with clay plaster and edged with wooden beams. The walls were apparently covered by textiles which fell onto the benches during the fire, leaving their impression on the mud-brick seats. Two hearths stood in front of higher raised benches flanking the door and backed by wooden panelling, with stone paving in front of them.

In the front centre of the hall a single column stood next to a small paved area with a sunken drain and, further along, a raised brick offering table, or perhaps a hearth, stood before a small platform reached by several steps. Just below the platform a tall iron tripod lamp and an elaborate wooden chair with carved panels of inlaid wood, and lathe-turned legs, was found.

At the back of this platform is a recessed entrance to a small room that may have been a sanctuary. Storerooms surround three sides of the building which may well have been the prototype of the later Achaemenian 'apadana'.

Somewhere around 800 B.C., the citadel, which is thought to have been allied with the Assyrians, was attacked and burned, probably by the Urartians, and the twentieth century excavators found vivid evidence of the suddenness and severity of the battle. Some forty skeletons were discovered just inside the entrance to the hall in which they had taken refuge, apparently killed when the burning upper storey collapsed on them. Other skeletons were also found scattered throughout the city, and on the crushed bodies cylinder seals and lion pins of bronze worn on the shoulder were among the many personal finds.

On the north side of the Lower Court in which Building II was found, stood a small structure (Building IV), which has a façade added later, consisting of twin porticoes flanked by tall stone stelae. Thirty people had been murdered on the roof of this building during the sacking of the city. On the east of this court stood an even older palace building (V), which was being used as living quarters for soldiers or domestic servants. (*Hasanlu: eighth season's work.)

Just across the street from Building II was another large structure (Burned Building I) which may have been a palace. As the site was cleared, in a small room to the south of the portico of the west wing, a man's hand and arm appeared from the rubble, the finger bones stained green from the verdigris of the bronze buttons on his gauntlet. He was found to be clasping an exquisite solid gold bowl which he had evidently been bearing from the burning building at the moment when the upper floor on which he was running gave way and crushed him with his two companions.[130] This unique and fascinating bowl is on display with other valuables from Hasanlu in the Treasure Room of the Tehran Museum.

Many other objects of gold, silver and electrum, as well as glass and ivory, were found in the burnt debris of the citadel, not to mention handsome grey-black pottery of the period 1000–800 B.C. that can be related to that of Khurvin (p. 60), Sialk (p. 170), Giyan[48] (p. 116), Kaluraz (p. 74) and Marlik (p. 73).

An earlier occupation by a different cultural group, with origins in the west, is characterized by painted buff pottery closely resembling 'Khabur ware' which originated in northern Mesopotamia and southern Anatolia; its makers seem to have crossed the frontiers of the Zagros foothills and settled in the valleys of the Solduz and Ushnu in the early second millennium at Hasanlu (Period VI) and at Dinkha Tepe. Trial trenches dug at three small village sites in the neighbourhood of Hasanlu—Hajji Firuz Tepe, Dalma and Pisdeli Tepe—confirmed the earlier neolithic sequence, part of which is known from Hasanlu itself.[41,42,43] (See Carol Hamlin on Dinkha Tepe, *Iran*, XII, 1974, and on Dalma Tepe, *Iran*, XIII, 1975.)

Dinkha Tepe, an elongated mound along the south bank of the Gadar river, is not easy to find and a visit involves fording several rivers. The Tepe is reached by a track from the main road between Hasanlu and Nagadeh (which is 7 km. south of Hasanlu), leading to Ushnuyeh in the west, a town which is probably of prehistoric origins. Before reaching the town however, where the road begins to curve to the north, you have to head across country westwards, asking for Dinkha village. Here Sir Aurel Stein carried out a trial excavation finding some second millennium jar burials and stone tombs.[156] More recently, however, Professor Dyson and Dr. Muscarella, the co-Director of the Hasanlu Project since 1968, made further investigations but nothing now remains of the large buildings originally found there.[120]

A few km. east of Dinkha Tepe, south of the village of Cheshme Gol by a small mountain, Qalatgah, with a spring at its foot, some eleven tumuli were noted during a preliminary survey at Se Girdan. Dr.

Muscarella investigated six of these;[121] Tumulus I has not yet been fully excavated; there were indications of plundering in Tumuli II, IV, V and VI, but in the lower levels the remains of stone tombs were cleared and found to be empty but for a small ring of shell in II and over 500 gold beads, three bronze axes and a bangle in IV. The skeleton of an adult male lying on his side with his legs contracted was found in the bottom of a pit in Tumulus III, the pit itself probably having been originally covered with a wooden roof. A fragmented silver vessel, a bronze knife, and a whetstone-sceptre with a feline head, as well as gold, silver, paste and stone beads, were among the objects found by the skeleton, but no pottery was discovered and so far only an approximate date near the sixth century B.C. can be assigned to the tumuli.

Immediately above the spring at Qalatgah, sherds of Urartian polished red ware and sherds of the same time-range as Hasanlu IIIA and B (c. 750–400 [?] B.C.) were found, with a small alabaster stamp seal of Urartian shape and design, which with other sherds would seem to indicate an occupation lasting into the Achaemenian period. At the spring itself, a re-used building block with six lines of a cuneiform inscription in Urartian was found. The inscription indicates the name of King Ishpuini and also of his son Menua, and may therefore date to the same period as the Kal-i Shin nearby and Tash Tepe (p. 97) inscriptions, helping to establish the line of the Urartian frontier south of Lake Rezaiyeh in the late ninth or early eighth century B.C. (See brief reports in *Iran*, VII, 1969.)

South-west of Ushnuyeh on the Iraq border, the Kal-i Shin stele stands on the high pass of the same name (first noted by Rawlinson, and then Stein). It was set up during the co-Regency of Ishpuini and Menua of Urartu between 815 and 807 B.C. and bears a bilingual inscription in Assyrian and Chaldean referring to a temple founded in 810 B.C. (and later destroyed in 714 B.C. by King Sargon II of Assyria). A military permit is required to visit this border site, which can be reached only by means of a rough track to the village of Hi, followed by a further climb of about 30 km. towards the head of the pass.

Among the many other sites surveyed or excavated by the American team in the Solduz area is Agrab Tepe, near Dalma village on the north side of the main ridge between Hasanlu and Nagadeh, to the east of the road. This site revealed an Iron Age III (seventh century B.C.) Urartian structure (see brief reports in *Journal of Near Eastern Studies*, 1965, and *Iran*, VII, 1969).

Nagadeh itself is a small town situated about 7 km. south of Hasanlu, and built partly on and around a citadel mound which is of the same type as that at Hasanlu. In Nagadeh, however, the mound has been continuously occupied to the present day. Stein found burnished and

Islamic glazed ware here, as well as jars similar to those in the Hasanlu cemetery.

There is a small provincial hotel and a petrol station here.

One can now take the old, rather rough road from Nagadeh eastwards to Mahmadya, and Mahabad. Mahabad is a large Kurdish town formerly known as Saujbulagh (a Government Tourist Inn was opened in 1970) and from here a track goes some 80 km. south to Saqqiz, the town closest to yet another famous archaeological site, that of Ziwiye.

In 1947, local villagers discovered a treasure of gold, silver and ivory in a container of bronze or copper. Different parts of the treasure are now to be found in the Tehran Archaeological Museum, in the Metropolitan Museum of Art, New York, in the Cincinnati Art Museum and in the University Museum, Philadelphia. The finds came from a steep hill dominating a valley, close to the village of Ziwiye which is some 40 km. from Saqqiz.

The site, which consisted of a citadel stepped in three stages, is probably of slightly later date than that of the Hasanlu citadel, and among other finds here were seventh century Scythian-type arrowheads. A flight of stone steps leads up to the highest point at the eastern end of the hill and the joint team of Dr. Crawford and Professor Dyson spent three weeks working here in 1964.

The site has been grossly damaged by commercial diggers who have toppled some of the huge circular column bases downhill from what may have been a palace with a portico decorated with glazed tiles. The mud-brick walls were at least 7·5 m. thick in places but there is little left to see today. The fortress was possibly built by the Mannaeans or by the Assyrians with whom they were allied.

Among the treasures allegedly from Ziwiye[70] were delicate engraved ivory plaques (partly burnt), gold bracelets, gold and silver fibulae, and a gold pectoral on which Dr. Helene Kantor has noticed similarities with Marlik's Tree of Life motifs and griffins (p. 73), and which R. D. Barnett sees as typical of Median art.[130]

From Saqqiz a road goes east through the mountains to Iranshah, 48 km.; and from here one can drive another 50 km. north-east to Takab and on to the extraordinary and spectacular Sassanian and Islamic site of Takht-i Sulaiman (p. 102).

Alternatively, from Mahabad, drive on to Miandoab, chief town of the area some 50 km. north-east of Mahabad. Several km. out of Mahabad, notice two rocky outcrops rising from the flat plain on the left (north-east) of the road. A side road branches off between the two outcrops, and on the southern face of the large one, to the south of the side road, is the rock-cut tomb of Faqraqa that may be late Achaemenian or post-Achaemenian in date. Two columns hewn out of the

1. (*above*) Guardian mastiff from Persepolis. (*In the Tehran Archaeological Museum*)

2. (*below*) Head of an Achaemenian prince— possibly Xerxes I (lapis lazuli). (*Photo: Iranian Archaeological Service*)

3. Bronze statue of a Parthian prince, from Shami, *c.* first century A.D. (*In the Tehran Archaeological Museum*)

4. Tepe Mil from the south. A late Sassanian palace near Tehran

5. Samiran. Assassin castle

7. Damavand. Tomb-tower of Sheikh Shibli. Eleventh century A.D.

6. Takestan. Mausoleum of Pir-i Takestan, near Qazvin

8. Silver dish from Mazandaran, late third century A.D. or early fourth century A.D., Sassanian. It depicts Hormizd I or Shahpur II employing the 'Parthian shot' in a lion hunt. (*In the Tehran Archaeological Museum, Treasure Room*)

9. Statue of Darius the Great *in si* found at Susa, Christmas Eve 1972, by the French Archaeologic Mission in Iran

10. Statue of Darius the Great. Detail of base with tributary nations in Egyptian cartouches. (*Both photos: Courtesy of the Délégation Archéologique Française en Iran: National Organisation for Protection of Monuments and Sites in Iran: Foundation Patek-Phillip in Geneva*)

11. Carved bone hilt from Tepe Sang-i Čaxamaq. (*Courtesy Dr. Masuda and Iranian Centre for Archaeological Research*)

13. Bastam. Gazelle head; Urartian red polished ware

14. Bastam. Urartian clay tablet (royal letter)

12. Detail of reliefs on the façade of St. Stephanos.
(All photos by courtesy of Prof. W. Kleiss)

15. Excavating large columned hall of Burnt Building II, Hasanlu. (*Photo: Courtesy of the University Museum, University of Pennsylvania*)

16. Nūsh-i Jan. Walls of Median fort showing arrow-slots

17. The Kharraqan tomb-towers from the north.
(*Courtesy of Mr. David Stronach, from* Iran, *Vol. IV, 1966*)

19. Hamadan. Sang-i Shir. Stone lion

18. Southern Gateway to Takht-i
Sulaiman. (Parthian)

21. Nūsh-i Jan. Interior of Central Building, east end of room. Original floor was one metre below the level of the ranging rod. (*By courtesy of Mr. David Stronach, from Iran, Vol. VII, 1969*)

20. Hamadan. So-called tomb of Esther and Mordecai

22. Coin of the last Sassanian king, Yazdigird III, defeated at the Battle of Nihavand, A.D. 642. (*From* Parthians and Sassanians, *Roman Ghirshman*)

23. Chahar Taq, Kazerun, showing 'squinch' in corner

24. Kangavar. Western terrace and remains of six columns of the Seleucid temple known in the first century A.D. as Concobar. Probably rebuilt by Sassanians after earthquake damage

25. Bisitun from the main highway (north-east)

26.
Nūsh-i Jan. Three quadruple spiral silver beads from the hoard hidden in the fort.
(*By courtesy of Mr. David Stronach, from* Iran, *Vol. VII, 1969*)

27. Taq-i Bustan. Investiture of Ardashir II, and the grottoes (part of the large one can be glimpsed on the far left)

28. Taq-i Bustan. Detail of royal boar hunt

29. Haft Tepe. Head of an Elamite Queen. (*Photo: Courtesy Prof. E. O. Negahban*)

30. Haft Tepe. Twenty-three skeletons *in situ* in a small tomb

31.
Susa. Fallen protome in the Apadana

32. Khurra (Khorheh).
Ionic capitals on
columns of Seleucid
or Parthian building

33. Susa. Partially-
revealed column base
in the Shaur palace,
1970

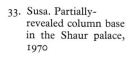

34. Foundation stone with Elamite
inscription discovered in 1970 when
clearing the main palace of Darius on
the Apadana mound. (*By courtesy of
the Délégation Archéologique
Française en Iran*)

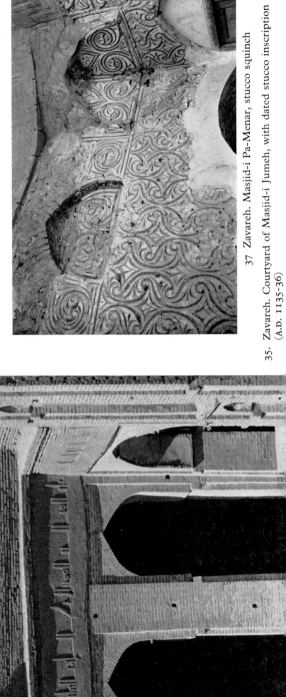

36. Sialk. South Mound from the south

37 Zavareh. Masjid-i Pa-Menar, stucco squinch

35. Zavareh. Courtyard of Masjid-i Jumeh, with dated stucco inscription (A.D. 1135-36)

39, Yazd. Nakhl in Maidan-i Chaqmaq

38. Nain. Stucco columns in Masjid-i Jumeh. Painted lettering on wall spells 'Ya Ali' (a Shi'ite invocation)

40. Isfahan. The Ateshgah, probably a Sassanian fire temple, with later, Mongol additions

41. Isfahan. Shahrestan bridge; Saljuq on Sassanian foundations

2. Tarik Khana, Damghan. Eighth-century purely Sassanian building. The slightly pointed arches are the first recorded in Persia

3. Damghan. Pir-i Alamdar. A.D. 1021

45. Tepe Hissar. Stucco decoration from the Sassanian Palace, early sixth century A.D. (*In the Tehran Archaeological Museum*)

46. Nishapur. Decoration from a ninth-century dish. (*In the Tehran Archaeological Museum*)

44. Bistam. Saljuq minaret

48. Pasargadae Treasure 1936. Found by a team led by David Stronach. Pair of gold earrings each with inset plates and three-sided pendants originally inlaid with turquoise coloured paste. About fourth century B.C. (*Photo: Olive Kitson, courtesy of Mr. David Stronach, from Iran, Vol. III, 1965*)

49. Pasargadae. Residential palace, with citadel and Zendan in the background

47. Pasargadae. Winged Genius on portal of Northern Gatehouse

51. Naqsh-i Rustam. Shahpur I, with Roman prisoners. Kartir the High Priest is seen head and shoulders only, on the extreme right

52. Bishapur. Prostrate figure of an Iranian found in 1975, under Investiture of Bahram I relief at Bishapur. (Photo: *Iranian Archaeological Centre*)

50. Naqsh-i Rustam. The Ka'bah-i Zardusht, Achaemenian

55. Persepolis. Fallen bull protome set upon the base of a column

53. (above) Persepolis. The Apadana
54. (below) Naqsh-i Rustan. The Ka'bah-i Zardusht and two of the royal
    Achaemenian rock-cut tombs (Darius the Great's on left)

56a. Persepolis. Immortals on Tripylon stair. Note the masons' marks above the heads of the first two figures

56b. Persepolis. Lotus symbol (from Apadana stair) showing mason's mark between flowers

57. Borazjan. Unfinished palace of Cyrus the Great

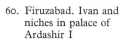

58. Siraf. Merchant's house with stucco decorated gateway and private mosque

59. Bishapur. (Sarab-i Qandil), Sassanian bas-relief

60. Firuzabad. Ivan and niches in palace of Ardashir I

61. Bam. Entrance to the walled town

62. Kirman. Restored Saljuq minar in Masjid-i Malik

63. Shahdad. Portrait-bust. (*Courtesy of Mr. Hakemi, and Tehran Museum*)

64. Shahr-i Sokhta. Steatite round seal. (*By courtesy of Dr. M. Tosi*)

smoothed rock surface form a portico to an ante-chamber, while three more columns stand between the funerary chamber and the portico. Within the chambers three recesses for coffins were originally closed by stone slabs.

Miandoab is largely populated by Kurds in their swaggering tribal dress. Hotels are of the simplest type. In 1973 the Berenj on Kh. Pahlavi was probably the best; or try the Ramsar, a little further along, where one can have a room with four beds in it for about 50 rials per bed, a communal washbasin in the corridor, and the best restaurant in town, particularly noted for its kebabs. Opposite is a bus station garage where one can also park a vehicle for the night for 20 rials. A new petrol station has been opened on the road going out of Miandoab to the north-east.

On the plain near Tash Tepe village, north of Miandoab, is the low mound that yielded an inscription of King Menua of Urartu recording his conquest of Meshtah. It is not known, however, if the inscription is original to Tash Tepe or if Tash Tepe itself is near Meshtah.

From Miandoab there is another road to Saqqiz, 98 km. to the south (p. 96) while the main highway to Tabriz runs almost due north, passing close to Maragheh, the first Mongol capital which also contains some Saljuq tomb-towers. (*Leilan.)

To reach Maragheh, drive directly to the pleasant little town of Bonab, which has a number of charming pigeon towers in the fields and vineyards around it. In the middle of the town a signposted turning to the right (east) takes you out onto a good road leading directly to Maragheh, which nestles in a fertile valley on the banks of the Sufi Chay river.

As you near the approaches of the town, a track up a steepish embankment on the left goes for some 2 km. to the little village of Tala Khan at the foot of a steep hill, on top of which Hulagu Khan, grandson of Chinghis Khan, built his famous observatory (A.D. 1259–1272), the Rasat-Khaneh or Star House. The sides of this hill contain a series of caves with interconnecting tunnels, that may have served as mausolea.[102]

Continuing along the main road into Maragheh one passes a petrol station on the right and the road then bends right over a bridge crossing the river, and into the Kh. Pahlavi. Maragheh means 'the village of pasturage', probably referring to the great herds of Mongolian horses pastured here in the thirteenth century; but the town itself is almost certainly of Sassanian origin, and possibly even Parthian or older. For a while it was the capital of Azarbaijan and the Caliph Harun al-Rashid built strong walls around it in the eighth–ninth centuries, although these are reported to have been destroyed in the tenth century. The Caliph

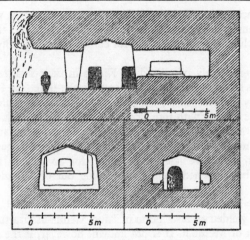

Fig. 17. Section of main cave, Observatory Hill, Maragheh.
(*By courtesy of Professor W. Kleiss*)

al-Mustarshid, a prisoner of Sultan Mas'ud who was Sultan Sanjar's nephew, was sent to Maragheh in 1135 but was killed by the Assassins on the banks of the river.

There were five notable tomb-towers in Maragheh—only four remain today, however, as the Timurid Quch-i Burj, or Koi-Burj, collapsed in 1938 and its base has been converted into a brick-kiln.

Oldest of the towers is the Gunbad-i Surkh—or Qermez—the 'Red Tower', which was built for Prince Abd-al Aziz ibn Mahmud ibn Sayyid of the local Ahmadi dynasty and completed in A.D. 1148.

(All the Maragheh towers have been described in detail by several authors.[128 (Vol. IV), 129,66a])

To reach the Gunbad-i Surkh, continue along the Kh. Pahlavi, crossing the main street of Kh. Khadju Nasr, and then pick your way through the narrow lanes on the right to a stream whose waters often smell strongly of wine from a nearby vintner's. On the northern bank is a large graveyard. Cross the stream by a footbridge and walk down the slope to the garden over whose walls can be seen the top of the tomb-tower. The kiln built into the foundation of the Koi Burj is half-way up this slope.

The soft red brick with its inset, carved terracotta panels and very sparing use of blue tiles gives a quiet majesty to this square mausoleum. Pope agrees with Schroeder and Godard that it is perhaps the 'most beautiful example of brickwork known';[129] the original octagonal pyramid roof has disappeared but the inner dome on stalactite squinches is well preserved and the building has recently been restored. A dated Kufic inscription over the doorway attributes the construction to the order of the 'Master of Azarbaijan'.

There are only the remains of a brick bench round the base of the interior walls of the mausoleum, but the crypt, entered by a low door on the south, has an interesting low vaulted brick ceiling.

This tomb is one of the earliest on which coloured glazed ornamentation appeared in the external decoration.

Two other towers in the town fall into the Saljuq period. These are the Gunbad-i Kabud (the Blue Tower) and, standing next to it, a circular tomb-tower locally known as the Burj-i Khohar-i (or Madar-i) Hulagu Khan—Tower of the Sister (or Mother) of Hulagu Khan. These are reached by returning to Kh. Khadju Nasr and turning north along it to the main cross-roads with Kh. Ohadi. Turn right (east) up Ohadi and take the first turning left, to a girls' school on the left of the road. You will be able to see the towers in a railed-off area beyond the school playground, but because the only access is through the school one must seek the permission of the Headmistress (or, if the school is closed, of the caretaker).

The second oldest of the Maragheh tomb-towers is the plain brick circular one on the right, finished, according to the Kufic inscription, with turquoise glazed brick over the richly decorated entrance, in A.D. 1167–8. Here the decorative facing has been given prominence over the brickwork. The elaborate doorway, partially hidden by a modern wooden one, faces the back wall to the north-west. Round tomb-towers became increasingly rare in northern Iran after the eleventh century A.D.

Neither Hulagu Khan nor his sister could have had any connection with either of the towers since they were built long before the Mongols came to Maragheh in A.D. 1256. The Gunbad-i Kabud, which local people mistakenly believe was the tomb of Hulagu's mother or sister, was built in 1196–7 and originally had a pyramidal roof with a stalactite cornice and a band of inscription. The main shaft of the tower is covered with an intricate network of dressed brick like a lace mantle, and the turquoise decoration is used only above this lacy brickwork, and for the inscriptions.

The remaining Maragheh tower is the Gunbadi-i Ghaffariyeh built in the early part of the fourteenth century. It stands within a modern wall on the banks of the river on the northern outskirts of the town, just beyond the early nineteenth century bridge.

There are a number of small restaurants in the main streets, serving good chelo-kebab.

In the Murdi-chai valley a few kilometres east of Maragheh, the fossilized remains of prehistoric animals are being found in profusion; from this area too comes much of the beautifully veined marble used in mosques all over the country, including the panels in the Blue Mosque in Tabriz (p. 79).

About 100 km. north of Maragheh the main road to Tabriz passes 3 km. to the east of Yanik Tepe, a largely prehistoric mound that was excavated by Mr. Charles Burney of the University of Manchester,[13] between 1960 and 1962. The Tepe is about 5 km. west of the village of Khosrowshah and close to the railway line and is one of at least fifty tepes found by Mr. Burney round the shores of the Lake Rezaiyeh, during a survey in 1958–9.

The excavations revealed a cultural sequence from the late Neolithic period (starting perhaps no later than c. 6000 B.C.) down to the beginning of Islamic times. In the latest period a massive structure, probably a citadel, was constructed of flat, square mud bricks; possibly it was Sassanian in date. The unusual feature of this mound however was the discovery of circular houses and granaries—some walls standing still to 2 m.—featured in the third millennium building levels. These were constructed of mud brick with a stone defensive wall around the town. Some intramural burials were found in the late Neolithic periods, but none with grave goods, while the remains of a second millennium cemetery at the foot of the west side of the mound had been largely destroyed by recent irrigation works. Here a few burials were found in shallow pits sometimes lined with mud bricks, probably dating from c. 1500 to c. 1100 B.C.

From Miandoab (p. 97) one can reach the unique site of Takht-i Sulaiman for which camping gear, food supplies and a four-wheel drive vehicle are necessary. Start off on the main Tabriz Road, crossing the bridge, but as you leave the outskirts of the town take the right-hand gravel road by the side of a large factory. The road improves after the first few kilometres and goes through very beautiful, fertile farming country and villages where the storks nest on the rooftops and kingfishers swoop across the road.

Driving through Shahindej (57 km.) where petrol is obtainable, and across rolling hills with magnificent panoramas, you make for Takab, about 77 km. from Shahindej, on a good gravel road.

Takab is a large village on the cross-roads from Sanandaj and Miandoab, with small chai khanehs offering the usual chelo-kebabs, fresh fruit and soft drinks. The petrol and diesel pumps are on the outskirts of the town which is very close to a prehistoric mound. It is from here on that the four-wheel drive is necessary and one should inquire at the petrol pump for the latest directions since the tracks are liable to change from year to year. Sufficient fuel should be taken for

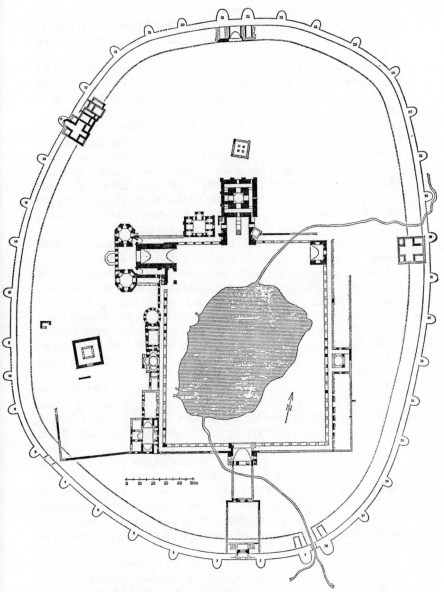

Fig. 18. Takht-i Sulaiman. Mongol period.
(*By courtesy of the German Archaeological Institute, Istanbul*)

the return journey of about 80 km.; or bargain to hire a jeep in
Takab, about 1,600 rials return (1973) taking about three hours each
way.

Drive back on the Shahindej road for 4 km. to a spot just short of a
large clump of trees on the left. On the right a rough cart track winds
across hilly, broken country, the usual route passing through the hamlets of Karakayah, Hassanabad and Ahmadabad; some nine or ten
river crossings are involved and, although these are low enough to ford
fairly easily in summer, the tracks can be very confusing and it is best
to make constant inquiries whenever you have the opportunity.

From the large village of Assadabad, one of many in this remote area
where the young men of the Literary Corps have introduced village
schools, as their gold and blue signs and the Iranian flag indicate, you
are within about 12 km. of the Zendan-i Sulaiman (Solomon's prison),
a conical hill looking something like an extinct volcano.

It was formed by the sediment from calciferous wells and rises from
a bare, rocky slope some 3 km. north of Takht-i Sulaiman.

Sherds comparable with those of Hasanlu (p. 91) have been found
at Zendan-i Sulaiman which was occupied as far back as 900 B.C.
The whole of the mountain was enclosed by walls and rows of rooms
and linking steps leading to what seems to have been a religious sanctuary on the top, where in prehistoric times a deep well filled the crater.
So far the site has not been culturally linked with Takht-i Sulaiman
(the Throne of Solomon), where the earliest pottery probably dates
back only to the sixth century B.C.

The track is now straightforward, passing through another large
village and across what are sometimes rather boggy, marshy fields.
It ends on a small terrace outside the massive, probably third century
A.D. walls, originally reinforced by thirty-eight high towers and refaced
in Mongol times, and the spectacular main gate.

This unusual site, which includes a Sassanian palace and fire temple
and Il-Khanid buildings grouped round a 'bottomless' lake of intense
blue, has been the object of archaeological excavations by a team headed
by Professor Rudolf Naumann, Director of the German Institute of
Istanbul, since 1959. The original survey, made in 1958, was carried
out by Professor H. H. van der Osten who led the first campaign in
1959 with Professor Naumann.[126]

The site was discovered in 1819 by the British traveller, Sir Robert
Ker Porter, but it was not until 1937 that it was thoroughly investigated
by Professor Upham Pope and D. N. Wilber for an architectural survey
by the American Institute for Iranian Art and Archaeology.[128]

There is nowhere to stay here except through camping in the fields
or the hospitality of a guest tent in the Archaeological camp just inside

the South gateway. This gateway is of special interest as it still retains some of its original facing, the large slabs with alternating stretchers and headers and the seven niches over the arch. Many authorities have seen these as derivative of arches on Roman city gates, but possibly they are of Sassanian origin influencing the Romans rather than the other way round. Through this gate runs one of seven water channels cut into the rock; only two of these now convey water down the slopes of the hill and it is unlikely that all seven were ever in use at the same time. Legend reports that despite the continuous rushing of the streams from the 'magic lake' the level never dropped but in fact the archaeological teams have noticed that the level does rise in winter. The waters of this 100-m.-wide lake have a high mineral content and drinking water is fetched from outside the walled area.

Some authorities believed this extraordinary site was the Parthian Phraaspa unsuccessfully attacked by Mark Antony and an army of 10,000 in 36 B.C. (current belief tends to place Phraaspa nearer Qaleh-i Zohak). It was Shiz to the Arabs and Saturiq to the Mongols and at all times was a great religious centre. Sassanian kings made a pilgrimage here on foot after their coronation at Ctesiphon near present-day Baghdad, to offer rich gifts and homage and receive the divine investiture at the great fire sanctuary of Adhar Gushnasp, the Royal Fire or Fire of the Warriors.

The German teams have gradually revealed many details of the Sassanian fire temple situated almost in the middle of the northern lake shore. Here later Islamic steps are seen today over part of the Sassanian fire temple which is entered through an arched door behind these steps. In a smaller, cross-shaped room leading east from the main chamber of the fire temple, a square basin is seen, whose corners may have supported columns and a canopy.

The walls of the fire temple are nearly 4 m. thick in some places, and made entirely of fired bricks held by lime mortar, but almost all the vaulting of the surrounding passages has collapsed due to robbery by villagers. There were at least four pre-Islamic building periods and recent work has revealed traces of a small hitherto unsuspected Achaemenian settlement, including the skeleton of a young man in the north-western corner of the Sassanian columned building to the north-west of the fire temple, concealed under a limestone deposit left when the lake flooded the area before the later occupation. More than twenty burial pits were found altogether in this location.

The first major buildings in the area of the fire temple, dating from the late Parthian or early Sassanian period, possessed broad mud-brick walls that were later levelled almost to their foundations to make way for new stone buildings with a somewhat different plan. The latter include large columned halls, complete with benches, podiums and basins, which bespeak the religious character of these constructions.

The outer fortifications in Parthian times were of mud brick and these were later enclosed by a second stone wall built by the Sassanians.

Another interior fortification wall surrounded the lake and the sacred buildings around it, while a gate, similar to the South entrance but in poor condition, pierces the outer fortifications to the north and here six clearly defined levels have been excavated. The whole main complex has been rebuilt and altered many times and it is difficult to date with certainty, but it seems there must have been several fire temples, halls, storage and side rooms. A great proportion of the rooms of the columned building was destroyed by the ninth century A.D. but those to the north had been restored and were in use as late as the twelfth century A.D. when some of the formerly open buildings were enclosed to make living quarters, and paved with stone or brick. Among the excavated finds are Sassanian coins, Saljuq 'moulded pottery' similar to that found in Nishapur, glass dishes, stucco reliefs and some very beautiful ninth to thirteenth century glazed metallic and lustre tiles and ceramics. (See *Iran*, Vol. XIII, 1975.)[4,96,136]

From Takht-i Sulaiman, return by the same route to Takab and continue the journey south. (Not recommended is the track east via Takht-e Bilkis Pass and Qeshlaq Jug to Nikpay on the main Mianeh-Zanjan road.)

One can drive from Takab to the small Kurdish town of Bijar where there is a petrol station (about 105 km.) and from here turn north-west on a track to Zanjan, on the main Tabriz-Tehran road, 156 km. and about seven hours driving from Bijar. Or from Bijar another track runs south for some 150 km. to join the main Hamadan-Kirmanshah road, but for preference drive from Takab south for 50 km. on a good gravel road to the Saqqiz-Sanandaj road making an interesting short diversion which carries you high over the rolling hills between fields of wheat and wild flowers.

About 25 km. from Takab, look to your right (west) and see in the middle distance the silhouette of two reddish limestone cliffs facing each other across a small valley, with higher hills in the distance. The northern cliff has a tall column of stone standing before it, while the southern one has a group of several partially detached columns. A small pile of stones by the side of the road marks a rough track and a signpost in Persian lists the names of the farms served by this. Drive along the track, always taking the left fork when it divides, and head in a wide sweep towards the back of the northern cliff which is known locally as Qalah Karafto. The tracks are rough and steep over undulating country and take one, after about 7 km. and perhaps twenty-five minutes, to the edge of a plateau overlooking a magnificent deserted valley and mountains. From here it is easy to walk down to a series of caves in the cliff, some of the higher of which have wooden steps or ladders.

These caves, visited by Ker Porter in 1818, and by Rawlinson in 1838, were surveyed by Stein in the 1930s,[156] and more recently by Dr. Von Gall.

For the main cave which is in the cliffs just behind the standing pillar of rock, climb up the wooden steps into a long dark passage leading off a large cave, and turn right into a corridor cut into the rock, where smaller steps lead via an upper level to a room with an inscription over the lintel. Stein translated the Hellenistic inscription as follows:

'Here resides Herakles; nothing evil may enter.'

A passage in Tacitus refers to the oracles of local divinities in this area, particularly of Hercules or Herakles, who was consulted by the Parthian king Gotarzes at the mountain of Sanbulos. The character of Herakles as the Iranian Verethraghna of the Avesta, or the Bahram of later Zoroastrian literature, was the genius of Victory who could also be identified with Mithras, and the caves were obviously used in connection with religious rites. They are extensive and quite complex and it is best to try to find a local guide—and of course you need some kind of artificial lighting.

The small rocks semi-detached from the southern cliff are weathered into curiously human caricatures and the whole place has a wild charm that makes it an intriguing picnic spot or camping place.

The main gravel road from Takab reaches a new asphalt road from Saqqiz to Sanandaj after about a half hour's drive from the Karafto turn-off. At the junction you turn right for Saqqiz and left for Sanandaj; a little further along the road towards Sanandaj is a signpost pointing to Fathe-abad. About 52 km. from the junction and a few km. south of the large village of Divandareh where diesel and petrol are available, cross a new bridge just outside the village and you will see a gravel road to the left, which goes to Bijar (60 km.).

Continue straight on for some 80 km. to Sanandaj, a large town of mainly Kurdish inhabitants and a great Darvish centre. The Abadeh hotel on the right of the main Kh. Pahlavi is perhaps the best of several small provincial hotels and has a courtyard where cars may be parked.

Sanandaj is built on the site of the old Sinneh which was the capital of Kordestan province and was called Sisar during the Middle Ages. It was also the site of a fortress built by the Abbasid Caliph Amin, but there does not appear to be anything left of old Sanandaj.

A track goes 128 km. west from here to Marivan which is 23 km. from the Iraq frontier, via Shahpur Dej, a large village in a small valley by a lake surrounded by mountains. The ruins of the old town

4*

known as Shahazur occupy the nearby Tepe Yasin, an important fortified town in the early Islamic period. As it was about half-way between Takht-i Sulaiman and Ctesiphon, this area was of considerable importance also in Sassanian times.

From Sanandaj there is a road going directly to Hamadan, about 180 km., and joining the Bijar track some 3 km. from the main Kirmanshah road. The track comes out about 22 km. west of Hamadan and there is a petrol station about half-way between Sanandaj and Hamadan, at Qorveh.

The road to Kirmanshah (p. 131) from Sanandaj continues south for 135 km. passing many prominent prehistoric tepes, some with the remains of later fortresses, and through very attractive country and colourful Kurdish villages.

NORDWEST-ANSICHT

Fig. 19. Qaleh-i Zohak, showing existing stucco and decorative brickwork, and suggested reconstruction of the Parthian Pavilion.
(*By courtesy of Professor W. Kleiss ref.* Archaeologische Mitteilungen aus Iran, *Neue Folge Band 5, Berlin, 1972*)

4 · Kirmanshah, Luristan

The road to Kirmanshah offers a pleasant drive in summer, but at least two high passes are often closed by blizzards and snow during winter. The first part of the highway, to Hamadan (400 km.), is, like the Tehran-Qazvin road, notorious for its heavy traffic and fatal accidents. Up to and beyond the frontier with Iraq, it follows the ancient Royal Highway used by countless invading armies in the past, and, as part of the old Silk Road, by merchants and caravans making the long journey from Europe as far east as Central Asia and China.

Leave Tehran by the Qazvin road and continue to Takestan (p. 53) and south past the junction with the Tabriz road. Some 57 km. from Takestan, at the village of Ab-i Garm where there are thermal springs, a turn to the right (west) for 33 km. brings one to two particularly lovely Saljuq tomb-towers at Kharraqan, less than 2 km. west of the village of Hisar-i Armani. The road runs parallel with the river Khar, and being liable to flooding is only suitable for four-wheel drive in late summer.

Described in detail[162] by David Stronach and T. Cuyler Young, Jr., with a discussion on the inscriptions by S. M. Stern,[157] the tombs were discovered in 1963 by William Miller and stand on open ground, 29 m. apart. Their external decoration classes them among the finest decorated brick monuments yet found in Iran, with the two earliest double domes known from this country, discounting the combination of a high conical roof with a hemispherical inner shell. A series of varied wall paintings, possibly of a later date, decorate the interior of the older tomb on the east (A.D. 1067–8).

The western tomb (Tower II) is dated to A.D. 1093 and both were almost certainly built by the same local architect, probably for Turkish chieftains of the Saljuq aristocracy whose precise names are unknown.

Both towers are octagonal with rounded buttresses, Tower I having the remains of two internal staircases built into two of its eight buttresses, reached by low doors inside the tomb chamber. The remains of an original brick bench can be seen at the base of each brick panel.

The later second tower has only one spiral staircase but its brick embellishment is more ambitious and may be compared with that used in the later Gunbad-i Surkh (p. 98), dated 1147, at Maragheh, which

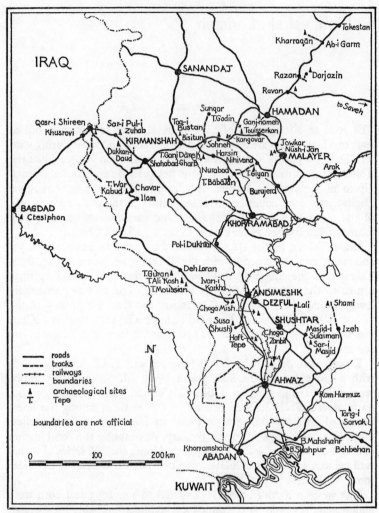

Map 5. Kirmanshah, Luristan and Khuzestan

appears to be the lineal descendant of the Kharraqan towers, while the twelfth century tomb of Khwaja Atabek at Kirman (p. 266) has the only octagonal ground plan from Iran claiming to be more sophisticated than that of Tower II.

The interior of Tower II is unplastered and contains an austere but pleasant brick mihrab which may be unfinished, on the south wall.

Returning to the main Hamadan road and driving through the earthquake zone where the government completely rebuilt villages after a particularly disastrous earthquake in 1962, one passes close to two interesting and pleasantly situated tomb-towers which may be considered worth a short diversion at the large village of Razan, 66 km. from Ab-i Garm. The pair of towers known together as the Darjazin (or Darazin) towers, consist of the Hud Tower, which may be Saljuq, nearer the main highway, and the Azhar, on the outskirts of the village of Darjazin, about 3 km. further east along the track from the main road, the latter probably Mongol.

As you approach Hamadan itself, one of the most elevated of all Iranian cities, delightfully cool in summer, very cold in winter, you see the impressive snow-capped Mount Alvand (3,570 m.) overshadowing the famous Median capital, ancient Hagmatana ('The Place of Assembly'), known to the Greeks as Ecbatana, the site of which is now covered by modern Hamadan. The main road bends to the west for Kirmanshah and the frontier, but you drive straight on into the city, which according to tradition was founded in the eighth century B.C. At that time, it is said, the royal citadel was surrounded by seven lines of fortification, each of a different colour, the two innermost being plated with silver and gold.

Cyrus the Great made this his summer capital after defeating its former ruler, his grandfather Astyages, in 550 B.C., but the Achaemenian palaces presumably lie under the buildings of many later conquerors including Alexander, the Seleucids, Parthians, Sassanians and Saljuqs. The Iranian Archaeological Service has already cleared old buildings on the mounds by the northern outskirts of the city, passed on the west as you drive in, but so far scientific excavations here are only in their infancy. Much Achaemenian treasure including two small foundation tablets, one gold and one silver, gold drinking vessels, jewellery, etc. (now mainly in the Tehran Museum) has been found here, often by illegal diggers.

Tobias, his dog and the Angel Raphael are traditionally supposed to have stayed in Ecbatana with Tobias's father's cousin, Raquel, whose daughter Sara he married before going on to Ray to collect a debt owing to his father.

There is a petrol station on Kh. Shahpur by which you enter the city, and another at the end of Kh. Ecbatana where it joins the Kirmanshah road. The best hotel is the Pahlavi Foundation's Bou Ali, which has a very cold pool and open-air restaurant (in summer) (900 rials double room with bath, 700 rials single) and a very poor annexe. It stands at the top of Kh. Abu Ali, and when visited in 1974 was the best hotel in Hamadan. The Taj, just off Maidan-i Pahlavi, charges 250 rials – no private bathrooms.

There are plenty of small restaurants near by, including the Chelo Kebabi Kakh on the left of Kh. Shahpur, and the Miami on Maidan-i Pahlavi itself, as well as the more sophisticated restaurant at the Bou Ali hotel. Much demolition and rebuilding plus renaming of streets is taking place and readers are advised that some information given here may already be out of date.

Among the early remains at Hamadan is a particularly famous stone lion, the 'Sang-i Shir', standing on a hill overlooking the town from the south-east and within walking distance of the Bou Ali Hotel. The now legless, much damaged lion, which for a time crowned one of the city gates in the early Islamic period, has been shown by Professor Luschey[112a] of the German Archaeological Institute, Tehran, to be of late fourth century date, most probably carved at the command of Alexander the Great to commemorate his general, Hephaestion, who died here. The mutilation of the lion is largely due to the clumsy attempts of a tenth century Buyid ruler to remove it. Candle grease is spilt in the dimples and hollows under the lion's mouth, for young women still burn candles and place small pebbles in the hollows as they petition for a husband. A Parthian cemetery has been excavated nearby. (See *Iran*, XIII, 1975.)

From the Sang-i Shir one can look across towards the Musalla, a prominent hill to the north-east, which is sometimes confused with the original mound of Ecbatana. One can also see directly north, among the streets at the foot of the mound on which the lion stands, the conical tower of a thirteenth century tomb-tower, the Burj-i Qurban, the key of which is kept in the Sina School in nearby Iskandipur Street.

In the same street as the Bou Ali Hotel is the modern mausoleum of the famous philosopher, poet and author of a medical encyclopaedia, after whom the street and the hotel are named. Ibn Ali Sina, known to the West as Avicenna, died here in A.D. 1037; his medical treatises were used in European universities at least until the sixteenth century, and a small museum of manuscripts and objects associated with him is attached to the mausoleum. The tomb of the mystic poet Sheikh Abu Said Dokhduh, Avicenna's host while he lived in Hamadan, is also housed in the same mausoleum.

Continue down Kh. Abu Ali to the Maidan-i Pahlavi and turn left to the next street, renamed Kh. Shahabbas. Just a few metres up here on the right can be seen the back of the so-called tomb of Esther and Mordecai, reached by a narrow lane to the right. The gate into the small garden surrounding the mausoleum is set in a high wall, and a resident caretaker, to whom a small fee is payable, has the key to the massive stone door of the shrine itself. Traditionally this is believed to be the burial place of the Jewish wife of Xerxes I (486–465 B.C.), Esther, and of her uncle Mordecai, but it is more likely perhaps that the present monument was erected over the supposed grave of a later Jewish queen, Shushan-Dukht, wife of the Sassanian, Yazdigird I (A.D. 399–420), and mother of that great hunter, Bahram Gur. Shushan-Dukht is believed to have founded a large Jewish colony in Hamadan (and also in Isfahan) and her tomb is visited by many Jewish pilgrims. An ancient Torah written on vellum is kept in the small inner room adjoining the tomb chamber, which contains two ebony tombs covered with many colourful velvets and brocades, while the presumed remains of either Esther and her uncle, or of Queen Shushan-Dukht and an unknown companion, rest in a crypt below. This can be glimpsed through a small hole in the floor, between the two tombs, into which one is expected to place an appropriate offering.

There are several antique shops in the alleys around the mausoleum, often with bowls and other vessels illegally excavated from the mounds in the city. Achaemenian remains are said to have been found when some old houses were pulled down at the northern end of Kh. Ecbatana, across the Maidan-i Pahlavi.

Carpet and leather-goods shops are on either side of this avenue, at its southern end, while the twisting lanes of a bazaar leading from the west of the street and connecting with the Kh. Baba Taher display the well-known modern pottery of Hamadan and excellent fruits and vegetables. (Incidentally Hamadan is famous for its wines made from grapes grown on the surrounding mountain slopes, but it is difficult to find them on sale in the city and one is mainly offered Qazvin wines in restaurants.)

At the north-eastern end of Kh. Baba Taher, also called Manuchehri, a small shrine stands surrounded by gardens, with a wide new road leading off to the right. Take this road, and as you go along it you can see on your right the back of the most glorious of Hamadan's Saljuq monuments, the late twelfth century (some think it is Mongol) Gunbad-i Alavian. It is reached by taking a cul-de-sac on the right, through the gateway to a girls' school, also on the right of the lane. In the playground stands the restored monument for which early morning light is required if one is to photograph the elaborate façade—try to visit on school holidays or before 8 a.m. on school days.

Believed to have been a Darvish monastery, it later became the mausoleum of the Alavian family who virtually ruled Hamadan for some 200 years. The tombs lie in the crypt reached by a staircase inside the tower, in front of the magnificent stucco mihrab.[88,129]

The entire façade of the building was covered with extraordinarily opulent stucco decoration in high relief depicting exuberant leaves, blossoms, vines and tendrils in closely interwoven patterns in which Pope sees the ancient invocation for abundance and fertility. Herzfeld writes of it: 'Here ornamentation through the fusion of all factors is brought to a most intense fortissimo. Words cannot describe it, it must be seen.' Which indeed it must.

The modern mausoleum of Baba Taher, a mystic poet who died in A.D. 1019, imitates that of Avicenna, rising on a mound to the north of this quarter.

About 12 km. south-west of Hamadan are two Achaemenian cuneiform inscriptions in the face of a spur of Mount Alvand, reached by driving up Kh. Dariush to a newly constructed roundabout, and following the road to the right. This is a particularly pleasant drive in summer, by the side of a stream with open-air tea houses disposed along the river bank.

The road ends below the two elevated inscriptions, which face north and are therefore best photographed when the sun is high. Known today as Ganj Nameh or the 'Treasure Book', since it was supposed that the inscriptions indicated the whereabouts of a hidden treasure, the two inscribed panels of Darius I (522–485 B.C.) on the left, and of Xerxes I (485–465 B.C.) on the right, actually pay homage to Ahura Mazda and list the lineage and conquests of the two rulers, in Old Persian, Neo-Elamite and Neo-Babylonian. Holes sunk into the rock at the sides of both inscriptions show where protective covers were originally attached, as at Persepolis.

The main road to Kirmanshah takes one over the Assadabad Pass which is often closed in winter, but the road itself is in good condition and is about 180 km. direct. However, the important Median site of Nush-i Jan to the south-east of Hamadan can be visited by a diversion which circumnavigates Mount Alvand, starting off on the Malayer road out of Hamadan. The road is excellent, being the main highway to Khorramabad (p. 118) and Ahwaz (p. 140). At 62 km. it passes a turning on the right for Touisserkan (p. 121) 34 km., which goes on to join the main Kirmanshah highway. One can take this road on returning from Nush-i Jan and visit another Median site, that of Godin Tepe (p. 121) at the same time. These two significant sites, together with that of Baba Jan a little further west (p. 116), show a series of characteristic architectural forms now associated with the central Zagros during the eighth and seventh centuries B.C., and each helps to illustrate the debt Achaemenian architects owe to this region.

For Nush-i Jan, continue through the village of Jowkar and at a point 20 km. short of Malayer, a track goes off to the west for 10 km. to Nush-i Jan, a steep-sided, partly natural mound some 37 m. high, which can be seen from the main road. The good fair-weather track takes you right to the slopes of the magnificent fortified settlement. The tepe lies midway between Naqilabad and Shushab villages.

The walls of the important Median buildings revealed by the excavations, directed by Mr. David Stronach in 1967 to 1974 have been
covered with a protective coating and roofed, and thus there is still
something well worth seeing at this unique site.

The rock outcrop of Nush-i Jan harbours much the oldest fire temple
so far associated with the plateau's Iranian invaders, marking the time,
near the middle of the eighth century B.C., when the Medes had already
begun to embark on monumental construction within their new homeland. The site was abandoned about the beginning of the sixth century
B.C. until its re-occupation by the Achaemenians who possibly only used
the summit of the mound as a look-out post. There followed another
gap until the Parthians made a brief appearance on the scene in the
first century B.C., possibly during a period of local unrest before they
felt able to move back to their less protected villages on the plain.

Four distinct Median structures were identified, reflecting an
occupation that probably lasted from the middle of the eighth century
down to the first half of the sixth century. At the very centre of the
mound stands the Fire Temple, a most distinctive building with a
stepped, lozenge-shaped ground plan. Entering by a single door and
porch in the south wall, the visitor had to bend low to pass into a
barrel-vaulted antechamber complete with a bench, basin and deep
wall-niche. Here one door in the west wall led to the base of a tall
spiral ramp running up to the roof, while another door led due northwards to the principal, triangular room of the temple, some 11 × 7 m.
in area and over 8 m. in height. This last room sheltered the large square
fire altar, set near the west bay immediately behind a low, protective
wall. In contrast to the standard three steps at the top and bottom of
Achaemenian fire altars, the Nush-i Jan altar has no lower steps but
only a plain square shaft surmounted by four steps, each leaning out
one above the other. It was made of white plastered mud bricks.

The unusual interior wall decorations of the main room include blind
windows with a mud-brick 'portcullis' effect and recessed crosses, as
well as scaffold holes which suggest that a high wooden platform might
have stood at two at least of the room's three corners. This same chamber
was found to have been filled with small stones placed carefully in
position to a height of 6 m. capped with alternate bands of mud and
shale. A thick protective seal of mud brick also ran over the room and
outside the original walls, possibly placed by Cyaxares or his son
Astyages (585–550 B.C.), following a Neo-Babylonian practice.

The south side of the once free-standing temple was surrounded
by a long curved mud-brick bastion some 7 m. high. Adjoining it on the
east is a fortress, still with its projecting buttresses and arrow-slits,
facing a street also carefully filled with shale.

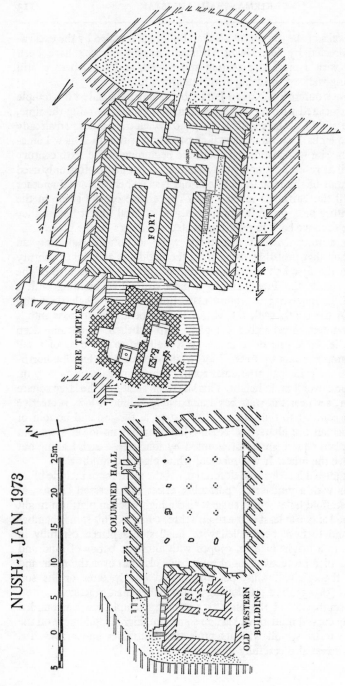

Fig. 20. Tepe Nūsh-i Jan. Plan of summit of mound showing, from left to right, the old Western Building, the partly excavated Columned Hall, the Fire Temple and the Fort.
(By courtesy of the British Institute of Persian Studies)

NUSH-I JAN 1973

N

5   0   5   10   15   20   25m.

COLUMNED HALL

OLD WESTERN BUILDING

FIRE TEMPLE

FORT

HOARD

Guardrooms, four magazines and a ramp (room 25) lead to a staircase covered with a corbelled mud-brick vault of which a small part is still visible. It was in the angle of the wall by the doorway in the south-east corner of the ramp that a small copper bowl containing more than 200 silver objects was found, still in its original hiding place covered by a mud brick. Quadruple spiral beads of types found in Marlik (p. 73) and Ziwiye (p. 96) and large double spiral pendants known only from the late third or early second millennium levels of Tepe Hissar IIIB (p. 196) were among the silver ingots and smaller scraps of metal. Dr. A. D. H. Bivar has suggested that not a few of the items from the hoard represent samples of an ingot currency used in Media before the introduction of coinage.[10]

Other finds elsewhere include bronze pins similar to seventh century Nimrud objects, possibly taken as loot from Assyrian cities, while a C.14 date taken from a piece of wood from the stone fill of the temple has given the date of 723 $\pm$220 B.C.[164,165]

At the west end of the mound are two further structures; the 'old Western Building' housing a second fire altar, and a rectangular columned hall 20 $\times$ 16 m. Four rows of three columns once supported the roof, while the walls possess buttresses and deep niches with quadruple stepped recesses. In 1974 a rock-cut tunnel descending from the hall at an angle of 30° was explored for a distance of 18 m. (See *Iran*, XIII, 1975.)

One can continue along the main road to Malayer, where there is a Government Tourist Inn, and on the main Khuzestan road for about 60 km. to Boroojerd. Here there is an interesting mosque, the Masjid-i Jumeh, with a Saljuq dome chamber and Qajar surrounds, and a so far unpublished Saljuq Kufic inscription in brick and stucco along the qibla wall of the dome chamber. Nearby is a tomb with the 'sugar-loaf' dome (like that over Daniel's tomb at Susa [p. 151]). This is the Imamzadeh Ja'far, and the tombstone inside, dated A.D. 1108, is believed by some to be later than the tomb itself. (See *Bulletin of the American Institute of Persian Art and Archaeology*, Vol. IV, No. 1, June 1935.)

Baba Jan Tepe, another very significant citadel mound of the early first millennium, lies almost due west of Nush-i Jan, in Luristan near the Sar-e Buzurg range of the Zagros mountains. A local tradition associates the range with Noah's Ark. The site can be reached by some cross-country driving through Malayer to just outside Nihavand, in the lovely valley where the last of the Sassanians, Yazdigird III, was decisively vanquished by the Arabs in A.D. 642. It was in or near Niha-vand in 1946 that a Seleucid stone stele was found with an edict of Antiochus III, establishing the cult of his wife Queen Laodicea. The stele is now on exhibition in the Tehran Museum.

Less than an hour's drive from Nihavand, Contenau and Ghirshman excavated Tepe Giyan[22] in the 1930s, a site occupied from at least the fifth millennium B.C. to c. 1000 B.C. (Drive for about 7 km. north and turn west at Kafresh, on to a gravel track passing through Dehgol; about 24 km.) Noted for its rich intramural graves, the site produced a striking corpus of painted third and second millennium pottery, the later vessels including tripod vases associated with Giyan III and slender, finely painted goblets of the 'Giyan II' style.

Next in time came the grey-black or black burnished wares of Giyan I that appear either merely as a new fashion or more probably as a new product of settlers from the north. In the topmost building level stood an imposing structure with architectural features that have been compared with others from eighth century Assyria. Ghirshman also attributes the partial destruction of the fortified town to a possible Assyrian assault in either the ninth or eighth century B.C.[58]

From Nihavand, the main road continues north for 58 km. to join the Hamadan-Kirmanshah highway near Kangavar. The easiest route to Baba Jan Tepe is from the main Kirmanshah highway, turning south for about 75 km. down the Harsin road to Nurabad, through exceptionally beautiful and dramatic country. Nurabad, a large village built round a tepe, is the local administrative centre. From here one can obtain detailed directions or a guide to Baba Jan Tepe which is reached by a poor and meandering track from Morabad village, also built on a tepe.

The several mounds excavated at Baba Jan have either been filled in or are collapsing so there is little to be seen of the imposing fortified manors and citadel revealed by Dr. Clare Goff, who directed excavations on behalf of the Institute of Archaeology, University of London, between 1966 and 1969. The whole region is extremely rich in prehistoric sites[156] and most prehistoric settlements were probably similar to present-day small hamlets where tribal groups spend part of the year in mud-brick houses supplemented by tents, migrating to warmer valleys in the winter.[177]

Baba Jan Tepe, which was occupied from at least the third millennium B.C., consists of a large central mound with smaller tepes to the east and south-west where a later town spread out along the flanks of the mounds into the fields.

Two fortified manors were excavated on the Central Mound, with long rooms flanking a central hall, roofed with a double row of columns down the centre, a small guardroom and a columned portico beneath the floor of which was found a horse burial. Dr. Goff draws[73] parallels between these buildings and those of the Burned Buildings of Hasanlu (p. 92) and of Nush-i Jan (p. 112). The horse burial was accompanied

Fig. 21. Tepe Baba Jan. Painted tiles from the walls of a chamber
in the East Mound.
(*By courtesy of Dr. Clare Goff, from* Iran, *Vol. VII, 1969*)

by pieces of harness, a bronze bowl and lamp, and was a later intrusion
into the probably eighth or seventh century manors, but such burials
were found also at Godin Tepe (p. 123) and Hasanlu (p. 92).

On the East Mound, two major contemporary buildings were
found, identified as a fort with a spiral ramp and stairs, as at Nush-i
Jan, and a building with a spectacular 'painted chamber' with 'blind
windows', a sophisticated fireplace and two stone column bases, each
of which probably supported a wooden shaft 90 cm. in diameter, painted
red like the walls of the chamber itself which was possibly a throne

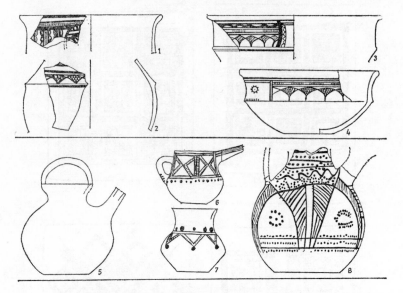

Fig. 22. Tepe Baba Jan. Representative pottery from Bronze Age (Nos. 1–4), Iron Age II (Nos. 5–7) and Iron Age III (No. 8) periods from Pish-i Kuh and Mahi Dasht. Scale 1:4.
(*By courtesy of Dr. Clare Goff, from* Iran, *Vol. VI, 1968*)

room or a temple comprising, with the fort, the residence of a local ruler.

The 'painted chamber' whose central area measured some 10·40 × 12·50 m., with an elaborately recessed, buttressed doorway to a small side chamber, was originally painted white with red-painted plaster superimposed, and a white floor. It was probably a two-storey building, and the ceiling of the ground floor had been decorated with a great variety of colourful painted tiles of buff clay and red and white designs; these had evidently fallen from the beamed ceiling when the building was partially destroyed by fire, in the first half of the seventh century B.C., possibly caused by Scythian invaders.

Some time late in the seventh century the elaborate site was covered with stables which in turn were burnt, and then the site was deserted until it was reoccupied briefly in the Achaemenian period; it was finally abandoned about the fifth century B.C.

The main road south from Nurabad reaches Khorramabad after 96 km., through country with many traces of prehistoric and Sassanian remains. Khorramabad was known as Diz-i Siah, 'The Black Fortress',

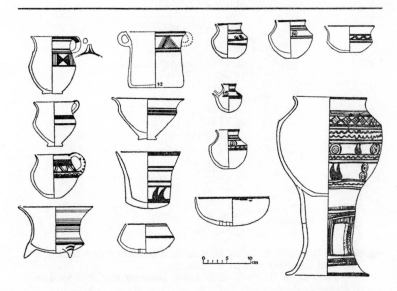

Fig. 23. Godin Tepe. Period III painted pottery, stylistically and technically
related to Tepe Giyan II and III.
(*By courtesy of Dr. T. Cuyler Young, Jr., from 'Excavations of the
Godin Project: Second Progress Report', R.O.M. Occasional Paper
No. 26. 1974*)

and the strong citadel on a mound in the centre of the town is to be
turned into a museum. A free-standing twelfth century Saljuq minaret
is seen in a garden on the south side of the main road, just past a petrol
station and a few hundred metres beyond the Khorramabad Tourist
Inn. A lane opposite the minar leads to the river and six intact arches of
a Sassanian bridge with probably ninth or tenth century restoration. A
similar, massive, almost intact bridge spans the Kashkan some 56 km.
along the good gravel road to Kudasht, west of Khorramabad. At 85 km.
a track to the left leads 2 km. to a village on the lower slopes of a rocky
spur, beside the stone foundations of Surkh Dum (see p. 129). Some
100 km. south of Khorramabad the main Andimeshk road passes
under the remaining lofty arch of the Sassanian Pol-i Dukhtar. This
great bridge was built by Shahpur I and restored in the Islamic period;
remnants of the massive foundations that supported eight other arches
still span the river. A pleasant little country inn, the Iran, on the left of
the road in Jaidar, just beyond the bridge, offers good local food and
clean, simple rooms. Continuing south one reaches Khuzestan.

As you drive north from Nurabad, for 75 km., the road goes, via
Harsin, to the Kirmanshah highway, near Bisitun. Harsin, a great centre

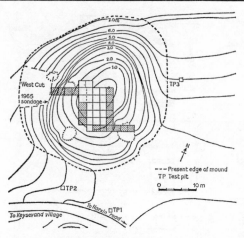

Fig. 24. Ganj Dareh Tepe. Shaded portions show extent of 1971 excavations.
Dotted lines, disturbances by villagers.
(*By courtesy of Dr. Philip E. L. Smith, Département d'Anthropologie,
Université de Montréal*)

for the famous 'Luristan bronzes', when they began appearing on the
market about 1928, has been identified as Shahpur Khast, a Sassanian
site of the third century A.D., and like so many small towns in the area is
built around a high citadel mound. A Sassanian podium, probably
supporting an outdoor fire altar, stands close to a nearby spring at
the foot of a mountain which has been partly levelled for an unfinished
bas-relief. A round basin is cut into the rock at the foot of the cliff
and it is thought possible that Shahpur I (A.D. 255–271) built a small
pavilion here. The whole area has been surveyed by Sir Aurel Stein
and Professor L. Vanden Berghe;[172,177] Sir Aurel Stein also noted and
made trial excavations as far south as Khorramabad.[156]

About 10 km. west of Harsin is the Early Neolithic site of Ganj
Dareh, situated close to the village of Kaysevand. Professor Philip
Smith of the University of Montreal found the site by chance during a
surveying expedition. Since beginning excavations after his initial
soundings in 1965, he has carried out four seasons of work here. The
site has proved one of the earliest known Early Neolithic mounds either
in Iran or outside Iran to have permanent architecture; a C. 14 test gives
a date of *c.* 8450 B.C. ± 150 for the lowest levels, and *c.* 6500–7000 B.C.
for the upper level.

Ganj Dareh has a valuable sequence of occupation that is beginning to
provide a new understanding of agricultural origins in the Zagros
mountain valleys between the years 8000 and 6000 B.C.

In one level, the sun-dried mud plano-convex bricks, nearly one metre in length, and laid between layers of mud mortar, were preserved in a conflagration so fierce—in the case of the earliest settlement at least—that it not only vitrified them, but even shattered flints. It also preserved the fragile, sun-dried pottery that would otherwise have been almost impossible to identify, thus challenging many earlier claims for a so-called a-ceramic Neolithic period.[149,150]

The walls of a complex series of small rooms still stood to nearly 2 m. in height, faced on both surfaces with mud plaster. An unusual form of walling was also found, in which alternating layers of mud and fine plaster were built up in strips and then plastered over. There was evidence of two-storeyed buildings with basements; under plastered living floors laid on horizontal beams, were found small cubicles, possibly for storage, and a few simple pots, although almost everything organic was destroyed by a fierce fire c. 7300 B.C. At another level, several rectangular mud-brick rooms with hearths, flint tools and some crude pottery are dated to c. 7000 B.C., at which time goats, but not sheep, were domesticated; besides their skeletal remains, hoof prints were found on a number of bricks. Here too a 'shrine' with two wild sheep skulls attached to a plastered niche recalls similar but later 'shrines' at Catal Huyuk in Anatolia. Among the several dozen human remains were those of adults and infants, mostly from level D, in both flexed and extended positions. Three extended skeletons, including a child's, were found inside a strange, elongated 'sarcophagus' of mud bricks, covered with a type of mud roof, while a human jawbone was discovered facing an intact pair of hands, apparently severed from the arms and lying palms upwards.

Other finds testified to the sophisticated use of clay in the eighth millennium B.C., including animal and delicately modelled Venus figurines, but no traces of obsidian, a commodity that had not yet reached this valley. (See *Iran*, Vol. XIII, 1975.)

If it is intended to go as far as the Iraq frontier, then by returning along the main highway to Hamadan, the sites of Kangavar, Bisitun and Godin Tepe may be seen on the way back. Assuming that the average reader will not be interested in visiting sites that are now merely overgrown mounds or hollows, one can leave Tepe Nush-i Jan to go back to Jowkar on the main Malayer-Hamadan road, and take the newly asphalted road west from here. It passes several imposing tepes and the small town of Touisserkan where there is a pleasant Mongol tomb-tower with a fluted conical roof, standing in a field about 1 km. on the western side of the town. The mausoleum contains a tombstone with an inscription in Hebrew.

Beyond Touisserkan the road (in 1974 still gravel surfaced), brings

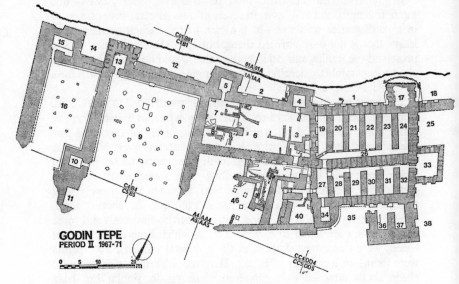

Fig. 25. Godin Tepe. The fortified Median manor with magazines (19–24 and 27–32) and towers (4, 5, 13, 15 and 17). Nos. 3, 6, 7, 8, were originally one sixteen-columned hall while No. 16 was an eight-columned hall. The Deep Sounding was cut between towers 4 and 5. (*By courtesy of Dr. T. Cuyler Young, Jr., R.O.M.*)

one after about 36 km. to Godin village, from which one can see, across the Gamas-Ab river which at times floods the area, the high, buff-coloured citadel mound of the third important Median site in this area. Dr. T. Cuyler Young, Jr., excavated this site from 1965 to 1973, sponsored by the Royal Ontario Museum, the University of Toronto and the Archaeological Service of Iran.

The eighth century B.C. citadel, probably that of a petty Median prince, with its bastions, towers and arrowslits, dominates the plain from a site occupied for some 4,000 years. Only the foundations of the thirty-columned, Period II throne hall remain, showing links with both the earlier monumental halls of Hasanlu IV (p. 91) and with the later plan of the 'Residential Palace' of Cyrus the Great at Pasargadae, 559-530 B.C., (p. 218). Well-preserved corridors are flanked by the magazines, with complete gateways into small rooms, while the remains of two fine staircases led to an upper storey of the fort.

About a thousand years earlier, earthquakes destroyed the town at a lower level where the skeleton of a man was found crushed by falling roof debris. Another skeleton with an arrow in his vertebrae, was that of a man whom medical evidence shows was paralysed and apparently died of starvation.

The cemetery, divided from the Central Mound by a dirt track on the southern edge of the town mounds, contains Iron Age I graves and a rectangular stone tomb open at the front, with a collapsed gabled roof and two burials inside. Outside was a complete horse skeleton, probably from the third quarter of the second millennium.[188]

The fifth and final season on this important key site in the archaeology of Western Iran ended in August 1973. In this year, excavations concentrated on three main areas: the Deep Sounding along the north edge of the Upper Citadel, the 'Median' palace and the Western Outer Town.

In the Deep Sounding, Period IV (2950–2400 B.C.), the remains of an open-air structure covering some 100 square metres was found. Here massive brick walls were lined with plastered mud-brick benches and floors, with, in one area, alternating bands of black and white paint on the walls. This striking structure originally stood on the edge of the highest point of the mound, the walls rising to a height of almost 3 metres, with at least five stages of reconstruction and replastering. Obviously it was a gathering place for people to sit, perhaps for religious, political or social functions.

To the east and south of this structure was an 'industrial' area of four small rooms each with an elaborate plastered hearth and other interesting features.

About two-thirds of the courtyard wall forming an oval around a Period V (3200–3000 B.C.) complex was found, originally about 33 m. long and 21 m. wide and entered from the south through a massive gateway flanked by small store-rooms. Here was a large courtyard with a monumental building containing a central rectangular room with niches and windows, and an elegant mud-brick plastered hearth. Similar structures were partially excavated here, all with well-laid mud-brick walls coated in white lime plaster. Nearly fifty tablets, some with numbers in wedges or dots, were found in this complex as well as many striking pottery vessels similar to those of the late Uruk and early Jemdet Nasr periods.

A small sounding revealed several other levels which entailed revising the original stratification; an entirely new culture, Period VIII (3850–3700 B.C.), rested on several building levels of Period IX (4100–3850 B.C.), the Seh Gabi Period (*Seh Gabi), while Dalma material, here called Godin X (4600–4100 B.C.) was found below the Seh Gabi deposit.

Work on the Upper Citadel cleared the remains of the Period II, Median fortified manor. In the south-east corner of the Great Columned

Hall, a small throne room with benches on four sides and a mud-brick throne seat in the north wall was found, as well as a kitchen with three large ovens and a drain, and other rooms that had been added to the original building.

The magazine area was completely cleared to reveal a doorway between Tower 5 and the sixth magazine, similar to those found at Tepe Nush-i Jan (p. 115); well-stratified pottery dated *c.* 750 B.C. was also recovered here. In the Outer Town area some six phases of architecture appeared in a deposit of about 2 m., dating from Period IV (2950–2400), to Period VI (3500–3200). Immediately below Period VI levels, virgin soil was reached. (For more complete details see *Iran*, Vol. XIII, 1975.)

The main Kirmanshah road lies some 5 km. from Godin village, and another 9 km. or so south-west brings you to Kangavar. There is a petrol pump a few metres up the first right-hand road into this Kurdish village, opposite a good chai khaneh. The famous Parthian temple of Anahita, the Mother Goddess and Goddess of Waters, known in the first century A.D. as Concobar, lies just off the main road, a little further on, where a sign indicates parking. Just beyond this, another turn right brings you into the village, with the north-western corner of the great terrace of dressed stone on the right of the street. Above, some six massive columns have been restored (the northern corner has been cut into by a mosque), while below the south face of the terrace, twenty-four columns have been re-erected opposite a pair of opposed staircases.

Noted by Sir Henry Layard and Flandin and Coste in the 1840s, this impressive site has been excavated since 1969 by a team of Iranian archaeologists directed by Mr. Kambakhsh Fard, a monumental task involving the purchase and demolition of houses constructed on the summit of the temple site, rehousing of villagers and handling of the huge blocks of superbly dressed stone. Many of these blocks bear graffiti and masons' marks of the Sassanian period and were apparently re-used in extensive rebuilding. Contrary to earlier beliefs, Mr. Fard's studies show the structure of the temple to be Iranian in nature and not occidental.

A Parthian cemetery was discovered below the eastern wall, while the temple platform itself revealed levels dating from Parthian to Safavid times, and include an early Islamic hamam, perhaps contemporary with that at Siraf (p. 251). While work continues on this remarkable site, photography is not permitted. (Brief report in *Iran*, Vol. XI, 1973, and 'Fouilles Archéologiques à Kangavar. Le Temple d'Anahita', *Bastan Chenassi va Honar-e Iran*, Nos. 9–10, 1972.)

31 km. further along this ancient highway is the Kurdish village of Sahneh, with a number of clean, shady chai khanehs on either side of the main road. From here one can visit two rock-cut tombs of probably

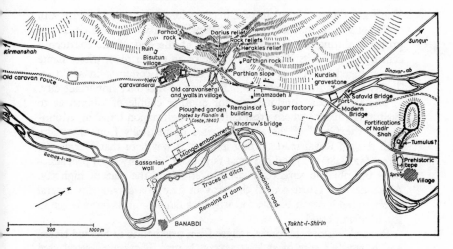

Fig. 26. Bisitun plan (*By courtesy of Professor W. Kleiss*)

fourth century B.C. or later date, popularly known as those of Farhad
and Shirin, a pair of legendary lovers. (Later dating of the so-called
Median tombs of Western Iran has been discussed by H. von Gall[54]
and David Stronach.[160]) The Sahneh tombs lie north-west of the village,
and involve a certain amount of scrambling up a rocky hillside. Take
the first turning right (north) off the first roundabout immediately
after crossing the bridge into Sahneh; turn right at the end of this
road, and then left (north again) at the small maidan which takes you
out of the town, to the slope of the hills behind. The track bends to the
left behind the last row of buildings, narrowing as it reaches a stream
and turns to run north, alongside, between a high bank and a drop
down to the water. A tarmac road brings you to a parking place.

High in the cliff on the left, beyond the opposite bank of the stream,
can be seen the square-cut opening to the larger of the two tombs. This
can be photographed with a telescopic lens from the track—either the
late morning or the early afternoon offering the best light. The stream
must be waded, and then there is a climb up the steep shaly slope to
the tombs which are virtually impossible to enter. The more important
of the two is decorated with a portico of two columns hewn from the
rock and it contains a vestibule with two niches for offerings, and
benches along the sides. The winged disc, symbol of Ahura Mazda,
is carved above the entrance. A burial chamber at a lower level, reached
by a shaft pierced in the floor of the vestibule, contains a single grave.

About 23 km. after leaving Sahneh a road on the right goes 58 km.
to Sonqor where there is an attractive tomb-tower, possibly Mongol.

The track crosses the plain of Dinavar, site of the tenth century A.D. capital of a small, independent Kurdish principality which was destroyed probably during the Timurid invasion at the end of the fourteenth century. Dinavar itself was on the site of an earlier town whose name was changed to Mah el Kufah after the Arab conquest in A.D. 640. Today there is little or nothing left to see of this once important city.

The main road continues on for another couple of kilometres to Bisitun (Behistan) whose great cliff, the 'Baghistanon Oros' or 'Mountain of the Gods' of the ancients, rises dramatically from the plain, with the old Royal road skirting its foot. It was here that Darius the Great (521–486 B.C.) had the most famous of his many royal proclamations inscribed in three languages, overlooking the ancient highway. Alexander the Great passed this way in 324 B.C., staying for several weeks in the Nisaean Fields, a nearby area famous for its horses even in the Median period.

Bisitun's history, however, ranges from prehistoric to Safavid times, and is worth a stay of at least several hours! There are several chai khanehs here, the most sophisticated one being the 'Persepolis', opposite the sugar-beet factory. From Bisitun to Kirmanshah, where there is a good modern motel, is only a twenty minutes' drive. Excavations at Bisitun were carried out by a German archaeological team led by Professor H. Luschey, revealing an important Median fortress.

The oldest remains of Bisitun lie on the northern side of the highway; to take them in order, as one approaches from the east, the first to be seen are those on the so-called Parthian Slopes on the right of the road, just beyond a large sugar factory on the left. A gentle slope leads up from the road to the base of the cliff and here Professor Wolfram Kleiss of the German Archaeological Institute of Tehran, detected the fortification walls of a Parthian settlement stretching down into the valley. Almost at the base of the cliff is a large, free-standing rock which has been carved on three of its faces, probably in the second century A.D. The least worn of these depicts a magus or priest wearing typical Parthian tunic and baggy trousers, pouring incense onto a small fire altar (on which Dr. Gropp of the German Archaeological Institute has recently noticed a worn and almost indecipherable inscription) while other Parthian figures stand on either side. From the rock one can look down across the main road to the river Gamas-Ab beyond a few scattered buildings and a clump of trees. Here are the remains of the stone piers of a Sassanian bridge that served the then main road to the east. As you look towards the bridge, the cliff of Bisitun curves away on your right, and at the base close to other Parthian remains, Professor Wolfram Kleiss cleared the fortification walls of a probable Median settlement. Above these last walls the natural rock platform still higher up the hill is approached by rock-cut steps, and a sharp climb up here reveals both a fire bowl and a rectangular ossuary of Parthian or Sassanian date.

Half-way up the face of the cliff behind the Parthian rock is the Ghar-i Khar (Donkey Cave) excavated by Professor Philip Smith in 1965.[149] This cave, some 27 m. long, had deep deposits ranging in time from the Middle Palaeolithic or earlier, down to the present day, covering a span of at least 35,000 years.[187]

The track round the base of this cliff towards the main road passes the opening of a much smaller cave at ground level (but still above the level of the road) which was one of the first caves to be excavated in Iran, in 1949, by Carleton S. Coon.[23,24] The track by which it is reached continues over the statue of Hercules and down to the cleft in the rocks opposite the Darius inscription. This small cave revealed traces of occupation of Neanderthal racial types, hunters of the red deer, some 40,000 or more years ago.

The statue of Hercules or Herakles was revealed in 1956 when the new highway was being lowered, and this somewhat bibulous-looking Seleucid figure reclines with a goblet in one hand and his club by his feet, watching the endless traffic on the highway. An inscription behind the figure dates it to the year 163 of the Seleucid era, that is, 148 B.C. A protective canopy erected over the carving makes the early morning the best time for photography. Seldom noticed is the fact that Hercules reclines on the back of a lion carved in shallow relief.

Just beyond the statue is the wicket gate behind which are the badly damaged and worn Parthian reliefs of Mithridates II (124–87 B.C.), on the left, showing four satraps paying homage to the King, and on the right a tablet commemorating the victory of Gotarzes II, who is shown on horseback, lancing an enemy, probably Meherdates whom he defeated in A.D. 50. Both reliefs have been mutilated by a seventeenth century A.D. panel.

The direct path to the Darius relief is also through the wicket gate (the key is usually with an old and knowledgeable member of the archaeological teams that worked here in the past, who is more or less permanently on duty at the small chai khaneh immediately opposite). The relief can be seen from the main road but binoculars are needed to pick out the details, wherever you are. Before 10.30 a.m. is best for practically all photography at Bisitun, the earlier the better.

To the left of the Mithridates relief as you face the mountain, the path winds up to a small platform terrace roughly 10 m. wide and of the same depth; the dry stone walls are closed by a second wall covered with mud bricks and the entrance is in the form of a ramp with steps. This was covered with debris from the cutting of the Darius relief in the cliff above and it was Professor Luschey[112b] who, in 1963, first noticed the fact that this was an artificial platform on which had once stood a mud-brick structure. He believes that this possibly early sixth century B.C. terrace was open, with a mud-brick balustrade around it, and that on the right and left of the entrance there may have been altars dedicated to the gods of fire and water.

This is the closest one can get to the Darius relief some 66 m. above, without some experience of rock-climbing techniques, and one can now appreciate the courage of Sir Henry Rawlinson who, in 1839, had himself let down by ropes from the top of the cliff, to copy the long inscriptions on the panels below. Darius is shown facing a line of royal prisoners with his foot on the body of his principal opponent, the defeated Gaumata. His proclamation, in Old Persian, flanked by Neo-Babylonian on the left and Neo-Elamite on the right, describes in detail his version of the dramatic story of the usurper Gaumata's attempt to pass himself off as Bardiya, Cyrus the Great's second son who had in fact been secretly killed by his brother Cambyses.

Darius, who had been acclaimed king by a council of nobles, fought nineteen separate battles before overcoming the last of his enemies. Darius also lists the 23 countries in his possession, and R. G. Kent[99] has published a full translation of the inscriptions.

It was Rawlinson's deciphering of the Old Persian text (following earlier work on Old Persian by such scholars as Grotefend) and his subsequent translation of part of the Akkadian (the language of the Babylonians), that gave the key to the Neo-Elamite and Old Persian inscriptions. In 1948, Dr. George Cameron, of the Oriental Institute of the University of Chicago, made a latex impression of the inscriptions thus ensuring complete accuracy.

Continuing on from the bas-relief round the foot of the mountain, one passes a Sassanian 'workshop' with roughly 1,000 scattered unfinished blocks of stone, many with masons' marks upon them. It is believed that the Sassanian king, Khusraw II, built a palace at Bisitun although the site has not yet been found, and that the Sassanian capitals now in the garden of Taq-i Bustan (p. 130) came from this building.[112c]

It was probably the same Sassanian king who, between A.D. 590 and A.D. 628, ordered what has been described as the greatest expanse of smoothed rock surface ever seen in Iran, the 200 m. broad and 55 m. high panel in the cliffs beyond the Darius inscription, at the spot known as Tarash-i Farhad. It was never completed, due probably to Khusraw's sudden death, but W. Salzmann of the German Archaeological Institute who examined the site in detail in 1965, entering the working chimney some 35 m. above the ground, believes that a fire temple had been planned in front of the panel and that possibly the capitals at Taq-i Bustan which were found in the village were intended for this building.

Meanwhile across the main road, almost opposite Hercules, one can see the once sacred spring, now a pleasant pool under the shady trees, and walking through the grove and across various small streams, one can reach the open land where a few traces remain of a Mongol kiosk, in which early fourteenth century glazed tiles were found. It is difficult now to trace even the ground plan as the land has been ploughed over. Beyond the kiosk are the foundations of a Sassanian embankment measuring more than 1,000 m. along the River Gamas-Ab. The foundations are 4 m. deep and 5 m. wide and consist of three rows of great stone blocks; it must once have been part of a monumental architectural design probably linking with gardens further from the river. The foundation piers of a Sassanian bridge can be seen to the north of the wall, following the line of a Sassanian highway which can still be traced, running across the bridge, to the east.

Professor Kleiss believes that this area formed part of a Sassanian 'paradeisos' for hunting wild boar, as depicted in the large grotto in Taq-i Bustan.

The track that leads down past the chai khaneh and spring continues towards the south to link with the old caravan road to Kirmanshah; on the outskirts of the hamlet, it passes a charming caravanserai built by Sheikh Ali Khan Zanganeh in A.D. 1685, one of the finest of its kind in Iran. It is still in use and from its roof the Terrace of Farhad can be very clearly viewed. Behind this serai, to the north, Professor Luschey found the remains of a Sassanian castle[112b] consisting of a small fort with space for pitching tents, which was followed by a fourteenth century Mongol serai on the same site, surveyed by Professor Kleiss.

Kirmanshah is 32 km. from Bisitun, and about 7 km. along the road you pass on the left the road to Harsin (22 km.); there is a bus-stop and a heavy vehicle check-point on the corner. (Ganj Dareh Tepe, p. 120, is about 13 km. down this road, which eventually reaches Khorramabad and Khuzestan.)

André Godard in 1930, and Freya Stark in 1931, made the earliest archaeological investigations in Luristan, followed by Aurel Stein in 1936 and E. F. Schmidt who worked at the ninth century B.C. sanctuary at Surkh Dum in the 1930s, finding many bronze votive offerings.[60]

In more recent years, ending in 1964, a Danish archaeological expedition under the direction of Mr. Henrik Thrane[115,167,168] carried out extensive surveys and excavations on some 30 sites in Luristan ranging in date from c. 6500 B.C. down to the first millennium B.C.

In addition a Belgian mission led by Professor Louis Vanden Berghe has now completed nine seasons of excavation and surface exploration in the more westerly valleys of Luristan (p. 132), documenting both the earliest and latest phases of local bronze production.[172,177]

Some 20 km. nearer Kirmanshah, from the Harsin turning, another road goes south (left) and about 2 km. along here, just behind a clump of trees on the right at a bend in the road, is a small mound, Tepe Sarab, one of over 250 prehistoric sites located in the area by a team led by Professor Robert J. Braidwood of the University of Chicago during 1958–60. The team was searching for evidence of the important transitional step in human history from food gathering to effective food production, which appeared to take place between about 15,000 and 8,000 years ago.[12] Clay figurines, pottery, ground stone, flint and obsidian industries found here recall the village farming community of Jarmo in Iraqi Kordestan; Sarab however seemed to have semi-pit structures probably of a temporary nature, and probably dates from about 9,000–8,000 years ago.

Only 5 km. further along the Kirmanshah road one reaches a roundabout. The left turn here goes past the oil refinery and into Kirmanshah itself, but turn right for the famous Sassanian grottoes of Taq-i Bustan, about 1 km. along the road, passing between the remnants of mud-brick walls believed to have enclosed another Sassanian paradeisos, probably for deer.

At the end of the road is an artificial pool fed by a 'sacred' spring welling from the rocky cliff behind, in which are the two grottoes.[50] The entrance is by a gate in the garden in front of the grottoes which are normally open from 8 a.m. to about sunset. A small charge is made for admission. If the entrance is closed, inquiries of the many children from the little Kurdish hamlet nearby will almost certainly produce the guardian within a few moments.

The carved capitals now known to have come from Bisitun, and other fragments of statuary, are scattered in the little garden. The early afternoon is the best time to photograph both of the grottoes and a bas-relief of the investiture of Ardashir II (A.D. 379–383) on the cliff wall just before reaching the grottoes. This relief shows the god Hormizd (Ahura Mazda) on the right, and a rare portrayal of Mithras standing on a lotus, with the sun's rays forming a halo, on the left. Ardashir II is accepting the ribboned diadem from Hormizd, and Mithras holds a ceremonial bundle of sacred twigs, known as the 'barsom', often depicted in religious scenes of later Achaemenian date. A vanquished Roman lies under the feet of Ardashir and Hormizd.

Next comes the small ivan artificially cut from the rock in the reign of Shahpur III (A.D. 383–388), son of Ardashir II, and the reliefs at the back show Shahpur III with his grandfather, Shahpur II (A.D. 309–379), on the right, together with an inscription in Pahlavi.

The largest of the ivans is unique in its decoration. It was probably intended to form the centre piece of a triple ivan of which the third small ivan was never constructed. The entrance is decorated with a fantastic 'Tree of Life' embodying Graeco-Roman acanthus leaves and possibly elements of Indian plants, according to Dr. Porada,[130] while in the centre a royal crescent is flanked by winged figures carrying ribboned rings.

On the right is an inscription commemorating the visit of the nineteenth century A.D. Qajar king, Nasir al-Din Shah. Inside the grotto are some of the most astonishing of all bas-reliefs in Iran. The back is divided into an upper and lower panel depicting below, in high relief, a king in full armour, holding a lance and riding an armoured charger. Most authorities believe this is Khusraw II (A.D. 591–628) on his favourite horse Shabdiz, although Erdmann took it to be King Peroz (A.D. 459–484). The upper panel depicts the investiture of the king, with Hormizd and probably the goddess of water, Anahita.[112c]

The two side walls depict what are perhaps the most vivid of all bas-reliefs, two royal hunts in enclosed paradeisos in a series of 'stills' —the left (facing the rear of the ivan) showing a royal boar hunt with the king in various stages of the chase, standing in a boat in the marshes, shooting an arrow at a herd of wild boar driven into the reeds by massed elephants, and accompanied by musicians in smaller boats. The opposite panel depicts the same king stag-hunting, mounted, like his nobles, on horseback, a royal parasol held over his head, while more musicians sing and play.

On the left wall, high up towards the rear, a much later, coloured and very poor relief shows the Qajar Governor of the Kirmanshah area, Mohammad Ali Mirza Dowlat Shah (A.D. 1822), son of the king, Fath' Ali Shah, with his two sons. (See *Taq-i Bustan* by Shinji Fukai and Kiyoharu Horiuchi, Vols. I & II, The Institute of Oriental Culture, The University of Tokyo, 1972.)

In 1970, a team of Iranian archaeologists led by Mr. Kambakhsh Fard excavated a Parthian cemetery on the summit of a cliff in the immediate area. About 50–60 m. immediately to the west of Taq-i Bustan, another Parthian site has been revealed on the hill known as Kuh-i Paroo. Obsidian flints and prehistoric pottery were among the finds in this dig which is being continued.

Kirmanshah (or, more properly, Kirmanshahan), was probably founded by Bahram IV in the fourth century A.D. and named 'city of the kings of Kirman' because Bahram had been governor of Kirman province during the reign of his brother, Shahpur III. The Sassanian city was somewhat to the north of the present town, nearer Taq-i Bustan, and was captured by the Arabs in A.D. 649.

Occupied by the Buyids in the tenth century, and then by the Saljuqs when it was the principal town of the province of Kordestan, it was destroyed by the Mongols in A.D. 1220. Six Sassanian capitals have been re-used in the Friday Mosque. (See A.M.I., Band 6, 1973.)

Today Kirmanshah is the capital of the province and a lively town, with striking Kurds in their national costume and rather fearsome looking Kurdish women with long ringlets, for all the world like Ardashir I's queen on the Naqsh-i Rajab relief (p. 222); they are usually friendly until you try to photograph them, and if they show signs of objecting, desist at once.

Close to the oil refinery, a sign on the right of the main road directs you to the Motel Glayol with a restaurant, a swimming pool and comfortable apartments with private bathrooms (about 700 rials double). The newer Darius Hotel in the centre of town offers double rooms with bath (700 rials inc. service) and has a good restaurant.

The Hotel Grand at the top of Ferdowsi (a continuation of the main street) near the Maidan-i Shah is clean, and very inexpensive; some rooms include a shower. There are a number of other two star hotels along the main road. Givehs, cotton slippers in many colourful patterns and designs, are good value at from 90 to 150 rials a pair, while in the covered bazaar tribal rugs, glims and saddlebags can be found.

There are no known monuments of interest in the town itself, but a bas-relief which Professor Vanden Berghe[172,177] attributes to the third century B.C. (Seleucid) carved over one of two adjacent hollowed niches in the Eshaqvand (Sakavand) rocks, which served as ostothekes or burial niches, can be seen near Deh-i Nau in the Kuh-i Sefid mountains south-east of Kirmanshah. The relief shows a priest praying at two fire altars and is reached from the road just south of Harsin (p. 120), a dirt road going 26 km. to the site, west of the Gamas-Ab. (*Eshaqvand.)

The road to Sanandaj and Takht-i Sulaiman (p. 102) runs north from Kirmanshah. For the frontier, westwards, leave Kirmanshah from the Maidan-i Shah, following the signposts to Khosravi, the actual frontier post. Qasr-i Shireen, the last town, is 182 km. away, along a road that crosses mountains, passing by prehistoric tepes, attractive Safavid caravanserais and relics of the many historic passages along this ancient highway. A good road goes south-east through Luristan to Khuzestan.

Shahabad-Gharb (formerly known as Harunabad), is a small town about 70 km. from Kirmanshah, built right up against a mound surveyed by Stein[156] who found bronze ornaments and dishes of Luristan type in the upper layers, and chalcolithic sherds of the third or fourth millennium B.C. lower down. (*Chogha Gavaneh.) There is a Tourist Inn here. A signpost in the main square indicates the road to Ilam in the heart of Luristan, which has become the chief centre for Professor Vanden Berghe's recent work. Ilam, about 150 km. from

Shahabad-Gharb, was until the 1930s known as Dih Bala or Husainabad, capital of the Lur chieftains, the Walis. Three palaces of the Walis are still in existence in Ilam, where there is also a tomb attributed to the father of Caliph Harun al-Rashid, who died in this region in A.D. 785. The Abbasid Caliphs made their summer quarters in Luristan with its good hunting and cool weather.

There is a Tourist Inn at Ilam. (*Shikaft-i Gulgul.)

About 25 km. to the north-west of Ilam, on the Shahabad road, is the village of Chavar or Chawar, near which are many of the sites, mainly cemeteries, dug by the Belgian team. In prehistoric times the dead were usually buried under the floors of their houses, or in pits on the edge of their settlements, while family or collective stone graves dating from the third millennium B.C. were in use in the necropolis of Bani Surmah,[178] near Chavar.

After the Iranian invasion from 1200 B.C. onwards, the dead were always buried outside their villages, as at the neighbouring site of War Kabud which marks the latest phase of the 'Luristan Bronze' civilization near the close of the eighth and the beginning of the seventh century B.C.

Tepe War Kabud is about ten minutes' walk from Chavar and in 1970 some graves were still open for inspection. The river Lashkan surrounds the necropolis which was dug in 1965 and 1966, when over 100 graves averaging 1 m. × 60 cm. in size were revealed. The tombs were of two types, one a simple pit in the ground, the other a funeral chamber lined with grey limestone ashlar, with the bodies placed in a contracted position, fully dressed and surrounded with their most valuable possessions which included magnificent bronze and iron weapons. Women had their gold, silver and bronze jewellery.

The much earlier necropolis of Bani Surmah, which was dug in 1967, lies along the banks of the Lashkan river, close to War Kabud, and extends over a wide plateau divided by depressions into three zones. Graves here revealed a previously unknown stage in the Bronze Age civilization of Luristan, dating from the mid third millennium B.C. in the last phase of the Early Sumerian period, and consisting of enormous funeral vaults, two or three of which are still open. Most measure from 8 to 16·20 m. long, and 1·70 to 3 m. wide, and were closed by enormous covering stone slabs, some weighing as much as 600 kilos. Pebbles were placed around each slab and the entire tomb was edged with solid counterweights. Inside, the thick limestone walls were perfectly finished, in staggered courses arranged so that each layer left a gap smaller than the one below, making the top of the tomb narrower than the bottom. These family or collective vaults contained only fragments of bone, but sufficient to show that the dead were buried fully clothed with all their personal possessions, and with an ample supply of food and drink for the after-life.

Professor Vanden Berghe believes these were Elamite tombs, and here for the first time was found the beginning of the Bronze Age in Luristan and proof that the archaic bronzes, formerly supposed to have been made in Mesopotamia and sent to Luristan, had on the contrary been made in Luristan itself, and exported to Mesopotamia.

Perhaps the most important find was that of a funerary statuette 19·2 cm. high, made of bronze and found in a cist tomb at Tattulban, near Chinan village. The statuette is a central demon-like creature with three double-faced heads, outstretched arms strangling two long-necked monsters appearing from the centre of its body, and two cocks' heads under the monsters' necks. It was discovered with many bronze and iron weapons, placed opposite the face of a warrior, and was the first to be found in a scientific excavation although there are many similar bronzes from clandestine diggers in private collections. The Tattulban statuette can be dated to *c.* 750–700 B.C.

Kulleh Nisar[179] was another necropolis investigated on the left bank of the Kalal river, 1 km. west of Chigah and 25 km. north-west of Bani Surmah—here a second phase of the Bani Surmah Bronze Period was revealed. Professor Vanden Berghe is continuing his excavations in an attempt to fill the 2,000 year gap between Bani Surmah and War Kabud. New roads are planned for this area which should make these sites more accessible. (For more recent work by the Belgian team and other archaeologists in the area, see p. 138.)

From the pleasant little town of Shahabad-Gharb, continue along the main highway to the west, passing through Khosrowabad after 16 km., a village which may have been on the site of a Sassanian palace, and possibly the ancient Tazar mentioned by thirteenth century historians. About 40 km. further on, the road climbs the Pai-i Taq pass (the 'Gates of the Zagros'), and after reaching the crest you can look down on your left to see the old road, now closed to normal traffic, winding below. A stone ivan is built into a curve of this road and is known as the Taq-i Girreh, possibly being a Sassanian relay station. From here a difficult track goes about 25 km. to the Sassanian fort of Qaleh-i Yazdigird (see E. J. Keall, *Iran*, Vol. V, 1967).

The road now descends to the plain and there is a pleasant little chai khaneh among some trees at the foot of the pass. About 10 km. further on, the road passes between two cliffs in a gap in the mountain, and as you emerge take a track immediately to your left, along the foot of the mountain to the edge of a graveyard. Look up at the cliff face and you can see a rock-cut tomb known as Dukkan-i Daud, 'David's workshop', which, with other rock-cut tombs in the area, used to be

Fig. 27. Rock relief, probably King Anubanini, at Sar-i Pul-i Zuhab, 21st–20th century B.C. or 23rd–22nd century B.C.
(*After Herzfeld, from* Ancient Iran, *Edith Porada*)

ascribed to the Median period but is now thought to be post-Achaemenian. The name is said to derive from a local tradition of a Jewish blacksmith who became a king and was buried here. The rectangular tomb is framed with stepped lintel courses, the smooth rock surface below bearing the carved figure of a magus holding the barsom. Both Stronach and Vanden Berghe relate this last figure to one found in the third century B.C. Fratadara Palace below the platform at Persepolis (p. 235). The tomb is best photographed in afternoon light.

About 3 km. further along the main road is the Kurdish village of Sar-i Pul-i-Zuhab. Captured by the Arabs when they swept triumphantly over the land in A.D. 640, the original settlement was renamed Holvan. Later it passed into Saljuq hands, in A.D. 1046, but the town was destroyed by fire and earthquake in 1149.

As you drive into the outskirts of the little town, some of the oldest known bas-reliefs in Iran can be found on the cliffs to your right.

These investiture and triumphal scenes may well have inspired the larger-scale reliefs of the Medes, Achaemenians and Sassanians, all of whom carved their proclamations and triumphs in similar high places within sight of every passer-by.

Take the lane leading round the back of a school to the foot of the cliff. The reliefs are small and there are two, one high above the other, on the eastern cliff facing the road. Early morning or late afternoon is best for photography here, and a telescopic lens is needed.

The upper relief which Porada[130] dates to the twenty-first or twentieth century B.C. probably depicts King Anubanini of the Lullubi tribes, whose territory was north of that of the Elamites, and whose artistic inspiration seems to stem from Mesopotamia. The king faces the goddess Inanna (Ishtar) who offers him the royal diadem. In her left hand the goddess holds a rope attached to two kneeling, naked prisoners. The king wears an unusual form of helmet and carries a crescentic-ended sword in his right hand. One foot is placed on the naked body of a prisoner while the eight-pointed star within a circle, symbol of Ishtar, is carved between the king and the goddess. In a panel beneath their feet, six other naked and bound prisoners walk in line and, as Dr. Porada has pointed out, their leader wears a feathered head-dress similar to that seen in some hammered Luristan bronzes of the early first millennium B.C. There is an inscription by the side of the prisoners, which is a later addition, and gives the name of Tar Lunni, possibly another tribal chief who made use of the existing relief to advertise his own conquests.

Below this relief is a very badly weathered Parthian relief of the vanquished Mithridates IV standing before Vologazes II or III who is mounted on a horse, with an inscription in Arsacid Pahlavi.

There are four other bas-reliefs of the Lullubi king at Sar-i Pul, all similar. Two are round the eastern cliff, one being high up and on a very dark, almost black patch of rock just below a large aperture in the rock. The two others are on the western cliff across the river, and must be reached by going back to the main road and over the bridge in the middle of the village, and down a track on the opposite bank of the river.

North-west of Sar-i-Pul, at Hurin Shaikh Khan, is an even older, undated triumphal bas-relief with an Akkadian inscription. The relief shows a Zagros tribal chieftain holding a bow in his hand and standing before two defeated prisoners. The inscription was added later and praises the conquests of Tar Lunni once again. (*Sar-i Pul.)

Just before reaching Qasr-i Shireen, about 30 km. further west along the main highway, which now runs through flat and, in summer, very hot country, you reach a Government Tourist Inn on the left of the road, with a swimming pool on the right. Near the pool, a footpath leads across a series of mounds to the massive Sassanian structure known as the Chahar Qapu (Four Doors), a huge fire temple, or as some scholars believe, a royal audience hall, built by Khusraw II, so solid that it has withstood centuries of earthquakes and Arab invasions. A great square building on the same plan as the usual Sassanian Chahar Taq, it measures just under sixteen square metres; it is made of rough stone bound with mortar, except for the four archways of baked brick. The dome has fallen in but the corner squinches, transforming the square base to a circular plan for the dome, still survive, and the whole gives shade now to shepherds and their flocks.

The foundations and lower chambers of a number of ruined out-buildings surround the Chahar Qapu which was only one of many structures standing in a vast park of nearly 300 acres, with gardens, pavilions, pools, wild-game reserves and palaces, the entire complex enclosed by an aqueduct in which flowed the waters of the river Hulwan.

The great palace of Khusraw, known as the Emaret-i Khusraw, lies across the main road, to the north-east of the Tourist Inn, a few minutes walk from it. Take a little footpath through orange and lemon groves by the side of a stream, and see the remains standing on a vast terrace across the fields to your right. Double ramps similar to the grand staircase of Persepolis (p. 226) formed the main approach to the terrace, at the eastern end of the platform. Approaching from the footpath, you first see the massive supporting terrace with some vaulted rooms on the south-west believed to have been either a menagerie or stables. The palace itself included the royal official and private apartments and in plan was somewhat similar to the earlier palaces of Firuzabad (p. 254) and Sarvistan (p. 258).

A columned ivan led from the eastern terrace to the public rooms including a square hall covered with a dome, with long, barrel-vaulted halls on either side. Then came a courtyard and the private apartments and servants' quarters, all grouped round some ten smaller courtyards.

The thirteenth century historian Yaqut called the whole complex 'one of the wonders of the world', but only a few years after Khusraw died the buildings were destroyed by the Byzantine emperor Heraclius in A.D. 628 and soon after came the end of the Sassanian dynasty; the hastily built palace of Shireen, 'the sweet', named after Khusraw's Christian wife, fell into ruins.

The small town of Qasr-i Shireen has no monuments earlier than the ruins of an early nineteenth century citadel, on a mound to the north. The jujeh kebab (chicken kebab) at the little restaurant of Karim, about 1 km. before the town proper, is highly recommended, but the best general food is at the Tourist Inn. There are a number of inexpensive

5*

small provincial hotels in the town, including the Marmar and the Ferdowsi.

Qasr-i Shireen, like the palace, is named after Khusraw's wife. It was captured by the Arabs only nine years after the attack by Heraclius, and virtually destroyed.

The border with Iraq lies at Khosrovi, about twenty miles further south-west, from whence the old royal highway continues to Baghdad, and ancient Ctesiphon.

Recent surveys in the Kuh-i Dasht area of Luristan, west of Khorramabad, by various archaeologists including Hamid Yazdanpanah, Dr. C. B. M. McBurney and Dr. Clare Goff, have revealed cave paintings dating from about 40,000 B.C. They are believed to be the only known examples between the Mediterranean and the Indian Peninsula and have been compared to those of Spain. Among others first shown to Dr. McBurney by Mr. A. A. Sarfaraz are those at Mirmalas on the west of the Kuh-i Sarun Massif, a few kilometres south-east of the town of Kuh-i Dasht. Six other decorated shelters were seen on the eastern side, including Bard-i Spid and Humian, where there were probably settlements some 10,000 years ago.

Also in the central Pusht-i Kuh area, on both sides of the nearby Kabir Kuh ridge Professor Vanden Berghe has been excavating Chalcolithic, Bronze and Iron Age remains. A large necropolis of cist graves of the last centuries of the fifth millennium B.C. were found at Hakalan, throwing new light on early burial customs. Enormous megalithic tombs were found in many Early Bronze Age cemeteries (2600–2500 B.C.), which with other Middle and Late Bronze Age tombs and second millennium Iron Age cyst graves, contained many grave goods showing a great diversity of cultures. (See reports in *Iran*, Vol. XI, 1973, *Archeologia*, Nos. 57, 63 and 65, 1973, and 'Cinquième Campagne, 1969, Prospections dans le Pusht-i Kuh Central' by L. Vanden Berghe, *Iranica Antiqua*, Vol. IX, 1972.)

5 · Khuzestan and the South-West

(See map, p. 108.)

Khuzestan is perhaps the easiest of all Iranian provinces to reach. You can arrive by air at the international airport of Abadan; by sea, on passenger-carrying cargo boats from Europe and India; and by rail at the adjoining seaport of Khorramshahr. A main highway as well as Iran's first major rail link connects Tehran with the Persian Gulf.

From Early Neolithic times this fertile region has attracted settlers; it is believed to take its name from the Khuz, a tribe probably already in occupation when the Achaemenians arrived to make this the province they knew as Susiana.

Elamites, Achaemenians and Sassanians all built royal cities here, often one above the ruins of the other. Remains of ancient irrigation works utilizing the waters of three great rivers, the Karun, the Karkha and the Diz, testify to the former prosperity of this mainly flat plain which is geographically an extension of Lower Mesopotamia and ancient Sumeria, reaching to the barrier of the Zagros mountains on the east and north. Today, Khuzestan's wealth comes mainly from the rich oilfields that have made possible modern hydro-electric schemes now helping to irrigate a long-neglected area.

The Abadan International Hotel, close to the airport, is usually very fully booked (900 rials single to 1,600 double, private baths, pool and restaurant). The nearby Caravanserai has similar rates. Others in Khorramshahr, linked to Abadan by a causeway across the river Karun, and in the town of Abadan itself, include the Anahita, overlooking the Karun, a pleasant Indian type of old-established hotel with rooms around a garden (700 rials double, with air-conditioning and bathroom). The Karoon is on the same road, on a first floor above shops (150 rials single, with air-conditioning, but no private baths). Further along still is the Persian Gulf Hotel with a night club and small garden and usually fully occupied by night club artistes.

Other hotels include the Bakhtiar, the Rukhane, the Kayvan and the Iran, all reasonably priced.

Travel agencies can arrange tours or hire cars but there is nothing of historic interest in Abadan, which is purely a product of the oil industry, dominated by the largest oil refinery in the world. Between the eighth and eleventh centuries in the Abbasid period, it was an important harbour, with many mosques which by the thirteenth century had already disappeared owing to the shifting of the river bed.

There is a small, modern museum with a twentieth century interpretation of the typical 'sugar-loaf' roof of the local shrines. It contains a collection of tribal costumes, artifacts and pottery from archaeological sites in Khuzestan, as well as a library. The Middle Elamite reliefs in the garden come from Qaleh-i Tul (p. 163).

From Abadan make first for Ahwaz (Ahvaz), the provincial capital straddling both banks of the river Karun about 100 km. north of Abadan. You can fly there or join an organized day tour by road, or hire a car independently to make the 90 minutes' drive along a good highway. The average cost for a hired car is 800 rials for the trip. It is possible to see the three major sites of Susa, Haft Tepe and Choga Zanbil in one long day from Abadan, but it should be remembered that in summer this area is very hot and in spring the road is subject to flooding which often completely cuts off Choga Zanbil.

Ahwaz takes its name from the Arabic 'Suq al-Ahwaz', 'The Market of Ahwaz', which is a corruption of Khuz; this tribe was still occupying the province when the town was captured by the Arabs in A.D. 638. Earlier, it had been the capital of an Arsacid Parthian princely state and during the Sassanian period after its capture by Ardashir I, it was known as Hormizd Shahr, or Hormizd Ardashir. The town was devastated during the Zanj rebellions against the Abbasid caliphate in the ninth century, was restored during the tenth century rule of the Buyid prince Adud al-Dowleh, and became a flourishing centre exporting sugar cane, and boasting a cathedral mosque. Its decline began in the sixteenth century and it is only within the last fifty years that it has regained some of its former importance, now becoming an industrial centre.

Today only the remnants of Shahpur I's bridge and dam across the river, along the right bank, testify to the antiquity of Ahwaz. The foundations of the dam were used in the building of a railway bridge.

There are a number of reasonable provincial hotels in the town itself including the Park on Kh. Pahlavi, the main shopping street (200 rials double room, air-conditioning and washbasin but no private bathrooms). There is a garden with a coffee bar, and a restaurant is in the main building. The Naderi in the same street also has a small garden and some rooms with private, European-style bathrooms (350 rials double with bath, air-conditioning 10 rials per hour). The new Khorram Hotel charges 700 rials double, with private bathroom and cooler, and the Royal on the corner of Pahlavi and Zahedi charges 200 rials double, some rooms with cooler, all with fans and washbasins.

Most foreigners, however, prefer the de luxe Royal Astoria on the river bank, opened in 1974, or the older Ahwaz International which is on the road to the airport. Both have a swimming pool.

The Shemshadeh restaurant in Pahlavi offers good Persian food such as fesenjan, koresht, chicken and kebabs at reasonable prices, and opposite this is the Karamat coffee house, with much the same kind of menu —the best tables are upstairs. Neither restaurant serves alcohol.

From Ahwaz one can take the popular minibus service to Susa for about 60 rials, but one needs independent transport to see all the sites in the area. The drive itself is rather dull until you reach Haft Tepe, the fascinating Elamite site dating from the mid second millennium B.C. which Professor E. Negahban, of the University of Tehran, has been excavating since 1965. (One can also reach Haft Tepe by train from Tehran or Abadan, but there is only one train in each direction daily, stopping for two minutes in the early hours of the morning and again in the early evening.)

By special arrangement, one can use the facilities of the Haft Tepe Sugar Factory canteen, just off the main road, and about 8 km. from the archaeological site. There is also an excellent Sugar Factory Club House and restaurant which welcomes visitors if advance notice is given. Consult a travel agent for this. A Museum designed on an Elamite plan and opened by Empress Farah in 1973, displays major finds including several striking life-sized painted clay busts, possibly of Elamite kings and queens, with inlaid eyes and bronze studs on leather-like bands round the hair.

The name Haft Tepe means 'Seven Mounds', although in fact the site covers more than a dozen mounds including several massive ziggurats, probably originally 25 m. high, royal graves, temples and palaces. During the first season a late fourth and early third millennium B.C. wall was uncovered, together with rough, coarse pottery that possibly dates from the sixth millennium. Painted ware contemporary with Djaffarabad (p. 152), a site near Susa, was followed by ware similar to that of the lowest Susa levels (p. 148), and this again by proto-literate Elamite and finally, characteristic second millennium B.C. Elamite pottery.

The discovery of the Haft Tepe site has filled one of the less well-documented periods in Elamite history, between c. 1500 B.C. and 1300 B.C.—just before the most illustrious period of the Elamite Empire, the thirteenth century B.C. which saw the construction of the impressive ziggurat of Choga Zanbil (p. 144). This was probably the city of Tikni.

The site is used as a training school for Iranian archaeologists, and if you visit during the season (winter and spring) you will no doubt find a willing guide. If the site is deserted, begin with the structures by

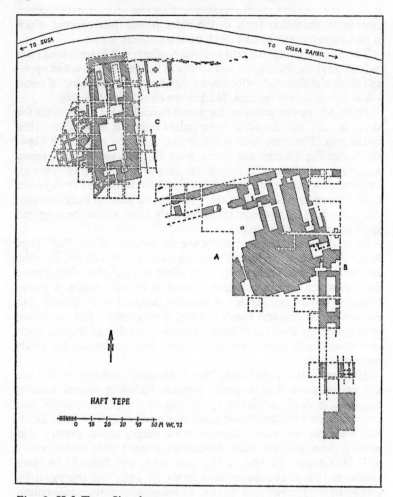

Fig. 28. Haft Tepe. Site plan 1973
A. Palace area, ziggurat foundation? B. Industrial area. C. Temple area.
(*By courtesy of Professor E. Negahban. Drawn by Professor W. Kleiss*)

the side of the main road, at the northern edge of the area, which was first revealed when work began on the road for the sugar factory.

Here you will see two tombs with vaulted roofs. The larger, eastern chamber, 10·30 × 3·25 m. in size and known as the Royal Tomb, contained twenty-one skeletons. A platform 60 cm. high covers four-fifths of the floor, with a channel running down one side, leaving an empty space at the rear. The platform was divided into three sections by low narrow walls pierced with holes to allow drainage into the channel.

Seven skeletons were lying side by side, all packed in ritual red ochre, with a few funerary objects in the first section. The smallest, and middle, section was empty, but at the back were two incomplete skeletons. A doorway behind the platforms led up a flight of stairs into the temple behind, which can be seen after climbing the ramp to the top of the mound. Near this doorway twelve roughly heaped, incomplete skeletons were found.

This is a particularly important tomb because it still retains one of the earliest known vaults, dated about 1500 B.C., that is, some 250-300 years older than similar arches at Choga Zanbil. Early morning light is best for photographing this tomb.

The second, smaller tomb lies parallel to and a little to the west of the Royal Tomb. Walk up the ramp by the side of the latter, turn right and you can look down on the open grave whose roof has disappeared but which has been given a temporary protective covering. Here fourteen skeletons can still be seen laid side by side like sardines, with nine others thrown carelessly on top of them.

In other rooms around the large temple behind the tombs, simple burials in the earth or in urns were found as well as a sarcophagus of baked clay bound with ropes and coated with bitumen. Below the paved brick floor of the hall behind the Royal Tomb there appears to be another as yet unexcavated room. A large portico leads off the hall, opening onto the brick-paved temple courtyards in the centre of which is a deep pit, dug by treasure hunters. Built of nine layers of baked brick, this was originally an altar; close by were found many fragments of inscribed stelae, one large portion still lying *in situ*, probably part of two major inscriptions which list the allowances of grain and animals to be given the priests in payment for services at the temple. Written in Babylonian cuneiform script using fourteenth century B.C. Elamite language, the inscriptions mention the name of King Tepti-ahar, possibly the ruler of a break-away group from the main Elamite centre at Susa (p. 148), where a brick bearing his name was found. Differing religious beliefs may have included human sacrifice.

Between the temples and the Museum is a series of huge courtyards, many with columns of earth supporting Sassanian skeletons found near the surface and left as evidence of prolonged occupation. In the Elamite level, kitchens and wells lie outside palace buildings whose walls were painted with yellow, red, black and white plaster. Here some 4,000 inscribed clay tablets, mainly accounts and treaties, were found, although some were obviously used for teaching, the mistakes pressed out of shape or preserved inside the clay. A massive wall surrounds the palace area, while outside, an industrial section includes two kilns for ceramics and metal, and a nearby well where the royal portrait busts and an elephant skull with tusks that had been partly carved for decorative use, were recovered.

Other finds have included a bronze plaque, possibly part of a door frame showing a warrior-king standing on a lion and holding a bow, with a quiver at his back. Behind him stands a priest while a nude woman kneels before him. The workmanship is characteristic of the mid-second millennium and has been compared with a figurine of the fertility goddess Ishtar found some years ago on the same site. (See short reports in *Iran*, V, 1967, and VII, 1969.) The work at Haft Tepe is being carried out in co-operation with the Institute of Archaeology of the University of Tehran.

From Haft Tepe it is advisable to take a guide or ask for explicit directions to the great Elamite ziggurat of Choga Zanbil (Choga is a local word meaning hill, while Zanbil means a large basket, which the unexcavated mound resembled). The site is about 30 km. from Haft Tepe, standing among low hills on the right bank of the river Ab-i Diz, a tributary of the Karun. Cross the railway track from Haft Tepe, and follow a signposted dirt road beside the Sugar Factory for some 20 km. across the plain; in normal conditions this is good enough for an ordinary car or small minibus. The astonishing ziggurat can be seen from the track.

Built by Untash Gal, King of Elam, about 1250 B.C., the massive artificial mountain was the focal point of his city of Dur Untashi, and was dedicated to the great god Inshushinak, 'Lord of Susa', symbolized by the form of a bull. Although now much denuded compared with its original height, the ziggurat remains the largest man-made structure in Iran and is perhaps better preserved than any comparable monument to be found in Mesopotamia.

Choga Zanbil was both a temple and a tomb and was built in the form of five boxes of increasing height, placed one inside the other. The tallest, innermost tower was 28 m. square at its base and nearly 50 m. high, with four monumental, vaulted brick doorways each over 7 m. high, leading into a complex of tombs, tunnels and chambers, some of which are over 15 m. long. On the flat top was a temple where the god Inshushinak was believed to ascend every night, and from thence to heaven. Along with much else at the site, the temples at the base of the ziggurat were pillaged by the Assyrian, Ashurbanipal, when he overthrew the Neo-Elamite Empire—and also destroyed Susa—c. 640 B.C.

Choga Zanbil consists not only of the ziggurat but of a large complex within an outer wall 1200 × 800 m., constructed around a sacred enclosure some 400 m. square and pierced by seven gates. Inside this enclosure were three temples and several paved courtyards with sanctuaries, as well as store houses containing weapons and ornaments. The ziggurat, with an outer base of 105 m. square, is built mainly of sun-dried brick bonded with cement and bitumen and was faced with glazed kiln-fired bricks of blue and green with a metallic shimmer, similar to those found at Susa. Glazed terracotta emphasized architectural details; wooden doors were decorated with opaque glass mosaics depicting prancing animals, and inlaid ivory mosaics were also used in the lavish decoration of this splendid structure which was discovered in 1935 by prospecting geologists of the then Anglo-Iranian Oil Company. In 1936–9, the French Archaeological Mission, headed by R. de Mequenem, worked at the site which was identified through the cuneiform inscriptions on many of the bricks found *in situ,* most of them repeating the name of Untash Gal. Professor Ghirshman[62] resumed the enormous task of revealing this site in 1946, and continued until 1962; since then the Iranian Archaeological Department has resumed restoration.

You can drive right up to a small guard house by the notice erected by the Mission, crossing the foundations of the city ramparts on the way. From here walk across the sacred enclosure to the inner courtyard surrounding the ziggurat which today has only three of its original five storeys. There is a steep staircase on the north-west side up which one can climb to the summit for a good view of the entire site.

Two temples dedicated to Inshushinak, and probably used only during the daylight hours, were found in the centre of the second storey on the south-east side, among many other chambers built into each side of the wide terraces.

Three ramps leading up the first, quite low storey were found on the north-east side, one at right angles and the other two on either side, laterally. Near these ramps, in the outer court, two bases were found on which two winged guardian genii, lying nearby, probably stood. On the north-west side of the ziggurat, opposite the approach staircase, stands a circular brick-built platform believed to have been an altar for animal sacrifices. Like the rest of the monument, this has been restored, but you can see some excellent examples of the cuneiform inscribed dedicatory bricks here, in the earliest known type of triple-arched niche. This was probably attached to the temple of Ishniqarab which was adjacent, with, next to it, the sanctuaries of Kiririsha the mother-goddess, and the god Huban. Some of these chambers are below the present level of the courtyards, around which were the kitchens and stores, and living quarters of the priests.

A gateway flanked by towers was found in the middle of the north-east wall surrounding the sacred enclosure, and another in the south-east wall has been called 'The Royal Gate' because of its impressive size and elaborate decoration. In the angle formed by these two walls the remains of four other temples were found, built side by side.

More than 100 cylinder seals were found in chapel buildings opposite the south-west façade, many of them made of deep blue glass possibly showing an Egyptian influence.

One of the most interesting finds, which can be seen in the Tehran Museum, is that of a humped bull or zebu, which was carefully restored by Madame Ghirshman, and which originally stood as a guardian before one of the gateways. Across the back of the creature is a dedication in cuneiform to the god Inshushinak.

About 300 m. from the Royal Gateway, walking towards the approach, eastwards, are the remains of one of three palaces, this one containing five underground, vaulted tombs. At the time of writing they have been bricked up owing to deteriorating brickwork, but it is here that the vaulted ceilings compare with those at Haft Tepe.

The charred remains of two cremated skeletons were found inside each of four of the tombs discovered intact, with one uncremated skeleton lying on a platform beside two of the cremated ones. Elamites were normally buried, indicating a change of custom for royalty, and it has been suggested that the queens followed their husbands to the funeral pyre, but no proof has so far been found that these were royal corpses.

The second palace is some 50 m. north-east, seemingly reserved for royal ladies, to judge from the many small rooms around the two courtyards; the third palace nearby consists of two courtyards each with four suites of rooms. All three palaces are different in style from those found in Mesopotamia, being much simpler in plan.

On the north-west side of the ziggurat outside the city walls, one can see traces of the elaborate system of irrigation that served the city, including reservoirs made of burnt brick and bitumen.

Between these and the ziggurat are a series of buildings believed to have included stables. (A small very condensed guide to this and Susa was published by the Archaeological Service in 1963.[117] A new edition is expected shortly, and should be available at the site.)

Returning to Haft Tepe, drive past the royal tombs along the main road for some 20 km., passing several prehistoric mounds among the sugar-cane plantations, and a paper factory, for Khuzestan is rapidly being developed, thanks to the hydro-electric power provided by the Pahlavi Dam at Dizful.

You will soon see the so-called 'Château' of the French Mission at Susa, built on a great mound dominating the plain to the north-west

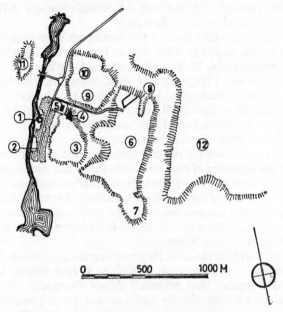

Fig. 29. Susa (Shush). Plan showing location of principal sites.
(*A. Labrousse*)

KEY

1. Daniel's Tomb	7. Keep
2. Village	8. Stratigraphic sounding
3. Acropolis	9. Palace of Darius
4. Archaeological Mission	10. Apadana
5. Museum	11. Palace of Shaour
6. Royal Town	12. Town of the Artisans

and looking like some medieval French castle. It was constructed by Jacques de Morgan at the end of the nineteenth century, using materials taken from the Elamite and Achaemenian ruins, to protect the Archaeological Mission from the very real danger of attack from marauding tribes. It is now occupied by the Mission for several months of the year.

When you reach a 'T' junction on the main road, with a chai khaneh and petrol station on the left, turn left to pass under a triumphal arch welcoming you to Susa (called 'Shush' in Persian). On the right is a Government Tourist Inn opened in 1970, and the only local overnight accommodation is available here.

A little further on is the village of Susa: (2)—see plan. On the left, the road winds up the hill to the team headquarters (4), past the small museum set in a garden, which it is probably worth visiting first. It contains many objects found both at Susa and elsewhere in Khuzestan, as well as a useful model of Susa itself.

Susa has been under more or less continuous excavation for a vastly greater period than any other site in Iran. It was identified by the British archaeologist, W. K. Loftus, who sank the first trial trenches in 1854. The famous French archaeologists, Marcel and Jane Dieulafoy,[36] began systematic excavations in 1884, and in 1897 Jacques de Morgan headed the first of the annual winter excavations, conducted ever since by the French Archaeological Mission, whose discoveries here continue to add to our knowledge of ancient Iran.

The Acropolis was the site of a modest prehistoric settlement dating back to the beginning of the fourth millennium B.C. At this moment the long-standing skill of the potters of Susiana had reached new heights and the tall, elegant beakers of Susa I, with their almost abstract, stylized bird and animal designs, represent the very peak of painted pottery production in prehistoric Iran. Excellent examples of such pottery can be seen in the Tehran Museum.

The next stage in the site's long sequence is equated with the middle Uruk period in Mesopotamia, while Susa C runs parallel to the late Uruk and Jemdat Nasr periods.[43] About the middle of the third millennium B.C., we already find evidence for a powerful Elamite kingdom which, at intervals at least, was able to challenge, and on occasion dominate, the contemporary city states of Mesopotamia.

The most prosperous period for Susa and Elam may well have been the thirteenth century B.C. however, when the major building programme of King Untash Gal, the founder of Choga Zanbil, did much to embellish the ancient seat of Susa. This same period also saw many of the major treasures of Babylon, such as the eighteenth century B.C. stele of Hammurabi, carried off to Susa by the victorious Elamites. While the original of the stele is in the Louvre, a copy stands in the Tehran Museum (p. 39).

About 640 B.C. disaster finally struck the Elamite kingdom when Ashurbanipal, the King of the Assyrians, laid waste all of low-lying Elam, destroying Susa by fire. At much the same time the Persians, ancestors of the later Achaemenians, were already beginning to make their power felt in this southern region, and by about 520 B.C. Darius, by now victorious over most of his rivals, had begun magnificent new constructions that were to include a citadel, a moated walled city, and royal palaces.

As soon as he approached the city, Alexander the Great received the surrender of Susa with its fabulous riches. Later it was the scene of his celebrated mass wedding when ten thousand Greeks and Persians were united in marriage. The Seleucids installed a garrison in the city and then it became a Parthian provincial capital. Devastated by fire during battles between the last of the Parthians and the first of the Sassanians, Susa next developed into a Sassanian provincial capital and a stronghold of Christianity under Shahpur I. It was destroyed under Shahpur II and never again completely rebuilt, although it was occupied by the Arabs who constructed a great cathedral mosque there. Finally Susa declined, and from the beginning of the thirteenth century deteriorated into no more than a series of crumbling ruins.

It is best to visit the high ground near the 'Château' (4) first in order to identify the general layout of the site which stretches almost to the horizon. The four principal mounds are signposted—they are the Acropolis (3), the Apadana (10), the Royal City (6) and the Artisans' city (12).

The Acropolis contains traces of civilizations dating from prehistoric to Islamic times and was the site of the main royal Elamite buildings and later an Achaemenian citadel. To the north-east stands the great 'Apadana Mound'—a vast artificial platform founded on the older remains of part of the Elamite city—where first Darius and later Artaxerxes II embarked on monumental palace constructions.

Crossing the corridors and rooms of the private part of the Achaemenian palace you reach the majestic ruins of the Apadana— the Audience Hall or Throne Room. Here the bell-shaped bases and other remains of 72 fallen fluted columns and capitals of immense bulls' heads, show clearly the similarity to the Apadana at Persepolis (p. 229) —the Susa Apadana having been even larger. The Persepolis palace, in fact, is now known to have been constructed immediately after the Susa palace, in part at least by the same craftsmen.

Glazed brick friezes in many colours decorated the walls of the Susa palace; the moulded reliefs depicted Immortals (soldiers of the Royal Bodyguard), lions and mythical creatures. (*Statue of Darius the Great.)

South-east of the Apadana is the mound known as the 'Royal City', in which Professor Ghirshman's deep sounding revealed some 15 layers of occupation, extending from the Islamic period back through Sassanian, Parthian, Seleucid, Achaemenian and Elamite times. Recent work has identified at least three more levels giving two time periods, c. 2100–1900 B.C. and 2700–2600 B.C.; several new graves found here establish that burial under house floors was standard practice in the last half of the third millennium B.C. The streets and house foundations exposed are of the Elamite city c. 1900 B.C.

Urn burials of children with Nestorian crosses marked on certain of the jars are thought to date from the time when Susa was an important Christian bishopric in the fourth century A.D. Indeed, the growth and power of Susa's Christian community ultimately led Shahpur II to destroy the city, a process involving the use of several hundred elephants.

Some eighth to ninth century A.D. Islamic structures over Sassanian buildings can still be seen near the western edge of the upper portion of the Royal City and here too were found Sassanian structures complete with decorative mosaics and bas-reliefs.

During the Achaemenian period the city was surrounded by particularly impressive fortified walls, the moat outside them being connected to the nearby river Shaur.

Further to the east lies the Artisans' City (12) where an early mosque, now disappeared, was revealed in the course of excavations.

On the Acropolis (3) a lone pillar of earth known as 'de Morgan's Pillar' has been left to show the extent of the early excavations here, while on the high ground between the pillar and the main mound, the famed Bengal Lancers built their barracks during World War I, leaving their own contribution to the existing stratification.

Excavations continue in this fascinating site, now under the direction of M. Jean Perrot, successor to Professor Roman Ghirshman who had already spent 36 years in active field-work in Iran before his official retirement in 1967 (in fact he still returns each year to direct excavations at Masjid-i Sulaiman) (p. 161). In 1970 an entirely unexpected discovery was made at Susa when tractors ploughing a field on the western bank of the Shaur ran into the bases of several stone columns (11).

This site, about 200 m. from the Museum, over the main road and across the only bridge spanning the river, proved to be another Achaemenian palace probably built by Artaxerxes II (404–359 B.C.). A track runs across the western edge of the audience hall which has now been partially revealed as a 64-columned hall. In no other place in Susa have so many column bases been found; those within the hall at least were new rather than re-used, although some had been repaired. Wooden columns, painted blue (traces of the paint have been found at the bases), stood on the stone bases. Pieces of coloured plaster walls in red and blue, some showing the head of a man, have also been recovered. Early Islamic mansions, a hamam and sugar cane refinery have also been found here. (See *Iran*, Vols. X, 1972 & XII, 1974.)

In 1970 also, while clearing an inner doorway on the axis of a southern entrance to the great palace of Darius on the Apadana Mound (9), two foundation tablets, measuring 34 cm. × 34 cm. × 9 cm., in perfect condition, were found under the foundations of walls which have now been partially reconstructed to give an idea of the original layout. One tablet is in Babylonian, the other in Elamite, and both give much the same information, virtually repeating previously discovered inscriptions. Darius the Great gives his ancestry, describes how he built his palace, where the workmen and the materials came from, and praises the deity, Ahura Mazda. In part the inscription describes how the foundations were dug to rock bottom, and rubble and gravel packed down to 40 cubits in depth; sundried and kiln-baked bricks were moulded by the Babylonians, and cedar wood was brought by the Assyrians from Lebanon to Babylon, whence Ionians and Carians (a people of Anatolia) brought it to Susa. The inscription continues: '. . . the gold which was worked here was brought from Sardis [in Anatolia] and from Bactria [in Afghanistan]. The blue precious stone [lapis lazuli] and the red [carnelian] which have been worked here, these were brought from Sogdiana [now in U.S.S.R.]. The unshining precious stone [turquoise] which has been worked here, this was brought from Chorasmia [U.S.S.R.]. The silver and the stone-wood [ebony] were brought from Egypt. The ornamentation with which the wall has been adorned, that was brought from Ionia. The ivory which has been worked here was brought from Ethiopia and from India and from Arachosia. . . .'

(For complete translations of the known foundation tablets from Susa, and for the work of the French Mission in general, see the more than forty volumes of the *Mémoires de la Mission Archéologique Française en Iran*.[116] Information about other work of the Mission is given in brief reports in *Iran* (Vols. V–XII).

Some idea of the splendours of the Achaemenian palaces can be gained by reading the Book of Esther in the Old Testament. The Ahasuerus who reigned from India even to Ethiopia, and whom Esther married, is thought to have been Darius the Great's son, Xerxes, or his grandson, Artaxerxes, and it was in the magnificent palace at Susa, the Biblical Shushan, that Esther lived.

Another Biblical association with Susa is the so-called Tomb of Daniel (1), the conical white sugar-loaf shrine just across the road from the archaeological site, standing on the east bank of the River Shaur. It attracts Muslim pilgrims who for centuries have regarded the Prophet's remains as having miraculous powers, particularly in preventing drought. At one time, by order of the Caliph Omar, the coffin is said to have been buried under the bed of the Shaur whose waters were diverted for this purpose, in order to prevent disputes as to who should possess the precious relics. When the Arabs first reached Susa in the seventh century, they found Daniel's coffin in the great citadel. In the twelfth century A.D. the Saljuq Sultan Sanjar is said to have decreed that the coffin be encased in an outer shell of crystal and suspended by iron chains from the middle of a bridge spanning the river. The mausoleum is believed to have been on the same site at least since the twelfth century, but has obviously been rebuilt many times.

Visitors are welcomed but women wishing to enter the shrine must wear a chador (ankle-length veil).

There are scores of prehistoric mounds protruding from the plains surrounding Susa, many of them noted by Sir Aurel Stein[156] and more recently by Professor Vanden Berghe,[172,177] while American, French and Iranian teams have recently collaborated in preparing an archaeological survey of Khuzestan.

Since 1969 Geneviève Dollfus of the French Mission, has been excavating an interesting early site at Djaffarabad, a low, ochre-coloured mound about 7 km. north of Susa, reached by a rough track across the fields west of the main road to Andimeshk, and a little north of a very large pudding-basin tepe. Abandoned about the time Susa was founded, c. 4000 B.C., this site has yielded a chronological sequence which extends backwards to the sixth millennium B.C. Djaffarabad, where work continues, has helped towards an understanding of social and economic developments during the fifth millennium B.C., the period immediately prior to the birth of towns. (See report in *Iran*, Vol. XIII, 1975, and *Appendix, Djaffarabad.)

A little further along the main Andimeshk road, an asphalt road to the west is signposted 'Deh Luran'. A short drive along this road brings you to the Sassanian city of Ivan-i Karkha, crossing a military airstrip and then a new bridge across the River Karkha (the Greek Choaspes). Here are the remains of the Sassanian bridge-dam of Pai-pol built by Roman prisoners captured by Shahpur I. Some 15 km. from the main Andimeshk road, the road forks, the right fork continuing on to Deh Luran, the left reaching, about 1 km. further on, the huge walled rectangle about 4 × 1 km. enclosing the fourth century city founded by Shahpur II after the destruction of Susa. Now there is only a series of grassy mounds to testify to its existence, unexcavated except for one corner where Professor Ghirshman found an important Sassanian palace during a short dig in 1950. The walls were covered with painted plaster murals and the palace itself, of bricks and mortar, was originally surrounded by gardens. It contained a square hall roofed with a cupola from which extended a wing 'divided into five sections by a series of arches thrown from one wall to the other, and parrying the thrust of the transverse barrel vaults'.[59]

A second trench revealed a pavilion with three ivans, the walls decorated with frescoes, an art form widely used in Shahpur II's reign. The remains of this barrel-vaulting, the springers and the vaulted windows, can be seen today standing on massive brick foundations on the right of the road. According to Ghirshman, this was probably the prototype for the transversal barrel-vaults thrown over the nave of Christian churches to be found from the shores of the Adriatic and

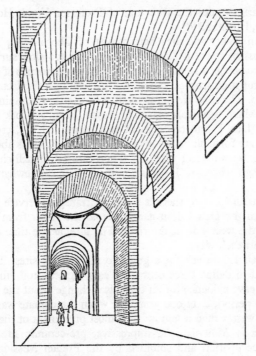

Fig. 30. Ivan-i Karkha. Reconstruction of the vaults.
   (*Gasche, after Reuther: by courtesy of R. Ghirshman, 'L'Architecture*
   Elamite et ses Traditions'. Iranica Antiqua. *Vol. V. Fas.* 2. 1965)

Mediterranean to Spain. This pavilion was later converted to use as a
mosque, the faithful assembling for prayer in the open before the central
dome over the open arches, just as Zoroastrians had stood before the
sacred fire burning below the dome. Only two other ancient barrel-
vaulted mosques are known for certain in Iran today, both of them in
the little village of Muhammadiyya (p. 176).

From the mounds of Ivan-i Karkha, looking south towards the Iraq
frontier, can be seen the remains of an early, undated brick tomb-tower
which Madame Dieulafoy in the 1880s identified as the Imamzadeh
Touïl, and which is worth an inspection. A track leads from the road
to the foot of the mound on which the tower stands, and one can see
the similarity of the upper construction to that of the typically Khuzes-
tani 'sugar-loaf' roofs today. Across the track from the tower rises a
large, prehistoric mound littered with fourth millennium painted sherds.

Turning back to the fork to Deh Luran it is possible, in dry weather,
to drive to several sites excavated by a joint Rice University-Oriental

Institute team under the direction of Professor Frank Hole of Rice University, Houston.[94,95]

The main prehistoric sites here consist of Choga Sefid, Tepe Sabz, Tepe Moussian and Ali Kosh (among nearly 300 sites surveyed over an area of some 1,000 square km.). They showed evidence of continuous human occupation from c. 7500 B.C. until well into the Islamic period, c. A.D. 1300. The sites are not accessible in winter when rains wash out the tracks which vary from season to season. From the fork near Ivan-i Karkha to Deh Luran takes about two hours' driving, crossing two rivers that are fordable in summer. Deh Luran village is about 20 km. beyond the second river crossing. There are two small chai khanehs in the village where it is possible to stay in somewhat primitive conditions.

From Dizful (p. 156) there is a regular transport service in pick-up trucks, from the Deh Luran garage across the street from the filling station on the west side of the river. The fare, at the time of writing, was 100 rials each way.

From Deh Luran ask for a guide to the various sites. The survey here helped to define three centres of early agricultural village settlements and gave evidence for an ecological change about the end of the Pleistocene period, c. 11,000 years ago when the climate was probably colder and wetter than it is now. The most prominent of the sites near Deh Luran is Moussian, an impressive, pre-ceramic site with late Akkadian occupation and sounded by the French Mission in 1905. Surrounding it are the remains of a late Sassanian town, now occupied by a lone gendarmerie post. Because it is covered by so many later periods it was not possible to carry out investigations on the earlier periods of Moussian during one season, so the smaller site of Tepe Sabz, also known as Haft Choga, about 20 km. west of Moussian, was selected for excavation in 1963. The four periods discovered here date from 5500 B.C.–3700 B.C., and include in period three (4500–4100 B.C.) a new type, Red-on-Red, which appears to be the imported Iranian 'straw-tempered ware' described as coming from Ras al Amiya.[161]

Of the two other sites where there is still something for the visitor to see, Choga Sefid and Tepe Farrukhabad are worth a visit. Choga Sefid, also known as Qalata, just outside Deh Luran and about 18 km. north-west of Moussian, still has the remains of walls and a platform. The three distinct phases found may prove to show connections with Chogha Mish (p. 157) and with sites across the Iraq frontier.

Professor Henry T. Wright, of the Museum of Anthropology, the University of Michigan, directed excavations at Tepe Farrukhabad, about 12 km. due south of Deh Luran on the banks of the Memeh river, in 1968. The site itself is almost large enough to be called a town, and is partly cut away by the river. It was probably founded about 5000 B.C., occupied more or less continuously until 3000 B.C., and re-occupied by the Elamites in the second and first millennium B.C. The team excavated in three places: two wide trenches on the south and in the eroded face of what was once the central town area, and a third on the north face.

Thirty-six layers were defined in one trench on the south-east, with the ceramics from the earliest levels similar to those of the upper layers of Tepe Sabz. A small portion of a private house was revealed, with a large building above it, possibly a granary, made of small mud bricks. Above this again was a badly eroded platform, partially cleared. A group of inhumation burials and many exotic flints, including some obsidian, were also found.

Part of a massive Uruk[161] (c. 3400–3100 B.C.) structure has been left in the centre of the south-west trench; this structure had been rebuilt many times and reached its maximum height probably in the Early Jemdat Nasr period (c. 3100 B.C.). The early second millennium occupation here, near the surface, revealed ceramics that may be related to those of the Third Dynasty of Ur, while a still later wall complex remains visible in the trench on the north.

Finally, at the end of Tepe Farrukhabad's long sequence a large building on stone foundations, constructed on top of the tepe, may have been an early Islamic fort.

Tepe Ali Kosh, known to the French Mission as Tepe Mohammad Jaffar,[116 (Vol. XXX, 1947)] lies about 3 km. due west of Tepe Farrukhabad. Its excavation has revealed three prehistoric periods dating from 7500 B.C., with a Susiana occupation uppermost.

In the third, Mohammad Jaffar phase (6000–5600 B.C.), pottery made its first appearance. Adult males were buried outside the houses, the bodies wrapped with pieces of coarsely woven flax material. A longer and more detailed collection of seeds and animal bones was made here than anywhere else in the world, and the lists of animals hunted and domesti-cated, of cereals grown and gathered, tools used and personal ornaments worn, make the reports on the Deh Luran excavations compulsive reading.[94, 122]

Back again on the main road to Andimeshk, one can make for this small town, about fifteen minutes' drive from the Deh Luran junction, turning left at the crossroads on the outskirts of the town and right for Dizful and Shushtar. By special arrangement beforehand it is possible to stay at the Khuzistan Water and Power Authority's Guest House near the first roundabout (ask for the 'Ab-o Bargh Mehmansarai'), but a new hotel, the Eqbal, on the corner of this roundabout offers reasonable, air-conditioned rooms with bath, for 400–800 rials. The railway station is at the end of a short street leading from the roundabout —Tehran is an overnight train journey from here.

A ten-minute drive brings one to Dizful on the Ab-i-Diz river, the 'Coprates' of the Greeks. The original bridge across the river was like the one at Pai-pol, built by Roman engineers taken prisoner by Shahpur I at Edessa in A.D. 260. Its foundations and piers still support the present structure. In the tenth century the city was known to the Arabs as Qasr al-Runash or al-Qantarah among other variants, and the present name derives from Dizpol, meaning 'fortress-bridge'. The bridge is about 450 m. long, the stone piers being Sassanian, but the twenty-two arches have been reconstructed during the early Islamic, Saljuq and Qajar periods. Many water-mills still function some distance upstream. A famous fortress built here in Sassanian times was used to imprison monarchs and the nobility.

An Imamzadeh, the Sultan Hussein, with a sugar-loaf roof, near the banks of the river, can be viewed from the bridge and the approach road.

The minibus to Susa starts from the Bank Melli, on the corner of the Maidan-i Mussalla as you drive into Dizful—the fare is about 15–20 rials. A small hotel, the Irandasht, is also on this maidan. Dizful, with its pavements sheltered from the fierce summer sun by arcades, and its colourful tribes in Bakhtiar and Lur dress, is a pleasant little town. In the old bazaar you can buy the Bakhtiar felt hats, 'kola numadee', and sleeveless overcoats, 'choga', in black and white or dark blue and white cotton or wool, for anything from 112 to 500 rials. Other good buys are large, Arab-style head scarves, 'khafiyeh', in black and white, for about 35 rials each.

From Dizful one can visit two particularly interesting sites, those of Jondi Shahpur, a royal Sassanian university city, and Chogha Mish, one of the largest early sites on the edge of the Susiana plain, to reach which you have to pass Jondi Shahpur.

One can sometimes find a taxi-driver who will make the trip to Chogha Mish from Dizful, charging about 400 rials. The road is often flooded in spring and is not easy to find. In good weather you can take the main road to Shushtar, driving for about ten minutes to the village of Shahabad, seen to the right of the road. This village is on the northern edge of the Jondi Shahpur site and one can see the sugar-loaf Imamzadeh Ya'qub ibn Layth on the outskirts of the village. The tomb-tower is on a small mound and is said to house the remains of an early 'Robin Hood' of Sistan province, who robbed the rich to give to the poor, and whose following eventually made him king of Sistan in the ninth century A.D.

Jondi Shahpur was not only one of the major Sassanian cities founded in Khuzestan, but its intellectual contribution to the world came to be

of signal importance. It was built by Shahpur I as a permanent settlement for many of his thousands of prisoners of war, mainly Romans,
and here too he built his royal palace. Some of the most brilliant minds
of the period were settled in the new city, including two Greek physicians who accompanied Shahpur's bride, daughter of the Emperor
Aurelian, and who introduced the Hippocratic system of medicine;
Professor Richard Frye suggests that among his prisoners Shahpur also
settled Christians from Antioch in 256 A.D., including their Bishop,
Demetrianus, thus forming one of the earliest Christian communities
in the country.[53]

The celebrated medical college of Jondi Shahpur is said to have been
founded by a Christian scholar, and later on Shahpur II, enlarging the
city, founded the university with its observatory and hospital. Here
Khusraw Anushirvan I received such famous scientists as the Seven
Sages of Athens in A.D. 529, and it is said that the Prophet Mohammad
himself recommended the medical skill of Harith ibn Kaldeh, an Arab
physician who had graduated from the Jondi Shahpur Medical Faculty.

Well into the Islamic period the university supplied physicians to
the Caliphates and it was because the Medical School trained so many
teachers for the new School of Medicine in Baghdad, as well as for many
new hospitals, that it was finally forced to close its doors.

Soundings were made here by Professors Robert Mc. C. Adams and
Donald P. Hansen[1] in 1963 with work carried out on the highest and
most prominent mound, Tabl Khaneh, where early Islamic sherds
including Samarra, imitation celadon, imitation T'ang splash glazes,
and a tenth century Nishapur type of ware were found. The large mound
at the north-west corner, Kashk-i Bozi, was also sounded. It seems probable that the city was surrounded on three sides by a canal or moat.

There is a track that will take a car along the top of the southern walls
of Jondi Shahpur, and after a further drive of about 6 km. along a
badly rutted track that often divides, one comes in sight of the high
mound of Chogha Mish, about 25 km. south-east of Dizful. A guide is
almost indispensable.

The name means 'Mound of the Ewe', and since 1961 a team headed
by Professor Pinhas P. Delougaz of the University of California, at
Los Angeles, and Professor Helene J. Kantor of the Oriental Institute of
the University of Chicago, has been working on this large, sprawling site.
(Professor Delougaz was still working at Chogha Mish when he died
of a heart attack in March 1975.)

Roughly rectangular, the site is orientated almost exactly north-south.
About one-third of its area consists of the steeply ridged northern
mound, more than 25 m. above the plain. Here Elamite period walls
more than 11 m. wide occur above Protoliterate and Prehistoric

deposits. The southern 'terrace' is less rugged, rising to about 8–10 m., with quantities of Protoliterate material. Here at the surface are occasional Parthian and Achaemenian remains, including some graves, but the main settlements were much earlier. In the north-west a solid mud-brick platform with projecting buttresses was excavated. To the east was a circular building about 11 m. in diameter and private houses, often rebuilt, separated by narrow lanes down which run drains of kiln-baked bricks. These structures are evidence that Chogha Mish was a city of considerable size in the Protoliterate period (c. mid fourth millennium B.C.) when writing was probably first invented.

Most significant are the cylinder seal impressions on clay, many of them in minute fragments which have been patiently preserved and reconstructed, providing invaluable clues to the habits and life of the people. One of these gives the earliest known evidence of music as an organized art-form, showing an orchestra and a vocalist, while another depicts a ruler with attendants, sitting in a boat, holding a rope attached to prisoners. Another shows women churning milk in a churn whose shape is similar to the pictographic sign 'GA' known to mean 'milk' in Sumerian, thus providing the first connection between symbol and the word.[31]

A mass of pottery ranges from tiny cosmetic jars to huge storage vessels. One vase displays at its two spouts reliefs of a snake biting the throat of a goat, suggesting conflict between the forces of the underworld and everyday life.

The Protoliterate civilization, identical with that of contemporary Lower Mesopotamia, was different from the earlier cultures on this site which had been inhabited for millennia, going through several stages. The earliest of these, unknown before it was identified and named as 'Archaic Susiana' by the excavators in 1963, is provisionally dated to c. 7000 B.C. and is characterized by highly burnished pottery often painted with elaborate designs. Chogha Mish is the only site so far providing an uninterrupted sequence of the prehistoric Susiana cultures which on other sites is represented incompletely.

Summing up in early 1974, the most important general results concerning the prehistoric periods were the evidence for the existence of a city of 45–50 acres during Middle Susiana, i.e., fifth millennium B.C., when the whole site was occupied; then came the so far inexplicable shrinkage of occupation to about one-third this size at the latest phase of prehistoric Susiana cultures (Late Susiana), before it was reoccupied in the Protoliterate period. Unexpectedly imposing architectural remains were found of the Middle, Early and Archaic Susiana periods. Another significant contribution of Chogha Mish is the wealth of new information concerning its connections with prehistoric Mesopotamia in terms of precise chronological correlations and the evidence of intensely close cultural contacts.

Early in 1975 intriguing fresh discoveries included an important Middle Susiana edifice destroyed by an intense fire which preserved storage chambers packed with jars and flint cores, indicating that this was an actual factory for the manufacture of implements and perhaps the first industrial centre in Iran.

A detailed interim report on the first five seasons will be published as *Oriental Institute Communication No. 22*, and see *Iran*, Vol. XIII, 1975.

From the main Dizful-Shushtar road, continue for about 40 km. to the ancient town standing on the left bank of the river Karun, yet another that boasts extensive Sassanian irrigation works. Here in Shushtar, which some believe to have been founded by Darius the Great and others by the first of the Sassanians, or by his son, Shahpur the Great, one can see the remains of the great bridge-dams and canals dating from the third century A.D., when the Roman Emperor Valerian was defeated by Shahpur I. The biggest of these works, an immense barrage of dressed stone and cement 550 m. long, could raise the water level by 2 m. or more. It is known as the Band-i Qaisar or Valerian's bridge and twenty-eight of its arches still remain on the left bank, seven standing on the right, seen as you come into the town from Dizful.

The river bed above the bridge was paved with huge stone slabs clamped together to prevent erosion. This paving, called Shadhorvan, was among the wonders of the world listed by the Arab invaders. The bridge was partly destroyed during a rebellion and irreparably damaged by several disastrous floods at the end of the nineteenth century.

At the beginning of the fifth century A.D. Shushtar became the seat of a Nestorian bishopric; it fell through treachery, after a siege of over six months, to Arab invaders c. A.D. 638 and its name was then changed to Tustar. Under the tenth century Buyid ruler, Prince Adud al-Dowleh, the city prospered and became famous for its fine fabrics. The great kiswa or brocade covering for the Ka'aba at Mecca was sometimes provided by the weavers of Shushtar. Later the city came under the rule of the Mongols.

As you cross the new bridge into Shushtar, the remains of the castle of Salasil, standing on a cliff on the edge of the river, beyond Valerian's bridge, come into view on the left. The new Government Tourist Inn lies directly below.

The outer walls of the castle date only from the eighteenth century A.D. but undoubtedly they rest on more ancient foundations, possibly Sassanian, with a medieval superstructure. Below the castle, two tunnels were cut in the Sassanian period, through which the waters dammed by the bridge flowed into another artificial channel called the Nahr-e

Darayan or Ab-i Mina, to irrigate land to the south of the city. Within the castle walls are only patches of cobbled and brick paving, some wells and water tanks and openings into underground chambers into which bold Shushtaris lower themselves by ropes to spend the hot summer nights—and to look for treasure.

Standing on the castle heights looking beyond the Tourist Inn, one sees yet another dam, the Band-i Mizan, with a small tower known as the Kola Feranghi, 'Foreign Hat', on the bank almost opposite the Inn. In the distance is a small imamzadeh known variously as Imamzadeh Golabi or Giah-Khur the 'grass-eater', a holy man whose body is said to have become green from existing entirely on grass.

From the castle too, one can see downstream the remains of Valerian's bridge. Upstream is the Sassanian Castle Aqili with its inscription.

Drive back into the town along the main road, Kh. Pahlavi, past a filling station on the left, to a roundabout, the Maidan-i Falukeh, and continue up the road. Inquire here to find out which of the narrow lanes on the right you should take for the ninth century A.D. Masjid-i Jumeh almost hidden behind a jumble of ancient houses.

The mosque is surrounded by a brick wall from the northern corner of which rises a charming brick and turquoise glazed brick minaret probably dating from the Il-Khanid period (thirteenth or early fourteenth century). The mosque, with its unusual buttressed façade, recently restored, and its portal, was founded in the reign of the Caliph al-Mu'tazz Bi'llah in A.D. 866 although it was not finished until between A.D. 1118 and 1135 in the reign of the Caliph al-Mustarshid. The flat roof of the prayer hall is supported by massive pillars and was originally thirteen bays wide, with eight bays of wooden columns parallel to the qibla wall. Today there are only six rows of massive diamond-shaped columns, the first two rows having disappeared. The mihrab and the wooden minbar, which is some 800 years old, are well worth inspection.

This structure is one of the few remaining mosques of Iran built according to the Arab plan; others include the Tarik Khana at Damghan (p. 195) and the Masjid-i Jumeh at Nain (p. 175).

Back to the Maidan-i Falukeh, continue driving now through the town which boasts a number of small imamzadehs, and reach the Band-i Gargar, also known as Do Pol—'Two Bridges', the older of the two being a small Sassanian bridge-dam across a Sassanian canal. The rushing waters in the canal, on the banks of which is a small, modern hydro-electric station, once used to drive some thirty flour mills. One can scramble down to the mills by a path at the side of the small shrine of Musa Ibn Ja'far on the town side of the modern bridge.

Crossing the bridge, the road continues towards Ahwaz and Masjid-i Sulaiman, passing on the outskirts of Shushtar, the ruined caravanserai of Aramat, often occupied by squatters, and a little further on, on the right, a pleasant ab-anbar or underground water reservoir. Almost opposite this is the sugar-loaf shrine known as the Qadamgah-i ('footstep') Khadre-zindah, where the son of one of the Imams, Hajji Khadre, is said to have spent a night.

A ten or fifteen minute drive brings you to a fork in the road, the right-hand branch going to Ahwaz, the left to the oilfield town of Masjid-i Sulaiman. It is possible to make an easy day trip from the Tourist Inn at Shushtar to the Parthian sites in the oilfield, preferably taking a picnic meal, although there are chai khanehs in the town, and a very comfortable Guest House belonging to the Oil Service Company of Iran for official visitors.

A road from Masjid-i Sulaiman to a new dam under construction in 1974, takes you, after some 35 km., to a desolate but lovely valley in the foothills of the Zagros mountains, where Bard-i Nishandeh, a great platform terrace of largely Parthian date, once supporting an important place of worship, was excavated by Professor Roman Ghirshman for the French Archaeological Mission.[61]

Professor Ghirshman first saw the site in 1950, and it was examined by Sir Aurel Stein[156] in 1936. In the Bakhtiari dialect Bard-i Nishandeh means 'Raised Stone', a vertical block of stone nearly 3 m. long, still standing near the site. Bard-i Nishandeh consists of the terrace with a sanctuary, a compact palace on a lower terrace, and a township. Two imposing flights of stairs, of which the northern is the best preserved, lead to the upper terrace which is some 21 m. high.

The approach by the lower terrace brings one to the foundations of what was probably a small palace or pavilion built by a local prince about the beginning of the Christian era. It has three oblong rooms with three doors opening onto a peristyle court with a portico, the roof of which was supported by two rows of eight columns, of which five remain. Some of the remnants of these columns are scattered around the site and bear crudely carved bas-reliefs and figures. Like the rest of the buildings here, the pavilion was destroyed and sacked, and several stone and bronze statues deliberately smashed. Nearly 5,000 bronze coins of the Elymaean period, concealed by three large blocks of stone, were found scattered under the threshold of the central door to the pavilion.

The massive retaining walls of the terrace can be clearly seen from the back of the pavilion. At the foot of the broad staircase leading to the upper terrace, a small cult niche was constructed on the left, flanked by a bas-relief of a king holding a sword before a fire altar. On the upper terrace there is a primitive podium possibly destroyed by earthquake and rebuilt, intended for a fire altar.

Many lifelike sculptured heads were found here and Professor

Ghirshman suggests that the nearly thirty statues had been set up to commemorate the faith of individual worshippers. Pilgrim flasks of enamelled pottery, bronze and silver rings and votive objects were also found.

Some 300 m. to the north of the platform, on a smaller height, is another terrace probably of Sassanian date, where the remains of a deep ivan with small rooms adjoining faced towards the higher terrace and fire altar. Godard[69,71] suggests this might have been a priest's house. Many of the carved stones from the site are to be seen in the small museum at Susa.

Mr. A. A. Sarfaraz recently found traces of an Elymaean temple c. 200 B.C., in the foundations of the Oil Company hospital at Masjid-i Sulaiman, Iran's oldest and major oilfield where the first well began operating in 1908.

Sar-i Masjid, the terrace-platform where Professor Ghirshman is still excavating,[63] is built against a hill on the left of the road to the airport. It supports a number of important constructions including three temples c. late third century B.C. to second century A.D. One is a large building of Parthian date with the remains of a columned portico on its north front, standing near the middle of the platform. A smaller, Hellenistic temple with a number of chambers is nearer the hill to the west; a large statue of Hercules throttling a lion—now in the museum at Susa—was among others found in the temple against the cliff.

The main approach is by the largest of several flights of steps, a majestic, wide staircase on the east side of the platform which is constructed of enormous blocks of stone. The possibility that natural gases from the oilfield once seeped from the soil at this point is not too remote and, apart from its commanding position, this same phenomenon may help to account for the particular location of the terrace.

Walls that are ascribed to the Achaemenian period have been found by the cliff, and portions of defensive walls with bays and salients remain on the south-eastern and northern edges of the platform; the southern portion of the upper terrace has been used as a Muslim grave-yard and for this reason will probably not be excavated. On the southern edge of the lower terrace, by a small flight of stairs, are the remains of a triple ivan, probably of late Parthian construction, from which the oil-field takes its name. (Ref. Reports by R. Ghirshman in *Iran*, Vols. VI, VIII & X, and *La Terrasse Sacrée de Masjid-i Solaiman*, by Ghirshman, Paris, 1969 and Henning.[84])

A third, more remote terrace or 'high place' is located at the beauti-fully situated site of Shami which was briefly excavated by Sir Aurel Stein in 1934, and which remains most famous for the magnificent bronze statue of a Parthian (Elymaean) prince, now in the Tehran Museum.

This site is reached either by driving south from Masjid-i Sulaiman, or east from Ahwaz, both roads converging at Haft Gel, and from thence on a dirt track, dangerous in places during rain, via Bagh-i Malek and Qaleh-i Tul (built round an impressive mound crowned with the ruins of a local chieftain's castle), to the small administrative centre of Izeh, in the Malamir plain. This takes about $4\frac{1}{2}$ hours from Ahwaz by Land-Rover. Entering the town, passing the Shahrdari on the left, a small hotel next door had to close in 1973, for lack of patronage. It may be possible to rent rooms in the town. Guides and horses, essential for further exploration, are available in Izeh. In 1971, the helpful Government official in charge of local archaeological sites was Mr. Abdolkarim Gheybipur.

It is worth while staying a few days in Izeh to visit the many interesting sites in the vicinity. For Shami, one takes the track north some 34 km. to the village of Piyun. From here one can reach the village of Mehrenan, in the Karun valley, where Dr. Klaus Schippmann found a bas-relief of a Parthian (Elymaean) warrior, in what may have been yet another temple complex. (Ref. *Archaeologische Mitteilungen aus Iran*, Vol. 3, 1970.)

The track to Shami continues east, towards the impressive bulk of Kuh-i Bilawa, and the remains of the royal paved highway, the Jadeh-i Ata Beg, can be seen near the track. On the right is a deep canyon, while at the top of the slope on the left, directly against the mountain, is the artificial terrace where the Shami statue was found. Below the platform, the ground is riddled with tombs, some of them roofed with long stone slabs probably originally surmounted by pyramids and cones. A number of these tombs of Parthian date were almost 4 m. long, over 2 m. high and about 2 m. wide. The walls were made of stone slabs placed one on top of the other, without mortar, and roofed by other immense slabs laid side by side. Godard believes that Shami was the royal necropolis of the Kings of Elymais.

The bronze statue, most important of all free-standing Parthian statues yet discovered, and usually dated to *c.* first century B.C.—first century A.D., was found with a number of other objects in a rectangular building on the artificial terrace. The structure probably originally had a vestibule with a columned portico, sacked and destroyed by fire.

In the same general direction, about 60 km. north-east of Masjid-i Sulaiman, beyond the limits of any motorable roads, the region of the Shimbar valley contains a number of sites dating between the first and seventh centuries A.D., first visited by Layard (see *Early Adventures in Parsia, Susiana and Babylonia*), that were later treated by both Herzfeld and Debevoise before being more thoroughly examined by Dr. A. D. H. Bivar in 1962. At the southern end of the valley the narrow gorge of

Tang-i Butan represents a classic mountain precinct. Here the chief relief shows a long line of figures divided into four groups in what appears to be a series of four separate investiture scenes carved at different intervals during the period of the second century A.D. In most cases the local Elymaean ruler stands beside a deity whose outward form is that of Herakles, although, as Dr. Bivar has stressed, the simultaneous presence of fire altars and *homa* utensils would indicate that 'the deity represented belonged essentially to an Iranian cult'.

The reliefs are accompanied by terse inscriptions in the Elymaean script together with later Kufic additions, all of which are discussed in some detail in 'The Inscriptions at Shimbar', by A. D. H. Bivar and S. Shaked.[8]

Above the reliefs Dr. Bivar discovered a pillar with a hollowed top that had most probably served as a fire altar, suggesting that the adjoining ruins of a stone building known locally as Qal'eh-i Dukhtar may have been part of a fire temple.

Also at the southern end of the valley, but on the eastern side, Bivar found more inscriptions near the Pul-i Negin, an artificial tunnel described by Layard[108] which drains this end of the valley. These last graffiti, on a large, isolated rock, were seemingly written in carbon ink with a normal reed pen, apparently in Parthian and Pahlavi, from perhaps the first century A.D. to the sixth or seventh century A.D. Still others, similar but better preserved and more numerous, were found in a rock shelter across a path in a defile called Tang-i Chilau on the eastern side of a ridge enclosing the eastern main Shimbar plain. Both the Elymaean script and Pahlavi were in evidence here, as well as some ink sketches of figures in typical Parthian dress.

Several interesting sites are within easy reach of Izeh; only 3 km. south-west by a shallow grotto called Eshkaft (or Shikaft)-i Salman, that can be seen from Izeh itself, are some Elamite bas-reliefs thought to date from about the eighth century B.C. A dirt track leads to the grotto in the Kuh-i Chalkhushk. Carved into the cliff to the right of the cave are two reliefs, one depicting King Khanni, a contemporary and probably a vassal of the Elamite king Shutruk-Nahhunte of Susa (717–699 B.C.), and his family, and the other, Khanni's Chief Minister Shutruru and his family. Inside the shallow cave two reliefs, badly worn by water dripping from the roof, are said to be those of King Khanni and his wife, both with inscriptions.

Some 8 km. across the valley, to the north-east of Izeh, the hamlet of Kul-i Farah nestles against the Kuh-i Bad. A large boulder in the centre of the hamlet depicts a huge, weather-worn figure with arms upraised in the gesture of worship, with rows of followers behind. Other boulders depicting hundreds of such figures stand in the narrow gorge behind the hamlet, all of the Elamite period. Animals too are depicted, and a dazzling display of similar scenes is carved into the cliffs, including one of King Khanni standing before a fire altar, others depicting the king on his throne, watched by hundreds of followers. Close by, the author observed a rectangular boulder into the surface of which, possibly at a later date, two circular fire bowls had been carved. A small relief on the southern side of the gorge shows a king upon his throne, with a long, well-preserved inscription.[174a] (See Additional Reading, de Waele.)

About 6 km. north of Kul-i Farah is an earlier adoration scene at Tang (or Hung)-i Nauruzi, dating from c. twentieth to eighteenth centuries B.C. together with an investiture and scene of respect by a local vassal to Mithridates I (171–138 B.C.). (For details, Ref. L. Vanden Berghe's bibliography in L'Archéologie de l'Iran Ancien, 1959; On the Track of the Civilizations of Ancient Iran, L. Vanden Berghe, Memo from Belgium, 104–5, 1968; and Elam, Pierre Amiet, 1966.)

Further south, some 54 km. north-west of Behbehan, which is on the main road from Ahwaz to Bishapur, several famous Parthian reliefs were found at Tang-i Sarvak, all on isolated rock boulders and dating from about 200 B.C. The route is difficult and at present only possible by Land-Rover and horses or mules. The Manager of the Government Tourist Inn at Behbehan can advise you regarding guides and transport for this journey. The most important of the reliefs were noted by Baron de Bode in 1841, but Aurel Stein gives a full account with photographs in Old Routes of Western Iran. Descending from the head of the valley, one sees first an isolated boulder on which are depicted two standing male figures and a figure reclining on a couch. Further down the pass the main group of sculptures is found on two large detached rocks on a small wooded terrace. The northern face shows another figure reclining on a couch accompanied by attendants, with traces of an inscription. In a lower register are three standing figures. The better preserved western face has three registers depicting an enthroned figure with standing figures to the right, probably a monarch with members of his court and family, standing figures in an attitude of worship, and at the right, a typically Parthian armoured horseman charging a rampant lion, with an inscription above its head. Below this, in the centre, a large standing figure grasps the throat of a seated lion.

The most outstanding of the reliefs is on the north-western corner of this rock, where a huge figure of a bearded man, possibly a Magus, is seen with his right arm raised towards a column fire altar, standing on a triple base, with an inscription of probable late Parthian date. Another relief seen on a nearby boulder shows an armoured knight on a charger, while about 1½ km. further down the valley is a small detached rock with more reliefs. Among these is a standing figure with his right arm raised above a fire altar. (See W. B. Henning, 'The Monuments and Inscriptions of Tang-i Sarvak', *Asia Minor* N.S. 11.2.1952.) Eric de Waele, who studied the site in 1973, reversed the order of viewing (approaching from the foot of the valley) and gave his findings in an informative paper at the Second Annual Symposium on Archaeological Research in Iran, held in Tehran in October 1973.

Behbehan can be reached from Masjid-i Sulaiman via Ram Hormuz, or from Ahwaz, about 200 km., on a reasonable main road with some interesting mountain sections. From Behbehan the road continues east to Shiraz (p. 208) via Bishapur (p. 238) and branches south to the Persian Gulf at Bushire (p. 245). (*Tepe Sohz.)

6 · Central Iran

Compared with the rest of Iran, there are few prehistoric sites along the old trade route through the middle of the country, from Tehran to Kirman, for it skirts the two great deserts of salt and sand, where water has always been in short supply. Today there are frequent bus services along the whole route and a less frequent train service from Tehran to Qum and Kashan, which one day may reach Zahidan and link up with the Pakistan railway system. Yazd and Kirman, as well as Isfahan, are linked by internal air routes.

There is one major archaeological site, perhaps the best-known of all and certainly one of the more ancient settlements located near the heart of the Iranian plateau. That is Sialk, excavated by Professor Ghirshman in 1933–7, on the outskirts of Kashan, 260 km. south of Tehran.

The road goes through the second most sacred city in Iran, that of Qum (154 km.), whose golden cupola over the Hazrat-i Masumeh (the Safavid sanctuary of Fatima) dominates the skyline. You drive out of Tehran along the Ray road, past the edge of the salt desert and by ruined serais and occasional bare tepes. Qum is not a city for the non-Muslim, especially during religious celebrations, and its sanctuary is strictly barred to non-believers, but it does possess a large number of attractive shrines which can be visited, including some seventeen Mongol tomb-towers and shrines (in fact, 444 descendants of the Imams are said to be buried in Qum). The Masjid-i Jumeh, whose Saljuq dome and later minarets can be seen to the east of the main road through Qum to Kashan, did have a dated inscription of A.D. 1133–4 but this has now disappeared.

Some people think that Qum was captured by the Arabs in A.D. 644, others that it was in fact founded by them in the eighth century. In A.D. 816 Fatima, the sister of Imam Reza, was travelling to meet her brother at Mashad when she was taken ill at Saveh, a small town to the north-west of Qum, and managed to reach Qum before she died.

Hassan-al-Sabbah, founder of the Assassin sect, is said to have been born in Qum; in A.D. 1221 the city's inhabitants were massacred by the Mongols.

Qum is noted for its pottery, its blue beads and its delicious jams. The best hotel is the Kasra on the north corner of the bridge, opposite

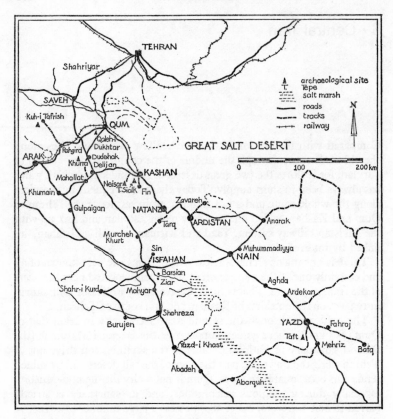

Map 6. Central Iran

the shrine, and from its roof one can (discreetly) have a good view of the shrine itself.

If you continue along the Arak road for some 33 km., you reach the junction with the main Isfahan road.

For Kashan, however, drive through Qum, crossing the river and passing a cluster of small, conical-roofed imamzadehs on the southern outskirts. It is about 104 km. to Kashan, through several attractive villages and by one or two splendid caravanserais, mainly Safavid. To the north-east in clear weather, the perfect, snow-capped cone of Iran's highest mountain, the extinct volcano of Mount Damavand, can be seen.

Kashan is a desert town and the bad-girs that funnel any breeze down to the lower, cooler rooms of the dwellings are a distinctive feature of this, and other desert cities. The most popular hotel is the Kashan, set in a small garden and reached by driving down the main Pahlavi avenue to the roundabout of Shishum-i Bahman where a signpost in English points right, to Bagh-i Fin, along Kh. Amir Kabir. Not far down this road, on the right, the hotel announces itself as the 'Guest House'. Clean, twin-bedded rooms, where you can also eat your meals as an alternative to the public restaurant, cost 800 rials, including a western-style toilet and shower in 1974.

Other hotels in the main street include the Hotel Saiya, almost next to the covered bazaar, clean with good Persian-style bathrooms but no private toilets. Here too food is served in your room in the traditional style—300 rials, extra for baths and meals.

Kashan is an attractive, typically Iranian town in which it is worth spending a night or two. It was believed to be the city from which the Three Wise Men set out for Bethlehem. Famous for its carpets, velvets, glazed pottery and tiles (the Persian word for mosaic tiles is 'kashi'), the city may have been in existence in Sassanian times, and, like so many others, it flourished under the Saljuqs and was destroyed by the Mongols. It was the Mongols, however, who revived it again, particularly encouraging the making of lustre faience tiles and textiles; the Ardabil carpet, now in the Victoria and Albert Museum, London, may have been woven in Kashan by Maqsud Kashani. And, although out of the period of this guide, it may be of interest to note that Shah Abbas the Great asked to be buried here next to his ancestor, Habib ibn Musa, on whose tomb are some fine thirteenth century tiles. Shah Abbas is believed to be buried in the crypt under a black marble tomb to the right as one enters the Mausoleum. Women require chadors to visit this shrine, which is in the Pusht-e Mashad district.

There are a few reminders of the Saljuq period here. One of them is the twelfth century Minar-i Zein ed Din, in Kh. Baba Afzal Kashani; a small plaster shop has been built into its foundations. Another is the twelfth century dome with the typical squinches, of the Masjid-i Jumeh, and its Saljuq minaret standing in the courtyard, dated A.D. 1073. A mihrab dated A.D. 1226, from the Masjid-i Maidan, is now in the Berlin Staatliche Museum, but the main structure of the mosque is Timurid. A few heavy piers in the west corner may date from the Saljuq period.

A small charge is made for entry to the shady Royal Gardens of Fin, some 8 km. south-west, down the Kh. Amir Khabir. The Safavid pavilions were constructed by Shah Abbas the Great and restored by the Qajars in the early nineteenth century. Mirza Taqi Khan, the brilliant reformist Prime Minister, was murdered here in 1853, in the royal hamam in the western corner of this typically Persian garden. A small museum is housed in one of the pavilions, and a Guide is published in English.

6*

Before reaching the gardens, about 5 km. from the Kashan Hotel, you will see the impressive South Citadel mound of Tepe Sialk, and the smaller Northern mound, on the right of the road, just beyond a few scattered houses and fields. In dry weather one can drive a car slowly along a track to the base of the main mound. There is a resident caretaker in a small building by this track.

The site was inhabited for some three or four thousand years, its earliest levels dating back to at least the fifth millennium B.C. One of the oldest known figurines of Near Eastern man was found here in the shape of a carved bone knife handle, depicting a man wearing a cap and a loincloth; it is now in the Tehran Museum.

In the first period of occupation the finds included carved bone and shell ornaments, a little metal work, stone axes and implements, and hand-made pottery that seems to imitate basketwork in some of its simple, painted designs. The dead were buried in a contracted position beneath their partly wooden huts, and the corpses were stained red (Sialk I, c. 5000 to 4500 B.C.). Next, in Sialk II (c. 4000 B.C.) came mud pisé dwellings followed by houses constructed of plano-convex bricks. The pottery was turned on a crude wheel, with black painted designs on a dark red ground depicting naturalistic animals, and a greater use of metal, similar to the Chesmeh Ali, Ray period (p. 48). The North mound was then abandoned and the bigger, Southern mound was founded (Period III, 3900–3000 B.C.), with the first evidence of trade (in shells, from the Persian Gulf), and many superimposed levels which produced prolific, beautifully decorated, long-spouted, wheel-turned pottery of a sophisticated type, stamp seals, and houses of rectangular mud bricks of a type still used today, the houses being painted white, with external, buttressed walls.

Many more precious objects were buried with the dead at this time, and copper was melted and cast in moulds.

A fierce fire, the ashes of which can still be found in the sides of the great mound, ended this period, probably with an invasion of new peoples who introduced a monochrome pottery identical in shape with that of Susa at the end of the fourth millennium (p. 148) and cylinder seals and clay tablets with proto-Elamite script (Sialk IV).

Then came a hiatus of nearly 2,000 years until there was a fresh invasion of peoples from the north-east who brought with them the art of iron work, towards the end of the second millennium B.C. At the same time these new invaders, probably Indo-Europeans, levelled the top of the mound and built a fortified mansion on stone foundations with alternating courses of crude brick and dry stone; a town came into being and the whole mound was surrounded by a wall flanked with towers. The dead, who wore leather helmets decorated with silver

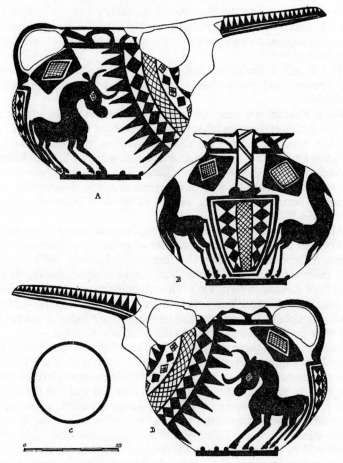

Fig. 31. Sialk. Vessel with long-beaked spout from Necropolis B, early 1st millennium B.C. (a) profile of right side; (b) back; (c) base; (d) profile of left side.
(*By courtesy of Professor R. Ghirshman, from 'Fouilles de Sialk'*)

plaques, were now buried in a necropolis away from the town. Over 200 tombs were excavated here and the remains of Cemetery B can be seen to the north-east of the citadel mound. The more important graves are dated from the tenth to ninth century B.C. and contained a notable series of beak-spouted, painted vases that appear to have been a luxury funerary ware of the period.

Somewhere around the ninth to eighth century B.C., the citadel was attacked and destroyed—although probably not by Assyrian forces as was once supposed—and thereafter the site was abandoned and never re-inhabited.[55,58,60]

This is still a fascinating and evocative site, with traces of walls and terraces and many sherds still scattered over the sprawling settlement.

From Kashan you can take a dirt road west to Delijan (84 km.) at the junction of the main Isfahan road. After about 15 km. from Kashan a rough track, unsuitable for ordinary vehicles, goes off to the left for a few km. to the village of Neisar. Here, on a nearby hill, is a heavily restored Sassanian Atesh-kadeh or Chahar Taq of the type from which the sacred fire could be seen from a great distance, thus serving as a signal or beacon to travellers, as well as the focal point of religious ceremonies.[68]

Although its precise date is not known, it is interesting to see that it makes clear use of a squinch in the zone of transition at the base of the dome. A form of wide gallery also runs round the dome.[71,177]

A more easily reached Chahar Taq can be seen at Natanz, on the road from Kashan south to Yazd. This charming mountain village about 85 km. from Kashan was protected by what may be a pre-Islamic castle, the Qalah-i Vashaq, standing on the crest of a steep hill skirted by the main highway about 10 km. to the north of the village.

In Natanz itself there is a Tourist Inn, petrol station and several chai khanehs, notably the Farvadin on the Maidan-i Shahrud, where there is always somebody anxious to act as guide. The main road skirts Natanz, but from it you can easily look down to the left and see the lovely minaret of the early fourteenth century Masjid-i Jumeh; a good road leads off to the left bringing you within a few metres' walk of the mosque which was begun in the Saljuq period as an octagonal kiosk against the south wall of the courtyard. In the Mongol period it was transformed into a 4-ivan mosque (A.D. 1304–5). Adjoining the mosque is the beautifully tiled portal to a monastery (khanehgah) which has disappeared, while in the same complex is the mausoleum of Sheikh Abd al-Samad al-Isfahani, A.D. 1307–8, with its pyramidal tiled roof. Close by is a large Husseiniyeh, an open-air theatre for the performance of religious plays during the mourning period of Muharram.

To get to the Chahar Taq, take the footpath along the side of the Khanehgah to the north, and follow it round to the left, past a cluster of dwellings. The fire temple lies immediately behind these, indeed, the houses are built onto part of it, and one can leave the path and walk behind the buildings into an orchard where the roofless Sassanian structure stands on a platform, some 2 m. high.

(Maxime Siroux gives details of other interesting Sassanian and Saljuq remains in the area between Kashan and Yazd.[147]) (*Ab-yaneh.)

There is another small Husseiniyeh close to the Chahar Taq, and there are usually one or two small 'Nakhls' here; these are wooden platforms with a heart-shaped wooden structure at either end, and during Muhurram they are covered with black drapes which entirely conceal the men who carry them in procession, much like the floats carried in the Easter processions in Seville, Spain, and possibly of the same origin.

North-west, across the fields, is an odd little mosque called the Masjid-i Koucheh Mir, surmounted by a curious canopy and perched on the very edge of a footpath along the side of a low hill. It contains a magnificent Saljuq stucco mihrab, quite out of keeping with its unpretentious exterior.

Natanz was a favourite hunting place for the Safavid kings, and from the Kashan road you can see a hunting lodge possibly of late Safavid date, sheltering several graves—on the hill to the north of the town.

The main road winds on from Natanz for about 10 km. to meet a junction where a right turn takes you about 67 km. to Moorcheh Khurt on the main Isfahan road; about half way along this branch road, near Tarq, there are the remains of a late Sassanian or early Islamic fort. Turn left at the junction from Natanz, and you drive 66 km. to Ardistan, believed to have been founded in Sassanian times, and an important, strongly fortified city in the tenth century. There is no hotel there but clean beds are available at the chai khaneh attached to the bus depot on the left of the main road as you drive in.

One of the earliest mosques to be built on the typically Iranian 4-ivan plan is the Masjid-i Jumeh here, but even earlier are two small mosques in nearby Zavareh which from the chronological point of view should be visited first. To do this, take a turning left (east) by the side of the Red Lion and Sun building, and drive along a reasonable dirt road for about 17 km. The road follows the old caravan route which eventually reaches Tabas (p. 206) and on to Khurasan.

Zavareh is known to have had a Sassanian fire temple and was an important trade centre in the Saljuq period. Today it is a forgotten little hamlet whose narrow streets and flat-roofed houses can have changed little in the last thousand years. Drive as far as you can along the road taking you into the hamlet, to a small square. Then walk through a short covered bazaar on your right, to the Masjid-i Jumeh with its stump of a brick minaret by the main entrance. You can climb to the top and onto the roof by a small door inside the mosque. An inscription in stucco round the upper part of the courtyard dates it to A.D. 1135-6, making it the earliest known dated mosque with a central courtyard and four ivans. There is a fine stucco mihrab, some lovely stucco fragments enhance the cradle vaults of the cloisters and the interior of the brick dome is quite majestic.

From the roof, looking south-east, one can see the minaret of the Masjid-i Pa-Menar, and it is an easy walk down the narrow lane by the side of the Friday Mosque, or one can drive there circuitously. The minaret of the Pa-Menar is almost complete and has a Kufic inscription in brick giving the date A.D. 1068–9, making it the second oldest known dated minaret in Iran. The oldest is at Saveh (p. 190).

The little Saljuq mosque itself, built round a rectangular courtyard, contains no less than six mihrabs and the remnants of some very fine stucco decoration with a few traces of the original blue colouring on the arches. Most of this is Mongol overlying Saljuq work.[67b,97,182] There is a fine Husseiniyeh between this and the Friday Mosque.

Back in Ardistan there are two notable monuments that must be seen. The first, as you drive in from Natanz, is the Masjid-i Imam Hasan, down a lane just south and east of the first roundabout. Here a handsome portal which originally had twin minarets—only one now remains—once led to a Saljuq Madrasseh; in the small mosque along-side is the badly damaged Saljuq mihrab which may be part of the original madrasseh and which bears a striking similarity to the main mihrab in the Masjid-i Jumeh in Ardistan.[97]

The decoration and inscription are probably of later date but the portal, the first known with minarets, is late twelfth century A.D. and according to Godard[67a] may be the earliest double minaret portal known.

Returning to the main road, continue to the second roundabout and just south of this a narrow lane leads westwards to the massive, rambling Masjid-i Jumeh.

The oldest part of this mosque is seen in the corridor leading from the door in the south to the mihrab room, which may have been built on the site of a Chahar Taq and later incorporated into a Saljuq kiosk mosque form in the twelfth century A.D. The lovely stucco mihrab was probably altered in the Mongol period. The prayer hall was built towards the end of the reign of Malik Shah (1072–92), and the simple brick Kufic inscription round the top of the mihrab room is dated A.D. 1158; that round the south ivan, leading to it, is dated A.D. 1160, about which time the kiosk mosque was converted into the 4-ivan mosque seen today.

Two other stucco mihrabs are in the two back bays of the south-east corner room. In the northern corner of the courtyard, between the north ivan and the later madrasseh on the west, are the remains of a restored Saljuq minaret.

From Ardistan to the next important town of Nain is about 95 km. You come into the town by a roundabout from which a good tarmac road goes off to the west, directly to Isfahan (147 km.), passing several villages with beehive roofs, Safavid caravanserais and the mountains on the north which look like cream puffs sprinkled with icing sugar. Later the road goes over a flat, salt-covered plain and, a few km. from Isfahan, passes the village of Gavart with its many pigeon towers. This village is noted for its fine carpets woven in the villagers' own homes and where one can usually watch the women and girls at work.

Nain was probably founded in the Sassanian period and was noted in the fourteenth century as being fortified—the remains of a citadel can be seen in the middle of the town, to the east of the main road. The town today is famous for its carpets and rugs, thought by many to be the finest in Iran. Inquire at carpet shops in the main street to visit home weaving sheds. There are also a number of pleasant chai khanehs including a large one near the first roundabout at the northern end of the town, opposite which the buses usually stop. There is an excellent Tourist Inn and a small local hotel, the Aria.

For the Masjid-i Jumeh, cross the roundabout to the Ardistan road and continue to the first wide turning on the right (north-west), at the end of which you can see the tall brick minaret attached to the mosque. The covered bazaar that formed the approach was pulled down in a road-widening scheme a few years ago. Almost opposite, covered entrances lead to a delightful Safavid mansion first noted by the author in 1966 and now being restored on Empress Farah's orders.

One of the most ancient mosques still in regular use in Iran, the Masjid-i Jumeh of Nain, was built perhaps *c.* A.D. 960 on the Abbasid design, with a central courtyard surrounded by porticos; the classic ivan type had not yet been adopted. The sharply pointed tunnel vaults are nearly three times as high as they are wide; the lower blocking walls and buttresses are modern, and the usual entrance is by a door under a modern porch by the side of the octagonal minaret.

The prayer hall and mihrab are ahead on the left, and several massive round columns by the mihrab are covered with exuberant stucco designs within the typical tenth century 'strap' patterns. The piers, the soffits of the qibla arches, and the mihrab are all covered with deeply carved, formerly polychromed stucco patterns probably deriving from Sassanian and early Islamic Mesopotamian designs, at times almost recalling the posts of a grape arbour laden with fruit.

A short gallery has been built recently under the central arch in front of the mihrab, while the fourteenth century carved wooden minbar next to it is also well worth inspection. Extensive restoration, revealing Abbasid brickwork, was observed in progress in 1974.

A new mosque has been built onto the north-western side of the court-yard, and stairs in the yard itself lead down to the underground prayer hall; other stairs by the southern door lead up to the roof. Other shrines in the town include the Gadamgah Pirniyeh with its splendid bad-girs.

Do make a short diversion to the enchanting little village of Muham-madiyya to the north-east of Nain, where the old, pre-Islamic town is thought to have been. Drive on through Nain's main street and take the first turning on the left, past the new mosque in a square near the exit from the town. 2½ km. along, this road brings you into Muhamma-diyya, snuggling in a hollow and dominated by the impressive remains of a castle on a hill to the north. Magnificent bad-girs rise from the domed roofs of the village and you should ask for the Masjid-i Jumeh and the nearby Masjid-i Sar-i Kucha.

Both are very plain, the Masjid-i Jumeh having a courtyard and cloisters, with a staircase on the far side, which leads down to a washing area with an open qanat (water channel) running through it. The main interest of this mosque is its underground prayer hall which would seem to be pre-Islamic, possibly Sassanian. A central dome rests on six columns, with a small open area on either side. This has now been completely restored so that none of the earlier work is visible, but the original ground plan has been carefully maintained. Part of the panels of the wooden minbar may date from the eleventh century A.D.

The Masjid-i Sar-i Kucha, a few metres north of the Masjid-i Jumeh, has no courtyard, but a very fine painted Kufic frieze running round the interior of the mosque, giving the names of the Companions of the Prophet, and verses from the Koran. In plan this mosque is an enlargement of the underground chamber of the Masjid-i Jumeh, in that it has a central dome, but the side areas have been extended to form barrel-vaulted side wings. Both mosques have been dated by Godard to the tenth to eleventh century A.D. and they are the only known mosques of their type, each ultimately descended from the barrel-vaulted Sassanian building at Ivan-i Karkha in Khuzestan (p. 153), with long, barrel-vaulted chambers divided into three. Fine cloth for abbas is woven and dyed here.

The road from Muhammadiyya continues along the old caravan route to Anarak where it joins the road from Ardistan to cross the Great Salt Desert to Tabas and on to Khurasan.

From Nain the new road continues south-east to Yazd, about 180 km., passing en route the picturesque village of Aghda with its mud-brick walls and citadel and small oasis of palms, and then skirting the little town of Ardekan. Carpets woven in private homes, and locally made pottery, are Ardekan's specialities. There is a good chelo-kebab restaurant on the corner of the main street, next to the bus depot, and a little further on, on the opposite side of the road, an unusually clean, public lavatory. On the new road is a petrol station.

About 35 km. from Ardekan, near a ruined caravanserai, a road on the left goes across the desert towards a range of low jagged mountains and this is the recommended road to Tabas (p. 206) and Khurasan.

Yazd itself is a large town, surrounded by mountains, and has been an important Zoroastrian centre since Sassanian times; in keeping with this distinction there are many fire temples and dakhmes (towers of silence) of more or less recent date to be found in the hills and villages around the area. The town's original name was Kathah from the Persian 'to hollow out', a reference to the deep moat that protected the ramparts; this old name is now given to the district of Yazd.

The town was probably conquered by the Arabs about A.D. 642, and in the tenth century it was noted as being a strongly fortified, prosperous city standing at the cross-roads of the most important caravan routes from Central Asia and India to the south and west. Marco Polo, who came here on his way to China in 1272, called it 'the Good and Noble City of Yazd'. Its brocades (termeh) and fine, handwoven silks are world-renowned. The cool, semi-underground weaving chambers where the termehs are fashioned can be found in the Sayed Fateh Reza district near the remains of the fourteenth century city walls to the east, and also in the north-west part of the city, but most are now mechanical.

There are several covered bazaars and, off the new, wide main streets, enchanting winding lanes with caravanserais, madrassehs and, in one case, a remarkable old serai converted into a home for the disabled. Yazd takes time to explore and a stay of several days would not be too long here. There is an air service from Tehran and eventually the railway line to Zahidan is expected to come through Yazd.

Probably the most comfortable place to stay is the Motel Safaiyeh on the southern outskirts of the town, about 5 km. along the Kirman road. A sign in English and Persian, at a modern roundabout, points to the Kh. Safaiyeh to the right, and a short distance down here, on the right, is the motel, set back in recently planted gardens, with a swimming pool and individual, well-furnished, air-conditioned and heated bunga-lows. A central block contains offices and a restaurant. An apartment costs 800 rials double (accommodation for drivers and servants is available at lower rates).

From the gardens of the Motel you can see, to the west, the hills crowned by several old Zoroastrian Towers of Silence with the barrel-vaulted charnel houses at their foot, where the corpses receive the last funeral rites before being exposed. However, many Zoroastrians today bury their dead in conventional fashion in a modern cemetery near the water-driven flour and henna mills in the vicinity.

Taxis in Yazd are cheap but if you have not got your own transport you may prefer to stay in the town. The Hotel Cyrus in Kh. Pahlavi offers air-conditioned double rooms with bath for 450 rials and has a reasonable restaurant and some parking space. Opposite is the newer Farhang Hotel with similar rates.

There are many interesting monuments in Yazd, most of them fourteenth century or later. The remains of the city walls of mud brick, probably begun in 1119 and rebuilt and enlarged in the fourteenth century, now surround a prison in the eastern quarter, reached by a road almost opposite the main PTT (Post and Telegraph) building in Kh. Pahlavi. There is a rather splendid, five-towered ab-anbar at the eastern end of the lane past the walls, and the clack of many looms guides you to the weavers in this quarter. Alas the ab-anbar is now spoilt by a new entrance.

The beautiful Masjid-i Jumeh at the end of a short cul-de sac west of the PTT office has what is believed to be the highest portal with twin minarets mounted above it and is perhaps the best-preserved fourteenth century building of any in Iran. It was built on the site of a fire temple in 1119 by the Atabek Ala al-Dowleh, but the original building was destroyed and most of what can be seen today was constructed in A.D. 1375, with later additions. Climb to the roof at the back of the portal for a splendid view of the city and surroundings. Immediately south-east of the mosque is the tiled dome of the Imamzadeh Vaqt-o Sa'at, all that remains of a famous fourteenth century complex of library, college and observatory. Over to the south-west the tall minarets flanking the early nineteenth century Takieh-ye Chaqmaq form a landmark; this is a grandstand from which the religious passion plays of Muharram are watched, and it is also the entrance to a small bazaar. It fronts onto a square leading off Kh. Pahlavi, on one side being the fifteenth century Masjid-i Chaqmaq. In front of the Takieh stands an enormous Nakhl, the wooden, leaf-shaped framework on a platform, which is rarely seen outside Central Iran.

On the eastern corner of this square is a particularly popular confectioner's where such local delicacies as 'grandfather's beard' (finely spun sugar), ghotab, bakhlava and many other candies and biscuits are made in huge ovens on the premises.

Most of the booking offices for long-distance bus services are on this part of Kh. Pahlavi while the colourful bazaars are mainly on either side of the Kh. Shah, opposite Maidan-i Chaqmaq. On the south of Kh. Shah is the Musalla 'Atiq or Safdar Khan, a reconstructed Chahar Taq[71] set in a large courtyard.

The Duvazdah Imam (12 Imams) stands in a small square reached by a narrow lane running eastwards from the Masjid-i Jumeh. This domed mausoleum dated A.D. 1036-7 is a plain, solid brick building (ask a local inhabitant to fetch the key for you) in which the interior of the squinch is composed of three arched panels, all blending upwards and outwards to carry the ring of the dome—an early and particularly striking use of the squinch, which most probably influenced the bold use that the early Saljuq architects made of this same feature. The 'quilted' style stucco panel above the mihrab and the remnants of the painted ceiling are unusually fine. In the same square is another, unrecorded neglected building of similar design, popularly called the Zendan-i Iskandar (Alexander's prison).

About 30 km. south-east of Yazd on the secondary road to Bafq turning left from the highway, one can see a very early mosque c. eighth to tenth century A.D. This very unusual early mosque is in the picturesque village of Fahraj which lies about 1 km. to the right of the road from which you can see the minaret of the mosque. It is built on the Arab rather than on the typically Persian plan, with three domes on the qibla side and two mihrabs with sparse decoration of moulded stucco. On the other three sides of the courtyard are double rows of arcades.

The mud-brick minaret is intact, built with a very striking batter, and has been slightly restored at the top. One can ascend by a staircase inside the mosque.

The main road from Yazd to Kirman (p. 264), 372 km., continues south, and there is a very indifferent Tourist Inn at Rafsanjan (260 km.). A turning branching off to the right, just outside Yazd, takes you south-eastwards to join the main Isfahan-Shiraz highway at a distance of 192 km. A new, straight road was under construction in 1974.

At Farahshah, near Taft, a Zoroastrian village amid orchards about 30 km. along this road, a Saljuq imamzadeh in the shape of an ivan standing on a platform may have been a Sassanian site.[144d] There are some charming caravanserais along this road and, after 135 km., one reaches the small town of Abarquh, a prosperous city on an important caravan route when it was seen by the geographer Istakhri in A.D. 950.

The first of several interesting monuments in this town today is the Gunbad-i Ali standing on a hill to the left of the road as you enter Abarquh. It is the earliest dated octagonal tomb-tower in southern Iran and is built of heavy rubble and roofed with a low dome. In appearance it is not unlike the Yazid tower at Ray (p. 48) and it is dated A.D. 1056-7 according to the Kufic inscriptions under the cornice and above the entrance. There is a mihrab inside the otherwise empty building which originally housed the tombs of the parents of one

Firuzan, Amir 'Amid al-Din Shams al-Dowleh, grandson of the Dailamite Nasr who served the local Buyid kings in the early eleventh century.[66b]

The remains of the old town of Abarquh are scattered around the tower, but follow the road into the present town and ask for the Masjid-i Jumeh. This is a classical 4-ivan mosque of which the oldest portion, the domed chamber between the south and east ivans, dates from the Saljuq period. The stucco mihrab in the east ivan is fourteenth century Mongol, and when this was built the south ivan was also lengthened with a cradle-vaulted prayer-room.

Inquire also for the Mausoleum of Pir Hamza Sabz Push which has been almost completely restored but contains a very lovely stucco mihrab of the twelfth century, originally surmounted by a high mantel similar to that of the Haidarieh at Qazvin (p. 55) now all but disappeared except for the lower portion.

Just outside the town on the western side, after passing a pleasant ab-anbar, you see the remains of a madrasseh with a pair of high Mongol minarets.

Now the road deteriorates somewhat between Abarquh and the main Isfahan-Shiraz highway which it joins after going through rocky valleys for about 56 km. A turn to the left at the junction takes you to Shiraz (256 km.), and to the right, Isfahan (235 km.). Making for Isfahan and Tehran, one passes a number of mounds and the remains of serais, tombs and forts, for this also was a great caravan route. Petrol is available at Abadeh, a famous caravan centre, about 25 km. from the Abarquh junction; there is also a small hotel in the main street and the remains of many large serais can be seen in the surrounding fields.

The most fascinating of all places on this road is surely the unusual village of Yazd-i Khast, 92 km. from the Abarquh turning. The remains of this 'skyscraper' mud-brick village crown a steep cliff that juts out into a deep, narrow gorge, like the prow of some giant ship. At the foot of the road there is a big chai khaneh and from here one sees not only the most dramatic view of Yazd-i Khast but also the fine Safavid caravanserai in the gorge, which is still in use.

As you drive up the hill, take the road to the left, round the base of the old village and into a small square where you can park. The modern highway skirts the town to the right.

Walk over a kind of rickety drawbridge across the deep cleft and then along the main street of the deserted town; there are plenty of small boys to guide you to the small Masjid-i Deh (or Masjid-i Khoneh) almost at the end of the rocky spur and approached through a ruined wall and by edging along a narrow crumbling footpath on the very edge of the gorge. Half of the mosque, repaired a few years ago, has already fallen over the cliff, but what remains is still in use and has very clearly been converted from a Sassanian Chahar Taq, with a stone minbar built against the rear wall, and a minute window looking out onto the gorge.

You can drive out from the square to rejoin the main highway by another chai khaneh opposite an Imamzadeh standing on a low mound. Some 20 km. further on the road passes another village, Aminabad, surrounded by mud-brick buttressed walls, and then more fortified serais. At Shahreza, 83 km. from Isfahan, there is a new Tourist Inn in the centre of the town—to the west of the main road—and on the northern outskirts of the town, a delightful Safavid Imamzadeh with an elaborate Qajar portico should be seen.

From Shahreza a road goes west into the Zagros mountains, to Burujen and Shahr-i Kord, and then circles back to Isfahan.

Between Shahreza and Isfahan is another largely ruined, walled village, Mahyar, with a large seventeenth century serai.

Some of the most splendid Saljuq minarets can be seen by diversions off the road in this area. For instance, about 27 km. before Isfahan, a track goes off to the right, south-east, to Ziar—keep bearing left where tracks join. At about 13 km. you pass the village of Jar or Gar, where there is a Saljuq brick minar on an octagonal base, dated by inscription to A.D. 1121-2. The minar has a double spiral staircase. The ruins of a mosque adjoin it, built by Sayyid Riza, Abul Qasim Ibn Ahmad. About another 10 km. brings you to Ziar, once a flourishing town but now merely a small village surrounded by cotton fields from one of which rises the remains of a mosque and a twelfth century minar described as one of the finest in Iran. It is some 50 m. high and divided into three sections by two balconies; the shaft is decorated with glazed and unglazed bricks. Less than fifty years ago the fields were covered with ruins of the old town, but farmers have destroyed all but the mosque and the minaret.

One can get to Isfahan by continuing back along the dirt track, keeping to the right at junctions, and past the village of Beshtar one continues on to reach the Shahrestan bridge (p. 184).

On the left bank of the River Zayendeh, in the same area as the Ziar minaret, is an early dated minaret (A.D. 1097-8) at Barsian, where there is also a Saljuq mosque.

The main highway from Shiraz to Isfahan, however, enters the city over the See-o-Se Pol (the Bridge of 33 Arches) which brings you right into the famous Chahar Bagh avenue, the main artery of one of the world's most enchanting cities.

There are a number of good hotels in Isfahan, but undoubtedly the most famous and romantic of all is the Shah Abbas in Kh. Shah Abbas Kabir, on the right of the Chahar Bagh ('four gardens'). This unusual hotel was converted from the Safavid caravanserai attached to the Madrasseh-i Madar-i Shah, formal gardens filling the centre of the courtyard with the addition of the new hotel on the southern side. Embodying the decorative arts of stucco, stalactites, miniatures, murals, mirror work and carving, from the Saljuq to the Qajar periods, carried out by Iran's finest craftsmen, this unique hotel with several bars and restaurants is a 'must' to visit, if not to stay in. (Prices range from 1,200 rials for a single room and bath, to 12,000 rials for a de luxe Presidential Suite in the converted serai.) There is a swimming pool and a traditional coffee-house with storyteller who recounts the great epics as you sip your tea on hot summer evenings in the north ivan of the serai.

Less expensive but comfortable and central hotels include the Irantour on Abbasabad avenue, across the Chahar Bagh, the small Arya facing the Shah Abbas, the good Ali Qapu and simpler Tus and Sa'adi on the Chahar Bagh. Across the river, the de luxe Kurush Hotel opened in 1971.

Pleasant restaurants include the Canary in the Maidan-i Mojassami, and the Sheherazad near the Irantour Hotel, as well as many coffee-houses along the Chahar Bagh.

Of all Iranian cities Isfahan is perhaps the most truly Persian in the sense in which westerners visualize the country of old. It is primarily a Safavid city and most of the many glorious buildings date from the time of Shah Abbas the Great; shopping in the enormous area of the covered Qaiseriyeh and other bazaars will yield all kinds of treasures from beaten and engraved silver, brass and copper, ivory miniatures and rugs, to a local type of nougat called 'gaz'; kalamkar, material hand-printed from old wooden blocks and many antiques are to be had.

Isfahan was probably in existence in the Achaemenian period—the Achaemenian city of Gabae is believed to have been here. It was certainly the capital of a Parthian province in the time of Artabanus V (A.D. 213–224) and during the Sassanian period the city became known as Aspahan or Sepahan (whence Isfahan) meaning 'the place of the army', since the district was used as an army camp and place of assembly. Sassanian crown princes were sent here to study statecraft and Yazdigird I, who had a Jewish wife, was probably responsible for settling a large number of Jews in the district which is still known as Yahoudieh or Jubareh, around the Saraban minar, in the north-eastern quarter.

The Arabs conquered the city about A.D. 640 and the Ummayads, followed by the Abbassid Caliphs, kept control of it until A.D. 931 by which time Isfahan was already famed for its silks and cotton weaving. The major part of the city at this time, known as Jay, was slightly to the east of present-day Isfahan, at Shahrestan. It was in Saljuq times that Yahoudieh expanded and became the centre of the capital, in the area occupied by the Masjid-i Jumeh. Several minor Persian dynasties ruled Isfahan during the tenth century A.D.; the Dailamites (Buyids) were perhaps the most notable and during their reign Isfahan is said to have had twelve bronze-covered gates through which elephants could easily pass, a thousand mansions and fifty mosques.

For a brief period Mas'ud, son of Sultan Mahmud of Ghazni, held the city in A.D. 1034, and in 1047 Tughril Beg successfully besieged it for a year and then made it his capital. He and his successors, Alp Arslan and Malik Shah, contributed much to Isfahan's architectural beauty.

Towards the end of the Saljuq period the city was under the power of the Assassins who killed Nizam al-Mulk, Malik Shah's famous prime minister, a great intellectual and founder of schools; Malik Shah himself was murdered by them in A.D. 1092.

In A.D. 1121 the Assassins set fire to the Masjid-i Jumeh, destroying its famous library. Isfahan escaped the first Mongol invasion but in A.D. 1235 their armies were let into the city by a member of one of the leading families among whom there had been religious rivalry for many years. In 1397 Tamurlane slaughtered some 70,000 Isfahanis, making minarets of their skulls.

Shah Abbas the Great made Isfahan his capital in A.D. 1598 and its glory lasted until the end of the Safavid period, in the early eighteenth century.

The remains of Isfahan's chief Sassanian fire temple may well have stood on an isolated, prominent rock outcrop that lies 7 km. to the west of the city, and some authorities believe it was a ziggurat.

To reach it drive up the Chahar Bagh, passing the Madrasseh Madar-i Shah, and turn left along the Khiaban-i Sheikh Bahai, marked by a sign-post to Najafarabad. On the right of the road, past the second roundabout where the built-up area ends, the possible site of the ateshgah dominates the entire area.

The easiest path to the extant mud-brick ruins winds round the back of the hill—the little (now much restored) round tower on the top was built by the Mongols in the thirteenth or fourteenth century, and may have been used later on as a signalling tower. (The difficult and still uncertain history of construction on the hill is discussed in considerable detail by Maxime Siroux.[145]) From the top one can see a number of attractive Safavid pigeon towers, a feature of the landscape in this district, and sometimes constructed to house thousands of birds whose droppings are collected once a year and used to fertilize Isfahan's famous melons.

On the return to the city, the so-called 'trembling minarets' of Junban are passed on the same side of the street as the ateshgah. They are Safavid minarets built on top of a Mongol ivan covering a tomb.

The site of the old city, which is now partly occupied by the village of

Shahrestan, is reached by driving eastwards along the banks of the Zayendeh Rud. If you keep on the northern side you will reach the splendid, time-worn Shahrestan bridge, the massive foundation piers of which are probably Sassanian in date.

At the northern end of the bridge are the ruins of what was probably a toll house. Until about 1915 there was a Saljuq minaret near the bridge, which was pulled down by the local villagers for the sake of its bricks. There is still a Saljuq tomb-tower, however, on a small mound by the village on the north bank, reached by walking from the bridge across a piece of wasteland, or driving down a narrow lane to the north. It is known as the Shahzadeh Ibrahim and Hussein and is an undated octagonal tower standing within a courtyard. It houses the remains of al-Rashid Bi'llah, the Abbasid Caliph murdered by the Assassins c. A.D. 1137–8, and his tomb is surrounded by a fine wooden 'zari' or grille, and still much venerated. A painted stucco Kufic inscription from the Koran runs around the lower part of the hemispherical dome which rests on a circle of sixteen arches.

In Isfahan itself, the few traces of the Dailamite city include the deep moat surrounding the citadel of Qaleh Tabarek, built by the Buyid ruler, Fakhr al-Dowleh, and the Dailamite doorway known as the Jurjir portal, which adjoins the Masjid-i Hakim. The citadel, whose buttressed walls were 8 m. thick, was pulled down in the 1930s, but here and there on the edge of the fosse, particularly by the bridge on the south-western side, one can see houses built into the thickness of the remnants of the wall, which lies to the east of the Masjid-i Shah.

The Jurjir portal is south of the Kh. Mohammed Reza Pahlavi at the end of the Bazaar-i Rang-razan (the Dyers' Bazaar). It can also be reached by going through the Qaisariyeh bazaar from the Maidan-i Shah and following the lanes to the north-west, asking for the Masjid-i Hakim which was built in the seventeenth century by Shah Safi's chief physician, on the site of the tenth century mosque of which only the Jurjir portal remains. Until 1955 even this was hidden behind mud-brick walls. It needs the morning light for photography from the narrow lane onto which it fronts.

The heart of the Saljuq capital was the Kohneh Maidan or Maidan-i Sabz, formed by the cross-roads of Kh. Abdol Razzak or Pahlavi, Sa'adi and Hatef, close to the Masjid-i Jumeh. Described by Pope as one of the greatest mosques in the world,[125] it best exemplifies the 'power and nobility of Saljuq architecture', embracing in actual fact more than 800 years of Persian architecture in its twenty distinct structures dating from the eleventh to the eighteenth centuries.

According to tradition, the first mosque on the summit of what was already a tepe, was built in the early eighth century, probably on the

site of a fire temple; it was enlarged about A.D. 842 by the Abbasids and
added to by the Shi'a Buyids in A.D. 908–932. The Sunni Saljuqs
rebuilt the mosque, keeping to the old plan, and the central core today
is virtually the same, with later decoration including onyx slabs,
added to the façades.

The oldest complete surviving portions are the magnificent sanctuary
and mihrab room built as an isolated kiosk by Nizam al-Mulk c. 1080,
on the southern side of the courtyard. This enormous dome rests on
deep trilobed squinches, a form developed from the Duvazdah Imam
at Yazd (p. 179), or perhaps even earlier Buyid styles (see A. Hutt in
Iran, Vol. VIII, 1970). The squinches in turn rest on huge cylindrical
piers crowned by what Pope describes as 'Abbasid-looking stucco
scrolls',[129] an observation recently confirmed when later plaster and
brickwork was removed by Italian experts from IsMEO. For some years
now a team led by Professor Umberto Scerrato has been excavating to
reveal unsuspected pre-Saljuq structures, while another team directed
by architect Eugenio Galdieri has carried out restorations (see 'Isfahān:
Masğid-i Ġum'a', 2, by Eugenio Galdeiri, IsMEO, 1973, and Iran,
Vol. XI, 1973).

This important work has identified almost the entire original fabric
of the early 'Arab-type' mosque which was gradually extended from
south to north around what was probably an open village square.
Under the big square Saljuq bricks of the south sanctuary floor,
fragments of painted Kufic inscriptions in vivid blue, red and gold,
were found, fallen from the Arab-type mosque, together with part of a
Sassanian column and early tenth century structures. On the north side
of the square, excavations have revealed remains of early Islamic houses
and a large, Sassanian style mansion with a courtyard and ivans and
typical late ninth century Buyid decoration. While work continues you
may see part of this excavation in the north-east corner in front of what
is known as the Gunbad-i Kharka, an exquisite small dome built by
Nizam al-Mulk's political rival Taj al-Mulk, and dated A.D. 1088. This
dome is a single shell which has survived without a crack for almost
900 years; of mathematically ideal dimensions, it is set on an octagonal
ring of sixteen panels, supported by trilobed squinches on slender
colonnettes built in one with the square base, unlike the structure of
the southern dome. The Kharka dome was quite possibly designed by the
contemporary mathematician (and poet), Omar Khayyam, who was
then resident in Isfahan. The tenth century Buyid phase of the Masjid-i
Jumeh was discovered when unusual trilobed columns, reminiscent of the
brickwork on the Jurjir Portal, were traced right round the courtyard.
Others, leaning perilously in the northern section, were found incorporated into massive rectangular brick columns, resting only on broken

mud-brick village walls or even over wells. However, little carbonide material has so far been discovered to support the traditional theory that the mosque was burnt by the Assassins in 1121. A trial trench is to be dug diagonally across the great courtyard to test the earliest periods.

Meanwhile, as you walk through this living monument to 1,200 years of Islam, look closely at the tremendous variety of brick vaulting, especially over the arcades and corridors by the southern entrance, with decorated Saljuq columns, brick end plugs and early stucco. Also notice the charming little Mongol stucco mihrab in a dark corner of the passage leading to the courtyard. Some particularly interesting brick end plugs can be seen in the arches of the east ivan, some of which were bricked up perhaps by the Safavids to prevent further movement of the structure which was built without solid foundations.

There is much more to enjoy in this impressive mosque, including the Mongol Il-Khan Oljeitu's marvellous stucco mihrab, A.D. 1310, the Safavid minbar by its side and behind, the beautiful Timurid winter prayer hall lit by golden sheets of alabaster.

Leaving the mosque, turn right through the covered bazaar into the Kh. Abdol Razzak. Turn left to the Maidan-i Sabz and cross over to a lane on the right where you can see the tall minar of the Masjid-i Ali. This minaret, some 50 m. high, was built in the late twelfth or early thirteenth century and the top has been restored. The portal of the mosque was built in 1522 by Shah Ismail, but the mosque itself is believed by Professor Luschey of the German Archaeological Institute, Tehran, to be pre-Safavid. A view from the roof of the mosque helps you to orientate yourself in this rather confusing district. The Saraban minaret is the tall one to the north-west and stands in a maze of narrow streets. Take a turning almost opposite the lane leading to the Masjid-i Jumeh, off Kh. Hataf, and bear right at the junctions. The name of the minar means 'Camel Driver' and it was built in the twelfth or thirteenth century as part of a now disappeared mosque. It is about 50 m. high and divided into three by two balconies of stalactites. The slender shaft is decorated with Kufic inscriptions and geometric designs of turquoise glazed bricks.

If you walk past this minaret along a lane leading north, then west, you will see another, earlier Saljuq minaret, the Chehel Dukhtaran, dated by a Naskhi inscription on the base to A.D. 1107–8. It stands within a small walled space, is 29 m. high, the brick shaft resting on an octagonal base and a Kufic inscription runs round the top of the minaret.

The tombstones of the assassinated Saljuq king, Malik Shah, and of members of his family and of his prime minister, Nizam al-Mulk, rest in a charming little garden in the Ahmed Abad quarter (also called the Dal Beiti or Dar-ul Bettikh), between the Kh. Ahmed Abad (an extension of Hafez) and Kh. Sa'adi. The graves were robbed in the seventeenth century and the tombstones displaced, but it is believed that in the simple, open-sided shelter the stones cover the remains of Sultan Mahmud and Turkan Khatun as well as those of Malik Shah and Nizam al-Mulk, both murdered near the close of the eleventh century.

In the same district is the Imamzadeh Ismail, one of a complex of buildings grouped round a courtyard approached through a short alley to the east of Kh. Hatef. From the main road one can see the very wide, shallow Turkoman dome covering the portal into the courtyard. On the roof of the Masjid-i Shaia, adjoining the Safavid shrine of Ismail, is the stump of a Saljuq minaret which, with the neighbouring vaults, was possibly built by Alp Arslan. The shaft of the minar is 2·65 m. in diameter, and the narrow tiled pinnacle is a later addition. From the roof too you can look down through openings to the tomb alleged to be that of the Prophet Isaiah, which was found in the ruins of the old mosque. This was the first large mosque to be constructed in Isfahan and was built by Abu'l-'Abbas the Mufti, in the time of Ali, repaired by Alp Arslan and restored in A.D. IIII–III2, according to an inscription found at the same time as the tomb.[148]

Much of the old quarter of Shahshahan or Babul Dasht is being demolished, but so far the domed building where Ibn Ali Sina (Avicenna, p. 110), is said to have taught when a Minister under Ala al-Dowleh Mohammad at the beginning of the eleventh century, still exists. From Kh. Modarres walk down Kouche Payeh Guldasteh on the south. The tiny Masjid-i Pa-Guldasteh on the left, contains the remains of a Saljuq minaret, 3 m. of which can be seen above the roof, the remaining 6 m. being concealed within the mosque walls. Just beyond this on the right is the so-called Masjid-i Ali Sina, next to a hamam. The exterior of Avicenna's dome is unchanged but the interior where once the brilliant intellectual held his classes, is now desolate.

The fourteenth century Dardasht is a tiled portal with twin minarets and adjoins a tomb-tower containing the defaced grave-stone bearing the following inscription: 'This stone was placed here by the high lady, Sultan Bakhte Agha, daughter of Amir Khosrow Shah . . . that God continues his help to his soul after his death, in Ramadan, year . . . .53.' Khosrow Shah was Governor of Isfahan in the mid-twelfth century A.D.

Another early relic is a long black carved stone set beneath the window of the Shrine of Ahmad, opening onto a lane in the Saroutaghi Bazaar to the south-east of the Maidan-i Shah. It is reached through the Chahar Souy-e Maqsud bazaar at this corner. The shrine itself is Safavid and entered from the courtyard which also houses a Qajar mausoleum, several graves and two typical Bakhtiar stone memorial lions. The carved stone beneath the window is dated by an Arabic inscription to

A.D. 1167, and was reputedly brought from an Indian temple by Mahmud of Ghazni.

About 3 km. along the Nain road from Isfahan, a track goes to the left for a further 3 km. to the village of Rahravan (pronounced 'Rahroon') where a tall brick minaret some 30 m. high stands in the fields to the north-east of the village. It probably dates from the twelfth century A.D. and the inscription is part of the Kalima, the Muslim confession of faith. (*Varzaneh.)

Other monuments still within easy reach of Isfahan, include the Sin mosque and its lovely Saljuq minaret, which incorporates the earliest dated exterior architectural faience of the Islamic period in Iran. It was built in A.D. 1131 and lies 24 km. north of Isfahan, along a dirt road linking up with the road to Natanz. The mosque also contains a small Saljuq dome chamber with a dated inscription above the mihrab.

About 25 km. to the south-west, starting along the Shiraz road and then bearing right for the village of Linjan, is an ancient Jewish cemetery said to date from the second century A.D. and still in use today. The village is on the site of the old town of Khan Lanjan, guarded by an Assassin[7] castle on the hills, while in the village itself is the remarkable, early fourteenth century mausoleum of Pir-i Baqran with its magnificent stucco mihrab and walls (A.D. 1303–1312).

There are, of course, literally scores of other enchanting and magnificent monuments to see in Isfahan, mainly of the Timurid and Safavid periods,[67c] and including the seventeenth and eighteenth century Armenian churches in Julfa, the Armenian quarter across the river.

One can drive back to Tehran on the fast main highway (and there is a frequent air service connecting Isfahan with Tehran and Shiraz), but it is more interesting to take the secondary road, about 190 km., to Gulpaigan (where there is a small, provincial hotel), leaving Isfahan on the Najafabad road. There is a Tourist Inn *en route* at Khonsar.

Gulpaigan is probably of Sassanian foundation and its name was changed at the time of the Arab conquest to Jorbahagan. It was an important town in the Saljuq period but the only evidence of this today is the austere Masjid-i Jumeh which was founded by Malik Shah's son, Abu Shoja, according to an inscription round the base of the dome, which is the only one known to refer to Malik Shah as 'Shahanshah'; it gives the date of building as A.D. 1105–1118. There is a fine stucco mihrab in the chamber under this dome, into which modern white plaster has unfortunately been inserted; the majestic dome chamber itself can be compared with those in the Masjid-i Jumeh at Isfahan (p. 185) and at Barsian (p. 181) and Qazvin (p. 55).

The mosque, which is reached through the covered bazaar, escaped additions, reconstructions and alterations until the early nineteenth century when the rooms surrounding the central court and the four ivans were built by one of Fath' Ali Shah's wives.

The free-standing minaret on a mound beside the main road, opposite the bazaar entrance, is dated c. A.D. 1100 and has a double spiral staircase in its cylindrical shaft which is set on an octagonal base. Each staircase is approached by a separate door. In front of the minaret stand two of the typical Bakhtiar stone memorial lions, probably commemorating an outstanding hunter or warrior.

Now one can continue northwards to Khumein, about 45 km., and here take the road to the east for Mahallat (55 km.) and Delijan which is on the main Isfahan-Tehran highway. One can cut off Khumein by taking a branch road used by heavy traffic, going to the right a few km. before reaching Khumein and coming out just west of Mahallat which is a large hill village of probably ancient foundation. It has a delightful spa, Mahallat Bala, set in landscaped gardens in a pleasant valley in the hills to the north. It is reached by a road from Mahallat which passes a fourteenth century Imamzadeh.

About 5 km. from Mahallat on the Delijan road, are the remains of a ruined castle and an early Chahar Taq, near a village called Ateshgah.[68,146]

Joining the main Tehran road at Delijan, drive north to Doodehak. From here you can reach a rare Seleucid or Parthian temple (?) at Khorheh or Khurra, about 13 km. off the main road along a gravel track to the west. It is indicated by a sign in Persian near the first chai khaneh on the left. The road goes through Doodehak and right, past a fine Safavid caravanserai, and over a small bridge of the same period. About 7 km. from the main road is a stream which can normally be forded. Pass the large village of Hajiabad and the remains of Parthian buildings crowning the hills to the left further on. Some 5 km. from these is Khorheh, and west of the village can be seen the two remaining columns of the intriguing structure, briefly excavated by the Iranian Archaeological Service in 1956.

The proportions of the columns with their Ionic capitals (there were probably twenty-four columns originally), seem to speak for local workmanship. You can see extensive remains of elegant stone mouldings, while the large number of human bones at the site represent one of its many mysteries.

Back on the main road, turn north for Tehran via Saveh. Or take the road to Qum, turning either at Neisar or the junction of the Arak road, a little further north. If you take the Arak turn to the left and eventually on to Hamadan, you will reach the village of Rahgird which is the starting point for a somewhat uncertain trip into the Kuh-i Tafrish mountains for an important, but difficult to locate, Chahar Taq noted by Godard and surveyed by Professor Vanden Berghe in 1964.

It is some 40 km. as the crow flies from Rahgird, near the village of
Navish in the Mihr Zamin plain, and 5 km. south of the valley of Burzu.
Vanden Berghe[176,177] thinks it may have been here that the famous
Adhar Burzin Mihr Fire of the Farmers was kept, rather than near
Nishapur as is generally believed (p. 199).

Continuing on to Saveh about 60 km. from the Arak cross-roads,
there are two extremely lovely, early Saljuq minarets to be seen in this
little town. It was once the winter capital of the last Iraq Saljuqs, at
the end of the twelfth century, after they had lost Baghdad. From the
tenth century Saveh was known as an important caravan centre, and
when the Mongols captured it in 1220 its famous library of astronomical
books was destroyed. This is another of the towns from which the Three
Wise Men are said to have begun their journey to Bethlehem.

Saveh was a great pottery centre and was visited by Marco Polo on
his famous journey to China.

Perhaps the oldest dated Saljuq minaret in Iran is by the Masjid-i
Maidan in the centre of the town, on the main square, and bears the
brick date of A.D. 1061. It contains a double spiral staircase. Another
twelfth century free-standing minaret is at the far end of the same
street, on the outskirts of the town, just outside the recently walled
Masjid-i Jumeh[71] which is being restored. The minaret with its many
bands of varied raised brickwork patterns, and brick inscriptions in
both Kufic and Naskhi, is dated A.D. 1110–11, and is probably the finest
of all Saljuq minarets. The gateway leading to the mosque is locked,
but the key is usually kept at the Masjid-i Maidan. The mihrab room
of the Masjid-i Jumeh is also of Saljuq foundation (A.D. 1110–11),
but was rebuilt by the Mongols; the remaining structure is Safavid.[71,129]

Alcohol is not normally served in Saveh chai khanehs, but just outside
the town on the left of the Tehran road, a retired Gendarmerie Captain
has opened a good chai khaneh, the Karun-i No, where excellent
Persian food and hard drinks were obtained in 1974.

There is a good road from Saveh (144 km.) westwards to Ravan on the
Hamadan highway, and a new petrol station about half-way along. A
fine example of a fortified stone Saljuq caravanserai can be seen about
96 km. from Saveh and some 10 km. before the village of Robat-i
Karim, after which it is named. It stands on the west of the road across
the railway track, and is probably late twelfth or early thirteenth
century, with remains of a mosque and water tank in the courtyard.

The highway to Tehran continues north for another 41 km., entering
the capital by the old Qazvin road in the southern quarter. On the way
one passes Shahriyar and Kenargard villages from which one can visit
the Sassanian fire altars at Takht-e Rustam (p. 60) and the prehistoric
tepes of Kara and Kaleh Dasht (p. 60).

7 · Khurasan

There are two highways from Tehran to Khurasan, both about the same length, but the better-surfaced and that used by the long-distance buses is the newer, northern route via Gurgan. The most interesting, however, is the southern road which follows the old caravan route, via Semnan, Damghan and Sabzavar, about 875 km. to Mashad, along what is at the time of writing a rather bad road.

There is an increasingly popular air service and a daily (overnight) train service to Mashad, a city housing the most sacred of all Muslim shrines in Iran, the Mausoleum of Imam Reza, the Eighth Imam.

Winter lasts a long time in Khurasan which is often cut off by heavy rains and snow. The area has also been devastated by severe earthquakes, not to mention countless invasions from Central Asia—the southern highway being the continuation of the old royal highway and the Silk Road to the Orient.

Probably the best time to visit this area is in late summer and early autumn when parts of the route along the edge of the desert may still be hot and dusty, but are negotiable.

From Tehran take the Damavand road (p. 61) to Firuzkuh, 137 km., or one can reach Semnan (220 km.) avoiding Firuzkuh and leaving Tehran on the Ray (p. 47) road. By going this way one passes through the 'Caspian Gates' of classical literature, just after Ivan-i Kay at 78 km. The Firuzkuh road, skirting the extinct volcano of Damavand, is really magnificent with its views of turquoise rivers and thick woods; Firuzkuh itself, a charming village strategically placed at the entrance to a narrow gorge, may be of Sassanian origin and the mountain peaks around are topped with ruined forts, some probably dating from the tenth century, the Dailamite period. Many of these castles were captured and used by the Assassins, and one of these guards the entrance to the gorge.

A left turn at the railway line would take you along an old mountain road to Shahi (p. 65) and the Caspian, passing the turns for the tomb-towers of Lajim and Resget (p. 63). Turning off the main road to the right, however, across the railway line, the next town of note you reach is Semnan, 82 km. from Firuzkuh and set in the midst of orchards. This too was probably of Sassanian origin and was an important

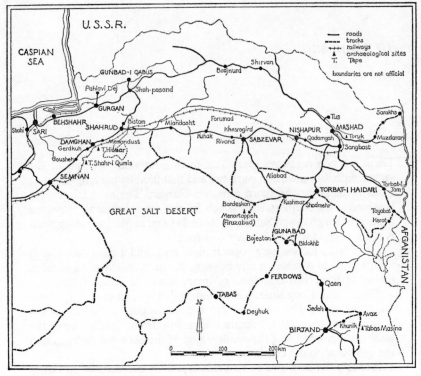

Map 7. Khurasan

staging post on the main caravan route to Central Asia. It was a Daila-
mite centre in the tenth century A.D. In 1036, Ghuzz Turkoman raiders
destroyed the town ramparts, but by 1046 they were rebuilt; sacked by
Mongols and Timurids, the town managed to survive after each crisis.
Some authorities believe the local dialect of Semnan to be a relic of Old
Pahlavi.

There is a comfortable Government Tourist Inn at Semnan, well
signposted and on the right of the main entry road. Other smaller
provincial hotels include the Talari, a little further along the main
highway, on the left.

There are many Imamzadehs in and around the town and a number
of interesting monuments including a charming Qajar city gate, the top
of which can be seen from the balcony of the Tourist Inn. A covered
bazaar and several mosques and shrines of post-Saljuq date are here,
and the remains of the mud-brick citadel can be seen rising in the
southern portion of the town. The swaying minaret of the Masjid-i
Jumeh, just inside the covered bazaar, can be entered by a small door
in the prayer hall of the mosque, to the right of the entrance, and it is

worth while asking permission to climb to the top for a superb view of the town and its surroundings. The minaret probably dates from the first half of the eleventh century A.D. and it is the only known Saljuq monument here. The mosque itself, repaired by one of Tamurlane's sons, was probably built on the foundations of a very early Ummayid mosque.

From Semnan you can take a round-about route, retracing your tracks as far as Firuzkuh, up to Shahi and Sari, then east to Gurgan (p. 66) and Gunbad-i Qabus (p. 69) and back through the mountains to Shahrud on the main southern highway, about 350 km. by this route.

Continuing directly east, however, and taking the desert road to Jandaq about 10 km. south-east of Semnan, cross the railway line for the small village of 'Ala. The top of a hitherto undocumented minaret first noted by Mr. Antony Hutt of the British Institute of Persian Studies, Tehran, in 1970 can be seen above the rooftops, standing some 10·25 m. high. It is similar in style to the minaret in Semnan in that it has no central column, the inner staircase revolving around itself, and Mr. Hutt believes that it may date from the twelfth century A.D.

Return to the main Khurasan highway which for a while runs along the edge of the Dasht-i Kavir (the Great Salt Desert), reaching Damghan after 114 km. On the way, by the village of Ahuvan, you see two serais, one on the north of the road in good condition, the other, on the south, is probably Safavid or older. About 40 km. further on another fine serai stands on the south-east of Gousheh hamlet, and from here a track runs for some 5 km. to intersect with another leading to the first major Parthian site examined in the north-east of Iran, that of Shahr-i Qumis.

Alternatively you can continue along the main highway for another 3 km. from which point the outlines of several mounds can be seen about 6 km. across-country to the south. A signpost in Farsi indicates a dirt road towards them and 3 km. after passing the junction of the path from Gousheh, another track leads directly west to the site, about 1 km.

Shahr-i Qumis has been reduced by flash floods but still sprawls across an area of some 7 × 4 km., the surface littered with sherds from the Saljuq to Iron Age periods. Mr. David Stronach and Mr. John Hansman carried out excavations on at least two large structures here.[80]

Early first century B.C. pottery and coins of the Parthian period were found in the vaulted mud-brick chambers that came to be used for funerary purposes, (Mound VII). These contained at least three forms of mud-brick vaults plastered over, with pointed and rounded arches of long mud-bricks. Here a strange type of burial was found in which human and horse skulls were mixed along with bones of various animals

7

including dogs, gazelles and pigs, all exposed before burial. A small cache of coins dated the burials to close on 70 B.C.

Parthian structures, including a fortified house, were followed by a short-lived Saljuq settlement destroyed in the Mongol invasion. The size of the city and its location on the highway linking Mesopotamia with Central Asia and India, suggest that it might be the site of the Parthian capital known to the Greeks as Hecatompylos, 'The City of 100 Gates'. Hecatompylos was one of the principal cities of eastern Iran, and it is recorded that it was there that Alexander of Macedon made his famous speech to his army saying that they would not return home but continue their march to the East.

About 2 km. from the centre of the original Parthian settlement is an enormous mud-brick monument some 56 m. in diameter. It is known locally as the Nagareh Khaneh, 'the house of the kettle-drum', and bears certain similarities in its plan to the round burial tomb of the same name excavated by Schmidt near Ray (p. 48). Also known as the Naranj Qaleh, 'the Tangerine castle' (probably on account of its upper radiating rooms), this building has yielded fine Saljuq pottery and was probably burnt during the Mongol invasion, (Mound I).

Another Parthian structure, Mound VI, some 50 × 30 m. in area, had the remains of six projecting towers, a large courtyard and a series of long, ground-floor rooms; in other seemingly secondary locations the work also revealed separate horse skull and human skull burials. The plan is not unlike that of other fortified mansions of the first centuries B.C. and A.D. that are found as far east as the region of the Oxus.[81]

One Sassanian grave was discovered in an upper chamber of one of the external towers of site VI, dated to the late sixth century A.D. by a coin of Hormizd IV. The very varied grave goods proved to include textiles, one of them with a fine rosette pattern, and others with chequered or striped design. (*See Appendix for sketch plan of site.)

Continuing eastwards along the highway to Damghan, 35 km., the cylindrical mountain of Gerdkuh can be seen almost all the way, on the left of the road ahead. This famous Assassin castle mentioned in Firdausi's epic Shahnama, and also by Marco Polo, was the centre from which the Assassins paralysed the entire district until the castle was finally taken in A.D. 1256 by the Mongols, led by Hulagu Khan (some say after a siege lasting 27 years and begun by Chinghis Khan). The easiest place from which to reach it is the village of Qadratabad, 15 km. before Damghan, and about the same distance from Gerdkuh to the north. Go through the village and out the other side and take the second rural track after the village, to the north. For this one needs a four-wheel drive. The track leads to a sizeable village, beyond which you have to pick your way across the open plain to the foot of the mountain, where the remains of a double curtain wall stand, said to have been built by the Mongols during their siege. There is a small tepe with some fortifications on it, to the right, and a gatehouse at the foot of the cliff. Go round to the east side of the mountain and here a track exists in parts, entailing a fairly stiff climb up to the top.

On the top are the remains of water cisterns, fortifications and part of the façade of a multi-storeyed residence. It is said that the besieged did not lack food or water, but had to surrender only when their clothes wore out. Half-way up the southern slope are rock-cut constructions popularly known as the Prison of Darius, while at the north-eastern foot of the cliff is a pile of mangonal balls used during the siege. Gerdkuh itself was probably fortified even before the Assassins, its earliest name being Diz-i Gonbadan.

The town of Damghan goes back to at least a very early Islamic date and in spite of its destruction and conquest by the Mongols, by Tamurlane, the Afghans and Nadir Shah it still contains a number of ancient buildings including what is accepted generally as the oldest mosque in Iran, the Tarik Khana (or Tari Khana). It is also known as the Masjid-i Chehel-Sotun ('forty columns'), and was founded about A.D. 760.

To reach this you turn right from the main square, Maidan-i Shishom Bahman, along a broad new road, on the right of which you can see the distinctive and very beautiful detached Saljuq minaret built in A.D. 1026–9 to replace an earlier square minaret that probably collapsed in a ninth century earthquake. The top of the existing minaret, with its many and varied brick patterns, has been damaged by lightning, but repaired.

Just south of the minaret, and separated from it by a modern wall, is the entrance to the ancient Tarik Khana, strongly reminiscent of a Sassanian building with its massive round columns, recently restored in part. It was probably badly damaged during the mid-twelfth century A.D. Turkoman invasion, and then restored on exactly the original Arab plan by the Saljuqs. An almost square courtyard is surrounded by arcades of tunnel vaults supported by brick piers nearly 2 m. in diameter and about 3·5 m. high. The slightly pointed arches are the first recorded in Islamic Iran but in many respects the burnt bricks and the columns are identical in size to those of the Sassanian palace at Tepe Hissar, 5 km. south-east of Damghan (p. 196).

This majestically simple mosque[67a] has been described as 'one of the most magnificent buildings in Islam'. The mihrab is at the back of the deeper, qibla wall with the minbar to its right, and worshippers can still be seen in this ancient building.

Back along the road towards the centre of the town, a small alley on

the right takes one into the narrow streets leading to the Masjid-i
Jumeh, also known as the Masjid-i Imam Hasan, which has been
rebuilt, leaving only its lovely Saljuq minaret, which probably dates
from the eleventh century although no date has yet been deciphered.
This too was struck by lightning in 1932 and has been repaired.

If you continue away from the town, down the narrow lane from the
Masjid-i Jumeh's covered entrance, you will soon reach a delightful
tomb-tower known as the Pir-i Alamdar, built in A.D. 1021 and the
oldest of its type south of the Alburz mountains.

A fine Kufic inscription in brick surrounds the base of the flat dome
which was probably originally covered by a conical roof. Round the
inside of the dome there is possibly the masterpiece of painted Kufic
inscriptions in Iran.

Return to the main square and the Kh. Pahlavi from which a short
turning takes you into a courtyard where there are three buildings, with
a fourth at the rear. On the right, at the far end, is the so-called Khanegah or Darvish monastery of Shah Rukh. Despite its Timurid inscription, the building is of Saljuq origin. Its interior has a dado of dark
green tiles comparable with Timurid work at Mashad. Of the two
other shrines in this courtyard, one of them, beside the Khanegah, is
the Imamzadeh Ja'far, again a building of Saljuq origin (there is
another, undated Imamzadeh Ja'far 8 km. outside the town to the
south). The third building, on the left as you enter the courtyard, is the
Imamzadeh Muhammad.

Walk round the back of the Khanegah of Shah Rukh and you will
find another circular Saljuq tomb-tower very similar to the Pir-i Alamdar. This is the Chehel Dukhtaran ('forty maidens'), also with a fine
Kufic brick inscription just below the dome, and was built by order of
Abu Shuja Isfahani in A.D. 1054–5 (446 Hegira).

There is a small provincial hotel, the Shahrdari, in Kh. Pahlavi.

To reach the celebrated site of Tepe Hissar, about 6 km. south-east of
Damghan, drive to the end of the road past the Tarik Khana to a track
on the left, running alongside the railway line which actually cuts a
section of the main mound to the south-east of an Islamic fortified
caravanserai. The smaller section on the north of the railway line is the
site of a Burnt Building[40], probably a fortified manor house, attacked
and destroyed at the end of the IIIB period. Here were found many
flint arrowheads and charred victims of the battle. (*Tepe Hissar:
sketch map and revised dating).

One of the key sites of this area, painted pottery from which was
discovered in 1880, Tepe Hissar was precisely located by Herzfeld in
1925 and dug by Schmidt in 1931–32 when over 1,600 prehistoric
burials were found, as well as the Sassanian palace.[139,140]

The main levels of the tepe date from *c.* 3500 B.C. down to *c.* 1700 B.C., and the third and second millennium strata of Hissar III may be said to have posed some of the larger problems of Iranian archaeology concerning the origin and dating of certain sophisticated metal products and techniques. Among the many metal finds here were five delicately wrought heads of moufflon, made of gold foil and apparently intended as decoration to be sewn onto garments. These were part of a hoard of precious objects associated with the latest III settlement, dated *c.* 2000 B.C. Beautifully painted black-on-buff conical bowls, now in the Tehran Museum, date from about 3500 B.C. and show connections with Period II at Sialk several hundred miles to the south-west. Also from this early period were pottery goblets decorated in stylized black on buff.

South-west of the mounds and south-east of an Islamic caravanserai are the remains of the Sassanian palace, partially excavated by Schmidt in 1931 and built on true Chahar Taq lines. It is entered from a court-yard, through a great central ivan supported by six massive brick columns similar to those in the Tarik Khana, and leading to a square, domed hall behind. Although the stucco decoration of this building has been compared with supposedly early Sassanian stucco forms, a coin assigned to Kavad I seems to show that the palace flourished at least in the first half of the sixth century A.D.

Rejoin the main road to Shahrud by taking a track north-west and some 21 km. further east, just off the road to the south of Mehmandust (which was the scene of Nadir Shah's victory over the Afghans in 1729), you will find a tomb-tower with decorated brick designs and a Kufic inscription dated A.D. 1096. Drive along a track between houses and a stream, but be warned that the path is often cut by deep irrigation ditches. The tower stands on the outskirts of the little town.

Shahrud, some 62 km. from Damghan, is a pleasant, modern little town on the railway line to Mashad, set amid woods and rich orchards and farmland at the foot of the Alburz mountains. There is now a comfortable Tourist Inn which provides accommodation with private bath and food at reasonable rates. It is on the left of the main road from Tehran, just before the crossroads leading to Sabzevar and Shah-pasand, outside the town. A good, inexpensive Persian meal with musical accompaniment can be had at the Colbeh Restaurant on the right of the road leading to Gurgan and the Caspian. Some 5 km. north of Shahrud along this road is the charming walled village of Bistam (pronounced Bastom), probably founded during the reign of the Sassanian king Khusraw II in A.D. 590.

The mud-brick walls of Bistam with their cylindrical bastions lie to the left of the Gurgan–Shah-pasand (120 km.) road.

On the southern outskirts of the village, by open land, is the Friday
Mosque adjoining a fluted tomb-tower built in A.D. 1313. The tomb-
tower is known as the Kashaneh and is the last of the great circular
fluted towers such as the Gunbad-i Qabus (p. 69) and Ray (p. 47)
towers and was built by Muhammad of Damghan. The mosque, founded in the Saljuq period, was restored in 1306 but the stucco mihrabs
in the cloister, and also in the Mongol mosque in the cluster of buildings
to the north, both date from the Mongol period.

The only Saljuq portion remaining among the southern group of
buildings is the very ornate brick minaret dated A.D. 1120, although part
of the adjoining mosque is also Saljuq. The two conical towers, several
tombs and small shrines with stucco mihrabs, and a madrasseh, all
grouped around a pleasant courtyard, are mainly early fourteenth
century. They are connected with Bistam's most famous son, the Sufi
Sheikh Bayazid who died in A.D. 874 and whose tomb is said to be the
one standing in the courtyard of the complex. (*Tepe Sang-e Čaxamaq.)

Turn back now to Shahrud and follow the Mashad highway to
Sabzevar, about 250 km. to the east. This time-honoured route along
the edge of the desert can be extremely dusty and hot. It has remained
almost unchanged for the last thousand years, but its monotony is
broken at Miandasht, about 114 km. from Shahrud, where the desert
really begins, and where, on the north of the road, is a splendid and
enormous, well-preserved caravanserai consisting of three separate but
communicating Safavid serais, well worth inspection.

About 70 km. further on, just by the hamlet of Kuhak, a rough track
goes north across the plain towards the mountains for some 25 km.,
following the line of the old Silk Road to China. It passes through the
enchanting little town of Forumad, famed during the Saljuq and Mongol periods for its important library and hospital. Here are the remains
of the richly decorated 2-ivan Friday Mosque typical of north-eastern
Iran, and built, it is said, on the site of an important fire temple. The
ruins of the splendid stucco decorations, said to have been too ornate
for prayers made there to be pleasing to God, stand now romantically
entwined by creepers and trees, and are mainly Il-Khanid, of the
mid-thirteenth century. Probably some parts of the mosque date from
the Saljuq period. (*Forumad.) Retrace the track to the main highway and, after passing an attractive serai at Mehr, the next monument of interest is the minar of Khosrogird dated A.D. 1111 on the left
of the road between Rivand and Sabzevar. This well-preserved, beautiful brick minaret, some 30 m. high, stands on a platform and is all that
remains of the twelfth century capital of the district, destroyed by the
Mongols.

Sabzevar, 9 km. further on, is a fairly modern town of caravanserais.

It became the capital of the district after the destruction of Khosrogird. Before this, the town was known as Bayhaq and was renamed in the thirteenth century. The Mongols destroyed it in A.D. 1221, and it was sacked again by Tamurlane in 1381 and yet again by the Afghans in 1723. To the north of the Masjid-i Pamenar, near the police headquarters, is a Saljuq minaret about 15½ m. high, with the ruins of an ivan attached.

Among the many small hotels here, the Arya on the main street appears to offer clean, reasonable accommodation.

From Sabzevar the road is now asphalted, climbing through barren hills and then across a wide plain with patches of cultivation. To the north-east are the famous turquoise mines of Nishapur and in the country around this town, so closely associated with the poet-mathematician-astronomer, Omar Khayyam, are many orchards and crumbling ruins.

Nishapur, 114 km. from Sabzevar, offers accommodation in a Government Tourist Inn right on the old highway running through the middle of the town. Nishapur itself is modern and virtually nothing remains of the ancient city of Sassanian origin. Its name probably derives from 'Niv Shahpur', 'the Good Deed of Shahpur', i.e. Shahpur II who rebuilt the city founded by his ancestor, Shahpur I, after its destruction by an earthquake. Yazdigird II made it his chief place of residence in the fifth century A.D. and it is generally believed that the Adhar Burzin Mihr, the sacred fire of the agriculturalists, was kept in a so far unlocated shrine in the mountains to the north-west of Nishapur. Other authorities, however, believe the sacred fire may have been in the Mihr Zamin plain south-west of Tehran (p. 190).

Probably destroyed and rebuilt more often than any other city in Iran, Nishapur, capital of the area, was the wealthiest city in the country during the ninth century A.D., after its capture by the Arabs in 651, when it was called Shahr-i Iran. By the end of the tenth century, it was producing some of the most attractive ceramics of the period. In A.D. 1037, Tughril Beg, the first Saljuq king, made Nishapur his capital and a centre of intellectual activity, with thirteen large libraries and one of the only two universities that accepted students from all parts of the then-known civilized world. Under the Saljuq Sultan, Malik Shah, and his famous Grand Vizier, Nizam al-Mulk, Omar Khayyam (who was born in Nishapur between A.D. 1038 and 1048, and died there in A.D. 1123) spent many years helping to compile a new solar calendar, the Jalali, which had an error of only one day in 5,000 years, as well as in establishing an observatory.

His tomb, an unusual modern edifice built in 1934 on the site of the original tomb, lies in a garden surrounding the seventeenth century

Imamzadeh of Muhammad Mahruq, about 4 km. south-east of Nishapur. Leaving the town on the main road for Mashad, you come to a
'falakeh', a roundabout; turn down a short road to the gardens and trees
which can be seen ahead on the left. There is a small entrance fee which
includes admission to the little museum in the grounds.

This is the area of old Nishapur, so thoroughly destroyed by the
Mongols that even cats and dogs were exterminated, and the entire city
ploughed into the ground. A little to the north of Omar's tomb is a
mound called Sabz Pushan which was partly excavated by the Metropolitan Museum of Art, New York, during the 1930s. Important
ceramics and stucco dating from ninth and tenth centuries A.D.[106]
formed a link between the Abbassid and Saljuq styles and more work
revealing much fine pottery of the same period was carried out on Tepe
Madrasseh, which lies close to the Imamzadeh of Farid-ud-din Attar,
1 km. south-west of Omar Khayyam's tomb, along a short, specially
built road immediately opposite the garden entrance.[82]

Farid-ud-din Attar was a mystic poet of vast productivity and renown
and, like his father, was a practising chemist. He was killed at the time
of the first Mongol invasion, c. A.D. 1221, when he is said to have run
for some distance after being beheaded by his Mongol captor, who, full
of remorse, built a tomb on the spot where the poet finally fell. The
present tomb is a seventeenth century building, restored in 1934, and
stands in a charming formal garden tended by a Darvish. The twentieth
century poet Kamal al-Mulk is also buried here, his unusual shell-like
mausoleum being designed by Professor Seihoon, the architect of Omar
Khayyam's mausoleum.

From Nishapur to Mashad you drive about 112 km. along a good
asphalt road, and several charming shrines lie on or near it. All are of
Safavid date although that of Qadamgah, about 28 km. from Nishapur
at the village of Mahmudabad, contains what is believed by the
faithful to be the footprints of the ninth century saint, Imam Reza.
Mahmudabad is a charming village of Sayyeds and the shrine is on a
small hill reached by a wide, shady turning on the left (north), in the
middle of the village. There is a very well-preserved and interesting
Safavid caravanserai on the left of this path.

At 72 km. there is a turning off to the right which goes south to
Torbat-i Haidariyeh and on to Sistan and Baluchistan.

About 4 km. after this, a diversion on the south of the road brings
you to Sangbast and the magnificent Saljuq mausoleum attributed to
Arslan Jadhib, Governor of the province and adviser to Mahmud of
Ghazni, but it is probably of early twelfth century date.[131]

The mausoleum and minaret can be seen among low mounds to the
south of the road which is now the Asian Highway. Close to a point

where the railway track crosses the Highway and the old Nishapur road forks to the right, a signpost points along a dirt track to Farimat and eventually links up with the road to Torbat-i Jam and Herat. The route to the monuments is apt to vary in bad weather and sometimes involves crossing the river bed, but it should be possible to drive direct to Sangbast from the main road.

The mausoleum stands among the ruins of many caravanserais and a recently deserted settlement, where the ground is thickly littered with potsherds. The tomb and its adjoining minaret—locally called the Mil-i Ayaz after the favourite slave of Sultan Mahmud—have been restored. The massive brick dome and four portals continue a style inherited from Sassanians, according to Pope,[128,129] and the interior Kufic inscriptions in brickwork, together with the various types of decorative brickwork in the dome and squinches, make this an exceptionally interesting building. It is possible that there was a high gallery at the base of the dome. The lone minaret, with its fine brickwork, may have been one of a pair originally attached to a mosque now long disappeared, and cannot be later than A.D. 1028. It can be climbed although the staircase is in bad condition.

The main highway branches north for Mashad and continues on south and east for Baluchistan and Afghanistan. To the left of the highway, about 17 km. from Mashad where a signpost in Persian and with a blue arrow points up a dirt track, less than 1 km. will bring you to the source of a spring, and a cluster of trees in a crack in the mountain. Here is the shrine of Khwaja Murad, in what was a delightful setting, a short footpath leading to the shrine itself, built against the mountain, with a little garden before it. The path is often lined with Rozeh Khans, dignified gentlemen in black or white turbans, who are professional narrators of the religious tragedies of the Karbala, for Khwaja Murad himself was one of the first narrators of the martyrdom of Imam Reza (p. 202). (Alas, the shrine has been recently modernized.)

Harsamat ibn Aiyin, called locally Khwaja Murad, 'Fulfiller of Vows', died in A.D. 832, only fifteen years after Imam Reza. His mausoleum has been restored but apart from the many pilgrims, particularly Baluchis and darvishes, picnicking under the trees, in an atmosphere which even the unsightly new café cannot really spoil it is interesting to learn that local farmers bring part of their harvest as offerings to the shrine.

About 3 km. further along the road, this time on the right, there is another mausoleum which is a restored Safavid building over the tomb of Khwaja Abbasalt Haravi, who is said to have been present at Imam Reza's death bed and who died about A.D. 851. His tomb attracts many devout pilgrims.

7*

Then, about 6 km. before reaching Mashad, over a bridge across the river Toruk, a track branches off to the right. Originally this went north-east to Sarakhs and the Afghan frontier.

Toruk in Arabic means 'cross-roads' and the trade routes from the Middle East, Central Asia, India and Afghanistan all met here. Consequently it was the site of many great caravanserais, a few of which, dating from the Safavid period, can be seen in the district. The forlorn remains of a fifteenth century Musalla (open-air oratory), whose ground plan is said to have been similar to that of the great hall of Shahpur's palace at Nishapur, stand in a field not far from a sugar-beet factory and a yakchawl which can be seen from the main highway.

From the outskirts of Mashad, near the petrol station standing in front of a picturesque ruined Ribat (fortified serai), the golden dome over the tomb of Imam Reza can be seen, and about 5 km. from the city, the Asian Highway passes a Government Tourist Camp.

Mashad, bitterly cold in winter and often cut off by snow and rains from all land communications, is surrounded by orchards and generally thought of as a holy city whose only interest lies in what has been described as 'probably the greatest concentration of religious buildings in the world'.[158]

It was built on the site of the village of Sanabad where the eighth Shi'ite Imam, Reza, died after eating grapes in A.D. 817. He was the son-in-law of Caliph Ma'mun who was the son of Harun al-Rashid (the famous caliph who himself died in Sanabad in A.D. 809). Imam Reza, whose father prophesied his murder, is believed by most Shi'ites to have been poisoned by Ma'mun. The Caliph, however, built a handsome mausoleum over the Imam's grave, close to his own father's tomb. Since it was said that a pilgrimage to Imam Reza's tomb would equal 70,000 pilgrimages to Mecca, Sanabad soon grew into a city whose name, Mashad, means 'the place of the Martyr'. There are now a number of good hotels including the air-conditioned Hotel Sina in the Falakeh Shomali on the perimeter of the sacred precincts and from whose roof views of the shrine can be taken, using a telephoto lens. The Sina also has a pleasant restaurant. Other hotels further from the shrine include the Pars and Bakhtiar, both in Kh. Pahlavi, and the Iran. By far the best hotel I have encountered in Iran, for comfort, food and service, is the de luxe Mashad Hyatt in Kh. Farah, opened in 1974. One can also stay by arrangement at the Electricity Club whose food, rooms and service were formerly the best and most expensive in Mashad. This is outside the town, near the attractive new Arya Mehr Park. The Kuh-i Sangi, on the hills overlooking the city, is an excellent place for lunch. (Unless regulations are relaxed in the future, it is forbidden to sell alcohol in the Holy City.) There are plans to build more hotels here, and to demolish and rebuild the entire area at present surrounding the Sacred Precincts.

The original mausoleum over Imam Reza's tomb was destroyed by Sabuktagin but rebuilt by Mahmud of Ghazni in A.D. 1009. It was later covered with tiles, some of them still visible in the innermost dome chamber, but the Mongols sacked the city in A.D. 1220 and most of the oldest part of the sacred complex now dates from the fourteenth century restoration by Oljeitu Khodabandeh. In addition to the shrine and various sanctuaries, there are two mosques and five madrassehs, as well as other buildings. Make inquiries at the Tourist Office concerning visits to the Sacred Precincts. In any event, it should be noted that in this city that attracts pilgrims from all parts of the Muslim world, dress should be ultra-discreet; long sleeves, stockings, and sober colours are strongly recommended.

The museum attached to the Sacred Precincts, and reached through a garden at the side of the lovely Gowhar Shad Mosque, contains among other exhibits an enormous, carved stone basin dated A.D. 1201 and some eighth to tenth century ceramics and metalwork.

Lively, covered bazaars offering Khurasan's famous sheepskin coats, velvets and turquoises, the latter cut and polished in the bazaars, surround the shrine and precincts in a huge circle. There are other interesting mosques and monuments in Mashad, but all of later date than Saljuq.

The ruins of the old city of Tus, important long before Mashad came into existence, lie about 26 km. along a road to the north-west, branching off right at 20 km. from the main northern route to the Caspian.

On the left of the road to Tus, about a kilometre from the ruins, is a massive mausoleum known as the Harunieh and locally supposed to be the tomb of Harun al-Rashid. In fact it is probably the tomb of the mystic poet el-Ghazali who died in A.D. IIII. With its Sassanian-type dome on squinches and deep vertical exterior channels, it is similar to the early Islamic Jabel-i Sang at Kirman (p. 266) but Pope[128,129] believed it was probably built in the early fourteenth century, while Herzfeld[89,90] thought it was begun by the Saljuqs before the Mongol invasion. Recent studies by Robert Hillenbrand have led him to the belief that a still earlier date could be defended for the central dome chamber and that the façade is no later than the Saljuq period. Professor J. M. Rogers favours the later date.[131]

The remains of the citadel of Tus lie on a mound to the left of the gardens at the end of the road. The modern mausoleum of the epic poet Firdausi who was born in Tus in the early tenth century A.D. is set in the midst of the gardens close to the citadel mounds.

Another tomb which attracts many pilgrims is that of Khwaja

Ra'abi, a disciple of one of the Companions of the Prophet Mohammad, and the leader of 4,000 armed men who went to the aid of Imam Ali. Ra'abi 'ibn Khothaym is buried in a shady garden about 6 km. to the north of Mashad, along a good main road which is a continuation of Kh. Pahlavi. His original tomb was visited by Imam Reza but was rebuilt by Shah Abbas the Great in 1617–18—its design is said to have inspired the architect of the Taj Mahal at Agra.

An ancient caravan road which connected Khurasan with Samarkand and Merv leads north-east from Mashad to the Afghan and Soviet frontiers, just before which are two splendid ribats or fortified caravan-serais. It is necessary to apply to the Ministry of Culture in Mashad, or at the Tourist Office, having brought suitable letters of introduction from the Archaeological Service in Tehran, for permission to visit the area. The road is perfectly good for a normal car in dry weather and the first of the monuments, a fortified caravanserai originally called Ribat Sahi, now known as Ribat-i Mahi, can easily be visited from Mashad, without a special permit.

This lies less than a kilometre to the left of the road, some 83 km. from Mashad, near Ismailabad village, and is identified by a small tower standing on a hill immediately behind it. In summer one can take a Land-Rover right to the site, crossing a dry but muddy river bed. This caravanserai of probable late eleventh-century date still has fragments of elaborate stucco decoration and was first noted by Godard (Ref. *Athar-e Iran*, IV, 1949), but not visited by him. It was photographed in 1966 by Derek Hill (see *Islamic Architecture and its Decoration*, D. Hill and O. Graber, 1967), and surveyed in 1969 by Antony Hutt, (ref. *Iran*, Vol. VIII, 1970). The remains of other early serais can also be seen along this route, which crosses part of the Turkoman Steppe in the area of the frontier town of Sarakhs, where one must present the permit to the Governor.

By arrangement with the latter it may be possible to spend the night at the Government Guest House. There is an interesting fourteenth century monument, the Gonbad-i Sheikh Luqman, in Sarakhs, and a more essential petrol station.

With written permission from the Governor, one returns some 57 km. back along the main Mashad road to a gendarme post, picking up a military guide here for the cross-country drive of some 6 km. to Ribat-i Sharaf. This magnificent complex standing in splendid isolation among the hills, was possibly built about A.D. 1120 and restored in A.D. 1154 according to J. M. Rogers.[131] It was very probably a palace with an outer and inner courtyard, both having four ivans and both equipped as mosques, each with a stucco mihrab still *in situ*. Elaborate stucco decoration and brickwork, and subtle patterns produced by the decorated stamped plaster joints, make this an outstanding Saljuq monument.

Some distance further east of the road between Ribat-i Mahi and Sarakhs, there are two small Saljuq towers or foundations of a cere-monial arch, known as the Do Baradar or Barar (Two Brothers), lying in a saddle of the ridge of mountains between the ruined palace Ribat-i Sharaf and the village of Muzduran on the main road. They are c. 12 km. from Chekudar village and were first noted by William Murrie Clevenger.[20]

A number of caves have been surveyed in the mountains around Mashad by Dr. Charles McBurney of the University of Cambridge, including a very large one high above the village of Moghan.[98]

South-east of Mashad, about 90 km. from the junction with the main Tehran road, we can see what some authorities believe to be the earliest known domed fire temple. This is the third century Sassanian structure called Baz-i Hur[68] standing on a rugged mound a short distance past a group of houses (Ribat-i Safid) on the road to Torbat-i Haidariyeh. The monument stands about 100 m. east of the road; wood, in a poor condition, can still be seen in the angles of the room; the remains of what was probably a surrounding wall can be found at the rear.[176]

The route to Sistan, south of the junction with the Tehran road, is dusty gravel, but in dry weather practicable for ordinary cars. The first sizeable town is Torbat-i Haidariyeh (well known for its felt mats), set in a fertile valley of cotton fields, surrounded by jagged mountains. From here a gravel road leads via Khaf, south-east to Tayabad near the Afghan frontier, served by local buses. About 6 km. past Torbat-i Haidariyeh is Khargird, a village with an enormous tepe on the north and opposite, the splendid fifteenth century Timurid Madrasseh Ghiassieh. The village also contains the scant remnants of a sun-dried brick Nizamiya, a four-ivan Saljuq Madrasseh-mosque built about A.D. 1154.[71] (*See Appendix for Sangan-i Pa'in, Zawzan, Tayabad, Kerat and Torbat-i Shaikh Jam.)

Continuing now along the main Zahidan road to the village of Shadmehr, you can divert and branch right (west) to the small town of Kashmar, about 57 km. There are a number of interesting monuments in the vicinity (ask for up-to-date information about roads from the local Minister of Education representative in Kashmar). Among others is a beautiful pre-Mongol minaret in the village of Firuzabad, also called Menar Tappeh. This is reached by first going to Bardeskan, about 50 km. west of Kashmar, and then taking a guide for the very bad track south-west. The minar shaft has an unusual inscription in brick, which has to be read sideways; the tepe alongside it probably contains the remains of the old town.

From Bardeskan there is a track north to Sabzevar on the Tehran road, but this is not recommended.

About 30 km. south of Kashmar, also, are a rock-cut road and the Qaleh-i Dukhtar, a much-ruined Assassin castle. The road south from Kashmar to Ferdows is a good, asphalted one—about 230 km.—and the town, which was very badly damaged in the 1968 earthquake, still has enough left of its ancient Masjid-i Jumeh to allow one to appreciate the original quality of its incised brickwork and red plaster. Most of the single, arched ivan remains and Robert Hillenbrand suggests a date of around A.D. 1200 for this.[92] There is no hotel in Ferdows but it is possible to stay at the new Municipal Guest House, if one asks the permission of the Mayor to do so.

From Ferdows several ancient caravan routes spread out to cross the great Dasht-i Kavir, the main one being to Tabas, formerly Golshan, known as the 'Queen of the Desert', about 190 km. away. Also known as the Gateway to Khurasan, it is surrounded by many palms and fruit trees and was the first Khurasan town to fall to the Muslims. The road is reasonably good and a Government Tourist Inn provides comfortable accommodation.

The ruins of an eleventh century fortress built by Abu'l Hassan Ibn Mohammad Gilaki can be seen in the town; the Assassins captured Tabas and occupied the castle themselves in the second half of the eleventh century, but they in turn were routed at the beginning of the twelfth century by Sultan Sanjar.

Most important of the monuments in Tabas, whose architecture flourished in the Saljuq period, are the two Saljuq minarets, with their faience patterns, flanking the portal of a twelfth century A.D. Saljuq madrasseh, the Madrasseh-i Do Minar. A regular bus service and thrice-weekly Pars Air plane carrying mail and half a dozen passengers connects Tabas with Mashad, while a good gravel road runs westwards to Yazd (p. 177) about 400 km. The road passes several oases and ruined serais, but there is no petrol station, except for an uncertain supply of cans sometimes to be found at wayside halts. About half-way along, the road divides at Ribat-i Pusht Badam, the right-hand or northern track leading by a roundabout route to Nain (p. 175), nearly 400 km. from this point. The left-hand, south-westerly fork goes on to join the main Kashan road 27 km. north of Yazd.

From Shadmehr (the junction of the Kashmar-Mashad-Zahidan highway), the road continues south to Gunabad, where there is a large, well-signposted Government Tourist Inn on the left of the main road as you enter the town. Continue down the main road for 1 km. to the Saljuq Masjid-i Jumeh, built in the first quarter of the thirteenth century and closely related to the early Ferdows mosque, with fine Kufic inscriptions. There is another Assassin castle within 30 km., reached by taking the road to Gaysur, one of the Gunabad complex of villages, but inquire at the Tourist Inn for the latest details of road conditions. From Gunabad, a road to the west joins the Kashmar-Ferdows road, about 53 km., while close to Gunabad, the village of Mand is famed for its pottery.

Some 100 km. south of Gunabad the road passes through Qaen, badly damaged in the 1968 earthquake, within reach of which are some eight Assassin castles. Many prehistoric mounds and ruins are passed on this road; between Qaen and the next large village of Bidokht keep a look out for the village of Sedeh about 52 km. south of Qaen, from whence a track to the east goes to Avaz, 109 km. away. This s the jumping-off point for Tabas Masina, a town with an Assassin castle in the mountains to the south. Carleton S. Coon excavated a prehistoric cave in this area, in 1949, near the terraced village of Khunik, about half-way along the track between Asadabad and Birjand. Dr. Coon's findings showed that, about A.D. 700, new converts to Islam moved into this area and built their mud houses outside a rock shelter into which they threw their debris. The roof of a smaller cave higher up was broken during an earthquake and the fill washed out into the larger rock shelter below, on top of the Islamic material, which sequence gave rise to some puzzlement initially. The smaller, upper cave had been used by hunters in the last glacial period but their tools and weapons were found above the later Islamic debris.[24]

The next town of Birjand is built around the remains of a citadel mound overlooking a dry river bed, on the banks of which is an extensive graveyard with some interesting mausolea and a small shrine. The Tourist Inn is down a turning to the right of the main highway as it leaves the town to the south.

From Birjand to Zahidan (p. 273) or Zabol (p. 282) the road passes through barren hills and desert scenery with occasional mud-brick fortified villages and castles, and increasing numbers of Baluch communities.

8 · Fars (1)

If the traveller to Iran visited only the provinces of Khuzestan and Fars, he would have seen what is virtually the essential heart of Iranian history. Fars (ancient Parsa)—homeland of the Persians and the source of the name so often given to the entire land—contains not only an enormous number of prehistoric sites with nearly 1,000 identified in the Marv Dasht plain alone, but the major Achaemenian and Sassanian remains in the country. Most of them are easily reached by road.

There are daily commercial flights from Tehran to Shiraz, the logical centre for touring the province, and several flights a week from there to Bushire on the coast, and on from there via Kharg Island to Abadan, Ahwaz and back to Tehran. Roads are improving all the time, particularly those linking the developing coastal ports with Shiraz. Over much of this area range the colourful migratory Qashqai and kindred tribes, moving in springtime from their winter camps in the warm plains around Bishapur and Firuzabad up to the cooler hills north of Pasargadae, and back again in autumn.

Driving by the good main road from Tehran and stopping en route at Isfahan would entail two days' actual driving, the entire distance being about 930 km. Comfortable buses make the trip in about 15 hours including stops, an overnight journey being the most convenient. T.B.T. and Levantour have air-conditioned buses with toilets and offer tea and soft drinks while travelling.

With its international festivals of arts and music and increasing number of medical and other congresses (the Nemazi Hospital and Pahlavi University's Medical Centre are world-famous), Shiraz is rapidly acquiring more expensive hotels of the de luxe category, including the Government Kurush (Cyrus), and the International, both away from the town centre and charging from about 1,350 rials double. There is also a large Government Tourist Inn and Hotel with tennis courts and swimming pool on the airport road, and a Tourist Camp with Continental-type tents, washing and cooking facilities, and a pool, on the edge of town near the tomb of Hafez. In the town centre, the Park Hotel with air-conditioning and swimming pool, just off Karim Khan Zand behind the BBC bookshop, is recommended (about 950 rials double), and less pretentious but still comfortable hotels include the Grand in Kh. Rudaki, close by (about 550 double with bath and air-conditioning);

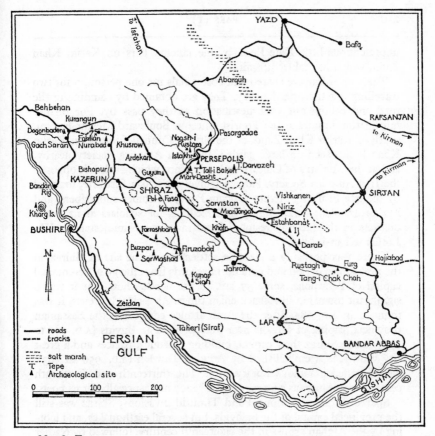

Map 8. Fars

cheaper still is the Ayra in Kh. Saadi (about 350 rials double with bath), with a roof terrace for summer dining. (Prices everywhere tend to increase annually.)

For eating out, Maxims in the Falakeh Gaz at the top of Mohammed Reza Shah Blvd., and the 103 in Kh. Anvari, south of Karim Khan Zand, are quite pleasant, but in 1974 there were as yet no restaurants of international standard. The Red Rose opposite the airport is popular in summer, as is the Shiraz Inn's garden restaurant by the pool. Meals and snacks can be had in clean surroundings, at the Milk Bar and Restaurant over the BBC bookshop on Karim Khan Zand.

One should not leave Shiraz without sampling the local Kholar wines, famous for centuries; most, but not all, are inclined to be sweet and do vary in quality but one sometimes finds a very acceptable white wine. For a delicious summer dessert try Faloudeh (or Paloudeh), an iced sweet served with fresh lime juice and highly recommended in the unpretentious little Kafe Reza, by the cinema Pars on Karim Khan Zand, which has tables upstairs.

Taxis in Shiraz are shared and cost 5 rials for one person, 7 for two travelling together, per journey. They are obtained by standing in the road and calling out your destination as they pass by. For further information inquire at the Tourist office on Boulevard Moshir Fatemi, south of Karim Khan Zand, at the British Council Library on Karim Khan Zand, set in a large garden, the Iran America Society nearby, and at the Ministry of Culture and Arts office which is almost opposite the Iran America Society. Pahlavi University's Asia Institute, founded by the late Professor Arthur Upham Pope, welcomes subscribers, and has an excellent small library and facilities for scholars at its head-quarters in the recently restored Zand mansion, Naranjestan, in Kh. Lotfala Khan-i Zand.

There was probably a sizeable settlement on the site of Shiraz in the prehistoric period and cuneiform records from the great ceremonial capital of Persepolis, some 57 km. to the north, show that it was a significant township in Achaemenian times. As a city, however, it was founded in A.D. 684, after the Arab armies conquered the Sassanian provincial capital of Istakhr near Persepolis. The Buyids (A.D. 945 to 1055) made Shiraz their capital, building mosques, palaces and a great city wall; it was embellished by Adud al-Dowleh (A.D. 950 to 983), who founded a famous library here. The thirteenth and fourteenth centuries saw Shiraz as a literary centre renowned especially for its poets.

Spared during the Mongol and Timurid invasions, Shiraz was still the provincial capital of the Safavids, but several earthquakes, and looting by the Afghan armies in the eighteenth century, followed by Nadier Shah's siege have resulted in the disappearance of almost all the pre-Muslim structures. Today most of the outstanding buildings of Shiraz date from the period when Karim Khan Zand made it his capital in the eighteenth century. A small museum was formerly housed in the charming little eighteenth century Pars Pavilion on Karim Khan Zand, and is expected to be rehoused in the Citadel (Arq) after alterations.

Just off Kh. Hafez in the Kh. Gowd-i Khazineh north of the river Khoshk there is a shrine originally built in the tenth century to house the remains of Shah Mir Hamzeh. It stands in a quiet courtyard entered from the street by a portico with beautiful carved wooden doors. An inscription said to have been carved by Tamurlane's grandson, Ibrahim, can be seen on a reddish stone in the portal.

The Masjid-i 'Atiq or Jumeh stands on the site of an earlier mosque founded about A.D. 890 by Amir ibn Layth (see Shahabad, p. 156). It was enlarged in the fourteenth century but the ivan through which the mihrab room is reached may be twelfth or thirteenth century. The

mosque is at the end of a courtyard in front of the Mausoleum of Shah
Cheragh which is on the maidan in the new Kh. Ahmadi in the south-
east quarter of the town. You pass also the Mausoleum of Mir Mohammad, brother of Ahmad who is buried in the Shah Cheragh shrine;
both were descendants of the Prophet Mohammad; reverent non-
Muslims may enter the modern shrines, ladies hiring chadors outside.

The unusual rectangular building in the centre of the 'Atiq courtyard is the Khudai Khaneh, 'House of God', which was built in the
fourteenth century and is said to imitate the Ka'bah in Mecca.

The New Mosque, in the same quarter, is one of the few pre-Mongol
structures in Shiraz and also one of the largest mosques in the country.
This is reached through a short lane on the west side of the Maidan-i
Ahmadi, leading directly into the huge, 100 × 200 m. courtyard, on
each side of which stands an ivan linked by cloister-like arcades decorated with mosaics. Practically all of this mosque was restored in the
Safavid period but originally it was the residential palace of a local ruler,
Sa'd Zangi (A.D. 1195 to 1226), and it was converted into a mosque
between A.D. 1201 and 1218 in thanks for the restored health of the
ruler's daughter. During this period, a poet named Mosteh-i-din lived
in a small house behind the mosque; he took his pen-name from his
patron and became known as Sa'adi. His tomb, a modern building in
an attractive garden on the east of Shiraz, is not far from that of another
famous poet, Hafez, who died about 1389. The road to the tombs,
like most places of interest in Shiraz, is well signposted.

Continuing past the tomb of Hafez and then past the Government
Tourist Camp, the road becomes a dirt-surfaced minor track which,
after about ten minutes' driving, passes the village of Abu Nasr, on a
hill to the left. The ruins on a hill just beyond the village are known
variously as Qasr-i Abu Nasr, or Takht-i Abu Nasr, or sometimes
Madar-i Sulaiman, and were excavated by C. K. Wilkinson[184] for the
Metropolitan Museum of Art during the 1930s. Most early travellers
such as Flandin and Coste[52] were chiefly interested in the three Achaemenian stone doorways which used to stand at this site but, as the
excavations of the Metropolitan Museum have shown, Qasr-i Abu
Nasr is essentially a late Sassanian and early Islamic foundation. Studies
carried out by Mr. and Mrs. Tilia of IsMEO prove in fact that the
Achaemenian doorways had been taken from the private palace of
Darius at Persepolis, presumably in order to embellish the much later
buildings at Abu Nasr some 50 km. away. These Achaemenian elements
have since been restored to their original positions at Persepolis.[140]

After some five or six minutes' driving further on the same track,
where the road bends round towards the low mountains on the left,
one comes to the site of some badly weathered Sassanian bas-reliefs

known as Barm-i Dalak. A stream divides the road from the cliff face
and there is usually a little chai khaneh set up under the trees opposite
the bay formed by the cliffs. On the east face of the cliff one can make
out the reliefs, about 3 m. high, depicting Bahram II with his wife
(A.D. 276 to 293). Early afternoon is best for photography which is
awkward because of the narrow terrace in front of the reliefs. A brief
inscription in Pahlavi, badly worn by water, is only decipherable in parts
and Dr. Gropp of the German Archaeological Institute has noted the
words, '. . . a man named Ardashir. . . .'

About 30 km. north-west of Shiraz, along the fair road to Ardekan
and Tal-i Khosrow, is an unfinished (or damaged?) Sassanian rock
relief near the village of Guyum. Mentioned by Herzfeld, and visited
by Vanden Berghe during his extensive surveys in the 1960s, it has more
recently been photographed by Dr. Georgina Herrmann of the B.I.P.S.
in 1967. Dr. Herrmann notes that the relief, which is about 9 m.
above the ground, is approached from a garden to which one must
obtain the key. It is possible to climb up on to a rock in front of the relief,
which should be photographed very early in the morning. It depicts
Bahram II on foot, raising his right arm in prayer, and is probably an
investiture scene.

North from Shiraz, on the road to Persepolis (on the main highway to
Isfahan and Tehran), one enters the plain of Marv Dasht, incredibly
rich in archaeological remains. From Pol-i Khan, the large bridge
spanning the river Kur, a good paved road to the left takes one up to
the new dam of Dariush Kabir, some 50 km. to the north. Near the
dam are the remains of an Achaemenian bridge and causeway, the stone
foundations of an Achaemenian residence, and a canal-head of probably
Sassanian date, the Sang-i Dukhtar, which is now being moved to a
fresh site south of the dam. K. Bergner first reported these considerable
monuments in the early 1930s, while more recent work on these sites
has been carried out by a Pahlavi University Expedition led by Dr.
Murray Nicol.

On the way, the road passes Ak Tepe, the tallest of the mounds in the
valley, where a long sequence of occupation extends from the fifth
millennium B.C. to Islamic times. In the southern face of the closest
rock ridge, Kuh-i Ayyub, one can also see a post-Achaemenian tomb
with a tall stepped façade and two small fire altars, one by the side of
the road, carved out of rock, and the other higher up, made with a
separate square stone placed in a hollow in the rock.

In a second bare ridge called Kuh-i Zakah two unique Sassanian
ossuaries have been carved side by side, each with a dog's-tooth
pattern incised around it. There are literally hundreds of these
repositories for bones in the mountains in this region, together with

an intriguing variety of rock-cut fire bowls and associated 'exposure platforms',[156,160,172,177] for the dead. (*Tal-i Malyan.)

Medieval travellers talked much of the 'Three Domes' in this plain, which are in fact the three flat-topped hills outstanding in this part of the Persepolis plain. Kuh-i Istakhr, the middle of the three, is a favourite Shirazi picnic spot with Sassanian and tenth century ruins on the summit. Enormous rock-cut reservoirs, roofed over on 20 columns, are said to have been able to supply a thousand men with water for a year. Here the citizens of Istakhr (p. 220), on the plain beside Naqsh-i Rustam, would take refuge in times of trouble—the Sassanians reportedly only surrendering to the Arabs when their reservoirs were damaged in an earthquake.

A little more difficult to reach, on the east side of the river, is the third mountain, Kuh-i Shahrak, almost at the southern extremity of which is a lone fire altar first noticed by Stronach in 1965.[160] Known locally as Sang-i Sanduk, 'the box-like stone', this rock-cut feature represents a close parallel to the famous twin Sassanian fire altars from neighbouring Naqsh-i Rustam. The principal shrine of this area, Imamzadeh Saf-i Muhammad, is close by.

Back on the main road to Persepolis, another 4 km. brings you to the large village of Marv Dasht. Not far to the south from here (about 15 km.) is the tenth century Buyid dam of Band-i Amir, built by Adud al-Dowleh. Water raised by this dam irrigated land for some 300 villages and it still remains in use. The many mounds around the site cover the remains of the medieval village.

On the south-west outskirts of Marv Dasht, several brick kilns have been built into the top of a large mound known as Tepe Sabz, which probably dates back to the second or third millennium B.C. The site is strewn with cultural debris and traces of prehistoric graves can still be seen.

The main road divides, the right branch going towards a range of hills bereft of any outstanding features. The full impact of the Achaemenian complex of Parsa—the Persepolis of the Greeks or, to give its later Iranian name, Takht-i Jamshid, that is 'the Throne of Jamshid'—is not apparent indeed until you are right at the foot of the great platform that supports the palaces.

About 2 km. before reaching the platform, you pass on the left, the Government's de luxe Hotel Darius, which has a swimming pool, and next door, a Tourist Camp with huts. An overnight stay enables one to enjoy the dramatic effect of sunset and sunrise over the palaces (two hours after sunrise and about the same time before sunset are best for photographing the famous bas-reliefs) and then to spend the second day seeing the earlier Achaemenian capital of Pasargadae, some 80 km.

further north, as well as the royal tombs and Sassanian bas-reliefs at Naqsh-i Rustam and Naqsh-i Rajab en route.

By starting from Shiraz early in the morning, all these separate sites can also be seen with much haste in one day. Chronologically it is preferable to visit Pasargadae first, and travellers coming by road from Tehran will automatically do so. Those approaching from Shiraz, with only one day to spare, should go straight to Persepolis and photographers should make for the bas-reliefs on the east wall of the Apadana, then stop at Naqsh-i Rustam, spend the rest of the morning at Pasargadae and return to Persepolis to see Naqsh-i Rajab between 2.30 and 3 p.m. for the best light, then completing the tour of Persepolis.

One can eat Persian food inexpensively at the Takht-i Tavoos restaurant, by the willow trees and pool just beyond Persepolis, and not far from a petrol station. Close to Pasargadae, lunch can also be taken (at any convenient hour) at the largest of the roadside chai khanehs in the village of Sadatabad. There is no hotel accommodation here.

Taking the oldest site first, continue along this road through lonely hills and valleys frequented by migrating tribes during the spring and autumn. The road enters the plain of Murghab, populated from prehistoric times, and the scene of Cyrus the Great's victory over his grandfather's armies in 550 B.C. Near a gendarmerie post there is a sign indicating the road to the left (west) which goes for about 6 km. skirting the village of Madar-i Sulaiman. Keeping to the left, the tomb of Cyrus is seen standing majestically in the open ground ahead. There is a small entrance fee.

The name of Pasargadae, given by the Greeks to the city, is now believed by most scholars, on the basis of Achaemenian tablets discovered in Persepolis, to derive from an original name, Pasragada, itself perhaps the name of the chief tribe of the Persians. It was here that Cyrus established his capital c. 546 B.C. and it was from this elevated valley, some 1,900 m. above sea level, that the Persian Empire really came into being.

As Sir Aurel Stein first noted in 1934, the plain was certainly populated by prehistoric communities in the fourth millennium B.C. The chalcolithic mound of Tall-i Nokhodi, about 800 m. north-west of the tomb of Cyrus, and on the edge of a small stream, was excavated briefly in 1951 by Mr. Ali Sami of the Iranian Archaeological Service, and more thoroughly by Dr. Clare Goff,[72] on behalf of the British Institute of Persian Studies, in 1961 and 1962; a pottery sequence partly related to that of Tall-i Bakun A was found, and several building levels, including houses and burials, were revealed, the upper two probably falling between 3200 and 2500 B.C. A few surface sherds appeared to relate to Vanden Berghe's 'Kaftari b and c' fabric.[172]

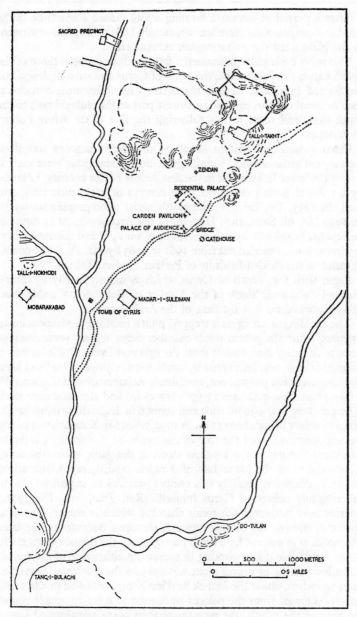

Fig. 32. Sketch plan of Pasargadae.
(*By courtesy of Mr. David Stronach, from* Iran, *Vol. III, 1965*)

After a period of intensive farming which ceased some time in the third millennium B.C., there was apparently little permanent settlement in the plain until the Achaemenian occupation.

The main Pasargadae monuments fall into four groups: those of the Citadel area, the Palace area, the tomb of Cyrus and surroundings, and the Sacred Precincts. In addition there is an Achaemenian rock-cut road or canal cut through the narrowest part of the Bulaghi pass to the south-west, and more or less following the line of the River Pulvar, to Persepolis.

Often visited and written about by nineteenth century travellers, the original archaeological soundings made at Pasargadae were carried out by Professor E. Herzfeld in the first decade of this century, followed by Sir Aurel Stein's site plans with surveys of prehistoric sites, and then, in 1935, Dr. Erich F. Schmidt's aerial photographic survey.[140] In 1949 Mr. Ali Sami, then Director of the Archaeological Institute at Persepolis, began a five-year programme of work,[132] and the most recent excavations were carried out from 1961 to 1963 by Mr. David Stronach, Director of the British Institute of Persian Studies, Tehran.[159]

Begin with the Tomb of Cyrus which is known locally as Qabr-i Madar-i Sulaiman, 'tomb of the Mother of Solomon', a name most likely bestowed on it at the time of the Arab invasion.

The building is set upon a stepped plinth recalling a Mesopotamian ziggurat, while the gabled tomb chamber bears at least some resemblance to funerary monuments from Phrygia and Lycia. But its massive, megalithic masonry, reinforced by swallow-tail clamps of lead and iron, is, as Stronach has pointed out, completely Achaemenian in character.[159]

The stone base measures 13·50 × 12·20 m. and the sepulchre itself is 5·24 m. long and 5·30 m. wide and about 6 m. high, the original height of the structure being nearly 11 m. In 1970, when Mr. Stronach was taking fresh measurements on the roof of the tomb, he discovered a hitherto unnoticed feature on the topmost stone of the gable above the door. This consists of the lower half of a much eroded, rayed disc about 50 cm. in diameter. Possibly this symbol provides an important clue to the religious beliefs of Cyrus himself. (Ref. *Iran*, Vol. IX, 1971.) Visitors may not enter the tomb chamber which is empty. One can, however, glimpse the interior through the open doorway in the later afternoon. It is entered by a small passage from the doorway, originally closed by double doors pivoting in sockets on either side of the frame. A shallow mihrab or prayer niche was cut into the south wall some 700 years ago when, under the Atabek Sa'd ibn Zangi, who died in A.D. 1226, various columns from the palaces were used to form an arcade round the base of the plinth, the monument then being transformed into a congregational mosque. Later still, more stone was brought from the palaces and elsewhere to construct the caravanserai that was excavated by the Iranian Archaeological Service. The columns have been removed and are being restored to their original positions.

Originally the Magi, guardians of Cyrus's tomb, lived within the surrounding gardens in a separate dwelling. The interior of the mausoleum, according to Arrian, was richly furnished; the embalmed body of the king lay in a golden sarcophagus on a gold couch, with a gold table by its side, on which various treasures were laid. Alexander the Great made several pilgrimages to the tomb.

Various classical writers mention an inscription on the tomb, no trace of which remains. According to Strabo this read: 'O man, I am Cyrus who founded the Empire of the Persians and was king of Asia. Grudge me not therefore this monument.'

From the tomb of Cyrus the road leads north-east passing the Residential Palace on the left, and ending at the Audience Hall. Both palaces were surrounded by protective walls until 1971 and are built on the oblong plan in contrast to the later, square plan of the Persepolis palaces. Only one tapered column of the original eight stands in place in the lofty central hall of the Audience Palace (or Palace 'S'), a stork's nest in permanent occupation on its top. Originally double-horned lion protomes formed the capitals. Four low-ceilinged porticos were also supported by columns, 48 supporting the northern colonnade.

On the doorways of Palace 'S', bas-reliefs of partly Assyrian inspiration can be seen, while on the south-east corner a stone shaft bears a cuneiform inscription in Old Persian, Elamite and Babylonian, reading, 'I Cyrus, the King, the Achaemenian [viz. built this]'.

Black and white limestone has been used with telling effect in both palaces and the doorways are also of black limestone, but exposure is beginning to damage the stone.

Outside, walk round the east wall of this palace and you will see the remains of a columned bridge discovered and excavated by Mr. Stronach and consisting of two opposed limestone side walls with five rows of three columns between them. Probably a light, wooden columned pavilion stood on the bridge, forming an inner entrance to the palace enclosure.

About 150 m. to the east and across the water channel which floods this area during winter rains, stands the Gate House, the least well-preserved of the palaces and probably the only monumental entrance to the area. Herzfeld found that the main doorways at either end of the building were flanked by colossal winged bulls similar to those on the Gateway of All Nations at Persepolis (p. 227) although no trace of these colossi remain. However, the most complete early Achaemenian bas-relief known, appears here in the shape of the unique four-winged figure on the eastern door jamb of the small, northern side chamber, best photographed in the afternoon. Early travellers record that it was surmounted by a trilingual inscription reading, 'Cyrus, the king the Achaemenian', and not a few writers in the past have taken it to be a stylized portrait of Cyrus himself. Today, however, most scholars are unanimous in the opinion that this grave, now much-worn figure, with its exotic Egyptian crown and Elamite dress, should be viewed as a guardian genius which, with others of its kind, was designed to protect the palace area from the entry of evil spirits.

Return towards the Residential Palace (or Palace 'P'), with its recently remounted columns. On the immediate right of the road 120 m. due north of Palace 'S', there is a rectangular platform of dressed stones forming the floor of a small building known as the Garden Pavilion, which was first found and excavated by Mr. Stronach in 1963. Near the southern arm of the south-east portico a tall, buff Achaemenian water jar was found, its upper portion destroyed by ploughing, but the lower half still containing an astonishingly rich treasure of 1,162 objects, including golden earrings and bracelets, necklaces and a silver spoon. All the principal pieces are housed in the Tehran Archaeological Museum and certain of them can be seen in the 'Treasure Room'.

It is possible that this was the personal jewellery of an Achaemenian noblewoman who had hidden her finery as Alexander the Great advanced on Persepolis in 331–330 B.C. On the grounds of style, at all events, the pieces can be dated from the second half of the fifth century B.C. to the middle of the fourth century B.C.

Finally at a distance of 230 metres to the north the palace area includes a third major building, the so-called Residential Palace, or Palace 'P'. The small mud-brick rooms that once flanked it to the north and south have now all disappeared, but the main structure consisted of a central hall with 30 stone columns on black and white square plinths. The stone floor is white, the door jambs black, and the lower half of a robed figure in the western doorway still bears part of an inscription identifying it as Cyrus the Great. Holes at the centre and the edge of the king's robe indicate that it was once adorned with fine gold hems. According to Mr. Stronach's most recent conclusions, the strangely asymmetrical plan of the Residential Palace, and the inferior quality of the western portico, can both be attributed to the fact that Cyrus never finished the monument—and that Darius, whose main building interests lay elsewhere, was not interested in completing the whole of the original concept. Traces have been found of red, white and blue plaster that was apparently used to cover wooden columns in some parts of the structure.

Darius also added the doorway reliefs in this building and the trilingual inscriptions upon them labelling Cyrus in the third person as 'Cyrus, the Great King, the Achaemenian'.

From this palace a new road on the original Achaemenian track leads north to the remains of the so-called Zendan-i Sulaiman or 'Prison of Solomon', of which the Ka'bah-i Zardusht at Naqsh-i Rustam is a better-preserved replica (p. 223).

The structure consists of an almost square tower built in the outward form of a three-storeyed house on a plinth of three steps. A flight of twenty-nine stone steps originally led to the single chamber in the upper half of the monument. Only one wall still stands to its full height. Although the function of this and the similar tower at Naqsh-i Rustam is still unconfirmed, Mr. Stronach suggests the form derives from temples in Urartu, thus supporting a religious rather than a funerary function.[159,163] A number of low, unexcavated mounds east of the tower may one day add still further information.

Continuing northwards, the road passes between two hills, the easterly hill forming the base of a great stone platform known locally as Takht-i Madar-i Sulaiman, or 'The Throne of the Mother of Solomon', which is fitted without mortar but with metal clamps, mostly now stolen. Excavations by Ali Sami in 1951, and more recently by the British Institute of Persian Studies, have revealed imposing stone staircases on the northern side of the platform and four distinct phases of occupation: the monumental phase of stone construction begun by Cyrus the Great (Period I); next, mud-brick constructions that lasted from early in the reign of Darius to c. 280 B.C. (Period II), when a number of these were destroyed by fire; a further phase of largely mud-brick construction that probably falls within the years 280 to 200 B.C. (Period III); and a brief final phase of early Islamic occupation (Period IV).[159]

Several coin hoards of the early third century B.C. were discovered, each associated with the thick debris of the Period II destruction. A beautifully finished, almost complete, grey limestone foundation tablet of Xerxes, in which he attacks the cult of the Daivas, was also found near the eastern wall of the Citadel where it was re-used as a drain cover. Masons' marks appear on many of the stones.[125b]

Thanks to the latest coins, from the reign of Seleucus I, the destruction of the Citadel can be dated to c. 280 B.C. and not, as had been supposed earlier, to the time of Alexander the Great. The early Islamic or possibly late Sassanian settlement on the crown of the Citadel includes a pillared hall with plastered floors and two square plastered column bases.

The Sacred Area lies about 1,200 metres to the north-west of the Citadel, beyond a range of low hills; however, the road past the Citadel, which formerly went right to the site, has been fenced off since 1973 and some ingenuity is required to negotiate the fence. It is hoped that the authorities will re-open the road and enable one to drive to the Sacred Area as in the past.

Crossing a brook, one sees at the western end of an enclosure the two free-standing limestone plinths.[49] The southern plinth has a flight of steps to its summit. These have been variously described as twin fire altar supports and as altars to Anahita and Ahura Mazda. A detailed survey and excavation in 1963, by the British Institute of Persian Studies, revealed the fact that black limestone additions originally embellished the white stone plinths; the northern plinth apparently never had a staircase and it may well be that, as in the scene depicted at Naqsh-i Rustam, the king mounted the steps of the southern plinth in order to worship before the sacred fire placed on the adjoining block.

The details of the stone dressing suggest that Cyrus the Great was responsible for the construction of both plinths, possibly as part of a larger plan which was meant to embrace a terraced mound 123 m. to the west. Herzfeld[87] thought this latter mound must have mirrored the Tomb of Cyrus, the uppermost mud-brick platform supporting a stone sanctuary but Mr. Stronach's excavations showed there were five terraces, walled with dry stone masonry, the fifth terrace being largely of mud-brick. The whole mound was probably approached by two staircases, one of which still partly remains on the north. Several of the lower terraces were probably paved. The terrace walls and those surrounding the precinct appear to have been substantially later in date than the altars. A small hoard of undated gold objects was discovered in the pavement of the fourth terrace, probably secreted at the end of the active life of the mound.

Mr. Stronach inclines to Erdmann's[49] view that the open summit of the terrace was a stage for sacrificial rites or support for yet another altar.

From Pasargadae return to the main road. A left turn to the north continues on to Isfahan and Tehran; go right almost to Persepolis, and about 4 km. before the mound of Istakhr appears (on the immediate right of the road) one can see in the walls of a gorge, on the far right of the road, several natural grottoes. The place is known as Tang-i Shah Sarvan and the grottoes contain what have been described as the earliest Parthian inscriptions yet known; but although within view they must be reached by a track close to Istakhr, going towards the north-west to the village of Hajiabad and then some 2 km. north of the village. The inscriptions are on several tablets in the first cave on the right, near the entrance to the gorge, and some of them have been attributed to the Sassanian, Shahpur I.

Istakhr itself is conspicuous by the one lofty column with part of a double-headed bull capital, which can be seen from the main road. Drive up by the small gendarmerie post to the top of the mound. The city of Istakhr was built on a prehistoric fourth millennium B.C. site and possibly the site of an Elamite town according to Schmidt.[140,141] It was occupied by Achaemenians, Parthians and Sassanians in turn, and here Ardashir I's grandfather, Sasan, a distant descendant of the Achaemenian royal line, was High Priest at the famous fire temple of Adhar Anahit; this was possibly the fire sanctuary at which the deities of water and fertility were worshipped. It was on the walls of this temple that Ardashir, first of the Sassanian dynasty, hung the heads of his enemies.

This single column still standing was one of a pair of the Achaemenian period which had been re-used in an early mosque that was supposedly built on the site of the fire temple. Istakhr, which is known locally as Takht-i Tavoos (Peacock Throne), was excavated in a limited fashion by Schmidt in the 1930s. The walled-in area covers 1,400 × 650 m. and the mound itself was partly surrounded by a moat filled with the waters of the Pulvar river. On the south side of the road one sees the remains of one of the original approaches to the site where large blocks of stone of partly Achaemenian origin were apparently used to bridge a major irrigation canal. The remnants of a Sassanian building of large stone blocks are on the north-east corner of the site, and Sassanian houses lie close to the surface in the western section, where Schmidt made his small excavation.

By the Seleucid period Istakhr was a provincial capital and a mint town, and continued as such until the end of the Abbasid caliphate in Iran. During the Arsacid (Parthian) period the sacred fire continued to burn in the temple which was probably the scene of the coronation of most, if not all, of the Sassanian kings, although Sarre[134] suggests that they were crowned at Naqsh-i Rajab.

In A.D. 640, Istakhr repulsed the first Arab attack, but was forced to surrender in A.D. 643, and soon afterwards its citizens rebelled, killing the Arab Governor. In A.D. 648–9 the town was once more captured and many of its inhabitants killed.[109,185]

Shiraz, which was founded as a city in A.D. 684, took the place of Istakhr whose power was broken; although it was rebuilt, it was only to be destroyed again by the Buyids in the tenth century when most of the survivors fled to Shiraz. By the twelfth century A.D. Istakhr was no more than a village of 100 inhabitants.[111]

In excavated materials, Istakhr has produced a fine range of tenth century Buyid pottery[106] including a distinctive moulded ware, and a number of coins.[142] Recently part of a large, high relief or even a statue, of a woman's left arm resting on a plump thigh, was found at Istakhr and may be Sassanian; it was probably used as building material in an early Islamic structure.

Only a few hundred metres west of Istakhr, where the road passes close to the cliffs on the south, is an inconspicuous cleft in the rocks, which can be all too easily missed. This is Naqsh-i Rajab, where four early Sassanian reliefs adorn the adjoining rock walls. On the left, Shahpur I is shown mounted on his charger, and although the face and head are damaged one can see the typical bunch of curls at the side of the head, and the high korymbos of royalty, believed to have consisted of a bunch of hair pulled to the top of the head and covered with a fine silk material, a hairstyle also used by the Parthians. Around the distinctive crown (a different style identifies each king), is the royal diadem fastened with long, fluttering ribbons flying out at the back.

The beribboned horse wears the typical pear-shaped 'balloon' hanging from the saddle. Known from the reliefs alone, this curious device was apparently stuffed with hair or some such light material since it is always shown streaming to the rear in all scenes of movement. An inscription in Pahlavi (Middle Persian) and Greek can be seen on the horse's chest.

The full-length figure immediately behind Shahpur's horse is thought to have been his heir, Hormizd I. The other eight figures may represent both the king's other sons and nobles; Dr. Herrmann believes they are all Shahpur's sons, or at least close relatives.[86] The relief was probably carved early in Shahpur's reign, possibly about A.D. 250.

On the opposite (right) cliff is another bas-relief depicting Shahpur's investiture; Shahpur on the right is seen receiving the royal diadem (the symbol of kingship), from the god Hormizd (Ahura Mazda), both the king and the god being shown to be mounted. This scene was possibly carved immediately after Shahpur's coronation on 20th March A.D. 242.

The back wall of the grotto depicts the investiture of Shahpur's father, Ardashir I, who appears on the left, standing to receive the diadem from the deity holding a barsom (bundle of sacred twigs). Some believe the figure with the high hat and ribboned diadem standing behind the king is his son Shahpur, and possibly an attendant with him, while the two small, badly damaged figures between the king and the god may represent Hormizd I, Ardashir's grandson, on the left, and a follower of Ahura Mazda on the right.

The most interesting thing about this relief is that it includes one of the rare portrayals of a woman, on the far right. Either Ardashir's queen or his mother, with a female attendant, stand with their backs to the investiture scene; the queen's hair is in ringlets and covered by a high Sassanian hat with a ribboned diadem. Like the supposed Shahpur, the queen holds her hand before her mouth in a gesture of respect.

Set a little back and to the left of this entire relief is the figure of

Kartir, High Priest and a powerful political figure through the reigns of several Sassanian kings. He also raises a finger in respect. An inscription in Pahlavi is carved by the side of this relief, and is similar in content to that of Kartir on the Ka'bah-i Zardusht at Naqsh-i Rustam. Noon to mid-afternoon is best for photography here.

Now cross the main road and take the turn to the north, crossing the small bridge over the Pulvar river. Immediately over the bridge to the left, and about 600 m. directly west of Naqsh-i Rajab, are the remains of an unfinished stone monument which Herzfeld was the first to suggest might have been intended as the tomb of Cambyses II (d. A.D. 522), son of Cyrus the Great. It is known locally as Takht-i Rustam, 'the Throne of Rustam', or Takht-i Gohar.

The basic dimensions of the two surviving tiers of stone are very similar in area to the lower tiers of the tomb of Cyrus. The centre of the monument was excavated by Herzfeld soon after 1930, although he failed to realize his intention of reaching virgin soil.[141] (*Palaces.)

Continue along the track from the bridge towards Naqsh-i Rustam—the name given to the great cliff face that bears the four rock-cut tombs of Darius and three of his successors; these are best photographed in the morning.

In a hollow in front of the tombs stands the enigmatic 'Ka'bah-i Zardusht' or 'Cube of Zoroaster', a monumental structure of black and white stone some 12·60 m. high, which was probably built by Darius soon after his accession, in careful imitation of the supposed royal temple at Pasargadae. The blind windows of black limestone give the structure the appearance of a three-storey building, although this too contains only a single, high, windowless room reached by a monumental external staircase. On the lower, outer walls, protected by screens, are a number of Sassanian inscriptions in Pahlavi, Sassanian, Parthian and Greek characters, including a detailed account of Shahpur's victories by Kartir the High Priest, who refers to the building as 'this foundation house'.[85,141] These inscriptions were revealed by Schmidt in the 1930s.

Controversy as to the function of the building still exists. While most authorities believe it to have been a religious edifice, perhaps a fire temple containing the sacred eternal fire, others think that it may have served either as a provisional royal tomb until the permanent tombs were finished or else as a unique repository for the royal standards or sacred texts.[138,143,163]

In the 1930s, Schmidt dug a trial trench in front of the tomb of Darius the Great, finding crudely built houses of the early Islamic period, c. eighth century A.D., minor Sassanian remains and, at the base of the deposit, Achaemenian walls composed of mud bricks of the same dimensions and with the same greyish-green plaster as others found on the Persepolis terrace. While clearing and lowering the ground level before the tombs in 1971, the worn reliefs of a leaping lion and an unfinished standing man were revealed about 10 m. west of Narseh's relief. (See M. Roaf, *Iran*, Vol. XII, 1974.)

Of the four rock-cut tombs, only one is identified by an inscription, namely that of Darius the Great, the third from the left as you face the cliff. Although different interpretations have been advanced, the tombs, from left to right as you face the same direction, are generally thought to represent those of Darius II (425 to 405 B.C.), Artaxerxes I (465 to 425 B.C.), Darius I (522 to 485 B.C.) and Xerxes I (485 to 465 B.C.).

Each of the tombs displays an identical façade which is seen at first as a tall, recessed Greek cross. Closer at hand, one finds balancing pairs of semi-engaged columns with bull protome capitals placed at the entrance, in imitation of the façade of an Achaemenian palace. Bas-reliefs above depict members of the vassal nations supporting the King's throne or platform, with the king himself standing in worship before a fire altar, facing Ahura Mazda, whose winged symbol floats above. The interior of the tomb of Darius contains several internal rock-cut bays, each with space for three separate sarcophagi.

This site, which first attracted the Elamites, also appealed to the later Sassanians who carved their bas-reliefs under and to the left of the Achaemenian tombs.

Beginning at the left, there is the investiture of Ardashir I (A.D. 224 to 255). Both the king and the deity are mounted, the god holding the barsom of sacred twigs in one hand and offering the royal diadem with the other; an Aramaic inscription appears on the shoulder of the latter's horse. Ardashir's beard is drawn through a ring; his horse has an inscription in Pahlavi and Greek on its chest and is trampling the last Parthian king, Artabanus V, while Ahura Mazda's horse tramples Ahriman, the epitome of evil. An attendant stands behind Ardashir.

Next, on the curve of the rock, comes Bahram II (A.D. 276 to 293) with his family (the queen, with ringlets, is the second figure from the left). This was carved over a neo-Elamite low-relief portrayal of which little can be seen save for an intact male figure on the right, and a seated queen, wearing a battlemented crown, on the far left. Dr. Porada dates these to between the ninth and seventh centuries B.C., although other authorities think they may be earlier. On the smoothed rock forming a wall in front of Bahram's companions, faint marks seem to show a skirted figure seated on a serpent throne (right) and other shadowy remnants of the original relief.

Look to the top of the cliff from this point, slightly to the right, and you will see one of the many different kinds of fire altars once used in this region; this particular example is in the form of a short column, probably one of a pair that originally stood here.

The next relief, under the first of the tombs, is of a battle or joust between two unidentified combatants; some think it is Bahram IV (A.D. 388 to 399) with his standard bearer on his left, and others that it is Hormizd II. The fourth relief, carved just to the left of Darius the Great's tomb, depicts Shahpur I (A.D. 241 to 272) on his horse; behind the king appears the head-and-shoulders of Kartir the High Priest, with an inscription added later, and before Shahpur is a standing figure with his arms raised and seized by Shahpur. This is possibly the Roman emperor Valerian, while kneeling in supplication is perhaps Philip the Arab, both these emperors being counted among Shahpur's distinguished prisoners. Hinz[93] believes Valerian is kneeling and Philip the Arab standing.

Immediately below the tomb of Darius are two reliefs, one above the other, both worn, and depicting equestrian battles. Some attribute these to Bahram II or Shahpur II (above), with Hormizd II below.

The last relief shows the investiture of Narseh (A.D. 293 to 302), standing on the left with the goddess Anahita offering the diadem. Behind the king, who was Bahram II's uncle, is a dignitary with an unfinished figure behind him. The small figure between the goddess and the king may be the crown prince, Hormizd. Beyond this relief an eighteenth century inscription was carved into an earlier panel of smoothed rock.

Round the corner on the left to the north-west of the tombs, the track continues and, after a few metres, passes two prominent rock-cut fire altars of the Sassanian period, both of which possess a deep rectangular fire bowl. In the cliffs above and around them are still other types of fire altar, and also rock-cut ossuaries in the small side valleys directly to the north.

To the north-east, along a track that runs past the tomb of Darius II, one also finds a number of flat exposure platforms with one or more rectangular troughs in which the corpses were exposed before the defleshed bones were placed in ossuaries. Some $2\frac{1}{2}$ km. further to the north-east is a small gulley called Darrehbareh with an Achaemenian quarry above it. Here a block of limestone was apparently made into a large fire altar with a curved profile resembling that of a Chahar Taq. Above, on a shallow rectangular slope of the cliff, are two other basins with distinct drainage troughs, while in the same area a second stone altar can be seen to the south.[160] Continuing along the track will bring you to the Hajiabad or Tang-i Shah Sarvan grottoes (p. 220). (*Altar.)

Returning to the main road by Naqsh-i Rajab, continue back to Persepolis or Takhti-i Jamshid as it is known locally.[52] A great many

volumes have been written on Persepolis, which was first scientifically
excavated under the direction of Ernst Herzfeld, and later by E. F.
Schmidt on behalf of the Oriental Institute of Chicago, from 1931 to
1939. In the 1940s the excavations were continued by the Iranian
Archaeological Service, directed first by André Godard and later by
Ali Sami. More recently, the excavations of the Iranian Archaeological
Service have been renewed under the direction of Mr. A. Tajvidi, while,
in cooperation with the Iranian authorities, Giuseppe and Ann Britt
Tilia of the Istituto Italiano per il Medio ed Estremo Oriente (IsMEO)
have been patiently restoring the damaged structure.

A small entry fee is charged and a condensed guide[133] by Ali Sami
is usually on sale at the site. D. N. Wilber has also written another
helpful guide.[181] Son et Lumière performances are given here.

It is perhaps possible that it was Cambyses II, the son of Cyrus the
Great, who chose the rock outcrop at the foot of Kuh-i Rahmat as the
site of a new dynastic home. But the massive terrace, built on three
different levels on a spur of the mountain, is essentially a supreme
monument to that great innovator, Darius the Great (522 to 485
B.C.).[127] (See also F. Krefter, *Persepolis Rekonstruktionen*, 1971.)

Look closely at the sides of the colossal platform, especially well
seen from the west and south sides where the meticulously fitted blocks
of limestone, of enormous size and weight, rise to a height of some
20 m. The terrace itself covers an area of 450 × 300 m. and an unfired
brick wall, possibly at least partly faced with polychrome tiles, was
built on top of the masonry wall. According to Professor Pope,[129]
the complex of buildings formed a ritual city whose very existence was
kept secret from the outside world at a time when the glories of the
other, secular, Achaemenian capitals of Susa, Babylon and Ecbatana
were well known. But in fact it must be by some strange accident of
history that Persepolis—known as Parsa to the Achaemenians—was
never mentioned in foreign records, for it was here after all that
representatives of all the varied peoples of the empire gathered to pay
homage, and bring tribute, to the King of Kings, probably each spring,
at the time of the ancient Now Ruz (New Year) festival.

It was Alexander the Great who, either by accident or design, destroyed the magnificent palaces, not long before the death of the last of
the Achaemenians, Darius III, in 330 B.C.

A complex system of drainage and water channels cut into the foundations of the terrace suggests that the entire layout of the complex was
designed in detail before any other construction work was begun.

Access to the platform is by a monumental double-ramped ceremonial
staircase, carved from massive blocks of stone (five steps are carved
from a single block 7 m. long), and shallow enough for the most impor-

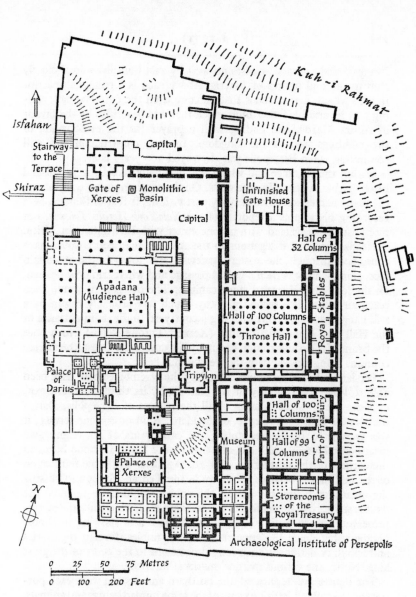

Isfahan

Stairway to the Terrace

Shiraz

Gate of Xerxes

Capital

Monolithic Basin

Capital

Kuh-i Rahmat

Unfinished Gate House

Hall of 32 Columns

Apadana (Audience Hall)

Hall of 100 Columns or Throne Hall

Royal Stables

Palace of Darius

Tripylon

Hall of 100 Columns

Part of Treasury

Museum

Hall of 99 Columns

Palace of Xerxes

Storerooms of the Royal Treasury

Archaeological Institute of Persepolis

N

0   25   50   75 Metres
0   100   200 Feet

Fig. 33. Persepolis. Plan.
(*After Hauser, by courtesy of Chicago Press*)

tant guests to be able to take their horses up. The stairs were closed at the top with gates whose hinges fitted into sockets in the floor, seen at the top of the northern flight.

At the head of the staircase is the **Gateway of All Nations**, built by

Xerxes I and guarded at east and west by vast bull-like colossi closely
akin to the bull figures of Assyria. Above each is a trilingual inscription in which Xerxes states that he completed the entrance hall, add-
ing that he and his father built much that was beautiful, by the favour
of Ahura Mazda, and ending with a prayer for the preservation of
the buildings and of the kingdom. In fact, construction was still
continuing when Persepolis was destroyed 200 years later.

Within the entrance hall which was originally roofed, well-polished
black marble benches line the walls. On the southern inner wall, among
the many names scratched here by past visitors, is that of Stanley, here
recording his role as a reporter of the *New York Herald Tribune*, but
more usually associated with his encounter with Livingstone in Africa.

Heads of official delegations to the Achaemenian court would have
continued through the eastern gateway and towards the mountain
face, along what was then a walled passage and where can now be seen,
on the left, several carved stone capitals. The delegations would then
reach an incomplete second gateway which was probably begun by a
still later monarch, before crossing a courtyard to the main entrance of
the Hall of a Hundred Columns (Xerxes' Throne Room) which bore
the brunt of the conflagration begun by Alexander the Great, the marble
columns being blasted with the tremendous heat.

Persian and Median nobles attending the ceremonies may have been
able to leave the Gateway of All Nations by its third, southern exit,
opposite the most fascinating of all the palaces of Persepolis, Darius
the Great's Hall of Audience, or Apadana. Built on a stone terrace, it
was completed by Xerxes during the early years of his reign. Two
inscribed tablets in gold and silver that were found in stone boxes in
the corners of the northern wall of the Apadana mark the foundation
of the building by Darius. Both are in the Tehran Museum. Crossing
the open area before the palace, the nobles would have mounted the
double staircase in the middle of the northern wall, which, like the better-
preserved eastern wall, is covered with bas-reliefs showing in almost
photographic detail the appearance of the nobles, foreign dignitaries
and tributary nations in their long processions to the court of the great
king. Notice the various masons' marks at intervals.

The figures are duplicated, the northern and eastern walls each portraying the right or left side views of the same human beings and animals.
Studying these and other realistic bas-reliefs at Persepolis one can well
visualize the colourful and impressive scene at the twice-yearly festivals
when representatives of the subject nations ranging from the Greek
islands to India, and from Central Asia to Ethiopia, brought their gifts,
the latter including exotic creatures such as giraffes from Abyssinia,
two-humped camels from Bactria in Afghanistan, and lion cubs from

Elam, together with golden ornaments, weapons, fine horses and still other tokens of homage.

The procession of the nobility would have entered the columned porch at the top of the stairs and then wound through the great hall, which is similar in design to the Apadana at Susa and large enough to accommodate some 10,000 people according to Herzfeld. They would have left through the eastern portico and gone down the second double-winged staircase to turn right to the Tripylon or Central Palace. From this they would have entered the adjoining Hall of One Hundred Columns from its southern side, and thus would face the visiting dignitaries as they entered at the opposite end of the Hall.

The original magnificence of these buildings can hardly be imagined even from the impressive portions still standing, for the great wooden doors were covered by delicately patterned gold plates; heavy curtains of gold lace kept out the draughts; glazed and terracotta tiles in blue, yellow and pink, portraying lions, bulls and plants, together with paintings on plaster, decorated the upper walls. Traces of colour have also been found on some column bases and stone walls and on the bas-reliefs of the staircases—the inside of the throat of a fallen lion capital near the eastern portico of the Apadana still shows distinct red colouring.

Guard and service rooms are on the corners, while the southern doors lead to Darius the Great's private palace, the supposed banqueting hall, and behind this the palace of the crown prince, Xerxes.

Of the original fluted and tapered 36 columns of the Apadana, only thirteen remain upright today, and of these most have lost their double bull protomes. The slender columns are nearly 20 m. tall. Another thirty-six columns on round bases supported the three porticos on east, west and north. The ceiling beams of cedar, ebony and teak were gold-plated, inlaid with ivory and precious metals.

The eastern staircase, approached from the north, shows first the classic and oft-repeated symbolic motif of a lion attacking a bull, then a cuneiform inscription of Xerxes, in Elamite and Babylonian, similar to the one on his Gateway. The same statement in Old Persian appears at the opposite, southern, end of the staircase.[99]

Next follow figures of Median (in rounded hats) and Persian (in crown-like headgear) officers who are preceded by Elamite guards or members of the Ten Thousand Immortals (the royal bodyguard), with chariot drivers, royal carriages and a throne, carried on the top row. On the southern section of the staircase, twenty-three scenes in three rows depict representatives of various countries in the Achaemenian empire, carrying or escorting offerings and also preceded by Court officials. Each section is separated from the next by a symbolic Tree of Life, the whole forming a virtual film strip showing us exactly

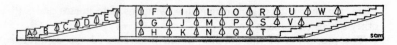

Fig. 34. Persepolis. Southern section of East Staircase of the Apadana.
(*After Schmidt*, Persepolis I)[141]

KEY

A. Kushiya (Ethiopians), with closely-curled hair and negroid features, carrying a vase and an elephant tusk and leading an okapi.

B. Putaya (Libyans), escorting a kudu with long curved horns, and a horse-drawn chariot.

C. Zranka (Drangianians), including a lancer with a shield and a long-horned bull. (Some believe these are Arachosians, mountain folk from Kirman region, and cattle breeders.)

D. Arabaya (Arabians), with textiles and a dromedary.

E. Skudra (Skudrians), lancers carrying shields, and a horse led by soldiers who wear classical type Thracian helmets.

F. The Asagarta (Sagartians), wearing tasselled caps (like those of the Cappadocians and Armenians), two of which are fastened under the chin like Balaclava helmets. They carry folded clothing and lead a horse.

G. Sugda (Sogdians) (or as some believe, Chorasmians), holding a short sword, bracelets and axes and leading a horse.

H. Hindush (Indians), wearing dhotis and one carrying baskets of vases, others with double-headed axes and leading a donkey.

I. Parthava (Parthians) wearing tunics and trousers, bearing cups and leading a Bactrian camel.

J. Gandara (Gandarians) with long capes, offering lances and a round shield and leading a humped bull.

K. Bakhtrish (Bactrians) in coats and full trousers of Median type, carrying bowls and leading a Bactrian camel.

L. Mudraya (Egyptians) (badly damaged section), leading a bull and carrying cloth.

M. Saka Tigrakhauda (Pointed-hat Scythians), armed and offering bracelets, folded coats and trousers, and a horse.

N. Yauna (Ionians), wearing cloaks with tassels over pleated robes, and carrying what may be beehives and skeins of wool or folded material.

O. The Harauvatish or Harakhuvatiya (Arachosians) with a dromedary, and bearing basins and lion skins. They wear knee-length baggy pants under tunics and their heads are swathed like the Aryans.

P. Suguda (Sogdians or Cicilians), wearing broad cummerbunds round long robes. They offer a length of cloth, cups, an animal skin and a pair of fine rams.

Q. The Katpatuka (Cappadocians). They wear cloaks pinned at the shoulders with Phrygian fibulae and their caps are like those of the Armenians and Sagartians. They bring folded cloaks and trousers and a horse.

R. The Haraiva (Aryans), their heads swathed in cloth, wearing tunics and boots and leading a Bactrian camel; they carry deep bowls and an animal (lion?) skin.

S. The Babirush or Babiruviya (Babylonians) wearing conical, long-tasselled caps, they bring a humped bull, woven fringed cloth and cups.

how the peoples of the vast empire dressed, their ornaments, weapons, hairstyles and the treasures of their homelands.

The Tachara (meaning 'winter palace') of Darius—it is so called in the trilingual inscriptions on its southern door jambs—is on a platform about 2 m. higher than the Apadana immediately to its north. This alone of all the other palaces on the platform has windows facing south from a portico with two rows of pillars. The original entrance to this small palace was by the two flights of steps on the south side. The palace was completed by Xerxes and a western staircase was added by Artaxerxes III, both staircases being ornamented with more bas-reliefs of tributaries and offerings.

These, like the huge bas-reliefs of the king and his attendants in the doorways, have been damaged by successive invading armies; the persons and robes of the figures were originally embellished with added jewellery, the crowns and edges of the robes adorned with gold and precious metals attached by golden nails. The winged symbol of divinity floats over the central inscriptions on the eastern wall and on the jambs of the eastern and western doorways where the king fights with mythical monsters. On the stone piers of the small rooms on the east and north, probably used for bathing and changing, the king's personal attendants are shown carrying such articles as a royal parasol, a scent box, towels and fly whisks. Cuneiform inscriptions round the stone window frames state that these were made 'in the royal house of Darius the King'. The stone walls were polished to a mirror-like shine and the floors covered with a bright red plaster, part of which can be seen in a corner of the northern rooms.

Notable visitors to this palace, including the Sassanian king Shahpur II, were unable to resist leaving a record of their visits in the form of inscriptions on some of the door jambs, and a number of early Islamic inscriptions point to a continuation of the same practice.

An unfinished palace of Artaxerxes III lies across the courtyard to the

---

(*Fig.* 34. continued)

T. Sparda (Lydians or Syrians), wearing finely pleated robes under cloaks fastened on one shoulder, boots and softly pointed caps. They bring vases, cups, bracelets and a chariot drawn by two small horses. The axle pin of the chariot is fashioned in the shape of the Egyptian god Bes.

U. Uvja (Susians) wearing the candys and a fillet round their hair; they bring a leashed lioness and two cubs, bows with ducks' head decoration and sheathed daggers.

V. Armina (Armenians) wearing belted tunics and trousers and tasselled caps like those of the Cappadocians; they escort a lively horse and hold a large vessel with griffin handles.

W. Mada (Medes), carrying a pitcher and bowls, a Median short sword, oval rings and folded overcoats and trousers, probably made of leather. (For detailed descriptions refer to Schmidt.[141])

south, and to the east of this, on the highest part of the platform and, like all the palaces, standing on its own terrace, is the main hall of the Hadish (literally, 'a Dwelling Place'), Xerxes' private palace which can be reached by a staircase from the courtyard.

The central hall of the Hadish with its 36 columns, approached by the northern porch with 12 columns, is surrounded by small chambers on the east and west, and has five doorways whose portals depict Xerxes entering or leaving the palace, accompanied by attendants. Not all the columns in the palaces were of stone; where it was possible to find tree trunks tall and strong enough, columns were made of these, standing on stone bases. The trunks themselves would be covered with painted plaster or gold leaf. These, together with the sun-baked mud-brick walls, roof beams and their mud-straw covering, have all disappeared with time, leaving only the stone elements of the construction.

The fact that both Xerxes' Hall of Audience and his private palace suffered heavily in the final fire has led some authorities to believe that Alexander started the conflagration in revenge for Xerxes' destruction of the Acropolis in Athens.[79]

Recent work by the Italian team[169,170] has revealed a palace of Artaxerxes III constructed on top of another of Artaxerxes I in the southern corner of the platform, practically completely destroyed by fire. At least thirty delegates were portrayed on the northern façade while the southern corner parapet is now complete with restored stone 'horns' discovered under debris at the foot of the platform.

South of the Hadish is a series of smaller, columned apartments of sun-dried brick which have been described as the Queen's apartments, but which were more likely to have been warehouses and stores for the Treasury.

There are two unexcavated mounds, one east of the Hadish and the other east of the Tachara, both of which await full explanation.

North of the Hadish is the Tripylon, the small Central Palace with its three entrances. The bas-reliefs on the main double staircase on the north depict Persian and Median guards with, on the inner surfaces, still other attractive reliefs of Median courtiers and nobles on their way to a banquet. There was another staircase on the south side of the palace, now moved to the Tehran Museum. On the portal of the eastern doorway Darius is shown on his throne, supported by representatives of 28 countries, and Xerxes the crown prince stands behind.[27]

From this palace one can look across almost the entire site, seeing on the south-east a small garden in front of the reception hall of the so-called Queen's apartments, which have now been restored and are used as a museum. (There is a public toilet here, as well as others which are by the main entrance to the platform.) The offices of the Archaeological Department have also been erected in this area.

The museum contains not only objects found in Persepolis but, in the right-hand galleries, prehistoric pottery and artifacts from nearby mounds including Tall-i Bakun (p. 235) and Tepe Shogha, and on the left early Islamic exhibits from Istakhr (p. 220). (*Museum.)

East of the museum, at the foot of the mountain face, is a self-contained complex of halls covering over 10,000 square m., including two large halls whose roofs were supported respectively by 100 and 99 wooden columns, and which is believed to have been the Treasury begun by Darius. Stone and clay tablets in Akkadian and Elamite[19] found here give details of exact wages in cash and in kind, paid to the men who built Persepolis, proving that this gigantic undertaking was constructed by free, paid labour, in contrast to contemporary monumental buildings in other countries where slave labour was the rule. According to Plutarch, Alexander the Great required 10,000 mules and 5,000 camels to carry the treasures of Persepolis to Ecbatana.

The better preserved of two identical bas-reliefs (*Reliefs) found on the east and south porches of the Treasury is now in the Tehran Museum and shows Darius on his throne with Xerxes and Persian nobles and attendants standing behind, and a Median official, probably the Chiliarch, the head of the Treasury who was also the Commander of the Army, standing with one hand raised to his mouth in a gesture of respect. Two elaborate incense burners stand between the official and the king.

Largest of all the palaces—70 × 70 m.—is the Hall of One Hundred Columns, immediately to the north of the Treasury, covered with some 3 m. of soil and cedar ash when it was first partly excavated by Mo'tamed al-Dawla Farhad Mirza, Governor-General of Fars, in 1878. Iranian archaeologists completed the excavation in 1940. Here only the column bases remain, badly scorched and damaged by the fire.

The bas-reliefs on the eastern and western doorways portray the monarch fighting a mythical animal—conceivably Ahriman, symbol of evil, who appears in various guises—with the winged symbol of Ahura Mazda hovering above. Those on the more important north and south portals show the king, in this instance Xerxes, on his throne, supported by representatives of the subject nations. The inner walls contain recesses of blind windows known as raf, or taqsheh, a traditional feature of old-style Iranian homes today.

The main entrance to the north, with its columned porch, takes one back through the incomplete entrance gateway and the passage leading to the Gateway of All Nations.

Between the Hall of One Hundred Columns and the mountains are buildings of sun-baked bricks forming the royal stables, guard room and

8*

domestic quarters—probably some 3,000 soldiers were garrisoned in Persepolis. Further north a 32-columned building with a columned porch faces the courtyard of the Treasury; other buildings in the extreme north-eastern corner included the royal chancellery and accounts offices where 30,000 tablets in Elamite were found.

Excavations and restoration still continue on this extraordinary site.

It is worth while taking an easy track up the slopes of Kuh-i Rahmat from the south-eastern corner of the Treasury, passing the remains of guard houses and a square well, to the rock-cut tombs tentatively ascribed to Artaxerxes II (405 to 361 B.C.), and further south to Artaxerxes III (361 to 338 B.C.). Both are empty save for the burial troughs cut into the rock. As at Naqsh-i Rustam, the king is shown worshipping before a fire altar, but on the southern tomb the small figures supporting the king's platform are each labelled. In front of the probable tomb of Artaxerxes II stand the remains of a small religious structure, while a two-leaved stone door and a long bronze trumpet from the more southerly mausoleum can be seen in the Persepolis Museum. From both these tombs one has a splendid bird's eye view of the entire terrace.

A track leads south over the mountain to a third rock-cut tomb that was never finished. It can be easily approached from the exterior of the platform, walking south along the track from which one can see the immense size of the terrace. In the middle of this southern wall is an important trilingual inscription of Darius the Great, unique in that the three versions are not exact translations but each gives some additional information. Together they assert that Darius, who gives his lineage and lists his possessions, built the foundations of Persepolis upon a hitherto unoccupied site.

Continue past the new excavations to the south-west and then cross a small stream closer to the cliffs. In an angle of the rock, hidden behind a tumble of rocks and young trees, is the unfinished tomb. Morning light is best for photographing this mausoleum which it is believed was intended to house the last of the Achaemenians, Darius III Codamanus.

The palaces under excavation on the plain below the terrace include one with inscriptions of Xerxes I, a temple, and other buildings of various dates. But Mr. Akbar Tadjvidi of the Iranian Archaeological Service has simultaneously carried out important work on the fortified walls that climb the mountain slopes to the east of the terrace, revealing many details of the original mud-brick construction and finding a significant new hoard of late Achaemenian seal impressions. (See Reports in *Iran*, Vol. VIII, 1970 & Vol. XI, 1972).

The remains of several early Achaemenian palaces have recently been found in the nearby plain. (*Palaces.) In addition, the nucleus of the so-called Fratadara Palace to the north-west of the platform, on the left of the Isfahan road, originally identified by Professor Herzfeld in 1932[89],[90] as that of a post-Achaemenian princeling c. 250 B.C., has been re-excavated. Work has disclosed a probably early Achaemenian palace with brick floors and walls which were re-used at the later date. (See report in *Iran*, Vol. XII, 1974.) The supposed base of a fire altar, a few foundations and column bases and the standing sides of a stone window are all that remains of the later palace. On the window are two badly weathered reliefs, one showing a man with both hands raised (one holding a barsom), and the other a female figure.

On the slopes of the mountain opposite this point is a quarry where an incomplete bull capital still stands *in situ*.

About 2 km. away is the chalcolithic site of Tall-i Bakun, possibly dating from between 4500 and 3500 B.C., which was first excavated by the Oriental Institute of Chicago in the 1930s. Particularly outstanding is the black-on-buff pottery including conical bowls painted on the exterior with the stylized, curving horns of the moufflon. Several excellent examples are on exhibition in the Tehran Museum.[107]

More recent excavations on the same site have been carried out by the Tokyo University Iraq-Iran Expedition in 1956-57; this same expedition also carried out further excavations on a considerable number of other sites in Fars.[44],[45]

Some 6 km. south of Tall-i Bakun, five private Achaemenian tombs have been cut into the side of Kuh-i Rahmat at a spot called Akkur-i Rustam.

About 12 km. from Persepolis, along the same southern side of Kuh-i Rahmat, is a delightful village called Maqsudabad located near the spring of Shah Abdullah. Two Pahlavi inscriptions dealing with the ownership of the spring are carved into the face of the mountain here.

Further to the south rises the humpbacked outline of Darvazeh Tepe, about 38 km. from Persepolis, but before driving to this, leave the track and follow the end of the mountain as it turns towards the rock-cut monument known as Qadamgah. Here, directly above a small spring, are two rock-cut stairways linking two terraces cut vertically into the rock. Along the back wall of the second terrace are three rows of five niches, badly damaged. Vanden Berghe suggests that this was an Achaemenian fire-cult monument, although others think it represents an unfinished tomb. (*Qadamgah.)

Back on the track to Darvazeh continue south, near the village of Kamjun, and only a little way from the great salt lake of Niriz. (From this point the drive back to Persepolis takes about one hour.)

Excavations are still taking place at Darvazeh Tepe under the direction of Dr. Murray Nicol of Harvard University. The site was first sounded by Professor L. Vanden Berghe[172] and noted earlier by Stein.[154]

It is one of the larger early mounds in Fars and covers approximately 63,500 square metres. At least seven architectural phases were revealed in the highest part of the mound during the first season's work. A series of C.14 tests provides a chronological framework from at least the beginning of the second millennium down to the middle of the first millennium B.C. Darvazeh Tepe appears to have been an industrial site producing ceramics, basically of the 'Taimuran/Shogha' wares which range through the entire history of occupation without a break. Possibly this site was occupied by an indigenous population not long before the founding of Pasargadae and Persepolis. The pottery found here includes the so-called 'Khabur' ware which was imported c. 1500 B.C. and a very fine, white-on-black painted ware not found in Iran before, which appears at Darvazeh c. 700 B.C.

Dr. Nicol and Mr. Paul Gotch carried out a survey of sites on the Persepolis plain and the Shiraz area in 1966, listing nearly 200 prehistoric and Islamic sites.[124] In addition a map showing the full range of the various occupational periods of the entire plain is to be published by Professor William Sumner, formerly of the recently established American Institute of Iranian Studies in Tehran, and now of Ohio State University.

9 · Fars (2)

(See map, p. 209.)

A splendid new highway from Shiraz to Kazerun begins by following the traditional caravan route but after climbing the Kotal-i Pir-i Zan ('the Pass of the Old Woman'), the first of two notoriously dramatic and dangerous passes, it follows a completely new route, from a small chai khaneh in the valley of Dasht-i Bagh. This avoids the second pass, 'the Pass of the Maiden', and cuts a formerly hazardous journey to a less dangerous one of about two hours to Bishapur. Buses from Shiraz, (Mihan Navad and Auto Kazerun, both in Kh. Nader), take a little longer and go on to Kazerun, but will stop right by the excavations. You might like to try the old, very poor, but picturesque route (by four-wheel drive), passing the historic Safavid caravanserai of Mian Kotal, now a gendarmerie post. This road approaches Kazerun from the south-east and from the final hairpin bends of the Kotal-i Dukhtar, Lake Parishan (or Famur), now part of a wild life and wetlands reserve, can be glimpsed and reached by a track south from the small bridge Pol-e Abgineh, with its Qajar relief at the foot of the pass. There are a number of chalcolithic and Sassanian sites in this valley and one arch of a stone Chahar Taq can be seen to the left of the road to Kazerun. This has been described by Maxime Siroux.[144a] Apart from small provincial hotels, a Tourist Inn is scheduled for Kazerun by 1975 and from here a drive of 21 km. east brings you to Bishapur.

If you drive by the new highway, however, you should make a short diversion to the remarkable Sassanian bas-relief of Sarab-i Qandil, noted by Mr. A. A. Sarfaraz in 1970. To reach this, turn right where the new highway joins the main Behbehan (p. 166)-Ahwaz (p. 140) road and after 2 km. take a track towards the hills on the left (west), negotiable in dry weather. Some 3 km. brings you to the Qashguli hamlet of Qandil where you may find the women weaving in tents. By four-wheel drive you can continue through the village a little further north on the old Sassanian road, to a stone ab-anbar of the same period. Then walk for less than one kilometre along the track by the Sarab stream, passing the Imamzadeh Sheikh Hussein which incorporates Sassanian stones in its lower walls, to the relief carved on a free-standing rock to the right of the track.

A king is depicted wearing a so-called 'Phrygian' or 'Parthian' cap, his right hand outstretched towards a female figure who offers a lotus, while to the king's left stands a male figure holding a ring in his right hand while his left hand rests on the hilt of his sword. There have been many theories regarding the identity of these figures; among them, Mr. Sarfaraz believes they represent Shahpur I, the goddess Anahita, and Kartir the High Priest (see his article in *Historical Studies of Iran, No.2*, Tehran, March 1973). Professor Vanden Berghe in 'La Signification Iconographique du Relief Rupestre Sassanide de Sarab-i Qandil (Iran)', Brussels, 1973, and Professor Richard N. Frye in 'The Sassanian Bas-Relief at Tang-i Qandil', *Iran*, Vol. XII, 1974, give a strong case for Bahram II with his wife and crown prince Bahram III, or a Persian noble. You need afternoon light for the best photography.

Back on the main road, turn south and drive about 10 km. to Bishapur, the 'Beautiful City of Shahpur'. Crossing the bridge as you approach from the direction of Ahwaz, you see the narrow gorge, which is the location of a series of important Sassanian reliefs, on the left. On the southern end of the bridge there are a chai khaneh and a small gendarmerie post, and above these on the top of a cliff are the remains of a Sassanian castle and rock-cut reservoirs. From here one can gain a good general view of the site on the opposite side of the main road.

The royal city was built on the Greek plan by Shahpur I in 266 A.D., six years after his triumph over the Roman emperor Valerian, according to a bilingual inscription in Parthian and Pahlavi that was found on one of a pair of columns dominating a presumed sacred area near the heart of the site. Bishapur was captured by the Arabs about 637 A.D. and soon lost its former importance; by the tenth century it was falling into ruins and most of its inhabitants had moved to Kazerun.

Five seasons of excavations between 1933 and 1940, by Professors Ghirshman and Salles, revealed a small but impressive section of this very large city, most of which is still buried. After a lapse of some years, the Iranian Archaeological Service began work here in 1968, under the direction of Mr. Ali Akbar Sarfaraz, and, for one season, under Mr. Jahangir Yasi. It is estimated that the city housed between 50,000 and 80,000 inhabitants; whereas the earlier French expedition revealed the remains of Shahpur's palace with its fascinating mosaics, a neighbouring temple and the above-mentioned votive area, the more recent Iranian work near the northern city wall has exposed a long stretch of the massive outer defences and early Islamic buildings constructed against the walls, as well as first millennium B.C. Elamite remains.

Walking from the main road, the city walls are on your right, and the core of the earlier excavations to your left and ahead.

Taking a track to the left you approach the remains of the great palace (see plan (1)). The cruciform-shaped hall, now open to the skies, originally consisted of a central chamber over 20 m. square, which was

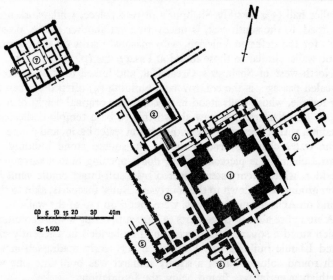

Fig. 35. Bishapur, 1974. 1. Shapur's Hall of Audience, 2. Anahita Temple,
3. West Mosaic hall, 4. East Mosaic hall, 5. Private palace of Shapur
6. Additions to royal palace, 7. Islamic religious building—
Madrasseh?
(*By courtesy of Mr. A. A. Sarfaraz, Iranian Archaeological Service*)

surrounded by four, triple-vaulted ivans; Ghirshman[56] thinks they
supported a cupola over the central chamber but Godard[71] takes the
view that it was unroofed. Around the walls, some of the 64 niches with
Greek key patterns and leaf scrolls in stucco, originally painted red,
yellow and black, can still be seen. A triple ivan opens onto a large
court to the east of the hall and when discovered it was still paved with
stone and bordered with colourful mosaics. The latter combine Roman
and Iranian motifs depicting nobles and ladies reclining on cushions,
the royal family, dancers and musicians. Some of these panels are in
the Tehran Museum, others in the Louvre, Paris.

Giving onto the same courtyard as this triple ivan was a second
palace (4), partially excavated before World War II put an end to the
French Mission's work here. Two niches showed traditional features of
Persepolis architecture, copies of those in the palaces of Darius and
Xerxes, while low reliefs on scattered slabs of stone that depicted charging horsemen had probably fallen from the façade. Adjoining the Great
Hall, to the south-west, another hall (3) has been completely cleared,
revealing red, blue and yellow paint traces on the walls, with half-
engaged columns by the southern entrance where some remnants of
mosaic flooring still remain. Next to this in turn, to the south-west, is a

smaller hall (5), possibly Shahpur's private palace, while work nearer
the road, to the south-east, is uncovering yet another palace, possibly
built for the defeated Valerian, with masons' marks on the enormous
stone walls, similar to those found at Pasargadae (p. 219).

North-west of Shahpur's Great Hall and linked to it by a recently
revealed passage, is the controversial building (2) often described as a
fire temple, whose walls stand in places to the original height of nearly
15 m. Mr. Sarfaraz has now shown this to be a temple dedicated to
Anahita, with a deep well below the central water basin, and connecting
stone water channels around the 14 m. square stone building: the
central chamber is pierced by four doors opening onto a surrounding
corridor, while twenty steps covered by a still-intact cradle vault lead
from ground level down to the courtyard. Bulls' foreparts, akin to those
found on Achaemenian capitals, were found on top of the walls.

A stone fire altar in three parts (a base supporting a short column on
which stood a square table), was found embedded in a recently excavated Islamic building (7). Probably a very early madrasseh-mosque
with round column bases; a square minaret was built into one wall.
Parthian material was found below the foundations.

The votive area previously mentioned lies further away from the
main road, past the new excavations and the team house with its small
museum, and along one of two main avenues meeting at right angles in
the centre of the town. Here, in a hollow just to the right of the avenue
which is flanked by the unexcavated ruins of buildings, stand two square
stone bases with a smaller base before them, and two broken columns,
now lying on the ground, but which originally stood on the larger bases.
Probably a lintel rested across the two columns on one of which one
can still see the clear inscription in Pahlavi and Parthian describing
how the Governor erected the monument, which included a statue of
Shahpur, in A.D. 266. Two small blocks of stone stood in front of either
column and probably supported fire altars. Masons' marks in Greek
characters can be seen on some of the stones.

Turning back to the excavations closer to the river, all the semicircular towers on the city wall have been restored with protective
sections built on top of the Sassanian. Originally the ramparts presented
a continuous façade of rounded towers with only 40 cm. between the
buttresses, some of which still stand some 3 m. high—the original height
of the towers possibly reaching fully 10 m. The wall and the towers
were coated with white plaster on fine, fluted stucco, with red and blue
plaster in the V-shaped spaces between the buttresses.

During the Sassanian period, many of the buildings in the city were
reconstructed and the outer face of the wall underwent changes which
included the removal of one tower in every three. The battlements were

extended in a smooth-faced façade pierced by high, narrow arrow-slits. At this time too a typically Sassanian building was constructed close to the outer side of the wall, beside the river, and here a central ivan with two wings and two corridors has been revealed, together with engaged columns on rectangular bases. A series of other buildings in this area, with its paved streets and an ab-anbar (an underground water reservoir) of the same dimensions as those built today include late eleventh and early twelfth century Islamic structures. Heavy grinding stones used for pressing oil can be seen *in situ*. (See short reports in *Iran*, Vol. VIII, 1970, & *Bastan Chenassi va Honar-i Iran*, Nos. 9–10, 1972.)

The Plan Organization of Iran has subsidized the excavations for five years, but detailed plans have been made by the Archaeological Department for work which could last for at least twenty years over this vast site that might well prove as spectacular as Persepolis.

On the other side of the main road the narrow gorge, through which flows the River Shahpur, was selected by the Sassanian kings for a display of six commemorative bas-reliefs. Two of Shahpur I's are on the right-hand bank as you walk up from the main road; one is badly worn and probably depicts Philip the Arab (who sued for peace in A.D. 244) kneeling before Shahpur's horse during the king's investiture by Ahura Mazda. The other, further along and set a little back and higher from the path, shows Shahpur on horseback in the centre panel, trampling the prostrate body of Gordian III; Philip the Arab (?) is again on bended knee before the king who holds the right wrist of another distinguished prisoner, believed to be the Emperor Valerian, standing beside the horse. According to tradition, Valerian was captured after a single-handed combat between the rulers. Choose morning light for photography. On the cliff above are the remains of a Sassanian castle.

The remaining four scenes which can be seen distantly from the heights of the castle, are on the opposite side of the gorge. Here, between 1973 and 1975, Mr. Sarfaraz removed a stone conduit which had not only made viewing difficult, but whose waters had badly eroded much of the carvings. The stream was diverted underground and a new, easier path constructed, resulting in the unearthing of hitherto unsuspected portions of existing reliefs.

Nearest to the main road is the triple victory of Shahpur I, now seen to be carved in a concave surface in five rows, showing Roman prisoners in the lower panels and Persians laden with booty in the upper. The fifth and lowest row revealed in 1975 shows horsemen on the left and men on foot on the right, almost all the human figures having lost their heads through erosion. Next comes the subjection of Arab tribes, with camels and horses, and Bahram II (A.D. 276 to 293), with an escort of Sassanian warriors, also damaged by the old conduit.

Third is a splendid investiture of what has long been taken for
Bahram I (A.D. 273 to 276) with an inscription in which supposedly
Narseh (A.D. 293 to 302) had his own name inscribed over that of
Bahram's. Below the king's horse, work in 1975 revealed the romantic
relief of a prone figure wearing a distinctive cap and resting his head on
his arm. Careful re-examination of the entire scene by the Iranian Centre
of Archaeological Research may soon result in positive identification of
both the king depicted and the figure being trampled by his horse.

Finally on the corner of the rock, another relief in several rows shows
Shahpur II (A.D. 309 to 379), seated in the centre, triumphing over an
Indian people or possibly the Kushans. Among the many other figures
seen here are prisoners, a man with a decapitated head in each hand, a
boy on a small elephant, warriors and courtiers. Try to see this side of
the gorge in the afternoon light.

These identifications follow those proposed by Vanden Berghe.[177]
(For other references, see Georgina Herrmann,[86] E. Herzfeld[87] and
W. Hinz.[93])

For Shahpur's Cave (Mudan), drive along the right bank of the river
for about 6 km. to orange groves by a ford opposite the Qashguli village
of Abdulla Khan. Fording the river, leave your vehicle behind the
village and follow a steep path to the wide-mouthed cave in the cliff
behind. Unless you scramble straight up, the climb will take about one
hour. The colossal statue of Shahpur, originally over 8 m. tall, has been
crudely repaired with cement and stands near the front of the cave
surrounded by broken fragments. Behind stretches the dark cavern with
a large Sassanian reservoir and tunnel, so far incompletely explored.
Ghirshman believes that Shahpur, who died in Bishapur, may have been
buried here but there is no trace of a tomb.

From Kazerun you can go south-west to Bushire on a new road
partially completed in 1974, or north-west to Ahwaz seeing a number of
interesting sites on the latter route. Some 30 km. from Bishapur you
come to the village of Sarab Bahram and about half a kilometre behind
this, carved on the steep sides of a mountain, above a rocky pool, is
the bas-relief of Naqsh-i Bahram which depicts Bahram II enthroned
and surrounded by the notables of his kingdom. You can see the site
from the road, looking east, and walk across the fields to the relief which
is best photographed in the afternoon.

About another 22 km. along the road and 7 km. west of the village
of Nurabad, on the edge of the plain of Shahpur and at the foot of the
Kuh-i-Pir-i Mard (Mountain of the Old Man), is a small, square stone
tower known as the Mil-i Adjahan or Dimei-Mil. Ghirshman identifies
this as a fire temple dating from the third to the first century B.C. and
it has certain marked similarities to the Achaemenian Ka'bah and

Zendan towers (p. 219). Among the differences, however, are an inner staircase leading to the roof on which fire altars may have been placed, and there are small landings inside the tower. From certain parallels with the masonry of the monumental stone temple at Bishapur, however, other authorities prefer a date in the Sassanian period.

About 12 km. from this tower, and 5 or 6 km. north-west of the large village of Fahlian (and about 200 m. west of Suravan), at the most westerly of the three hamlets known collectively as Jin-Jin, Aurel Stein[156] first noted the ruins of an Achaemenian pavilion with black limestone column bases decorated with lotus flowers, a reminder that the royal road connecting Susa and Persepolis ran along here. The site is a low tepe about 80 × 60 m. in area and has at least one exposed column base still visible near the summit. It was the scene of a preliminary survey conducted by Kikuo Atarashi and Kiyoharu Horiuchi on behalf of the Tokyo University Iraq-Iran Archaeological Expedition in 1959.[5]

There are many more sites in the immediate vicinity, including Tepe Mohammad-Qasim by the river. This yields reddish-brown polished ware of possible Achaemenian date. Large stones and black column bases have been found on the skirts of Kuh-i Dol, south-west of Tepe Suruvan, although here many of the stones appear to have been incorporated in the houses of the nearby village.

Aurel Stein commented on the Kurangun Elamite rock reliefs, first noted by Herzfeld in 1924, which stand about 10 km. from Fahlian but are separated from it by a river. To reach them, continue along the new Bishapur-Ahwaz highway which by-passes Fahlian. The old road goes off to the left and can be taken for Jin-Jin, which lies beyond Fahlian and where the remains of the Achaemenian pavilion mentioned above can be seen. Beyond this diversion, however, the new highway continues, and just past a track on the right, going to Yasuch, another track on the left leads to the village of Seh-Talu near which are the Kurangun reliefs.

On the way, the track passes near a flat-topped mountain on whose summit are the remains of the Qaleh-i Sefid, 'the White Castle', dating from the Islamic period but probably on older foundations. The mountain has traditionally served as a place of refuge for local tribes, since it has springs and pastures. Near the path up the mountain and close to the summit, there is a small fortified building which is probably Sassanian, on a partly artificial terrace.

Beyond Qaleh-i Sefid is Seh-Talu village where the river turns west, forming a right angle. Behind the village is the cliff on the further side of which, near the summit, are the Kurangun reliefs which involve a climb to the summit of the rock, edging along a narrow flight of rock-cut steps.

Herzfeld[87] attributes the reliefs to the reign of King Puzur Inshushinak, *c.* 2400 B.C., but Vanden Berghe[172] feels the principal relief probably dates from the fifteenth–sixteenth century B.C. This shows two divinities surrounded by worshippers; one figure is seated on a coiled serpent throne, and wears a horned head-dress; he pours water from a vase onto the heads of worshippers. The second (left-hand) relief shows the faithful descending from the mountain and Vanden Berghe dates this to *c.* eighth century B.C. To the right of the relief are two small buildings partly carved out of the cliff face.

Close to the old Fahlian road, about 3 km. east of the Kurangun reliefs, but some 1½ km. off the new main highway, is the mound of Tula Sepid (Tal-e Sepid). Elamite town walls of brick have been found here, with cuneiform inscriptions, dating between 1500 and 1000 B.C. Around this area are many chalcolithic mounds, and Alexander the Great is thought to have taken the mule route from Tula Sepid towards Shiraz when he defeated Ariobarzanes, before seizing Persepolis.

Beyond Tula Sepid, the road climbs through the Tang-i Sangur and over the pass of the same name, at one time blocked by a wall of large, unmortared stones. It was possibly near here that Alexander defeated the Uxians, a tough mountain tribe that is said to have exacted a toll from all who traversed the royal road.

In the fertile valley of Deh Now, near the small settlement of Mansurabad, a winding mountain track leads northwards through Mamasani tribal country, past various remains of suspected Sassanian or early Islamic date, to the impressive rock-cut tomb known as Dai-i Dukhtar, or 'the nurse of the maiden'. Discovered by Herzfeld in 1928 and often ascribed to one or other of the Achaemenian ancestors of Cyrus the Great, the tomb is now thought to be post-Achaemenian in date. Here two pairs of semi-engaged columns, surmounted by late Ionic capitals, flank the entrance to an empty tomb chamber consisting of an upper and lower room. Access, as Stein has noted, is more than difficult.

About 22 km. further along the main road from Deh Now, near the village of Basht, are the remains of a Sassanian bridge over the Tang-i Brin, a little upstream. An early Islamic bridge about 100 m. downstream spanned the river with two arches resting on a central pillar, but only a single block of masonry now remains.

There are still other Sassanian remains in this area. North-west of the plain, on the borders of Fars and Khuzestan, are the ruins of a Sassanian town, possibly Darkhid, at the western end of the limestone cliffs of Kuh-i Sharrafi near the entrance to the Tang-i Malium gorge, and on the right, a few km. before reaching Dogunbaden. The remains of a square stone building with an inner courtyard can be seen in the eastern part of the town, while to the south-west are the ruins of a fort, with bastions and buttresses. Within the fortress is a well with an underground channel which supplied the garrison.

Dogunbaden lies just across the provincial boundary, in Khuzestan. On a mound to the left of the road, just before Dogunbaden, however, is a Sassanian fire temple, known locally as the Chahar Deh. This building, once covered by a dome, exhibits the typical square plan of a Chahar Taq with a wide arch piercing each of its four walls. Other notable features include a surrounding, cradle-vaulted passage and a large, vaulted ivan on the south-east.

From the village of Dogunbaden one can drive 150 km. south along a poor road to the little port of Bandar Rig on the Persian Gulf, with a turning off to the Gach Saran oilfield; or continue west to Behbehan, 70 km. (p. 166), and on to Ahwaz.

From just north of Kazerun one can take the new highway to Bushire, some 172 km. to the south-west through wild and desolate mountains. (*Borazjan, Tal-i Mor, Sang-i Siah.) Bushire, a hot and humid area, not recommended for a summer visit, lies on the tip of a peninsula and is on the regular Iran Air route from Abadan, via Kharg to Shiraz. It was on this peninsula then called Mesembria, that Alexander's admiral, Nearchus, anchored in the fourth century B.C. On the southern outskirts of the town past dilapidated eighteenth century mansions, are the remains of the earlier Partho-Sassanian city of Rishahr which some scholars think was named after the Sassanian fortress of Riv-Ardashir, and others attribute to the earlier Elamite 'rishair' (great). Now it is merely a huge embankment with a broad ditch and remains of mud-brick walls rising some 9 m. round a hollow square with remnants of Portuguese and Safavid constructions. One edge of the fortress has fallen into the sea by the small but important harbour which it guarded and from whence several Sassanian kings launched naval attacks.[180]

Remains of the important Elamite town of Liyan lie under nearby mounds, while about 4 km. south-east of Sabzabad (the side of the old British Residency), reached by 10 km. of good tarmac road from Bushire, are the ruins of an Elamite temple first excavated by the French Mission about 1911 and where local occupation probably lasted from c. 2500 to 1200 B.C. and possibly a thousand years earlier by Proto-Elamites from Susa. [116 (Vol. XVI)] Unfortunately the huge citadel mound lies between two naval establishments and is therefore not easily examined. In 1969 Martha Prickett discovered a prehistoric mound towards the south of the peninsula which yielded sherds of Hajji Muhammad and later Ubaid styles.

The Tourist Inn and Persian Gulf Hotel offer reasonable accommodation and there are several smaller hotels in Bushire itself.

From Bushire one can fly three times a week to Abadan, via Kharg

Island where there are a number of interesting sites. However, since this is a protected area, special permission must be obtained to stay here—arrangements can be made through the Security Police or through the courtesy of the Oil Service Company (O.S.C.O.) who operate their own guest house and other facilities for official visitors.

This small coral island which is now one of the world's largest crude oil tankering terminals, was probably part of the Elamite dominions from the third millennium B.C. onwards. In the first century A.D. Pliny's reference to a temple of Neptune on the island of Aracia may well be linked with Kharg.

In 1959 the I.O.O.C. (now Oil Service Company), invited the French Archaeological Mission to survey Kharg before its development, and Professor Ghirshman's findings were published in a condensed form in a small booklet available from O.S.C.O.[57]

Two megalithic dolmen tombs dating from about 1000 B.C., hewn out of rock, stand in isolation on a high ridge in the central portion of the island. Fragments of some fifteen skeletons were found in one of these, while the other was empty. A Roman coin points to continued re-use however, probably down to at least the fourth or fifth century A.D.

Several courses of stone, forming the four sides of a small building erected on the central ridge of the island, have been taken to be the remains of a temple of Poseidon. Now there is only the trace of a podium within, while outside, in the south-east corner of the ridge, a square basin has been cut into the solid rock. About 100 m. to the north of this there is a cistern dug into the rock, with water channels to guide the rainwater. At one time a spring gushed from the ridge and formed a lake which could have contained as much as ten million gallons of water.

By early Sassanian times the original stone building had fallen into ruins and a Sassanian Ateshkadeh or fire temple, dated by a coin of King Hormizd II to about the beginning of the fourth century A.D., had been built on its debris. Constructed of rough stones and mortar—the materials usually favoured by the Sassanians—this building has now been crudely restored with cement.

Some 100 m. to the south of the domed Ateshkadeh—the permanent repository of the sacred fire—are the remains of an open-sided pavilion (Chahar Taq) where the fire would have been displayed to the public.

In the early Muslim period the fire temple was used as a mosque, a mihrab niche being cut into the side of the wall facing Mecca.

The ridge overlooks, to the north, a charming Muslim shrine with the typical southern sugar-loaf roof and a small dome behind. The rear tomb chamber of the saint, Mir Mohammad, may date from the tenth century A.D., possibly built on a Sassanian structure, and the remainder with glazed Mongol tiles, is probably early fourteenth century.

Around the base of the rocky prominence on which stands the fire temple, are more than eighty tombs hollowed out of the rock. The shallow circular openings are astodans or ossuaries in which Zoroastrians placed the defleshed bones of their dead. The large man-made caves with rectangular entrances, having the Nestorian cross inscribed above their openings, were early Christian tombs.

Most interesting, however, and best photographed early in the morning, are the two large Palmyran tombs used for multiple burials. The façade of the southern tomb was probably destroyed at the time of the eighteenth century Dutch occupation when columns and pilasters of the two large tombs were broken down to serve as building materials for a Dutch citadel and fortified town on the north-east tip of the island. The façade of the eastern tomb is almost intact and was designed in the same style as that of a domestic dwelling of the same period, c. second century A.D. The main entrance in the centre is flanked by jutting-out false windows over which a dog-tooth frieze is carved, and by square pillars with capitals between the 'windows', all combining elements of Parthian and Sassanian architectural features.

Beyond the entrance hall are three rows of alcoves above each other, cut out of the rock, and here embalmed bodies were laid, each alcove being closed with a slab of stone. The vestibule and the central chamber are divided by a triple ivan—a feature now most clearly seen in the southern tomb.

A partly obliterated bas-relief on the wall facing the entrance of the southern tomb shows, if one can discern it, a figure reclining on a couch, supporting itself on one elbow resting on cushions, and holding a drinking cup in its hand, reminiscent both of the Seleucid Hercules at Bisitun (p. 127) and of a bas-relief in the underground chamber in the Atenatan in Palmyra itself, dated A.D. 229. A smaller figure stands at its foot and there are other, much defaced small figures along the lower edge. Opening into the two projecting sides behind the relief are more alcoves, the side of one of which shows a badly worn bas-relief of what may possibly be a tutelary genius standing on a globe, holding out one arm as though making an oblation. Vine branches encircle the tomb on the right of this relief.

These tombs bear such similarity to the classical tombs of Palmyra that they were almost certainly constructed as hypogea for a colony of Palmyran traders on the island. Kharg thus probably formed one of the most southerly trading links for merchandise brought from India and China and then transferred at Kharg to Palmyran vessels which took it up the Euphrates to caravans transporting the goods finally to the Mediterranean ports and on to Rome.

(Palmyra, an important commercial city on an oasis between Damascus and the Euphrates, about 140 km. east of Homs, was a centre of Graeco-Oriental art with strong Parthian influences.)

Extensive burial grounds on the eastern part of Kharg were probably dug into the rock at the end of the Sassanian period or later, the individual graves being covered with slabs of stone and sealed with plaster. Some of these still contain skeletons.

During the Sassanian era, from the third to the seventh century A.D., a sizeable Nestorian Christian community existed on Kharg; the most important Christian centre of Iran in the third century A.D. was in the town of Dev-Ardashir about 12 km. from Bushire on the mainland. In the fourth century A.D. the Nestorian sect was the only orthodox creed accepted by Iranian Christians, and among them only monks were allowed to remain unmarried, the clergy being forbidden to take the vows of celibacy.

On the barren western coast of Kharg there are the remains of a monastery and church, mainly constructed of dressed stone. There is a triple nave, in the Sassanian style, and probably the three vaulted roofs that covered them were between 6 and 7 m. high. From the entrance, five steps lead down from the narthex (a railed-off portico for women, penitents and those persons under instruction) into the main section of the nave; a second flight of four steps goes from the further end of the nave into the choir, a square chamber surmounted by a dome. Under this dome (the entire building is now roofless) was the altar; a hollowed-out circle in the plaster floor still contained fragments of dark stone from this altar when it was discovered. To the left is a small chamber where the eucharistic elements were placed and where there is a small basin and a drainage hole. Walls here rise to some $2\frac{1}{2}$ m. and include a complete, arched alcove. On the right of the choir was the diaconicon at the far end of which, in two corners, stood a bed and a reliquary, the latter in the corner to the right of the bed, facing it and built in stone and plaster with a small opening large enough for a man's hand. Probably monks who had to spend a number of nights in the sanctuary touched the relics through this opening.

In the spacious corridor leading from this chamber, the remains of three terracotta lamps, attached to supports with bitumen, were found. Off the passage was the sacristy and the detached rooms at the southern end with a stone bed, were probably occupied by a gatekeeper.

The bones of four adults, thrown haphazardly into a tomb sealed with plaster, were found in the floor of the side aisle on the north of the nave. It is thought they might have been bones of Christian

martyrs brought from the mainland when the church was consecrated.

The walls of the church were decorated in stucco, much of it in pure
Sassanian style and similar to the stucco on Taq-i Bustan (pp. 130–1),
suggesting a date of the fifth or sixth century A.D. The communicating
doors had a Nestorian cross carved over them. Two long chambers
behind the sanctuary probably held scrolls for the library, in numerous
niches arranged in three levels. Adjoining this to the east was a Capitu-
lary chamber with corridors on three sides, a low bench round the four
walls and a large vaulted recess in the north corner probably for the
official seat of the monastery's Superior.

The monastery itself formed the outer wall surrounding the church
and it contained some sixty cells, each of three small chambers, in one
of which stood a low platform or bed of stone and plaster. A few hundred
metres from the church, a number of small ruins each surrounded by a
wall were probably the homes of the married clergy.

Rainwater was trapped in holes dug at the foot of the eastern slope
and conveyed through underground channels. Wells provided irrigation
water for the small fields made by building dams across the gulleys,
and vines were planted in holes hewn out of the rock and protected from
the wind by low, circular walls. Below the terraced vineyards (now a
public park) Mr. Sarfaraz identified a Sassanian-period circular
ab-anbar.

Further down the coast of the mainland is perhaps the most interesting
of all sites in this part of Fars, the eighth to tenth century A.D. port of
Siraf, which a British team sponsored by the British Institute of Persian
Studies under the direction of Dr. David Whitehouse excavated from
1966 to 1973. The site, which is a little difficult to reach during the
spring and after heavy rains, is some 200 km. south of Bushire. There is
a daily bus from Bushire, leaving round about 8 a.m. and arriving by
the early afternoon, in Taheri, the modern fishing village. Partly Shi'a,
partly Sunni, the latter women are distinguished by their black masks.
Taheri in 1974 boasted no public accommodation and one had to camp
or depend on local hospitality. As the bus emerges from the winding
Kunarak gorge it passes the excavations on either side of the road.

The ruins of ancient Siraf (traditionally associated with Sinbad the
Sailor) were discovered in 1808 by James Morier [118] and have since been
seen by other visitors including Sir Aurel Stein [155] and Professor Vanden
Berghe.[172] As a result of Dr. Whitehouse's excavations, Siraf is now
known to have been a Sassanian port probably serving Gur (p. 254) to
which it was connected by road, and was possibly a naval base with a
massive fort that may have been built by Shapur II *c.* A.D. 360. In the
tenth and eleventh centuries Siraf was still a flourishing port, a

prosperous and imposing city second only in importance to, and almost as large as Shiraz, although only a narrow strip of land less than 500 m. wide between the sandstone ridge to the north, and the shallow bay, is suitable for habitation.

This fascinating site lies between the modern village, dominated by

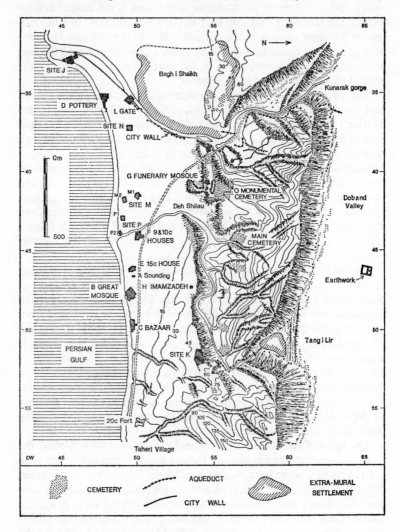

Fig. 36. Siraf. General plan of western part of city.
(*By courtesy of Dr. D. Whitehouse from* Iran, *Vol. XII, 1974*)

the Shaikh's fortified mansion, and the Kunarak valley. Beginning at the western tip of the bay you can see at Site J, what appears to have been a military complex with a large warehouse or caravanserai and hamam and at Site L, a Sassanian gate on the city wall. South of this, on the shore at D and eroded by the sea, was an industrial area of pottery kilns, while east of the gate the team revealed what appears to be a Basilica, perhaps a Nestorian church, N. Across the road on a spur of rock which further inland overlooks the astonishing Shilau valley and its hundreds of rock-cut graves, is a thirteenth century funerary mosque, several times rebuilt. Immediately to the north is the monumental cemetery O, with the remains of some forty stone mausolea, probably built in the ninth and tenth centuries and comparable in size with the tomb of Ismail the Samanid at Bukhara. These tombs were intended for the collective disposal of the dead and contained skeletons of both sexes and all ages. In one tomb were the remains of at least fifty-two persons, many of whom seem to have suffered from sickle cell anaemia.

Down on the shore again, by an oval depression used as a rubbish tip then a cemetery, south-east of the monumental cemetery, Site M includes a massive early Islamic building richly decorated with stucco and with narrow cubicles round a large courtyard. In a lane outside the building are a number of latrines. Perhaps this was an office block, or maybe a brothel? Nearer the sea, at Site P, a small Khanegah and mosque with part of a staircase to a minaret, was later abandoned and, until the eleventh century, used as a factory for processing whale blubber, judging from the thick black deposit still seen on floor and walls, and the pits for large storage vats.

A curtain wall probably built in the tenth century as an emergency defence, connects the Khanegah and factory. Not far from this, a little to the north-east on the far side of a footpath, is Site F where you can walk along paved lanes between the nearly 6 m. high walls of once splendid mansions in the early Islamic merchant residential quarter. With interior courtyards, some with remains of pillars that supported upper galleries, stucco decorated walls and one house by the footpath boasting its own private mosque and handsome portal with half-engaged columns facing the main street, this is an evocative area whose architecture still shows unmistakable Sassanian ancestry.

About 400 m. further east on the very edge of the sea and partly eroded by it, lies the Great Mosque B, built over a massive early Sassanian fort or fortified palace with remnants of the covered bazaar and a hamam around it. The piers and foundations of the Mosque, built shortly after A.D. 803–4, have cleverly been left intact while the Sassanian structures were excavated, revealing fifty-two rooms and four courtyards in a lightly fortified outer enclosure. The monumental east entrance of the inner fort has been exposed with at least two periods of construction, and can be seen just in front of and below the square base of the minaret. There are double arcades on three sides of the large mosque courtyard and an arcade five bays deep on the qibla (west) wall.

Site K is a terraced area on the crest of the ridge, behind the outskirts of Taheri village and reached by a footpath. Here is a Sassanian curtain wall to the south and at least four palaces on two terraces overlooking more rock-cut graves and ossuaries inland. The earliest mansions date from the Sassanian period, with other early Islamic buildings, probably governors' residences. The Upper Building with more than thirty rooms on different levels, revealed a fascinating plastered wall on which many graffiti had been scratched, including one of a three-masted ocean-going boat.

A vast quantity of finds includes Chinese porcelain, coins from Spain, Russia and Syria, and glass and lapis lazuli. (See [180] and reports in *Iran*, Vols. VI, 1968 – XIII, 1975.)

A coastal highway is under construction between Bushire and Bandar Abbas. While there are no known prehistoric sites here, there are charming fishing villages such as Bandar Lengah and the nearby picturesque shipbuilding port of Bandar Kung. From Lengah a track goes north through the Lar area connecting with Jahrom, Fasa (p. 258) and the Shiraz road. But inland is still wild and isolated country and only well-organized escorted parties should attempt this route.

From Bandar Abbas an excellent highway runs due north to Kirman (p. 264) and a jet airport, first-class Gameroon Hotel on the outskirts and the less expensive but good Hotel Naz in Kh. Reza Shah Kabir and others less sophisticated in the city, make this a pleasant stop. The early morning seaside market is thronged with local women wearing black or red leather and cloth masks of varying designs. Almost opposite Bandar Abbas are the islands of Hormuz and Qishm with their Portuguese remains. Qishm, which has been under excavation by the Iranian Archaeological Service, directed by Javad Babakrad, has yielded pre-historic, Achaemenian and Sassanian sites, is in a Protected Area, not accessible to visitors.

Bandar Abbas itself dates only from the time of Shah Abbas, although Minab, some 110 km. east, across the bay, and reached by a rough track which is flooded during the rains (new roads are promised soon), was the most important centre in the area in ancient times and today is set in an extremely lovely palm grove. From here a road continues north to Jiraft and eventually joins the main Kirman-Bam road.

There are various tracks inland between Bushire and Bandar Abbas, taking one into the country between the old Sassanian highway from Firuzabad and the new one from Kazerun to the coast. Archaeological discoveries are still being made in this area but any projected journey requires considerable organization beforehand, guides, and in some cases the hire of mules.

One can see a number of sites in the area south of Shiraz, by starting off from that city on the road leading to Firuzabad itself, 116 km. to the south. The road begins by being asphalted but soon deteriorates into a gravel road which goes through attractive country frequented by migrating tribes. About 104 km. from Shiraz is the narrow gorge known as Tang-i Ab and half-way through this, perched on top of the cliffs on the left-hand side of the road, is the Qaleh-i Dukhtar, a fortified palace probably built by Ardashir I before his victory over the Parthian ruler Artabanus V. Remains of the defensive walls formerly blocking the roadway can still be seen. From the road one can see the tunnel now cut by the new road, connecting the well-shaft about 20 m. deep, with the river. Several tracks lead to the castle, the shortest being a fairly stiff 20–30 minutes' scramble from the west. The complex occupies three terraces, and from the lowest, containing the defences, you climb by a well-preserved staircase to the second and a courtyard surrounded by rooms. On the third terrace are the main palace buildings including the formerly barrel-vaulted ivan some 21 m. long. At the eastern end is the round tower with its façade of long, narrow niches, its inner square chamber with most of its dome intact, and decorations of stucco 'Egyptian' grooving. (*See Appendix for plan.) For details see 'Qal'a-ye Dukhtar bei Firuzabad', by D. Huff. *A.M.I.*, 4, 1971.

Just before emerging from the gorge where the cliffs narrow, you can see a bas-relief on the opposite bank of the river, by the remains of a Sassanian bridge. It shows Ardashir's investiture, with the king standing before a small fire altar on the other side of which is the deity Ahura Mazda. Behind Ardashir is a small page with a fly whisk and then three male figures, probably his sons. The best time to photograph this relief is mid to late afternoon.

A most attractive chai khaneh with tables set out under the trees overlooks the river just beyond the relief, and past this again, about 1 km. down the road and difficult to see even when looking for it, is an immense relief over 20 m. long, depicting Ardashir's battle with Artabanus, carved in low relief high up on the wide rock face. Early morning light is the best in which to see and photograph this. When the river is not too high, leave the car by the side of a rock-cut trough, scramble down to the river bed, and walk along it for a few metres until you have passed the reliefs on the opposite cliff. Attempting to ford the river elsewhere can be dangerous even in summer. If in any doubt, ask at the chai khaneh for a guide. One can cross the river where a series of rocks narrows the flow, and find a fairly easy footpath some way to the east

of the reliefs, climbing up a gradual ascent to a narrow platform immediately beneath them. Once you are here, the fascinating details can be
seen—the largest and probably the earliest of all Sassanian reliefs,
shows three pairs of combatants, all mounted on chargers: Ardashir is
unseating Artabanus V whose horse turns a somersault; Shahpur,
behind his father, defeats Artabanus' grand vizier, and, behind these,
a Sassanian page tackles a Parthian, with his arm around his opponent's
neck.

The cliffs fall away after this, and now from the road one can see
across the river the domed palace of Firuzabad, reputed to have been
built by Ardashir some years before his great victory over the Parthian
king in A.D. 224. It is possible to drive or wade across the river to the
palace which stands on an eminence before a small pool fed by a spring
that once watered formal gardens, or take the gravel road from Gur.

Built of rough-hewn stones bonded with mortar, the palace is a
mixture of architectural styles. Its uneven walls were smoothed with
plaster and the niches inside were ornamented with the same kind of
'Egyptian' grooving seen at Qaleh-i Dukhtar. It is a massive building,
one of the most important in Persian architectural history, with walls
some 4 m. thick and measuring 104 × 55 m. Facing the pool is a façade
of semi-engaged columns of Parthian style, and over a tangle of fallen
rubble one sees, and enters through, the great central ivan whose
approach is flanked by two small cradle-vaulted rooms on either side.

The ivan leads into the middle of three square domed halls and one
can clearly see what have been described as the earliest known examples
of the squinch, in which the problem of placing a round dome on a
square or rectangular base was solved, a feature that spread much later
to Europe. Pope[129] has described these as the earliest known Persian
domes.

These halls were the official apartments. A small ivan leads out of the
Central Hall to a large courtyard round which is a series of barrel-
vaulted rooms presumed to have been the residential section of the
palace, with distinctive 'key-hole' doorways and decorative motifs;
in the most westerly room, reached through the domed chamber
immediately in front of it, a staircase can still be mounted to the roof
and the galleries around the domes.

To the south of the palace, between it and the present town of
Firuzabad, lie the remains of Ardashir's city which he called 'Ardashir
Khurrah', or 'the Glory of Ardashir'. The name was later contracted to
Gur. It was this city—founded after Ardashir had brought all the petty
princes of Fars under his own rule—that finally roused the fears of
Artabanus V and led to the Parthian's disastrous attempt to crush his
dangerous vassal.

The 'Glory of Ardashir' was built on the typical Parthian circular plan, rimmed with a ditch and earth ramparts, the whole over 2 km. in diameter and forming a perfect circle with gateways at the four quarters. Several dry-weather tracks go across the site which is divided by two main roads. At the original centre of the city stands the imposing core of a square tower some 30 m. high and 10 m. square, made of rough-hewn stones and known as the Minar of Gur. On one side are traces of a spiral staircase[154] which Dr. D. Huff believes was inside the originally 20 m. square tower. On the summit some authorities believe a sacred fire burned in full view of the public; others maintain that the tower was a symbolic fortification, a visual expression of the king's power and authority.[50]

About 100 m. north-east of the tower is a platform of finely dressed stones 25 m. square and known today as Takht-i Nishin. Dr. Huff has shown that this had a cruciform inner chamber covered by a dome of about 15 m. diameter, with several ivans or extra rooms around, and may have been identified with Ardashir's fire temple.[59, 71] (See also 'Der Takht-i Nishin in Firuzabad', by Dietrich Huff, *Archaeologischer Anzeiger*, Heft 3, Berlin, 1972.)

The present town of Firuzabad, which stands on its own early foundations a kilometre or so to the north-east, was also known as Gur until the tenth century when the Buyid ruler Adud al-Dowleh renamed it as Firuzabad. It fell into ruins in the eleventh century and never regained its former importance on the great caravan highway from the Far East to the Persian Gulf. Today it is a Qashqai tribal centre with little trace of the once fertile fields of world-famous roses.

Several small cafés in the town offer excellent Paloudeh (or Faloudeh), the iced sweet of frozen vermicelli served with pure lemon juice, which the writer has eaten here with impunity. Beyond Firuzabad there are fair roads to Kunar Siah, Farrashband and Lar, through desolate country; for exact directions and as a precaution in case of breakdown, it is wise to consult the local police or gendarmerie.

Of the many fire temples in this area, of particular interest is the magnificent complex near the village of Kunar Siah, discovered by Vanden Berghe in 1961, which must have been one of the principal fire worship centres of Fars, possibly even that in which the Bahram fire for the entire district was kept. Kunar Siah lies on the ancient road that formerly linked Firuzabad with Bandar Taheri (Siraf), south of Firuzabad and about 18 km. from the entrance to the Gardaneh Salvakhi gorge. Standing on high ground near the river are several buildings within a sacred enclosure measuring some 70 × 45 m.

The fire sanctuary of rough-hewn stone, 10 × 8·80 m. and 4·70 m. high under a dome that rests on massive walls, consists of an enclosed

room with two doors; the eastern door, almost destroyed, led into a
passage connecting with the square Chahar Taq some 14 m. to the
south which is surrounded by an ambulatory. There are priests'
dwellings and stores to the east and south of the Chahar Taq, while
3 km. to the south are the remains of Sassanian (?) caravanserai.

Of the known nineteen Chahar Taqs in Fars Province, several lie in
the Farrashband Plain, but none so well preserved as the Kunar Siah
complex and the journey is only recommended for those with a special
interest. Most of these monuments were probably built by Mehr
Narseh, an official at the courts of Yazdigird I and Bahram V. [172, 173, 177]
Several can be seen from the main, unmetalled road which winds for
60 km. from Firuzabad to the west. (A new road should be completed
soon.) Temperatures here are extremely high in summer.

About 10 km. south-west of Firuzabad as the crow flies, near the
village of Nowdaran, is a small Sassanian building and the ruins of a
Chahar Taq. The former, domed and very similar in style to a Chahar
Taq, can be seen standing in fields close to a range of low hills;
constructed of rough-hewn stone, with an ambulatory and a dome, it
was probably restored and modified in Safavid times. Stein supposed it
to be Islamic but Vanden Berghe who saw it in 1960, includes it in his
lists of Sassanian fire-cult monuments.[173,176] The remains of the
Chahar Taq and other ruins are scattered in the surrounding fields.

One of the most rewarding areas to explore is that around Sar Mashad
and the Buzpar Valley. Until recently only accessible by four-wheel
drive and mule from the Farrashband district, thanks to oil exploration
there is now a good road from Jereh. It is probably best to start from
Kazerun, taking the road south-east to Baladeh village and on to Jereh,
about 50 km. from Kazerun. Here the new road begins by the bridge,
going south-west across rugged country to a new bridge over the
Dalaki river. About 10 km. across the hills beyond this bridge brings
you to a plain covered with extensive ruins and the small village of
Huseynabad. A track to the right (north-west) brings you after about
12–15 km. to Sar Mashad. Here is an unusual bas-relief with a long
inscription and depicting Bahram II protecting his wife and son against
the attack of two lions or possibly the same lion shown once as it is
wounded, and again as it sinks to the ground.[84]

From Huseynabad, the Oil Company road continues for some 10 km.
over rugged hills to the narrow Buzpar Valley. Leave the road in the
centre of the valley and go right (north-west) along a reasonable track
(a normal car can make it with care), for some 12 km. to the small white
limestone tomb of Gur-i Dukhtar. The total distance from Kazerun is
roughly 95 km. but these distances are only approximate.

First noted by Professor Richard Frye in 1948, it was examined in

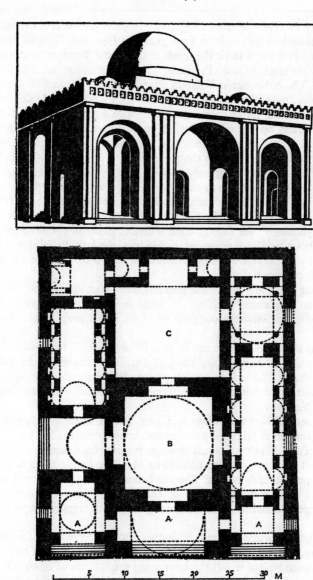

Fig. 37. Sarvistan Palace. Plan and elevation showing reconstruction (after Reuther). A – Triple Iwan, B – Reception Hall, C – Courtyard in the Residential Quarter.

(*By courtesy of Professor R. Ghirshman, from* Parthians and Sassanians)

9

detail by Professor Vanden Berghe twelve years later and discussed by
Mr. Stronach in his article on Pasargadae, in *Iran*, Vol. II, 1964. Mr. S.
Shahbazi believes it to be the tomb of Cyrus the Younger, *c.* 401 B.C.,
built by his mother Queen Parysatis, whose reigning son was Artaxerxes
II (see 'The Achaemenid Tomb in Buzpar', *Bastan Chenassi va Honar-e
Iran*, Nos. 9–10, December 1972). The tomb, a small, gable-roofed
chamber resting on three receding tiers with a single entrance facing
north, stands on the edge of what was a fair-sized Sassanian town,
apparently covering an Achaemenian settlement. The mausoleum bears
a remarkable resemblance to the tomb of Cyrus the Great, although it is
smaller and simpler, being only 4·45 m. high, 5·10 m. long and 4·40 m.
wide, compared with ¦Cyrus the Great's tomb which is 10·60 m. high
and 13·20 × 12·20 m. in area. Vanden Berghe believes the tomb was
probably that of Cyrus the Great's grandfather, Cyrus I, but as Dr.
Carl Nylander[125] has shown, from a careful study of the shape of the
clamp-holes and the advanced techniques used to fit joining stone
surfaces together, the building cannot have been erected any earlier than
the fifth century B.C.

Among the many Sassanian remains here, Vanden Berghe[172,176,177]
noted an important building of rough-hewn stones showing close
links with the Sarvistan complex (p. 259), and known as the Kushk
Bala.

Many other monuments can be seen from two roads to the south-east
of Shiraz. First comes Pol-e Fasa, 18 km. from Shiraz, where a signposted unmetalled road to the left goes to Sarvistan and later splits to
reach Niriz and Kirman, Fasa, Darab and the main Kirman-Bandar
Abbas highway.

The second is at the village of Kavar, 61 km. from Shiraz, where a
road takes one to Jahrom by a more southerly route (132 km.).

The Pol-e Fasa road winds through magnificent country, skirting a
great salt lake known as the Baharlu or Maharlu, on the edges of which
are heaped mounds of salt. The sandstone hills are pitted with caves
and the road traverses valleys of cotton and grain, with occasional
large tepes, ruined serais and, later on, bare mountains ringing a broad
valley.

Sarvistan (ancient Khavristan) is about 80 km. from the main Shiraz
highway, and is now no more than a large village in the midst of orchards.
In the main square stands the interesting mausoleum of Sheikh Yusuf
Sarvistani, known locally as Imamzadeh Pol. The building itself is
astonishingly similar in style to a Sassanian Chahar Taq and has an
inscription dated A.D. 1283. Its open-sided, square, domed structure is
supported by carved stone columns in groups of three which again bear
a striking similarity to those in the nearby Sassanian structure. The back

of the mausoleum is attached to a ruined, rubble structure of probable Mongol date.

There is little doubt about the age, only about the purpose, of the Sassanian buildings that lie south-east of Sarvistan and can be reached by a fair track marked by an Oil Company sign pointing south, from the main road 6 km. east of the town. One can see from some distance the domes of the fifth century A.D. buildings, thought by many to be a hunting lodge or small palace built by Bahram V (A.D. 420 to 440). Constructed of stone and mortar, the façade has three ivans opening outwards, behind which lay a square hall with long narrow rooms on either side, and a central courtyard with other rooms grouped around it; the ground plan is similar to that of the Firuzabad palace (p. 254) except for its many side entrances; its unique aspect lies in the springing of the vaults which are supported by thick, rectangular columns on short round columns. Between these were semi-domes on squinches, the top of the vaulted niches supporting the barrel vaults roofing the corridors.[50]

Godard believes this might have been a reception palace, one of many built by Mehr Narseh, Bahram Gur's minister, who also built the Chahar Taqs at Farrashband. More recently Oleg Grabar[74] found its construction and decoration remarkable, with its extraordinary use of piers supporting the vaults of the façade, and the designs and stucco decorations representing an important step in the development of Iranian architecture. He notes that each one of the halls and rooms is architecturally different from all the others. Comparing the complex with Qasr-i Shireen (p. 136) and the Kunar Siah (p. 255) fire temples set within an enclosure of courts and apartments, he suggests that Sarvistan too was some kind of sanctuary, an example of a royal style of architecture being transformed for religious purposes, although he has no conclusive evidence for this interesting theory.

The main dome, built of baked brick, rests on corbelling which ensures a perfectly circular dome and is a most clear example of this highly developed method of Sassanian construction.

Many mounds and traces of buildings surround the Sarvistan 'palace' which has been largely restored. Potsherds litter the ground, and not far to the south-east more Sassanian remains can be seen on a mound at the base of which chalcolithic sherds prove the site to have attracted settlers over thousands of years.

From Sarvistan the road undulates south-east over an easy pass on to the village of Mian Jangal or Mian Gol, about 30 km. from Sarvistan, passing the huge Tepe of Kharmguh on the north. From here various tracks across country take one to a number of Sassanian remains.

[A few kilometres past Mian Jangal the road is joined by a track from the right which descends to the valley and small town of Fasa. In the tenth century the town was almost as important as Isfahan, with a great mosque and a thriving textile industry. Nearby is the large mound of Zohak close to which Achaemenian, Hellenistic and Parthian remains have been found.

[About 14 km. south-west of Fasa there is a Sassanian dam across a gorge, from which a path leads up the mountainside to the spur on which stands a massive Sassanian fortress, the Qaleh-i Gabr, together with a collection of buildings within a great wall that included a one-domed structure.

[From Fasa a number of tracks, some of which are being improved, lead in various directions; one takes the more southerly route back to Shiraz via Khafr but the first part of this road is rough, crossing a very bad pass between Fasa and Khafr, and is not recommended. Another runs south-east to the date-palm town of Jahrom (about 75 km.), via Hosseinabad and Baba Arab, on quite a good gravel road. There is a Government Tourist Inn at Jahrom, standing on a knoll on the right just before reaching the town, which is hidden among the palms. Jahrom was once a famous commercial city on the old caravan routes, renowned for its prayer rugs and tapestries. The Friday Mosque is probably of tenth century origin but its Saljuq minaret, like two Sassanian castles, has disappeared. Possibly the Qadamgah behind the town embraces the remains of an Atesh-kadeh.

[The road, which at the time of writing was in poor condition, continues south through Lar to Bandar Lengah. From Jahrom another road to the left, some 4 km. north of the town, also reaches Shiraz via Khafr, and this route is partly asphalted for about the first 30 km., followed by some 70 km. of roughish road until one reaches the last 20 km. of asphalt again before Akbarabad. About 12 km. south-east of Kavar a charming walled garden on the right of the road surrounds the tomb of Pir Bokeh. This stands behind a modern stone building and offers a pleasant picnic spot among the cypress trees.

[From Fasa again a road, at present only a rough track, continues to Darab 110 km. to the south-east. About 27 km. from Fasa, by the fortified village of Shehsh Deh, several prehistoric mounds can be seen, and some 19 km. further along the valley a track from the village of Dogan, once an important tenth century city called Darkan or Zarkan, fortified under the Saljuqs but sacked in 1345 by Atabek Ali Mozaffar, leads for 22 km. to Irij.

[This village, set among orchards and vineyards, lies 3 km. south of the ancient city of Shahr-i Ij, by the banks of a small river. The remains of aqueducts and cisterns still lie around the river, as well as city walls and the ruins of a town gate to the north. A mosque carved out of rock, set into a rock grotto, can be found on the right bank of the river, to the north.

[East of Dogan is the ruined fortress of Habs-i Isfandipur, on the crest of a rocky spur, where columns, rock-cut cisterns and other remains of probable Sassanian or early Islamic date can be seen. Continuing eastwards to a fertile plain surrounded by mountains, about 12 km. before Darab one can already see to the north-east the great circular ramparts, in places 12 m. high, that surrounded the early Sassanian city of Darabgird, built, like Firuzabad (p. 255) on the Parthian circular plan. The city wall was some 1,850 m. in diameter with a deep ditch 55 m. wide, and was pierced by four gateways.

[In the middle of the town a citadel stood on a mound, while near the north gateway are the remains of Sassanian stone arches and of a rock-cut aqueduct which supplied the town with water by means of a canal from Ij. This city was abandoned in the eleventh century.

[At the foot of a cliff known as Naqsh-i Rustam Darab, between Darabgird and the present-day town of Darab, a spring forms a quiet pool before the cliff face, into which is carved another early Sassanian bas-relief. Since it must be viewed from across the pool it is not easy to see the details with the naked eye and most authorities have attributed it to Shahpur I, believing that it depicted his triumph over the Roman emperors Valerian and Philip the Arab. Dr. Herrmann, however, offers the suggestion that it shows Ardashir I (who was military Governor of Darabgird during his father's lifetime and before his battle with Artabanus V). Dr. Herrmann[86] thinks the relief was probably carved in Ardashir's final decade and some years after the Naqsh-i Rustam carving near Persepolis (p. 224). It shows the Sassanian king on his horse, with a fallen enemy by its side; the king, extending one hand to touch the head of an old man, has an escort of Persians behind him. Other figures include a younger man with one arm stretched towards the king, and like the old man he is wearing a royal diadem. Among the Roman Emperors defeated by Ardashir were Severus Alexander and Maximus Thrace.

[About 6 km. further south-east, at the foot of the same ridge, the so-called Masjid-i Sang (Stone Mosque) has been carved out of the rock, with an altar niche at the east end, a nave and transepts in the shape of a Greek cross, suggesting that it may originally have been a Nestorian Christian church. It is known that a Nestorian bishopric existed at Darabgird during the Sassanian period.

[An inscription cut into the rock is dated A.D. 1254 indicating the chamber's use as a mosque at a later period.

[There is a pleasant Government Tourist Inn in Darab.

[From Darab a new road links up with the main road from Kirman to Bandar Abbas, joining it at Kahgum.[154] Along this new road, between Rustagh and Furg, at the entrance to a gorge known as the Tang-i

Chak Chak, are the well-preserved remains of a great fire temple complex comprising a Chahar Taq and a closed Ateshgah, known as Qars-i Dukhtar.[172,176]

Back on the Sarvistan road, leaving the turn to Fasa on the right, continue to Estahbanat through valleys and hillsides planted with cotton and fig trees. On the way, about 4 km. from the fork to Fasa, just before the new road enters Tang-i Karam, look over the fields to your right, across a stream with stepping stones. Under a lone tree on the right of the old road is a Sassanian column shaft, probably a fire altar, cut out of the limestone terrace on which it stands. As noted by several travellers including Stein and Ouseley, there are very worn inscriptions in two medallions on the sides of the shaft, with perpendicular lines of Pahlavi script, recently worked on by Dr. Gropp of the German Archaeological Institute, Tehran.

Some 650 m. from the column, close to the new road, are traces of a wall across the gorge, and a fortified hill called the Qal'a-i Dukhtar, with possibly a ruined fire monument by the pool.

At Estahbanat, a charming small town with an ancient history but no historic monuments to prove it, the road goes through the main square where an enormous plane tree shades a Qajar mosque. There is another Government Tourist Inn on the outskirts of the town. Near the Pir-e Morad shrine is a Government pottery centre and in the town, numerous family potteries. In the hills to the north-west are many fossilized fish.

A track leads from Estahbanat, south-east through the mountains, for about 24 km. to the ruins of Shahr-i Ij (p. 260).

Prehistoric mounds, including a large tepe to the right of the Niriz road, and Sassanian remains can be seen in the surrounding hills and valleys. Niriz, another Qashqai tribal centre, is only 40 km. from Estahbanat, driving through fertile valleys of fig trees and cotton, and winding through mountains with glimpses of the large Bashdegan Salt Lake on the left. The tenth century Masjid-i Jumeh of Niriz can be seen from afar as you approach the valley ringed with mountains, and a turn left from the main road, onto the Kh. Souraya, takes you into the town.

There is a large petrol station on the left, and a little further on, on the right, is the Government Tourist Inn, built, unfortunately, without any provision for parking.

The Masjid-i Jumeh, on the outskirts of the town at the end of Kh. Pahlavi, is according to Godard[67a,71] the only ivan mosque identified in the west of Iran, being of a type which originated in Khurasan, and is the earliest single barrel-vaulted ivan mosque known in the country.

It consists of a great vaulted archway open at one end, with a stucco mihrab in its closed end, standing in the middle of the southern wall of a peaceful courtyard in which grows an ancient cypress tree. According to the historian Muqaddasi, the original mosque, consisting of the ivan, was built in A.D. 951 on the site of a fire temple. The mihrab inscription mentions several stages of construction of the mosque, beginning in A.D. 972 to 973, but it is not easy to determine how much of the original structure remains. The mihrab in its present state is no earlier than the Saljuq period. The side aisles and south ivan were added after the tenth century, probably at the same time as the minaret which springs, as it were, from the flat roof in the northern corner.

At the time of writing the road from Niriz to Sirjan on the main Kirman–Bandar Abbas highway is very poor, deteriorating into the following of tyre tracks across the salt desert. The road skirts another salt lake before climbing a 2,300 m. pass and descending to the quaint little village of Qatru, about 50 km. from Niriz. Qatru's mud-brick houses cluster round the high mud-brick walls of the citadel which is now part of a large gendarmerie post.

It is best to inquire here for the 'good' northerly road to Sirjan, via Vishkaneh (pronounced Bishkaneh), a three to four hours' drive across the hard-packed salty sand of the Kavir. The southern route, intended for heavy vehicles, takes at least two hours longer and passes occasional ruins, deserted mud huts and black, jagged mountains pitted with caves, before emerging onto the Bandar-Abbas road some 17 km. south of Sirjan. There is a Government Tourist Inn and a petrol station here, and the main highway goes north-east to Kirman, 177 km. and south to Bandar Abbas, 385 km.

10 · Kirman, Baluchistan, Sistan

Kirman, a desert city with an altitude of some 1,800 m., is still famed today as in the past for its carpets. It stands on the edge of the great Dasht-i Lut and is reached by a regular air service from Tehran, or by a long (1,060 km.) road journey (the roads, although gradually being improved, are not completely asphalted, and so the luxury long-distance buses do not normally run on this route, but there are a number of provincial bus services).

Kirman is traditionally said to have been founded by the first Sassanian king, Ardashir I—he called it Beh-i Ardashir which was later corrupted to Berdeshir. Captured by the Arabs in A.D. 642, it was fortified by the Buyids who were driven out by the Saljuqs in A.D. 1041. The province was sacked by Turkoman Ghuzz raiders in A.D. 1187 and the provincial capital transferred from Kirman to Zarand, 87 km. to the north-west. A local dynasty ruled from Kirman under the Mongols, then the city passed in turn into the possession of the Mozaffarids, Timurids, Qara and Aq Qoyunlu tribes from Azarbaijan, the Safavids (who gave it the name of Kirman), Uzbegs, Afghans and Qajars.

At the time of writing, the best hotel is the Sahara in Kh. Zabol, in the south-west quarter of the town. Prices here range from about 400 rials (double without bath), to about 700 rials (double with bath). Of the many smaller, typically provincial hotels, the Arkhavan in Kh. Khazemi (*not* the Arkhavan Guest House in Kh. Shahpur) is reasonable. Others can be found in Kh. Pahlavi (formerly Shahpur). Much needed new hotels are planned for the future. The municipality restaurant, Khaneh-i Shahr, in the new Maidan-i Valiyad, is probably the best in the district. The Masjid-i Jumeh and the tiny Pa-Menar, both fourteenth century, must not be missed, nor the Ibrahimiyeh Madrasseh and hamam, and the well-restored Safavid Ganj-Ali Khan complex in the bazaar, including a mint, serai and hamam, the latter now a fascinating ethnological museum.

There are few buildings of the Saljuq period or earlier in Kirman but among the earlier monuments is the Masjid-i Malik, a classical 4-ivan type of mosque entered from the south side of Kh. Sheshum-i Bahman. The Saljuq mihrab room of this mosque, which was originally called the Masjid-i Tabrizi, is built on a square plan, covered by a dome, and according to Hill and Grabar[91] appears to have been founded in the

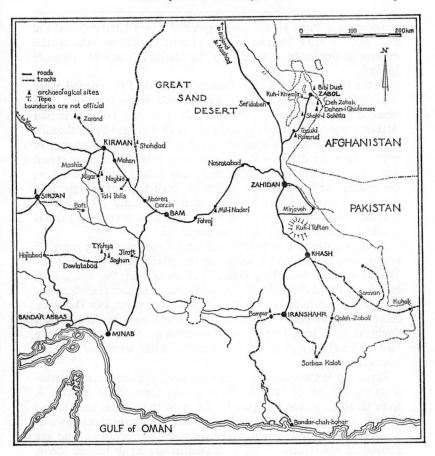

Map 9. Kirman, Baluchistan, Sistan

latter part of the eleventh century; apart from a few fragments, the
major part of the building and the stucco mihrabs are twelfth century.
The other mosque constructions date from the thirteenth century and
were restored in the sixteenth century and more recently.

On the roof, three very fine Saljuq stucco mihrabs stand side by side
(under cover) and can be seen if you ask for the key to the stairs.
Some $7\frac{1}{2}$ m. of a single, late eleventh century Saljuq minaret originally
free-standing, and recently described by Mr. Antony Hutt of the
B.I.P.S.,[97] can be seen from the lane along the east side of the mosque,
reached either from the side door or from the main street. The minar,
9*

standing on a stone plinth, is incorporated into a later wall and the shaft bears a brick 'diagonal basket pattern' similar to those on the minaret at Bistam (p. 198) and on the Masjid-i Jumeh at Semnan[99] (p. 192).

Of the Masjid-i Bazar-i Shah, founded during the Saljuq period, there is nothing left save an arcade along one side of the courtyard. The remainder has been rebuilt. However, the twelfth century Khwaja-i Atabeg Barghush, a Saljuq tomb-tower much damaged by earthquake but restored, stands in a maze of narrow lanes in the northern quarter not far from the Masjid-i Bazar. The tomb-tower is normally closed but there are plenty of helpful neighbours willing to fetch the key; the exterior walls with some decoration, including sparse light blue faience, are octagonal, but inside the plan is rectangular, the walls are covered with elaborate stucco, with inscriptions in stucco, and there is a mihrab with a few light blue faience insets.

In the middle of a cemetery containing some interesting engraved tombstones, is the building known as the Jabel-i Sang, the Gunbad-i Jabaliyeh or the Gunbad-i Gabr. It is reached by the Kh. Zarisf, running eastwards from the Maidan-i Arq past the ancient fortifications. Nobody has yet discovered its true origins but it is possibly Dailamite and certainly pre-Saljuq according to Mr. Hutt, with the oldest known double dome in Iran. Its purpose is unknown but Pope[129] sees a strong Sassanian influence in the design. Local tradition attributes it to the Zoroastrians.

Returning to the town along the same road, you can reach the ramparts and remains of Sassanian fortifications attributed to Ardashir I, from turnings on the left (south). Close to the road is the Qaleh-i Dukhtar and a steep climb to the top of the ridge further back is worth while for the splendid view of the town and surroundings, and the remains of the Qaleh-i Ardashir. Sassanian and Early Islamic sherds litter the ground here.

A fair road from the north-west of the town goes some 87 km. to Zarand, passing a Zoroastrian tower of silence after about 7 km., off the road to the right. Zarand was famed in the tenth century for its fabrics, and from 1187 to c. 1222 was the provincial capital. An attractive little town set in a fertile valley edged with craggy red mountains, it has a Saljuq minaret dated by Hutt to the late eleventh century and possibly slightly older than the Malik minaret in Kirman. The Masjid-i Jumeh, built in the eighteenth century on the site of a tenth century mosque, is in the bazaar, and the remains of the minar are set into the inner walls of this later building. Only one quarter of the exterior of the minaret with its brick patterns is visible and now it serves as a staircase to the roof of the mosque. It is surrounded by alternate round and stellate flanges and

Hutt[97] believes it may be the prototype of the Qutb Minar in Delhi, begun in A.D. 1193. A reasonable road goes to Tabas (p. 206) from here.

Another Saljuq minaret first mentioned by Sir Percy Sykes[166] is found at the domed village of Nigar south of Kirman. Here too is a similar series of stellate flanges, but it is over a century later in date. To reach Nigar, drive past the airport south-west, down the splendid new highway to Sirjan and the coast. Migrating tribes are often seen with their caravans in this area. About 70 km. from Kirman, near Mashiz (also called Bardsir) a signposted track goes off to the east, 18 km. to Nigar. As you drive into the village, the remains of the Saljuq citadel can be seen on the right of the road but only two of its four corner towers survive.

The Saljuq minaret, which Hutt dates to about A.D. 1216, has a pattern in dark and light blue on its truncated shaft, with inlaid faience tiles and a Kufic faience brick inscription in turquoise, of the 97th Surah, the Surah of power. An inner staircase leads to the roof.

The mihrab, which Sykes was told had a date of A.D. 1218, has now quite disappeared from the mosque adjoining the minaret, but next to the mosque is an old hamam (baths) which may either have been built on the Saljuq foundations or even be the original Saljuq hamam, in which case it is a very rare specimen. It is still partially in use.

About 19 km. along a rough, jeepable track going from Nigar to Kirman (it was the old highway to the Gulf), Professor Vanden Berghe examined a Chahar Taq perched on a small hill dominating a wild and isolated region. This large Sassanian monument, which was in a good state of preservation, is in two distinct portions. One is the Chahar Taq proper with its narrow ambulatory, and the other, a rectangular annexe, which is a feature resembling the narthex of a Nestorian Christian church. For this reason Vanden Berghe[176] believes it might have been converted to that use. About 23 km. east of Nigar (following rough tracks across the desert) are the remains of the Saljuq town of Ghubayra, founded on a prehistoric settlement, which Dr. G. Fehervari of S.O.A.S. began excavating in 1971. (*Ghubayra.)

In the valley of Bardsir, some 30 km. south of Mashiz, lie the prehistoric mounds known as Tal-i Iblis ('Devil's Mound'), where exploratory excavations were carried out in 1966 by an international expedition directed by Professor Joseph Caldwell on behalf of the Illinois State Museum and supported by the National Science Foundation.[17,18] Some 2,300 m. above sea level, the excavations were part of an attempt to verify an earlier discovery of late fifth millennium B.C. smelting of copper from ore; new discoveries made on these mounds may push the date back even further, but occupation seems to have been continuous from c. 4400 to 400 B.C. The site, like so many others in Iran, was examined first by Sir Aurel Stein[155] who dug a trial trench here in the 1930s. Large sections of the mounds had also been dug less scientifically by farmers who used the soil for fertilizer.

Among other finds were a large pre-Islamic pottery kiln of mud brick with a sophisticated system of vents, and pottery similar to that of the early third millennium, with links with both Mesopotamian Jemdat Nasr and Uruk sites. A guide is essential to locate the site.

Continuing down the Bandar Abbas highway, from Mashiz, for about another 100 km., the road passes close to Sirjan where there is a Government Tourist Inn. From the main road one can see to the south-east the low, reddish cliff called Qaleh-i Sang, a rocky eminence rising above the plain and surmounted by a great medieval stronghold, the citadel of the medieval town. The fortress resisted a siege by the Timurid armies for two years. At the foot of the citadel a monolithic minbar with an inscription dating from this period (A.D. 1387) can be seen.[166]

About 5 km. east of Qaleh-i Sang the ancient city of Sirjan, which was the capital of the province from late Sassanian times until the tenth century A.D., is being excavated by a team from the British Institute of Persian Studies, Tehran, which began work in 1970. Here a large palace has been revealed, possibly the mansion of the governor, with fine tenth and twelfth century stucco and evidence of coin minting nearby.

About 350 km. from Kirman, a little south of the village of Hajiabad, on the main Bandar Abbas road, a poor road leads east to the area of the Ab-Dasht. Not far from here Professor C. C. Lamberg-Karlovsky of the Peabody Museum, Harvard University, began work on Tepe Yahya. This is the largest and most imposing pre-Islamic mound yet found in south-eastern Iran and lies in the attractive Soghun valley, by the side of the Kish-e Shur river in a district well off the beaten track. However, Auto-Taj buses now run daily from Sirjan via Hajiabad to Soghun village where the team has its headquarters one kilometre from the site. The journey takes about six to seven hours from Sirjan. You must take camping equipment and food for your stay.

In 1973 Miss Martha Prickett surveyed the nearby Rud-i Gushk district, finding over fifty archaeological sites within a 100 sq. km. area, dating from 4500 B.C. (Period VI of Tepe Yahya), well over half of the sites dating from 3900 to 3400 B.C. At the same time Dr. Robert Raikes made a hydrological survey, noting many stone dams and large cairn burial fields.

Excavations are still continuing but already there is important evidence of trade communications between Tepe Yahya and centres in Mesopotamia, the Indus Valley and the Persian Gulf in the third millennium B.C.

Some 20 m. high and with a nearly perfectly circular base with a diameter of 190 m., this site has an extensive mud-brick platform on its summit which apparently formed part of a first century B.C. to first century A.D. citadel, Period I being of Partho-Sassanian date.

Period II is now dated 500–300 B.C., and this, together with its location, has suggested the strong possibility of the site being that of ancient Carmania, the former Achaemenian provincial capital visited by Alexander the Great on his return from India.

Period III appears to have been c. 750–500 B.C., while Period IV covers a long period from c. 3400–1800 B.C.

Next comes Period V A–C from c. 3800–3400, and then Period VI with pottery similar to that of Bampur V and VI (p. 276) and Susa D (p. 148), and with a great number of carved steatite bowls, stamp and cylinder seals, many of them unfinished. Period VII has several building levels sub-dividing the period into at least three phases and is referred to as the 'Yahya Period'; it has characteristic pottery, red-slipped with black painted geometric designs with no ready parallel. Some other wares of this period can be compared with Tal-i Iblis (p. 267) and Bakun A (p. 235).

Period VIII consists of three major superimposed neolithic levels and a massive wall almost 2 m. wide; the rooms of the lowest level so far exposed are mid-fifth millennium B.C. Pottery finds here date back to the late sixth millennium B.C. and from the lowest excavated level a unique female figurine—a goddess?—28 cm. high, of green speckled steatite, was found resting on a bed of about 30 flints, near a bone spatula and three stone arrow straighteners.

Excavations in the second season emphasized the importance of Period VI, where new finds included a steatite double axe with an eagle carved on each blade, a common motif on Susa D pottery; and cylinder seals of the late and middle third millennium as well as a finely carved cylinder seal of the same period, closely related to Akkadian-type seals from Mesopotamia, with what seems to be a vegetation god wearing a horned helmet, and his hair tied in a bun. An etched carnelian bead of the type found in both the Indus Valley and Mesopotamia, together with pottery similar to painted wares from Bampur (p. 276), Shahr-i Sokhta (p. 280) and possibly Mundigak in Afghanistan and Sialk (p. 170), give more evidence of trade and communications with both east and west. Perhaps at this time, the third millennium, Tepe Yahya belonged to part of the greater Elamite political confederation.

In the fourth millennium Period VII, the settlement appears to have flourished without the need for fortification walls of any kind.

This compact site, consistently occupied for over five thousand years, giving it a far more venerable history than that of any world capital

today, is evidence that the south-eastern area of Iran, for so long considered insignificant and sparsely inhabited in ancient times, must in
fact have been extremely important. It may well be eventually identified
as a key city in the area called Magan, to which the Akkadian king,
Naram-Sin, sent a trading expedition, buying wood, textiles and copper
ore.

In 1973 a series of substantial brick platforms over 100 sq. m. in
area (Period IIB), similar to Achaemenian structures was discovered
immediately above Period III. The site is temperate in climate and excavations are carried out during the summer months.[104,105] Work during
the 1970 season revealed the unique find of 30 blank writing tablets
stacked in a corner of a newly-excavated chamber, with seven inscribed
tablets in proto-Elamite script nearby, offering convincing proof that
the tablets were written at Yahya itself. Professor Dyson conservatively
dates these to c. 3200 B.C.

Other finds included Persian Gulf seals similar to those associated
with the Indus Valley civilization, and steatite 'hut' bowls (bearing
incised motifs resembling huts), of a type found at Susa and many
Mesopotamian sites. Till now their origin was unknown but many
unfinished examples were found at Tepe Yahya, as well as an extensively
quarried steatite mine nearby, thus indicating that the bowls were in
fact exported from Tepe Yahya. (See *Iran*, Vols. X, 1972 & XII, 1974.)

About an hour and a half's drive east from Tepe Yahya, between
Soghun and Boluk villages, is the Tang-i Mordan gorge which Sir Percy
Sykes noted as a major pass, probably that used by Alexander the Great.
Around this area are a fantastic number of cairn burials.[103] What is
most fascinating is the unusual rock art which Professor Lamberg-
Karlovsky has photographed and described (in *Archaeology*, Aug.–
Sept., 1969). Lavish and prolific hunting scenes are engraved on the
sides of the gorge, showing lions, hunters, camels and ibex with stylized
sweeping horns as part of the body.

It is possible to find tracks for a jeep continuing east to link with the
road from Minab, on the Persian Gulf, to the Kirman-Zahidan highway.

There are a number of other prehistoric sites around Kirman, including Tepe Langar, 30 km. to the south-east on a track between Jupar
and Mahan. Here Professor Lamberg-Karlovsky excavated a burial
with an exceptionally finely woven piece of flax material still wrapped
round a corpse. C.14 tests date the material to c. 4100 B.C.

From Kirman to Zahidan, the international highway to Pakistan
consists of some 543 km. of passable but uncomfortable, ridged and
dusty road. Some 42 km. from Kirman the road passes through Mahan,
a town well known in the tenth century A.D. but of which the oldest
relics known are the delightful group of buildings forming the shrine of

Nur al-Din Nimatullah, a Sufi Darvish, d. A.D. 1431. Next door a caravanserai was being converted to a Tourist Inn in 1974.

The road now climbs over a couple of passes, one of them some 2,500 m. high, just before Naybid, and goes through several small oases and fortified hamlets, including the large village of Abareq which has the ruins of a castle on a hill to the south of the road.

Just after Naybid, about 50 km. from Mahan, a track to the north along rough river beds, leads via Gowk for some 285 km. to Shahdad, but a shorter, 150 km. road from the fair-weather track at the Shahdad intersection about half-way between Kirman and Mahan, is scheduled for completion in 1975. Shahdad (ancient Khabis), a large oasis of date palms and orange trees, with a small hotel, is on the very edge of the great Lut desert. About 6 km. to the east a joint team from the University of Tehran Geographical Research Institute and the Iranian Archaeological Service, led by Mr. Ali Hakemi, has been excavating since 1968 one of the most intriguing of all prehistoric sites, exceptionally rich in finds, although with little or no architectural structures.[78] Several great floods in the fourth millennium B.C. destroyed the habitations and most skeletons, but left bricklined graves, potters' kilns and many artifacts testifying to a high degree of civilization. (*Shahdad.)

In the village of Darzin, about 175 km. from Kirman, a petrol station was almost completed in 1969 and a track to the south from here leads to the Persian Gulf via Jiraft (formerly known as Sabsevaran) where there are Government experimental agricultural farms. Famous in Saljuq times, Jiraft rapidly declined after the Mongol invasion. The track continues on to Minab.

The only sizeable town between Kirman and Zahidan is Bam, about 35 km. from Darzin. It boasts an attractive Tourist Inn which makes it an excellent overnight stop. The unique walled town and inner walled citadel can be seen from some distance and a turn from the main road to the north takes one right into the new town, past the Tourist Inn set back on the right of the road, in a garden of orange trees and cypresses by the corner of the first roundabout. The Governor's office and the police station are housed in a new building on the right of a large square, further along the road, and on the left is a petrol station. There is a small, old-style hotel, the Sayaa, in this street.

Dates from the Bam palmeries are now being canned and shipped to Tehran and elsewhere, and the mast and local nan (bread) are particularly good.

The famous citadel, which, perhaps more than any other place in Iran, conveys the vivid impression of a living medieval fortified town, is reached by continuing down the main street to the northern outskirts

of the town, then turning along a dirt track to the right—or else through
a maze of twisting lanes behind the bazaars.

The crenellated walls with their intricate gateways are superbly
preserved and, although the city is believed to have been founded in
the Sassanian period, most of the present-day remains are Safavid.
In the seventh century A.D. the Arabs occupied Bam, and by the tenth
century it was described as impregnable, the citadel containing three
mosques and many great mansions. In fact it was taken by the Saljuqs
towards the end of the eleventh century after they had diverted the
course of the stream along one side of the fort.

Bam was a great textile centre in the Middle Ages, attracting merchants and craftsmen from all parts of Iran. Today one can wander
through streets and bazaars, ruined houses, shops and mosques and
climb up into the magnificent citadel parts of which were surveyed by
Mr. Hutt in 1969. It was here that the last of the Zand dynasty sought
refuge in 1794, only to be handed to his enemy, Agha Mohammad
Qajar, who first blinded, then killed him.

It is essential to take adequate supplies of water and fuel on the next
stage of the journey east.

About 30 km. along the main road east, towards Zahidan, the large
oasis of Zahedabad lies just off the road to the south. Close by this are
the ruins of Narmashir, mentioned in the tenth century as another of
the great trading centres of the area, and capital of the district, with
many palaces and mosques. It was probably destroyed by Tamurlane's
armies in the fourteenth century.

A few kilometres further on, a bad track goes south to the Makran
district of Baluchistan.

Ruined serais and forts and occasional villages appear in the weathered
sandstone landscape, until after the village of Fahraj, with its palms
and pomegranates, its mosque and gendarmerie post and ruined castle,
the desert, covered with a layer of salt, really begins and one can
expect to be stopped by occasional travellers begging for water or fuel.

At about 300 km. the remains of the Mil-i Naderi stand in splendid
isolation on the south of the road. This brick tower may be one of a
series built in A.D. 1073 to guide travellers across the Kirman desert.
Some scholars would, however, date it several centuries later. The
foundations of what are said to have been another signal tower lie on
the north of the road some 14 km. beyond the village of Shurgaz. After
Kahurak gendarmerie post, about 50 km. from Shurgaz, the flat
stony desert is relieved by sand dunes, and then the road climbs into the
mountains and through a gorge to Nasratabad, one-time capital of
Sistan, where one of many health check-points is usually based during
cholera epidemics (either in Iran or across the borders). Be prepared to

swallow anti-cholera capsules regardless of the possession of valid health documents.

Zahidan, 333 km. from Bam, is a new, border town that is linked by several flights weekly to Tehran via Mashad or Kirman. The highway runs north to Mashad, and east across the Pakistan frontier. Baluchi tribesmen from both Iran and Pakistan mingle with Pathans and Afghans, their tribal costumes rivalled by those of the many unconventional travellers from the West, hitch-hiking or driving dilapidated vehicles to India and Nepal.

A single-track railway from Quetta, Pakistan, terminates at Zahidan and there are long-standing plans to continue the line to Tehran, linking it with the existing track which is now edging its way towards Yazd.

Zahidan is an essential stopover for any excursions contemplated either south into Baluchistan proper, or north, to the Italian excavations in Sistan, and a 20-roomed Tourist Inn was opened in 1974.

An excellent Tourist Accommodation Camp provides inexpensive but comfortable tented rooms on the outskirts of the town. In Zahidan itself, the long-established Tourist Rest House in Kh. Shahpur was founded by the late Mr. Abbas Ali Valaii, of both Iran Air and the Tourist Office. Reminiscent of Indian dak bungalows, double bed-sitting rooms cost 150 rials per person, and are grouped round a small courtyard with a shower, toilets, and three washbasins in the yard itself. There is no restaurant but a large communal refrigerator is available for the convenience of guests. A few more modern rooms have been built in an annexe across the road.

The Tourist Office in the main Kh. Pahlavi will provide the latest information on local road conditions, permits or letters of introduction to gendarmeries and local officials who should be informed in advance before travelling in certain areas. They can also help with arranging transport, the hire of cars or Land-Rovers, or finding seats on long-distance buses. On a normal week-day this office can also arrange a visit to a local handicrafts centre where Baluch women in their everyday tribal dress are trained to weave and embroider, in traditional designs, articles suitable for sale to the general public. Some fine examples of Baluch embroidery can also be found in the small covered bazaar running in an L shape between Kh. Pahlavi and Kh. Alam.

Several modest hotels are found around this central but noisy area. Among them is the Park Hotel, with space for parking some vehicles, and a reasonable restaurant. Here a double room costs 120 to 140 rials for each person. This hotel stands in Kh. Shahpur, close to the crossing with Kh. Pahlavi, locally known as Chahar Rah Che Kunam? or 'Cross-roads What shall I do?', a favourite lounging place for the locals on lazy afternoons.

A signpost in English is sited here, and on the next intersection of Pahlavi and Alam opposite the covered bazaar there is a bus-terminal with auto-repair workshops nearby. Further along still, towards the Tourist Office, are more bus depots and the gendarmerie station with, between them, the Hotel Karamati which offers good chelo-kebab (rice and kebabs) in a clean restaurant, and two-bedded rooms with washbasins for which the charge is 80 rials per person.

Opposite this hotel is Mehboob's dairy, which sells excellent mast in small, handmade earthenware bowls.

There are a number of as yet unidentified prehistoric mounds and ruined castles in the picturesque Baluch hills and valleys south of Zahidan, notably at Sarbaz Kalat where there are no less than three forts with sherds dating from Sassanian to Safavid periods, but there are no known sites of great importance here. Travelling is difficult, possible only by four-wheel drive, mainly along dried river beds in summer, and unmarked tracks. Accommodation is non-existent.

One can, however, drive to Bampur where there is a citadel and a prehistoric mound, close to Iranshahr, one of the hottest places in Iran, over a fair dirt road through some wildly beautiful country. There are no hotels in Iranshahr and letters of introduction are needed for overnight stays. Camping out, except within private compounds or gardens, is not recommended.

The road goes via Khash, 194 km., passing at about 83 km., near the village of Dehak, a track to the east, which joins the main road into Pakistan. Camel scrub desert and low hills give way to a gradual pass about 2,100 m. high through a tangle of mountains not far from the active, twin-coned volcano of Kuh-i Tuftan to the east which is 4,043 m. high and larger than Mount Etna.

A few small settlements and the sprawling black nomadic tents are seen at intervals. At about 125 km. the road enters a plain dotted with weirdly shaped outcrops of jagged hills. Ahead are misty hills through which the road climbs and finally enters the small, new town of Khash. A petrol station is on the right of the road and on the left, further along, is the Bakshdari, the office of the local government official. In the same grounds is a new guest-house, for government officials—and with a letter of introduction from Zahidan it may be possible to have overnight accommodation here. One can buy food at nearby shops—good eggs, mast, bread and tomatoes but no butter—and cook one's own meals in the kitchen, which also has a refrigerator.

It is not advisable to drive in this area during the heat of the day in summer months, nor during the hours of darkness.

From Khash to Iranshahr is about 180 km., the switchback road running west for much of the time, through largely uninhabited and

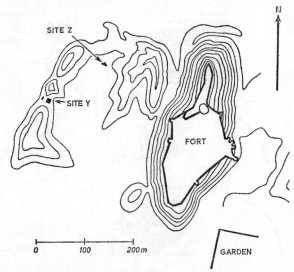

Fig. 38. Bampur. Site plan of excavations.
    (*By courtesy of Miss B. de Cardi. From* Iran, *Vol. VI, 1968*)

spectacularly varied and attractive country. Black mountains, one 12 km.-long pass with hairpin bends, winding gorges filled with partridges and stunted tamarisk trees, and two or three Baluch villages—all these are typical of the scenery in this region. The drive takes about 3½ hours.

Iranshahr is a pleasant, small town, with no hotel; but with introductions one finds a ready welcome at the Army Officers' Club Guest House (Bashkar Mehman-sara), near the gendarmerie station and at the very end of the main street, by the mud-brick wall of the army post.

The Club is set round a garden where meals are taken during the evenings, and on hot nights beds are placed outside on the terrace. The charges are nominal.

There is a petrol station on the road leading out of Iranshahr to Bampur, which is about 25 km. to the south-west on a fast but switchback dirt road. It continues as a rough track down to Bandar Chah-Bahar on the coast.

Along this road one sees the first round wicker frame huts covered with reed mats, that are a feature of the Makran coast; a Government irrigation and experimental farm straddles the road about 20 km. from Iranshahr and from here one can already see the Bampur citadel on its high mound to the right of the road.

The citadel is reached by a narrow track from the one main street

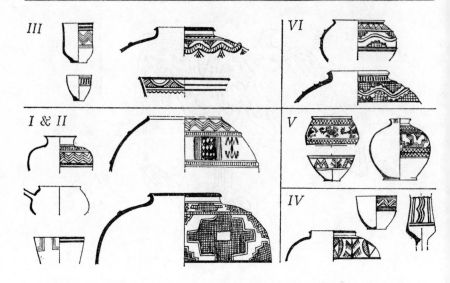

Fig. 39. Bampur. Diagram illustrating the pottery characteristics of Periods
I–VI (not to scale).
(*By courtesy of Miss B. de Cardi, from* Antiquity, *Vol. XLI, No. 161,
March 1967*)

of Bampur. A few little shops in this street sell exquisite pieces of Baluch
embroidery made in the Lashari district.

The walled citadel is a miniature Bam, and the fort itself, and the
mound on which it stands, have not been excavated but there is much
prehistoric pottery lying here, as well as later sherds. The ruins probably
rest on a series of earlier forts which in turn cover a prehistoric settlement. However, the excavated prehistoric site lies immediately to the
west and north-west of the fort, surrounded by sand dunes. This and
other prehistoric mounds in the Bampur valley were noted by Sir
Aurel Stein in 1932[155] and later by Professor Walter A. Fairservis
Jr.[51] The Bampur mound, with its perennial water, is near the intersection of several caravan routes.

Miss Beatrice de Cardi,[28,29,30] of the Council for British Archaeology,
led a small archaeological team in 1966 to reveal a sequence of six
successive periods, basing her relative dating on comparative material
from sites in Afghanistan and Oman, extending from about the second
quarter of the third millennium B.C. to *c.* 1900 B.C.

Two sites were excavated here: the first, site Z, lies among early Muslim graves north-west of the fort, the other, site Y, among the mounds to the south-west of Z. The earliest levels of Z contained no structures, but sun-dried mud-brick buildings with mud-plastered walls were found in Period II, rebuilt in the later period when five successive floors were laid, with a succession of hearths. New buildings were erected on a different plan in Period IV, after which the site was abandoned until newcomers arrived. Marine shells found in this level indicate contact with the Makran coast in Period V. After a short interval this last stage was succeeded in Period VI by an occupation layer containing much pottery; this layer was badly disturbed when used as a cemetery in early Islamic or later times.

Trench Y was opened across the line of Stein's earlier sounding, showing that his original trench had cut through a rubbish dump of Period VI and had not reached virgin soil. Miss de Cardi's excavations revealed a well-preserved kiln, carved steatite, a metal stamp seal and small animal figurines together with numerous oval clay sling stones. The decorated pottery of Periods II to V can be connected with contemporary painted wares of Afghanistan and Pakistan, while geometric and zoomorphic motifs were common throughout the Bampur sequence, including some from Period II that were reminiscent of Susa I and others, from Period III, related to Mundigak IV in southern Afghanistan.

Incised grey ware and painted wares suggest links between Bampur IV and the pre-cemetery levels of Shahi Tump across the border in Pakistan Makran, and with other sites on Umm-an-Nar off the Oman coast. Ceramics of Period V include types similar to those of the Kulli culture, in Pakistan.

On the evidence of new pottery types at the end of Period IV, it seems that newcomers arrived at Bampur, possibly from the Helmand river area in Sistan, north-east of Baluchistan, apparently forcing the original inhabitants to abandon their possessions. Similar pottery has been found among grave goods at Khurab, another site examined by Stein some 13 km. east of Bampur, from which also came one of the earliest representations of a camel. This appeared on a cast copper-arsenic shaft-hole axe of c. 1900 B.C.

It is possible to return to Khash from Iranshahr, by a longer (over 400 km.) round-about track via the hamlets of Sarbaz Kalat and Qaleh Zaboli; but although providing interesting scenery, there are no known noteworthy archaeological sites on the route, and nowhere to stay. Moreover, since much of the track lies along river beds, it is unsuitable for any but four-wheel drive vehicles in dry weather, and impassable in wet.

Along the track between Qaleh-Zaboli and Khash, two tracks lead off to the south-east, meeting at Saravan and continuing to the border. A new road is being built to Chaharbahar on the coast.

From Zahidan a good dirt road goes north-east, 211 km. to Zabol, passing a number of extremely interesting prehistoric sites. Arrangements can be made with the Tourist Office in Zahidan to stay at the comfortable Government Rest House on the right of the road and almost opposite the police post, as you enter the town of Zabol.

This is in the midst of a largely treeless region which from April until November endures temperatures around 50°C, with the 'Wind of 120 Days' raging from the end of May until the end of September. In winter freezing blizzards sweep across the bleak landscape, and temperatures drop to 20°C, yet it has been a fertile plain supporting great cities and many settlements, and has attracted a wide range of archaeological research.

In the early years of the present century, G. P. Tate, Sven Hedin, Percy Sykes and Aurel Stein, all commented on the many remains here. More recently, Professor Walter A. Fairservis Jr. worked here[51] with an expedition in 1949 and 1950, noting over 100 archaeological sites. For some years, too, the Italian Archaeological Mission, under the general direction of Professor G. Tucci, has been excavating important sites in Sistan, revealing the richness of this border land which Dr. M. Tosi has aptly described as 'the country of Dead Cities'.

The area near the Afghan border is watered by the Helmand, Hari and Farah rivers forming, in winter, a marshy lake known as the Hamun. Winds and sand have eroded most of the buildings and pottery in the sites here, leaving mainly surface remains, ranging from the third millennium B.C. 'Burnt City' of Shahr-i Sokhta, to the spectacular Parthian palaces on Kuh-i Khwaja.

Sistan was known in ancient times as Zaranka or Drangiana, and was renowned as a farming area. Drangians served in the Achaemenian armies invading Greece in 480 B.C., and Alexander the Great took the province a century and a half later, with little opposition.

Under Parthian rule, when the area was occupied by the Sacas, Drangiana was known as Sacastene, whence Sistan, and a local ruler, Gondophernes of the house of Suren Pahlav, c. A.D. 20 to 48, has been associated with the legendary Iranian hero Rustam. (Some think that Gondophernes was Caspar, the leader of the 'Three Wise Men' who journeyed to Bethlehem for the first Christmas.)

Under Sassanian rule, Sistan's importance as a religious centre increased and great irrigation schemes were also carried out in this period. After the Arab invasion, c. A.D. 652, when many Zoroastrian monuments and temples were destroyed, the capital was moved from the

Sassanian Zaranj (Nad-i Ali) to Zahidan (not present-day Zahidan which was formerly known as Dozd-Ab, but another city close to the Afghan border and to Zabol). A local dynasty, the Kaianis, assumed power under the Saljuqs, and their descendants still live in Sistan today.

It was in Sistan that Tamurlane received the wound that permanently lamed him, while fighting the Kaianis; in revenge for the Sistan rebellion he destroyed Zahidan as well as many fortresses, and, most drastic of all, severely damaged the vital irrigation system, which his successor, Shah Rukh, destroyed completely, thus turning the district into a desert.

Most of the scores of prehistoric sites[65] are south of the Hamun delta, that is, south of Kuh-i Khwaja. At the time of writing, an official guide to southern Sistan (a Baluch who knows all the sites in the area) can be picked up at Tasuki, a village on the road from Zahidan to Zabol, but make inquiries at the Tourist Office in Zahidan for confirmation. The road winds through a valley close to the Afghan-Pakistan border, and the distinctive, triangular Mountain of the Black King, Kuh-i Malik Siah.

The road divides after some 84 km., the left-hand fork continuing to Mashad, the right going to Zabol. Tasuki lies about 35 km. along this right fork, about 5 km. past Gird-i Gah gendarmerie post. From Gird-i Gah an early Islamic brick wall can be seen on the east of the road, about 20 minutes' drive across the sand dunes. This is probably Ram Rud, noted by Stein in 1916[153] and not so far excavated, but believed to be late Sassanian and possibly the remains of the Sassanian capital of Ram Shahrestan; it was occupied until the early nineteenth century.

Continuing east, across the desert, one can see the ruins of Qaleh-i Gird further east still, about half an hour's drive from Ram Rud. This was a large, circular fortified settlement with well-preserved towers and walls. About 3 km. to the north are two large and well-preserved fourteenth century buildings about 5 km. from the Afghan border. Both these sites are worth a visit.

From Tasuki continue north, and after 1 km. turn east to Tepe Rud-i Biyaban, a long, low black mound off the road. Discovered by the Italian Mission only in 1966, this seems to have been the site of a prehistoric pottery factory dating from the late Bronze Age and corresponding to Shahr-i Sokhta III and IV (p. 280). Here some fifty large downdraught kilns have been isolated from the enormous third millennium B.C. urban centre of Shahr-i Sokhta.

Separated from Tepe Rud-i Biyaban by an arm of the ancient delta, with considerable vegetation growing in it, is a second mound with a large Islamic building on the top, some 40 × 50 m. in area.

Three other mounds seen along this road are of no great interest, but some 24 km. further you will see the immense series of light-coloured mounds looking like natural eroded sandhills, along the left (west) of the road. They form the important prehistoric settlement of Shahr-i Sokhta where a team under the direction of Dr. Tosi has been working since 1967, after Professor Scerrato, in 1960, suggested excavating here.

Aurel Stein first noted this site in 1916. It is about 20 m. high and stretches along a north-south axis. Two caretakers guard the site and here, as on most other sites where work is still unfinished, photography is not allowed except by special permission. For this one should first contact Professor Tucci at IsMEO in Rome or the Italian Institute in Tehran.

At the end of the season which lasts from September to December, all excavations on this, one of the best-preserved early cities in the world, are covered with protective reed mats.

The sprawling site is covered with terracotta sherds and alabaster and stone and bronze objects (which visitors are strictly forbidden to pick up), and Stein supposed the erosion had removed all traces of buildings, leaving only the heavier ceramics. However, the high salinity of the ground creates a slight difference in colour and the buried mud-brick walls appear whitish, thus making it possible to recognize a network of walls extending over some 2,000 square m.

Excavations began with some 1,800 square m. in the middle of the mound, revealing a group of rectangular buildings with walls over 3 m. high, doors, windows, staircases as well as burnt roof beams and straw mats, all well preserved. Winding alleys separate some of the buildings, and pottery of various periods related to that of the Bampur Valley (p. 276), Mundigak in Afghanistan, Mohenjo-daro in the Indus Valley and Tepe Yahya (p. 269), among other sites, was found here.

Later excavations on the highest part of the mound revealed a well-preserved building of some 500 square m. with massive mud-brick walls also over 3 m. high, and a new period in the cultural sequence, undocumented in the previous excavations. Two staircases to an upper terrace store were found to have their rims strengthened with timber edging. The building met a dramatic end in a violent fire which brought about the collapse of roof beams, wall plasters and floors, and on the floor of the northernmost and isolated room one man, with a stone pestle still grasped in his right hand, was trapped and killed under burning debris. His skeleton, fallen among Period IV buff pottery, was completely burnt within a few hours of death, a fact proved by the carbonized brain in the exploded skull.

The cultural sequence of Shahr-i Sokhta as so far revealed is divided into four periods. Period I is late chalcolithic with biochrome buff and red/black-on-grey ware painted with geometric designs, close to the Geoksyr Culture (Namazga III of the South Turkmenistan sequence). Among other exciting finds were three sealings of cylindrical seals very close in type to the late Uruk or Jemdat Nasr period, c. 3100 to 2900 B.C.

Periods II and III, with pottery developing into black-on-buff and black-on-grey wares, showed the wide use of stamp seals, metal, timber and stone tools, clay anthropomorphic and theriomorphic figurines, and a striking bronze figurine of a woman carrying a jar on her head. This period is related to Namazga IV and Bampur I–IV (p. 276).

Period IV, dated to the first quarter of the second millennium B.C., saw the introduction of the fast wheel, new types of stamp seals and anthropomorphic figurines, and greater architectural skill. This period has been associated with Bampur V–VI and even with the Umm an-Nar Culture of the Oman peninsula (p. 277).

This fascinating 'Burnt City', which must have been an important producing centre for objects of sandstone, alabaster, and lapis-lazuli and other semi-precious stones exported to cities of the Fertile Crescent, fills a definite place in the cultural geography of the third millennium B.C.[171,105] (*Shahr-i Sokhta.)

(For further details, see reports in *Iran*, Vols. VIII–XI, 1970–3.)

The guardian at Shahr-i Sokhta will also guide you to Qaleh Rustam, a group of some 15 sites reached by driving across the bottom of a hard clay lake $5\frac{1}{2}$ km. south-west of Shahr-i Sokhta. Here, by an attractive, ruined eighteenth–nineteenth century A.D. village, are the remains of quite a large settlement—perhaps even of a city—with fragments of beautiful brickwork, a massive earth rampart, and various brick structures, as well as more than eight prehistoric mounds clustered around the site. One extremely important find made here by Stein was a Sassanian silver coin of Queen Boran (A.D. 630–631), found near the northern base of a massively built brick rotunda that once supported a dome. Professor Fairservis dates the brickwork as late Sassanian.

With an early morning start from Zahidan all the previous sites could be seen in one morning, continuing on to Zabol, some 60 km. from Shahr-i Sokhta. The road goes through a fertile valley with a levy post at Lutak. From here it is about 10–15 km. to a T junction where a signpost indicates a right-hand track going east into the important village of Sehkuh, headquarters of one of the four Sirdars of Sistan, about 3 km. along the road. One can see the fortified city of Qaleh-i Sam ahead and to the right, some 5 km. away. It lies within a rectangular moated fortification on the south of the track, the magnificent main gateway with twin cylindrical towers being right on the road. This city, first noted by G. P. Tate in the early years of this century, then by Fairservis in his survey of 1949–51, was more closely examined in

1964 by the Italian Archaeological Mission. The Italian team uncovered two building levels, the earliest being Parthian with Greek
inscriptions appearing on the local burial urns, and the later being
Sassanian.

From the Qaleh-i Sam it is less than half an hour's drive to Zabol.

Among the many sites within reach of Zabol, where the Italian
Archaeological Mission maintains its field headquarters, there are two
or three of outstanding interest. The easiest to reach is that of the famed
Holy Mount, today known as Kuh-i Khwaja, standing in the flat plain
to the south-west of Zabol and visible from the main road even as far
south as Shahr-i Sokhta.

The best time to visit Kuh-i Khwaja is in the early morning; to
reach it, drive back along the Zahidan road for about 6 km. to the bridge
over a canal, and soon afterwards take the right fork on a good, hard-
topped road for some 20 km. In winter the plateau is surrounded by a
virtual lake and the only access is by reed boat; be prepared to bargain
firmly with the boatmen before being ferried across. In summer, the
waters recede and it is sometimes possible to take a four-wheel-drive
vehicle along the narrow paths through the high reeds, passing abandoned boats and millions of tiny, croaking frogs. Alternatively and perhaps better, follow tracks to the left of the reeds and circle them until
you reach the south-eastern face of the plateau and a small village where
the negahban (watchman) will no doubt accost you.

Although authorities state categorically that no permission is required
to visit the site, the negahban usually makes obstinate demands for a
stamped permit and it is as well to be prepared to meet his request in
one way or another.

Such a prominent site has of course been noted throughout history
but Stein was among the earliest to survey it, in 1917, followed by
Herzfeld. Venerated by Zoroastrians and Muslims this Mount is
particularly intriguing for the extraordinary remains of the Parthian
and early Sassanian royal complex known as Ghagha-Shahr, one of the
three sites surveyed by Stein on Kuh-i Khwaja. Weathered almost
silver white, the living quarters grow out of the lower slopes on the
south-east, and above and behind them is a palace of sun-dried brick
with a fire temple set within the highest point. Herzfeld[90] discovered,
removed and copied a series of unique coloured frescoes in the long
gallery of the palace buildings, taking them to be Parthian, first century
A.D., influenced by Graeco-Bactrian art. A line of gods adorned the
window-wall, with spectators in full profile around the windows,
while a king, with his arm around his queen, was shown three-quarter
view on the back wall. Stein[153] believed the frescoes were early Sassanian and Ghirshman[59] sees in the 'Three Gods' a further indication of

Graeco-Roman influence, with a counterpart in Sassanian bas-reliefs of the same period.

Some of the earliest ivan halls known were constructed in the palace here, which consists of rooms built around a huge rectangular court entered from the south. Right and left are the vaulted ivans and ahead, in the northern portion of the palace, the long gallery of wall-paintings. Behind this again is a platform on which stood a square fire temple surrounded by a corridor.[21] The palace and palace-temple complex is Parthian in date, with evidence for a restoration of the palace in Sassanian times. G. Gullini[76] suggests that certain parts of the present structure date back to the Achaemenian phase, but this claim still remains more than doubtful.

On the summit of the plateau above the palace complex is a small Parthian fort called Kok-i Zal, while another fort, the Chehel-Dukhtaran, on the southernmost spur, probably dates from the same period.

A large number of other ruins remain on the summit of Kuh-i Khwaja which derives its name from that of a saint (said to be a descendant of Abraham) whose shrine is at the extreme north of the summit, attracting many pilgrims especially during the Iranian New Year, in mid-March.

East and south-east of Zabol lie scores of other sites, mostly unexcavated or with little that can now be seen. One of the most important of these is Tape Shahrestan, a huge, unexcavated Sassanian site with three Islamic levels above, but with not much to be seen today.[51,153] It is not easy to find, but it is reached by driving east along the fairly good road to Bibi Dost. The ruins themselves stand on a ridge west of the Band-i Sistan. From here, it is not far to the spectacular site of Dahan-i Ghulaman.

It takes about one hour to drive the 35 km. to Bibi Dost, where there are some dramatic remains to be seen, and you should inquire for Deh Burzak. The wind here is said to blow more fiercely than anywhere else in Iran, and all the tombs in the extensive cemeteries around Bibi Dost are eroded, like the pottery and the glazed remains inside. A shrine here attracts many sick pilgrims, brought to the spot from Zabol by antiquated buses. Here one sees the ruins of Deh Zahidan—which some authorities believe was the ancient Zaranj, one-time capital of the province—spread over an area of 20 km. The city was destroyed by Tamurlane and his successors, and the ruins lie south-east of Bibi Dost. They incorporate a number of walled forts, a citadel, a great gateway and mosque and, at Mil-i Kasimabad, a few km. north-west of Deh Zahidan, a minaret with inscribed bricks which gave the name of Malik Taj al-Din, the Elder, who died in A.D. 1163–64; the name of his great-grandson, Malik Taj al-Din Harab, was also given, together with the

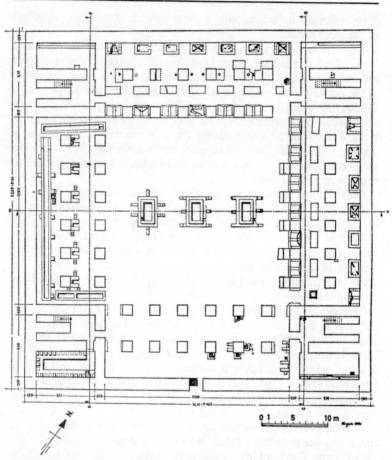

Fig. 40. Dahan-i Ghulaman. Plan of Building No. 3, 1963 (late period).
(*By courtesy of Professor U. Scerrato, from* East and West, *Vol. 16,
Nos. 1–2, March–June, 1966*)

date of construction, A.D. 1199. Most unfortunately only vestigial traces
of this minaret remain.

From here a difficult track goes to Shahrestan but it is advisable
to return to the main road, to Deh Zahak, crossing the bridge and
continuing on to Deh Qaleh-Nau and Deh Ziarat where two caretakers
live, who will guide you to the nearby sites. Even before reaching Deh
Zahak the huge mound of Shahrestan can be seen on the east of the
road, right on the Afghan border but unreachable from here due to the
many canals that cut the road.

One of the most spectacular of all sites in the area is Dahan-i Ghulaman, discovered in 1960 by Professor Umberto Scerrato who directed the excavations there on behalf of IsMEO in 1962 (presided over by Prof. Giuseppe Tucci). The site has been identified as an Achaemenian city, possibly the Zarin mentioned by Isidore of Charax and Ctesias, the capital of the province of Drangiana.

Dahan-i Ghulaman, which means 'gateway of the slaves', is about 2 km. from the village of Qaleh-Nau and it forms a terrace some 4–5 m. above the surrounding land. The eastern part of the city appears to have been divided into two unequal parts dominated by a massive elevation called Qabr-i Zardusht, with a large rectangular room inside.

The city seems to date from the sixth–fifth century B.C., in the reign of Darius the Great or of Xerxes, his son. It stretched for about 3 km. in an east-west direction, and among the first 27 buildings revealed— all with their entrances facing the protected south, or else provided with a wind-break against the fierce, 120 day wind—was a sacred edifice of a type without parallel in Iran's early history; others included private houses and a new type of public building with a courtyard surrounded by a portico on all four sides, which may have served as a storehouse or some kind of military barracks.

Building No. 3, the Sacred Building, lies in the eastern half of the city and is of mud brick, almost square (53·20 × 54·30 m.), with a single entrance on the south. The porticos are made up of two rows of square pillars with square corner rooms with staircases, almost all still coated with plaster, and the whole is of a typical Achaemenian style, particularly close to the northern courtyard area of the Treasury of Persepolis (p. 233), although carried out in less sophisticated materials.

Three large, rectangular-shaped altars stand in the middle of the courtyard, each on a pedestal mounted by steps, and hollow inside where the flame was fed through a hole in the base. Rows of altar-ovens of two distinct types stand in the porticos, with sacrificial tables or altars before some of these. Fragments of burnt animal bone prove that animal sacrifice formed part of the religious rites, possibly a cult embracing three divine beings such as Ahura Mazda, Mithras and Anahita. Still earlier ritual fire altars were found in 1973.

There are parallels too with buildings excavated by Soviet archaeologists in Central Asia, especially with the Achaemenian site of Kobadian I.

Houses built on the same plan of a central hall surrounded by four oblong and four corner rooms, incorporated private domestic shrines. The pottery includes hand-made rose-red and orange cups and jars similar to those discovered at Nad-i Ali across the border in Afghanistan, which Professor Ghirshman excavated in the 1930s, and which was also thought possibly to be the lost capital of Zaranj.

Dahan-i Ghulaman was apparently not fortified and seems to have had a comparatively short existence. It was abandoned quickly but in an orderly fashion, possibly due to changes in the course of the river Helmand bringing prolonged drought and the movement of sand-dunes which creep relentlessly across the area today, smothering everything in their path.[135]

Although maps show a road joining Zabol with the main Khurasan highway at Saidabad, this was not in existence in 1974, when one had to return along the road to Zahidan as far as the junction, 84 km. before Zahidan itself, and then turn sharp right (north) for the road to Mashad (p. 205), some 1,000 km. away.

Appendix I: Additional Material Indicated by Asterisk in Text

page 56

SAGZABAD AND ZAGHEH: Since 1970 Professor E. O. Negahban has been directing the excavations of the Institute of Archaeology and Department of Archaeology of Tehran University at a number of ancient settlements situated 60 km. south of Qazvin. The oldest mound, Tepe Zagheh, represents one of the earliest permanent settlements on the Iranian Plateau.

To reach these, drive down Kh. Rahahan and turn off on a good gravel road to the right, just before reaching Qazvin railway station; a sign points to a sugar factory and there may be others indicating the Tehran University project. About 30 km. along this road, in the Safavid caravanserai of Mohammadabad, splendidly restored by the University and lying to the left on the outskirts of the village of the same name, the teams have their residential headquarters. The sites are reached from the village of Faizabad about 20 km. further along, where a meandering and somewhat confusing track to the right, takes you about 11 km. to the excavations.

The most obvious of the three sites is the main mound of Sagzabad 7 km. north of Sagzabad village. Pitted by much clandestine digging its finds have supplied the antique markets with quantities of inaccurately dated material. A narrow deep trench to virgin soil here gave a total of thirty-six levels dating from the first half of the fourth millennium B.C. to Achaemenian times. An earthquake in the mid third millennium destroyed stables here, where collapsed walls are found on many crushed animal bones.

Three hundred metres to the west is Tepe Gabristan where a settlement extended from the mid sixth millennium B.C. to the late fourth millennium, with one major gap of five hundred years. The surface of this mound had been dug into by a late second and early first millennium cemetery, probably that of the Iron Age peoples who occupied Sagzabad. Work on this site is now being directed by Drs. Y. Majidzadeh and A. Farzanegan.

In the sixteen levels and four major periods, much interesting pottery has been found including Giyan Vc and Vd and Protoliterate bevel rim bowls, large straw-tempered grey ware dating *c.* 4000–2500 B.C. and in levels 8–10 (Period II), pottery is related to Sialk II, 4 and 5.

The early fifth millennium settlement here consists of many one- or two-roomed houses with hearths, some with kilns for smelting metal, while finds included crucibles and moulds for a double axe. Close by, the excavators found the burnt skeleton of a man who had failed to escape a severe conflagration.

Period IV, levels 11–16, is typified by one-roomed houses with a raised central platform supporting a hearth, and storage compartments at the rear. Here the walls were of moulded mud bricks measuring 33 × 33 × 10 cm. and walls and floors were plastered and white-washed.

Tepe Zagheh lies about 2 km. east of the main mound. Return on the track towards Faizabad for about 1 km. and then take a track to the left, ending at the site which only protrudes for half a metre above the present ground level. In a trench dug to virgin soil at 6·50 m. below the summit, seventeen levels were distinguished and a radio-carbon date of 6269 B.C. ± 150 was obtained only 2·50 m. below the surface. Dr. Reza Mostowfi conducted the initial excavations, finding 5th millennium Sialk I and II (p. 170) or Chesmeh Ali (p. 48) ware at the surface.

Walls of the self-contained houses are made with sun-dried plano-convex bricks 60 × 20 × 10 cm. (others measure over 80 cm. long) with grooves made by drawing the fingers along the wet clay so that when dry the bricks interlocked. Similar bricks have been found at Chogha Mish (p. 157) and Ganj Dareh (p. 120). Many houses contain intra-mural burials, the dead often lying in red ochre and covered with stacked plano-convex bricks. One young girl of 17–19 years, is among the fifth millennium skeletons, with a turtle shell, cut in half by a still protruding bone blade, at the foot of the body. Such grave markers for a young virgin were a tradition observed in some parts of northern Iran and in Egypt.

Many workshops with smooth plastered floors and drainage channels, rectangular burnt plastered platforms and sunken storage vessels have been found here, with numerous figurines, bone gaming pieces, implements and pottery including large late sixth and early fifth millennium 'knobbed' vessels. Recently Drs. S. Malek Shahmirzadi and M. Golzari have been directing work here. (See *Iran*, Vol. XII, 1974.)

page 63

RESGET: The dating given here for the Resget tower is Godard's, but according to Dr. A. D. H. Bivar who made a more recent visit to Resget (see 'The Tomb at Resget: its architecture and inscriptions', *The Memorial Volume Vth International Congress, Iranian Art and Archaeology, Vol. II*, Ministry of Culture and Arts, Tehran, 1972), the damaged inscription does not give a date. Based on analogies in Saljuq architecture, Dr. Bivar believes the tomb to have been built some hundred years later, in the reign of the Sultan Sanjar. Bivar also reports that from the new road, a walk of about 2 km. only is necessary to reach the Resget tower. (See also 'Tomb Towers and Inscriptions in Iran', by Mary E. Burkett, *Oriental Art*, Vol. XI 2, 1965.)

page 77

QALEH-I ZOHAK: For an interesting and perhaps adventurous cross-country trip to a unique cliff-top site, drive to Siah Chaman, some 63 km. along the road to Tabriz, from whence a rough track will bring you eventually to the unusual Parthian pavilion called Qaleh-i Zohak, noted by Colonel Monteith in 1830 (*Journal of the Royal Geographical Society*, Vol. 3, 1834). Ten years later the tireless Sir Henry Rawlinson visited the pavilion, while more recently, Professor M. T. Mostafavi and Dr. Klauss Schippmann have examined it (Schippmann, *Archaeologia Iranica VII*, *Miscellanea in Honorem*, R. Ghirshman, Leiden, 1970). However, the most detailed study has been made by Professor Wolfram Kleiss whose full report appeared in *Archaeologische Mitteilungen aus Iran*, Neue Folge Band 6, 1973.

It is not easy to find this site but Professor Kleiss suggests taking a four-wheel drive vehicle from Siah Chaman along the rough track westwards to Sar-eskand, about 24 km. From here the track continues for some 14 km. to the railway station at Khorasanak (sometimes a request stop only, but you could take the train from Tehran to this point). Now continue north-eastwards along a footpath by the river Karangu, which follows the railway line, to the second tunnel. A guide from Khorasanak is advisable. Just before the tunnel is a bridge from which you can climb to a large Sassanian fortress, beyond which you can see the Parthian pavilion. This is the shortest but most difficult route involving about an hour's walking. If there is not too much water in the Karangu, you can ford the river, taking the old road and seeing the pavilion high above the winding gorge, on the cliff-top. The road leads up to the pavilion and between the end of May and the autumn is an easy two and a half hours' walk.

The main structure is the Parthian brick pavilion with its fine stucco ornament dated to about the first century A.D. and which Minorsky believed might have been ancient Phanaspa (Phraaspa). Traces of painted frescoes showing women's heads have been seen here and the typical open arches and Parthian barrel vault (there is no squinch as in later Sassanian monuments) lead some authorities to believe that this may be the prototype of the later Sassanian Chahar Taq, with stucco or carved capitals. The decorated brickwork on the façade and the interior stucco have been compared with Assur, as well as with Hatra and Kuh-i Khwaja (p. 282). (Ref. Minorsky, *Bulletin of the School of Oriental and African Studies*, *XI*, London, 1943–6.)

page 80

MUJUMBAR: The new main road to Marand leaves Tabriz by the railway station, but for Mujumbar you should turn right before this, taking the old road to the airport but leaving this road immediately after crossing the old bridge, and turning right again along a good road skirting the air base. This road proceeds north-west into the mountains. After about 38 km. you reach Mujumbar; the chapel is on a hill to the east of the church itself.

page 85

BASTAM: Probably a small Urartian garrison was stationed here in the seventh century B.C. when King Rusa II ordered the building of a fortress to block possible invasion from the river. A path from each fortified gate led up to the inner citadel on the crest, where the Governor resided. To the south of the citadel, warehouses contained great storage pithoi, while one of several terraces south of these again, may have been the site of the Haldi Temple mentioned in inscriptions. Two more inscribed clay tablets, apparently royal letters from King Rusa to a palace official, were found recently in an unusual rectangular building. This was constructed like a caravanserai with rooms round an inner courtyard and might have been a royal guest house. The settlement was probably destroyed by the Medes between 600 and 500 B.C. and the site then abandoned.

In Sassanian times a cemetery was established near the North Gate. (See *Iran*, Vols. XI, 1973, XII, 1974, and XIII, 1975; 'Excavations at Bastam, Iran' by Stephen E. Kroll, trs. William G. Doty, *Archeology*, Vol. 25, No. 4, October, New York, 1972, & Professor W. Kleiss in *Archaeologische Mitteilungen aus Iran*, Neue Folge Band 6, 1973.)

page 90

KORDLAR TEPE: Taking the road east to Lake Rezaiyeh, a drive of 13 km. brings you to the village of Kordlar. Turn right here and drive along a dirt road through the village to the large mound which can be seen from the road. Two school buildings lie at the foot of the tepe. Professor Dr. Karl Kromer from the Institute for Prehistory at the University of Innsbruck, began excavations here with a joint Austrian–Iranian team in 1972. A trial trench revealed layers dating between *c.* 3500 and *c.* 800 B.C.

The three main periods cover the Iron Age, with its four building levels ending in destruction by fire at the end of the 1st millennium B.C.; the Middle Bronze Age c. 1900 to 1400 B.C. with polychrome painted ware; and lowest of all, the Chalcolithic period c. 3500 B.C. with monochrome painted pottery and obsidian arrowheads.

Recent excavations have concentrated on the Iron Age period in the north-eastern part of the site, with, in the lowest level IV, a large brick building which in level III was fortified by two towers; later still it was rebuilt as a massive, square fortress along the east side of the inner town wall running south to north. This level II was finally destroyed by an immense fire dated by C.14 to c. 1010 ± 80 B.C.

The topmost level I revealed the outlines of huts in a small settlement, dated by pottery finds to the ninth century B.C., including an urn burial, the vessel having a deliberately made small hole (perhaps for the escape of the soul?), a ninth century B.C. type of burial common in Eastern Middle Europe but until now, unknown in Iran. Other similarities with this culture included double-handled pottery with 'bosses' ('boucle'). Work on Kordlar Tepe continues under the direction of Professor Dr. Andreas Lippert. (See *Iran*, Vol. XI, 1973.)

page 94

HASANLU: EIGHTH SEASON'S WORK: The eighth season of work in 1972 revealed many interesting facets of life in Building V, which proved to have a large columned hall with an altar on which stood a small column—both features had been plastered more than 100 times. Round this were four column bases and some brick paving. Behind the hall was a large storage room complete with jars.

The floor of the anteroom to the hall was stained green from the urine of horses, the skeletons of four of which were found in the columned hall itself; while in the northern corner of the lower court just outside Building IV, was found the burnt body of a man by a pile of bronze horse harness.

In this same area, in an angle of the wall of Building V, was found a 'box' reached by a small stone staircase, and many times plastered with white. Inside were the skeletons of a young man and a woman embracing, and dated c. 800, the time of the great fire. Small pieces of brick and plaster filled the 'box' and one theory suggests the couple were lovers who were suffocated when they crawled into a storage bin to escape the conflagration that destroyed the building.

(See reports in *Iran*, Vols. XI, 1973 and XIII, 1975 and 'Hasanlu 1972', by R. H. Dyson, *Proceedings of the 1st Annual Symposium of Archaeological Research in Iran*, Tehran, Nov. 1972.)

page 97

LEILAN: Less than 10 km. along the road north to Maragheh you can see about 3 km. across the fields to the village of Leilan. It is reached by a track to the east. Believed by some to have been the Parthian capital of Ganzaka, Leilan villagers have for centuries re-used the many Parthian column bases found in the vicinity, and these are particularly noticeable in the mosque. Professor Kleiss also saw here a Urartian painted rhyton in the form of a lion, and surveyed a mud-brick dam just north of the village, as well as noting other remains in the area. (Ref. *Archaeologische Mitteilungen aus Iran*, Neue Folge Band 5, 1972.)

page 123

SEH GABI: Seh Gabi, where in 1971 Louis D. Levine began excavations on behalf of the Godin Project, was named for the nearby village of Seh Gavi (Three Cows). It is reached by taking the road to Shahnabad, crossing the small Safavid bridge of Pol-e Shekasteh on the south side of the main Hamadan road, east of Godin Tepe. Turn right immediately over the bridge and keep to the right, past a deserted village and along the south bank of the river, then follow the track inland to a river bed, normally dry in summer. Here, to the left, is Shahnabad village, 6 km. from the main road, but instead, turn right, possibly driving along the river bed or a rough track, seeing already several tepes in the distance to the right. Drive towards these, reaching the village of Seh Gavi after 2–3 km. and from thence another half kilometre to the nearest tepe. The track is extremely muddy in winter.

Basically a late Neolithic site, Seh Gabi comprises a group of small mounds, chosen to help clarify the earliest levels of Godin Tepe, some 6 km. to the south-west. The 1973 season revealed a level named 'Shahnabad', tentatively dated c. 6000–5500 B.C. Here were found walls preserved to over a metre high, and some of the earliest material yet seen in the Kangavar Valley, including coarse, chaff-tempered, hand-made vessels, some with triangular painted decoration. Next came the 'Dalma' period, named for its striking painted pottery similar to that found at Dalma, near Hasanlu, and painted in black, brown and red on a cream slip. In this level dated c. 4600–4100 B.C., infant burials wrapped in fragments of textiles were found inside pottery vessels, while in the 'Seh Gabi' level, tentatively dated c. 4100–3850 B.C., small but substantially built plastered houses, together with sling pellets and fragments of red deer antlers, were revealed.

On another of the mounds, structures of the Godin VII date included a large building with at least eight rooms and walls preserved to a height of almost 2 m., several doorways with lintels, and in one room, the second and third-storey floors preserved *in situ*. Crucible fragments, some with copper still adhering, indicated metal working at this time. A test trench at Godin Tepe confirmed the sequence so far proposed for the Seh Gabi mounds. (See *Iran*, Vol. XII, 1974.)

page 132

ESHAQVAND: Four-wheel drive is recommended, as the poor track, partly alongside the Gamas-Ab, is liable to flooding. Drive along the Harsin road from the main Bisitun-Kermanshah highway, for 5 km. and immediately after crossing the Harsin bridge, take the dirt track to the right. (Another track from Ganj Dareh, (p. 120) joins this road at 8 km. from the bridge.) After 16 km. the track leaves the Gamas-Ab, turning due east for 5 km. At this point (21 km. from the bridge), you can see the burial niche in the high peaked mountain left of the road. Leave the vehicle, jumping a creek to walk some 40 to 45 minutes to the cliff (Faratash), set in a most attractive valley. Late afternoon is best for photography.

page 132

CHOGHA GAVANEH: In 1970, Mr. M. Kordevani began excavating Chogha Gavaneh, the imposing tepe nearly 25 m. high, in Shahabad-Gharb, for the Ministry of Culture and Arts, Archaeological Department. Dug into by houses constructed on its sides, and by much illegal excavation, recent work suggests that this might be the long-sought Shimash mentioned in Assyrian annals.

The team has been concentrating on the central portion where an important private mansion, perhaps that of a prince or governor, was revealed. The many objects found here include a bronze sword with a Babylonian inscription reading 'Palace . . .' and the end of a proper name, 'day'. Other finds include a cylinder seal with three lines of Babylonian inscription dating to the second millennium B.C., and a statuette of the Elamite goddess Kirisheh, wife of Gal, who with Inshushinak formed a trinity.

Two-storeyed buildings of sun-dried brick (occasionally with burnt brick) have living-rooms around one large central chamber on both floors. The burnt buildings and most of the objects found here belong to the period between the ninth and seventh centuries B.C. when the region was in the midst of frequent savage attacks from the Assyrians. Probably the inhabitants of Chogha Gavaneh fled to the mountains at such times, taking their personal belongings with them. (See 'Les

Fouilles de Tchogha Gavaneh' by M. Kordevani, *Bastan Chenassi va Honar-e Iran*, Nos. 7–8, Autumn 1971.)

page 133

SHIKAFT-I GULGUL: About 30 km. south-west of Ilam, at Shikaft-i Gulgul, Professor Vanden Berghe recently discovered an unusual Assyrian rock relief depicting a king, possibly Esarhaddon (681–669 B.C.) with the symbols of Sin, Ashur and Enlil, with two of the 'seven planets' and a long, badly damaged cuneiform text. (See *Iran*, Vol. XI, 1973.)

page 136

SAR-I PUL: Mr. Leo Trüempelmann of the University of Munich, has recently studied one of these inscriptions which has been published by Professor D. O. Edzard, Munich.

p. 149

STATUE OF DARIUS THE GREAT: On Christmas Eve 1972 the top of a unique statue of Darius the Great was revealed at the gateway of a four-columned portal by the massive east retaining wall of the Apadana platform, between the Apadana and the Royal City. Inscriptions by Xerxes on the column bases of the portal state that the gateway was built by his father, Darius the King.

The statue (whose head, probably broken off at the time of the Arab invasion and so far still missing) originally stood at least 3 m. high and was presumably one of a pair on either side of the royal gateway; only the footing for the second statue has been found. The Darius statue, the first large piece of Achaemenian sculpture in the round to have been recovered, bears identical inscriptions on the typically Persian robe in the usual Old Persian, Elamite and Babylonian. The statue and its rectangular base also bear six inscriptions in Egyptian hieroglyphics. On the opposed long sides of the base of the statue we find the kneeling figures of representatives of twenty-four countries of the Persian empire, each identified by a separate oval cartouche.

'Sma' symbols, flanked by the gods personifying Upper and Lower Egypt, appear on the front and back of the base under the giant sign of 'heaven', with the statement, addressed to Darius, 'To you is given all power, stability, all health and gladness of heart. All lands of the plains and of the mountains are reunited under your (royal) sandals. To you is given Upper and Lower Egypt, who offer their adoration to your beautiful face, like unto the god Ra, in eternity.'

By the right foot, another Egyptian inscription reads, 'His Majesty has consecrated this long-lasting statue fashioned in his likeness so that the memory of his spirit would dwell forever next to the Sun God' (Atum of Heliopolis).

Analysis shows the statue was carved in one piece with the base and was made of crystalline sandstone almost certainly from the Wadi Hamamat in Egypt, which provided stone for other statues and stelae erected along the canal built by Darius from the Red Sea to the Nile. Depicted in the classical Egyptian attitude with the left foot advanced, the king is shown in entirely Persian dress but probably wore the 'pshent', the Egyptian royal crown which was also worn by Artaxerxes III.

Carved towards 500–490 B.C., the statue shows for the first time the actual cut and construction of Persian dress, hitherto only seen in bas-reliefs. (See 'Une Statue de Darius Découverte à Suse', *Journal Asiatique*, Paris, 1972, and *Iran*, Vol. XII, London, 1974.)

At the time of writing (1975) the statue is on display in the entrance to the Archaeological Museum in Tehran.

p. 152

DJAFFARABAD: By the end of the fifth campaign in 1973, the occupation of Djaffarabad could be seen more clearly. Level 5 showed that the site was occupied by one very large mansion on a compact plan with at least fifteen individual rooms and kitchens, all interconnecting, surrounding a large central chamber possibly used for communal living and partially divided in two. In one section were workshops with basins and tubs for the making of clay figurines, and there appear to be comparisons with Chogha Mish 'early Susiana' levels (p. 158). At the end of this period, the structure was rebuilt, most of the new walls resting on the old ones (level 4), while during the next period, level 3m-n, only a pottery workshop was found at Djaffarabad. It was again inhabited at the beginning of the fourth millennium B.C. but now the building plan differed completely from the first period of occupation and was less dense, with fewer rooms built round an open central space.

p. 166

TEPE SOHZ: There are many prehistoric and later sites in the foothills of the Bakhtiari mountains and north-east of Behbehan, including some Buyid-Saljuq monuments in the Banovar area. In 1970, the Oriental Institute of the University of Chicago conducted a brief excavation of the large mound of Tepe Sohz, 7 km. north-north-east of Behbehan. This site, which has a large mud-brick terrace probably constructed in the late fifth or fourth millennium B.C., was never occupied after the middle of the fourth millennium (Middle Susiana). (See *Iran*, Vol. XI, 1973, and A. A. Bakhtiar, 'Newly reported Buyid-Saljuk monuments in Khuzestan and Isfahan', *Memorial Volume* (2), *of the Vth International Congress of Iranian Art and Archaeology, 1968.* Tehran, 1972.)

p. 173

AB-YANEH: One of the most attractive to visit is in the village of Ab-yaneh, which was completely Zoroastrian right until the time of the intolerant Safavid Shah Ismail I in whose reign most of the villagers emigrated to India or to Yazd. Even today their costume, way of life and ancient dialect are still practically unchanged.

Drive for about 42 km. to Dehji, along the road to Natanz, south of Kashan; a few km. further on, see a good new gravel road to the west, before the Hinjan bridge, where a sign in Persian indicates Ab-yaneh and the magnificent Barzrud valley. Some 25 km. along this road, passing Hinjan village, you reach Ab-yaneh at the bottom of a gorge dominated by a small Mongol fort. The main street goes right through the remains of the 'ateshkadeh' or temple, open on three sides and with a broken dome. This structure probably dates from the late Sassanian period and was built in two stages (see also Siroux, 'Anciennes Voies et Monuments Routiers de la Région d'Ispahan', Cairo, 1971).

Originally isolated and constructed in three tiers, houses now abut on its walls, while the third element was destroyed about 1945. One storey remains below road level, with a tiny room, while remnants of three elements can be seen in the domed road level hall from which one can see the ground plan of the first Chahar Taq, reached by a stairway to the second structure under the central element of the hall.

About 300 m. from the ateshkadeh, on the same lane, is an interesting mosque with a probably Safavid entrance and corridor, and next to it, below the present building, another mosque believed to be pre-Saljuq, with an exceptionally beautiful and unusual carved wooden mihrab protected by a sheet of glass.

p. 188

VARZANEH: Due south of Kuhpayeh on the Nain road, another early twelfth century Saljuq minaret can be found by the Timurid mosque at Varzaneh (about 100 km. east-south-east of Isfahan on the Zayendehrud). There is also a bridge here with possibly Sassanian piers at the last crossing before the Gavkhaneh salt lake. (See Siroux, 'Anciennes Voies et Monuments Routiers de la Région d'Ispahan', Cairo, 1971.)

p. 194

SHAHR-I QUMIS.

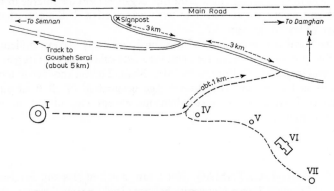

Fig. 41. Shahr-i Qumis. Rough sketch plan, not to scale, showing the central excavated mounds. I, Nagareh Khaneh; IV, Parthian mound; V, two-storey Parthian building; VI, fortified mansion; VII, Parthian mound with intact pointed vaults.

p. 196

TEPE HISSAR: An article in *Iran*, Vol. XII, 1974, gives a revised dating for some of the Tepe Hissar periods. ('The Radiocarbon evidence for the terminal date of the Hissar IIIC Culture', by C. H. Bovington, R. H. Dyson, Jr., A. Mahdavi and R. Masoumi.) In 1971, Professors Dyson and Sumner visited the site to take fresh samples of ash which

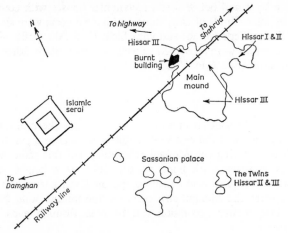

Fig. 42. Tepe Hissar. Rough sketch plan of site. (Not to scale.)
10*

gave the dating of the end of Hissar IIIC as early in the second millennium B.C. A hiatus of about 500 years between the end of Hissar IIIC and the beginning of the Iron Age began around the middle of the nineteenth century B.C. and may have coincided with the end of the Indus Valley civilization.

The burnished grey ware of the third and early second millennia B.C. found in north-eastern Iran and variously called Hissar, Gurgan or Eastern Grey Ware Culture, is found at Shah, Tureng and Yarim tepes as well as Hissar, and the Bronze Age occupation of all these sites seems to have come to a simultaneous abrupt end in the second millennium B.C.[40]

p. 198

TEPE SANG-E ČAXAMAQ: Just 8 km. north of Bastam, Professor Seiichi Masuda of Tokyo University has been leading a joint Irano-Japanese team in excavating the early site of Sang-e Čaxamaq since 1971. Two mounds lie 150 m. apart, the smaller, West Tepe being the oldest with five layers. Floors covered with lime plaster were often painted red and one house had an oven. Another had a square, stepped hearth that may have been intended for a sacred fire, while a third had no fireplace but a small room with clay figures of the mother goddess among others on the plastered floor. In one case the floor had been replastered twenty times. Fragments of pottery were found here and a C.14 test gave an early sixth millennium B.C. date, corresponding to Sialk I or II (p. 170).

The larger East Tepe has six layers, with several human burials in the surface layer and below these, rectangular houses with courtyards and nearby kilns. Finds of clay, stone and bone objects were similar to those of Yarim Tepe (p. 69) and with Sialk II. Sickle shafts with fine animal decoration were recovered as well as bone knife handles carved in human form. (See *Iran*, Vol. XII, 1974.)

p. 198

FORUMAD: The south ivan is now believed to have been first built in the Saljuq period and the east wall of this ivan contains a pointed arch portal filled in during the Mongol rebuilding. On this same wall the Saljuq basket-weave brick bond is still visible to a height of 4 m. Apparently the original ivan collapsed and the lower part of the Saljuq walls now carry the Mongol structure. On the mihrab wall, traces of earlier Saljuq plaster decoration can be seen through gaps in the Mongol stucco.

p. 205

SANGAN-I PA'IN, ZAWZAN, TAYABAD, KERAT AND TORBAT-I SHAIKH JAM:

The desert village of Zawzan is somewhat difficult to find, reached by a virtually non-existent track south across the desert, and a local guide is advisable. The track leaves the road about 17 km. from Khargird and some 8 km. before Sangan-i Pa'in where there are two twelfth century Saljuq mosques, one of which is now a school. The other, the Masjid-i Gonbad, dated to A.D. 1140–1 by Godard (*Athar-e Iran*, IV, Paris, 1949), has a splendid stucco mihrab, and both mosques have been more recently studied by Robert Hillenbrand. (See 'Mosques and Mausolea in Khurasan and Central Iran', *Iran*, Vol. IX, London, 1971.)

The Baluch village of Zawzan is some 30 km. south-east of the main road, via Abbasabad, Assadabad and Kuzneh where there is a gendarmerie post. Some 4 km. beyond Kuzneh the two great ivans of the Malik Mosque pierce the sky against an enormous tepe surrounded by domed mud-brick houses. A damaged inscription on the magnificent qibla wall was read by Godard[71] as A.D. 1219–20, making it the forerunner of the great two-ivan mosques of Khurasan.

Continuing along the Tayabad road, you pass Kerat with its Saljuq minar standing on an octagonal base to the left of the road. The minar has a circular shaft with a door half-way up.[37]

At Tayabad there is a Tourist Inn and a fifteenth century shrine containing a tiled inscription by the Timurid Shah Rukh. Some 60 km. further north on the main Mashad road at Torbat-i Shaikh Jam, is the shrine of the Sufi Shaikh Ahmad who died here in A.D. 1141. The oldest part of this splendid complex, recently restored, is the dome chamber built A.D. 1203–4 or 1236 but the main portion is Mongol or Timurid with tile additions by Shah Abbas the Great. (See *The Architecture of Islamic Iran; the Il-Khanid Period*, by D. Wilber. Princeton, 1955 and 'The Chronology of Turbat-i Shaikh Jam', by Lisa Golombek, *Iran*, Vol. IX, London, 1971.)

p. 213

TAL-I MALYAN: One can also reach Tal-i Malyan by a poor track alongside the gendarmerie post on the road to the dam, but it is a tricky drive of some 46 km. through Darashuri Qashqai country; a more straightforward route is from a point on the main highway about 28 km. from Shiraz, just north of the refinery. Here a good dirt road goes to the north-west, about 46 km. to the village of Tell-i Bayda, then 6 km. north to Malyan village.

Since 1971 Professor William M. Sumner has been leading a joint

Irano-American team here, sponsored by the University Museum, University of Pennsylvania, with additional support from Ohio State University, the Metropolitan Museum of Art and the Ford Foundation.

Preliminary excavations on this huge sprawling site whose defensive walls covered about 1,000 acres, have definitely identified Tal-i Malyan with the Elamite capital of Anshan, based on Dr. Erica Reiner's reading of inscriptions on bricks and tablets from the site. This supports John Hansman's theory, in his article 'Elamites, Achaemenians, and Anshan', *Iran*, Vol. X, 1972. Huge Proto-Elamite and Middle Elamite buildings discovered here have led to the reconsideration of the generally accepted idea that early Near Eastern Urban civilizations were exclusively located in Mesopotamia. Walls were painted red with fragments of frescoes in yellow, black and red stepped patterns and fireplaces and doors covered with white plaster. Some seven phases of pottery dating from *c.* 5000 B.C. have been identified in the valley,[172] and finds include cylinder seals and Proto-Elamite, Old Babylonian and Middle Elamite (?) inscriptions on alabaster and on baked bricks. Many female and animal figurines were also found, together with a beautifully made small white stone foot; obsidian and copper-bronze tools and fragments of steatite hut pots, plus a quantity of exotic imported material indicate that Anshan was an important trading centre and it was certainly the hub of at least seventy-seven known occupied sites in this valley in the third millennium B.C. Many parallels have also been found with Susiana at the end of the second millennium B.C.

An intense fire destroyed many rooms in a substantial building less than one metre below the surface. Work is continuing at this important and interesting site. (See reports in *Iran*, Vols. XII, 1974 and XIII, 1975 and 'Cultural Development in the Kur River Basin, Iran', by W. N. Sumner, Ann Arbor, 1972.)

pp. 223 and 234

PALACES: In 1973, a tractor working in the field 170 m. east of this monument, hit a white limestone column torus. Excavation by Mr. and Mrs. Tilia who, since 1965 have been working on restoration of many Achaemenian monuments, and later inspection by Professor Carl Nylander of Bryn Mawr College, led to the discovery of early Achaemenian palace foundations with a twenty-eight column portico and a main hall with at least four rows of eight columns, plus a smaller portico on the other side of the hall and Achaemenian baked bricks and ceramics (see 'Discovery of an Achaemenian palace near Takht-i Rustam to the North of the Terrace of Persepolis', by Ann Britt Tilia, *Iran*, Vol. XII, 1974).

Further exploration in the area has revealed two more early

Achaemenian structures; one of huge blocks of black and white lime-stone with workmanship similar to that of the Pasargadae palaces, lies about 100 m. to the west of the new Darius Hotel, while still more column bases and round white tori of another early Achaemenian palace have been found in a field behind Bagh-i Firuzi, a little further west, and all only just below the surface.

It would seem that contrary to earlier ideas, the plain around Persepolis was well populated with a number of splendid palaces, probably of noblemen and members of the royal family, even before Darius began work on the great terrace. No doubt more will now be discovered, but of some 400 sites of various dates, identified in an aerial survey by Erich Schmidt, almost all have been ploughed out of existence within the last few years of intensive cultivation.

p. 225

ALTAR: Paul Gotch noted a 'high altar' complex of several rock-cut altars at Imamzadeh cemetery, about 8 km. from Naqsh-i Rustam, with a number of interesting features. Traces of cave paintings were also seen nearby. (See 'The Imamzadeh High Altar and Subsidiary Monuments', by Paul Gotch, *Iran*, Vol. IX, 1971.)

p. 233

MUSEUM: Often overlooked are the incised 'walking lions' and unfinished rosettes on the borders of Xerxes' robes, on the bas reliefs of the southern doorway. Thousands of sculptural and architectural fragments, mainly from Xerxes' One Hundred Column Hall, were used as a foundation for the floor of the portico and the main hall of the building. A square opening in the portico floor shows the original red-coated floor of Darius' time.

p. 233

RELIEFS: Fascinating detective work on the part of the Tilias has proved that both the Treasury bas-reliefs were re-erected there, after removal from their original positions, which was in the centre of the Apadana staircase façades[169] (see Fig. 34).

p. 235

QADAMGAH: One can also drive to this site more directly from the main road to Pasargadae, just north of Istakhr. Here, by two ostodans in the rocks to the east of the road, a track takes you after about one hour, to Qadamgah.

p. 245

BORAZJAN, TAL-I MOR, SANG-I SIAH: About 12 km. north of
the small town of Borazjan, near the village of Nazar Agha, Mr. Sarfaraz
found in 1971 the remains of an Achaemenian palace or pavilion known
locally as Sang-i Siah, possibly built by Darius the Great. The route,
along a river bed, is only possible by Land-Rover during dry weather,
but a more easily seen Achaemenian pavilion is just off the main road
about one kilometre south of Borazjan.

To the east of the road a track branches off to a clump of trees by the
hamlet of Charkhab, about 500 m. Here Mr. Sarfaraz and his team
discovered twelve column bases in a hall some 18 m. wide; exquisitely
made of black and white limestone with round tori of black basalt, these
column bases were covered by only 1½ m. of soil and were apparently
part of a palace probably begun in 529 B.C. and left unfinished on the
death of Cyrus the Great about a year later. A solid embankment has
been built to protect these remains from the effects of frequent flooding.
(See 'Un pavillon de l'époque de Cyrus le Grand', by A. Sarfaraz,
Bastan Chenasi va Honar-e Iran, Nos. 7–8, Autumn 1971.)

Continuing beyond the embankment, the huge tepe of Tal-i Mor can
be seen, where remains of an Elamite citadel probably of the second
millennium B.C. have been found. Other remains of the Sassanian
period have been noted in the surrounding fields.

A drive of some 70 km. south brings you to the important Persian
Gulf port of Bushire.

p. 267

GHUBAYRA: Lying at the junction of the Chari and Ghubayra rivers
in the eastern part of the Bardsir Valley, Ghubayra site consists from
north to south, of two prehistoric mounds, a stone tower, many mud-
brick ruins including a large building known as the Keshmeshkhaneh
(raisin-house), two octagonal imamzadehs and a fortress called
Qaleh-i Khan.

Pottery dating back to Tal-i Iblis second and third millennia B.C.
types was found in the lowest levels, but the main excavations dealt
with the early Islamic period, eighth to fourteenth centuries A.D. A
Central Citadel mound, an extensive industrial area with metal-
workers' furnaces and brick kiln have been revealed, while a large
variety of pottery including much slip-painted Samanid type ware, as
well as glazed oil lamps, coins, bronze implements and late Sassanian
silver coins, are among the many finds at this site where work still
continues. (See reports in *Iran*, Vols. X, 1972, XI, 1973 and XIII, 1975.)

p. 253

QALEH-I DUKHTAR

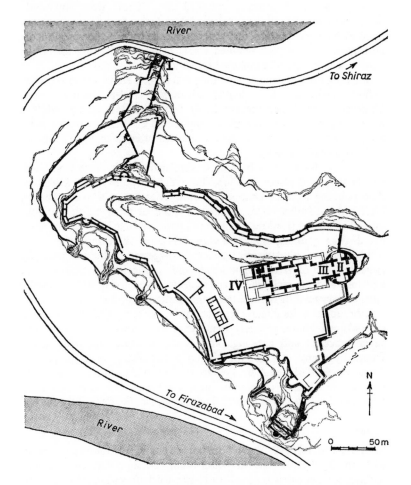

Fig. 43. General plan of Qaleh-i Dukhtar, near Firuzabad. I, deep well
shaft; II, tower; III, ivan; IV, palace entrance?
(*By courtesy of Dr. D. Huff, German Archaeological Institute, Tehran*)

p. 271

SHAHDAD: Most striking and unique among the many finds at
Shahdad were a number of remarkable third millennium B.C. near
life-size statues of painted, unbaked clay. These were apparently
portrait studies of both men and women and were found lying in graves
lined with unbaked bricks, face to face with the corpses they presumably
portrayed. Some graves retained traces of hessian matting under the
bodies, which were accompanied by various grave goods.

Smelting furnaces and many fine metal objects show that in the same
period, Shahdad was a highly advanced metal-producing centre.
Unusual metal dishes portray lively fish, deer and snakes, while a
metre-long finial with an eagle on top, bears a metal flag portraying a
religious scene of a fertility goddess and her attendants, seated lions, a
bull, sun, stars and water.

Many of the artifacts bear close similarities with those from such
widely separated places as Elam, Tepe Yahya (p. 269) and Mohenjo-
daro pointing to trade connections from Mesopotamia to the Persian
Gulf and the Indus Valley. Some 700 different pictographic symbols,
incised or seal impressions on plain red pottery, some in groups of up to
five distinct symbols, indicate a very early form of writing.

That this was a matriarchal society is suggested by the exceptionally
large number of fertility goddesses and female figures portrayed in
figurines and on seals and metal objects. Even today in the nearby
village, boys take their mother's name rather than that of their father.

Other finds include many steatite bowls, one apparently a model of a
cube-shaped building; finely made cups and bowls of local marble,
silver bracelets and ear-rings and beads of agate and lapis lazuli.
Hopefully many of these will be on public display once the present
Archaeological Museum in Tehran is able to devote all its space to
pre-Islamic objects. (For more details see also 'La Civilisation du
Désert de Lut' by Pierre Amiet, *Archeologia*, No. 60, Paris, July 1973.)

p. 281

SHAHR-I SOKHTA: Shahr-i Sokhta is a city of superlatives. To begin
with, the hard layer that Sir Aurel Stein had supposed to be natural
sedimentary deposit was actually a 20 cm.-thick deposit of salt, sand and
clay sealing an archaeological site averaging some 7 m. thick, and thus
preserving the 5,000-year-old city 'as if kept in a pot of pickles' as
Dr. Tosi so aptly observed.

Walls that were at first supposed to be foundations proved to be at
roof level, with every room crammed with finds. Over two million
potsherds have been recorded, pottery from the lowest levels showing

links with Soviet Turkmenia and that of the latest (*c.* 1900 B.C.), with the Indus Valley civilization. Two specialists have spent three years studying the 25,000 stone tools and five palaeontologists are working with the thousands of animal bones. In fact, of the 25 experts working on the site, only 10 are archaeologists, the others including geologists, nuclear physicists using palaeomagnets and uranium 238 to date specimens, and other specialists from countries as diverse as the Soviet Union and Japan, making this a truly international effort.

Paleobotanists have floated more than 6,000 kilos of earth and sifted every bit of the city's extensive sewage system, microscopic study proving that practically every plant and animal living in the area today existed there 5,000 years ago.

Forty-two thousand clay figurines, all freshly made and unfired, had been deliberately broken and thrown away, perhaps as offerings to a sacred shrine? One industrial area produced thousands of unfinished lapis lazuli beads plus flint tools, blades and drillers for their manufacture. By far the largest known Bronze Age cemetery of the Near East, covering some 42 hectares, was found on the south-western side, with literally tens of thousands of graves of four main types; (a) simple oval pit, (b) rectangular pit lined with bricks, (c) small chambers built with a transverse wall inside a larger pit and eventually covered with lintel bricks, and (d) subterranean chambers cut in the side of a large oval pit, the access closed by a small brick curtain wall. All were preserved by a 20–30 cm. salt 'concrete' layer.

It could well be that Bronze Age Sistan was the mythical land of Aratta, Uruk's rival in a cold war over the lapis lazuli trade in the first half of the third millennium B.C.

Towards the end of Shahr-i Sokhta's long existence, the Helmand river changed course by 90 degrees, resulting in the ultimate abandonment of the city.

Work is likely to continue here for many decades to come. (See also 'Shahr-i Sokhta and Tepe Yahya; tracks on the Earliest History of the Iranian Plateau', by C. C. Lamberg-Karlovsky and Maurizio Tosi, *East and West*, Vol. 2, Nos. 1–2, Rome, 1973 and 'Shahr-i Sokhta; a Charge and a Chance for Urban Archaeology' by Maurizio Tosi, *Proceedings of the 1st Annual Symposium of Archaeological Research in Iran*, Tehran, Nov. 1972.)

Appendix 2 : Chronological and Historical Table
showing principal periods
of main sites

B.C.	*South*	*North*
6000	ALI KOSH Agricultural villages, Neolithic stage Handmade ware	TEPE SARAB HOTU CAVE HAJI FIRUZ (nr. Hasanlu) GODIN TEPE VII
5000	CHOGA MISH Early phases of painted pottery (*c.* 5000–3500 B.C.)	GODIN TEPE VI
4000	YAHYA TEPE VI (nr. Kirman) (*c.* 4000–3800 B.C.) YAHYA TEPE V (*c.* 3800–3300 B.C.) (a-c equates with Tal-i Iblis II and III) Obsidian TAL-I IBLIS II and III (nr. Kirman) Early metallurgy SUSA A Painted pottery (Style I) Copper tools, stamp seals TALL-I BAKUN (nr. Persepolis) Painted pottery	DALMA TEPE (nr. Hasanlu) PISDELI TEPE (nr. Hasanlu)
3500	SUSA B Potter's wheel	SIALK III, HISSAR I Painted pottery, potter's wheel, copper tools, stamp seals
3300	YAHYA TEPE IVC (*c.* 3300–2900 B.C.) Inscribed tablets	GODIN TEPE V Potter's wheel
3000	SUSA C Urbanization, cylinder seals	SIALK IV Influence from Susa, decline of painted pottery

B.C.	*South*	*North*
	SHAHR-I SOKHTA (nr. Zabol) YAHYA TEPE IVb (*c.* 2900–2600 B.C.) (equates with Susa C) 'Hut pots', steatite bowls, Persian Gulf seals	

Bronze Age

B.C.	*South*	*North*
	SUSA D Polychrome pottery (Style II) Elaborate tombs with chariot burials First Dynasty of Awan	HISSAR II Appearance of burnished grey pottery
	YAHYA TEPE IVa (nr. Kirman) (*c.* 2600–2200) (equates with Shahdad) Incised and stamped ware	GODIN TEPE IV YANIK TEPE EB-I Circular buildings
2500	SUSA, Akkadian suzerainty Fall of Susa, probably at hands of the Guti	HASANLU VII Painted orange ware
		HISSAR III TURANG TEPE Metal-work; spread of grey pottery
2000	Third Dynasty of Ur dominates SUSA. Destruction of Ur by Elamites OLD ELAMITE PERIOD Elamite kings of Simash alternately warring and allied with rulers of Isin, Larsa, Eshunna dynasties	
		HASANLU VI Painted buff pottery comparable to Khabur ware
1500	MIDDLE ELAMITE PERIOD Occasional Kassite incursions.	GODIN TEPE III

B.C.	*South*	*North*
	Elamite expansion. Untashgal, *c.* 20 years± 1230 B.C. HAFT TEPE (nr. Susa)	Painted ware

Iron Age

B.C.	*South*	*North*
	CHOGA ZANBIL (nr. Susa) Kidin-Khutran, *c.* 1230 B.C. Shutruk-Nahhunte *c.* 1170 B.C.	HASANLU V Appearance of grey pottery Button base period contemporary with Sialk V (A), Giyan I
	Shilhak-Inshushinak *c.* 1160 B.C.	MARLIK (nr. Caspian Sea)
1000	NEO-ELAMITE PERIOD	HASANLU IV contemporary with Sialk VI (B)
	YAHYA TEPE III (*c.* 1000–500 B.C.)	
800		Urartian incursions
	Rise of Medes in Central Iran	
		BASTAM (nr. Khoi) Urartian
	all near Hamadan $\left\{ \begin{array}{l} \text{GODIN TEPE II} \\ \text{NUSH-i JAN TEPE} \\ \text{BABA-JAN TEPE} \end{array} \right.$	
c. 640	SUSA sacked by Ashurbanipal	
		ZENDAN-i SULAIMAN (nr. Hasanlu)
	Scythians in Iran	
612	Defeat of Assyrian empire by Medes and Babylonians. Destruction of Nineveh.	ZIWIYE (nr. Hasanlu) Gold treasure
		HASANLU III
c. 590	Cyrus II born of union of Mandana, daughter of Astyages of Media, and Cambyses, son of Cyrus I of Anshan (Fars)	

THE ACHAEMENIANS (550–330 B.C.)

B.C.

550   Cyrus II, the Great, defeats Astyages his grandfather, at Cyrus's capital of PASARGADAE. Media becomes part of the Achaemenian empire.

547   Cyrus the Great defeats Croesus of Lydia; Lydia becomes subject to the Persians.

539   Cyrus the Great conquers Babylon and its provinces (Syria).

c. 530/29   Cyrus killed in battle.

525   Cambyses (Cyrus the Great's son) conquers Egypt.

522   Darius the Great suppresses the revolt of Gaumata the Magian, marries Cyrus's daughter and extends his empire to the Nile and the Danube. Ceremonial capital of PERSEPOLIS founded.

513–12   Scythian campaign led by Darius, and Persian bridge-head in Thrace.

486–330   Xerxes I (son of Darius the Great). The Greek wars. Artaxerxes I; Darius II loses Egypt; Artaxerxes II; Darius III Codamanus, last of the Achaemenian dynasty.

334–330   Alexander the Great conquers the Achaemenian empire, and partially burns PERSEPOLIS.

323   Death of Alexander.

THE SELEUCIDS AND PARTHIANS (c. 312 B.C.–A.D. 224)

B.C.

312–281   Seleucus I Nicator founds the dynasty.

250–174   Foundation of the Arsacid dynasty of Parthians in Khurasan followed by struggle for power between Seleucids and Parthians. Parthians take possession of Seleucid satrapies.

174–127   Mithridates I expands the Arsacid empire of Parthia. Phraates II defeats the Seleucids in 129 B.C.

124–91   Mithridates II and the height of the Parthian power.

91 B.C.–   23 kings reign, and there is a gradual decline of Parthian
A.D. 110   strength along with the rise of Roman influence in the East.

53   Crassus is crushed at Carrhae in his attempt to conquer the Parthian empire.

A.D.

114–224	Parthian empire declines and Artabanus V, last Parthian monarch, is defeated in hand-to-hand battle with Ardashir I, the ruler of Fars and Kirman, and founder of the Sassanian dynasty.

THE SASSANIANS (A.D. 224–642)

224–241	Ardashir I; makes Ctesiphon his capital and expands his empire, with Crown Prince Shahpur at his side.
241–272/3	Shahpur I; defeats several Roman emperors and captures Valerian in 260.
310–379	Shahpur II; continues victories over Rome.
461	Relations are established with China.
531–579	Khusraw I; introduces internal reforms, and the Sassanian empire reaches its peak.
608	The first Sassanian armies before Constantinople.
614	The Sassanians conquer Jerusalem and bring part of the True Cross to Ctesiphon.
619	The Sassanians attack Egypt.
629	Heraclius conquers Dastadjird. Khusraw II is murdered at Ctesiphon.
629	Heraclius returns the relic of the True Cross to Jerusalem.
630	The Prophet Muhammad enters Mecca.
632	Yazdigird III is chosen Great King at Istakhr.
637	The Arabs conquer Ctesiphon.
642	Final defeat of the last Sassanian king, Yazdigird III, by the Arabs at the Battle of Nihavand. Yazdigird's heirs flee to China.

A.D.

EARLY ISLAM (c. A.D. 651–1000)

660–750	Umayyad caliphate.
744–749	Shi'ite revolt led by Abu Muslim from Merv to establish the Persian Abbasid caliphate.
750–1258	Abbasid caliphate with the capital at Baghdad from 762.
892–999	Samanids, former Governors of the Oxus region, extend their dominions.
945–1055	Buyids rise to power near Shiraz, and govern Kirman and Iraq.

962–1040   Ghaznavids assume power in the east, seizing territory from the Samanids.

THE SALJUQS (c. 1000–c. 1218)

1000   The Saljuqs invade Transoxiana.

1031–1040   Tughril Beg defeats the Ghaznavids.

1055   Tughril Beg conquers the Buyids.

1063–1072   Alp Arslan captures the Byzantine emperor in 1071.

1072–1092   Malik Shah rules during the height of the Saljuq empire which extends from the river Oxus to Arabia.

1118–1157   Sultan Sanjar, last of the notable Saljuq rulers.

THE MONGOLS (1218–1334)

1218–1220   First Mongol invasion under Chinghiz Khan.

1231   Second Mongol invasion.

1256–1265   Hulagu, grandson of Chinghiz Khan, founds the dynasty at Maragheh, Azarbaijan.

1295–1304   Ghazan Khan, and the final Mongol conversion to Islam.

1304–1316   Oljeitu founds a new capital at Sultaniyeh, near Qazvin.

1334   Abu Said and the end of the Mongol Dynasty.

A.D.
THE TIMURIDS (1370–1502)

1370–1405   Tamur conquers Iran from the north and by 1392 governs Khurasan, Herat, Azarbaijan, Iraq, Isfahan and Shiraz.

1405–1447   Shah Rukh, governing from Herat, conquers the Oxus region.

1408–1453   The rise of the Qara Qoyunlu Turkomans in the west, expanding to include Fars, Iraq and Isfahan (1598).

1461   The Ottoman Turks enter the north-west and push the Timurids to the east.

THE SAFAVIDS (1491–1722)

1491–1524   Shah Ismail founds the dynasty in 1502.

1587–1628   Shah Abbas I defeats the Turks in the north, conquers Baghdad and transfers his capital to Isfahan.

1694–1722   Shah Hussein, last of the Safavid line.

1736 to the present day

1736–1739	Nadir Shah, brilliant commander, becomes Shah; conquests in Afghanistan and India.
1750–1779	The Zand dynasty rules from Shiraz.
1779–1925	The Qajar dynasty, ruling from Tehran.
1925	Reza Shah (the Great) founds the Pahlavi dynasty and begins modernizing the country. He is succeeded by his son
1941	Mohammad Reza Shah, Pahlavi.
1951	The Shahanshah begins distributing his personal lands and follows this with his 12-point 'White Revolution' with its widespread reforms.
1967	The Coronation of H.I.M. Mohammad Reza Shahanshah Arya Mehr and, for the first time since the Sassanian era, of the ruler's consort, Empress Farah.
1971	Iran celebrates the 25th Centenary of the Foundation of the Persian Empire.

(Compiled, with amendments and revisions, from *Ancient Iran*, by Edith Porada in collaboration with R. H. Dyson, and *Persian Architecture* by Arthur Upham Pope.)

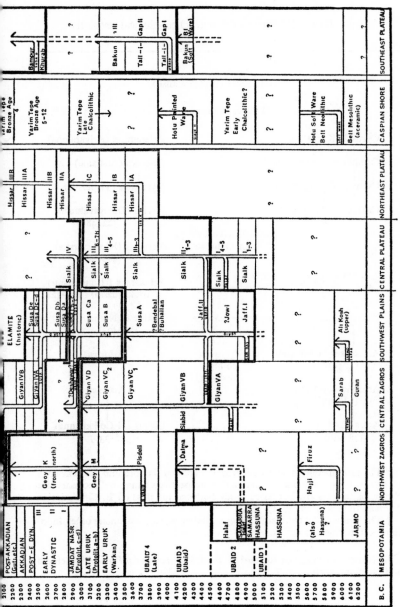

Ceramic traditions. Arrows show ongoing ceramic traditions; solid lines mark approximate beginning and end of major ceramic horizons; south-east plateau should be read as if next to central plateau. Caspian shore is an isolated unit. By courtesy of Professor Robert H. Dyson, Jr., from *Chronologies in Old World Archaeology*, 'Problems in the Relative Chronology of Iran, 6000–2000 B.C.'

GENEALOGY OF THE ACHAEMENIDS

(After Kent, *Old Persian* 158 with chronological revisions)

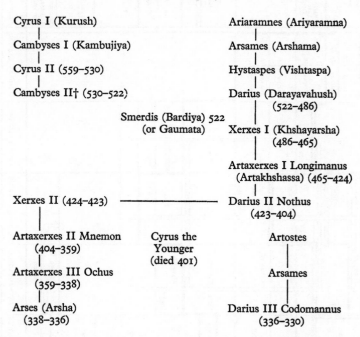

Achaemenes (Hakhamanish)

Teispes (Chishpish)*

Cyrus I (Kurush)

Cambyses I (Kambujiya)

Cyrus II (559–530)

Cambyses II† (530–522)

Smerdis (Bardiya) 522
(or Gaumata)

Ariaramnes (Ariyaramna)

Arsames (Arshama)

Hystaspes (Vishtaspa)

Darius (Darayavahush)
(522–486)

Xerxes I (Khshayarsha)
(486–465)

Artaxerxes I Longimanus
(Artakhshassa) (465–424)

Xerxes II (424–423) ———————— Darius II Nothus
(423–404)

Artaxerxes II Mnemon
(404–359)

Cyrus the
Younger
(died 401)

Artostes

Artaxerxes III Ochus
(359–338)

Arsames

Arses (Arsha)
(338–336)

Darius III Codomannus
(336–330)

* The introduction of another Cyrus and another Teispes into the genealogy of Cyrus I (his grandfather and father respectively) may be necessary for chronological reasons, but there is no evidence for this; cf. E. Cavaignac in *Journal Asiatique*, 239 (1951), 364.

† The naming of a child after his grandfather was known among other Indo-European peoples.

By courtesy of Professor Richard N. Frye, *The Heritage of Persia*, Weidenfeld and Nicolson, 1966.

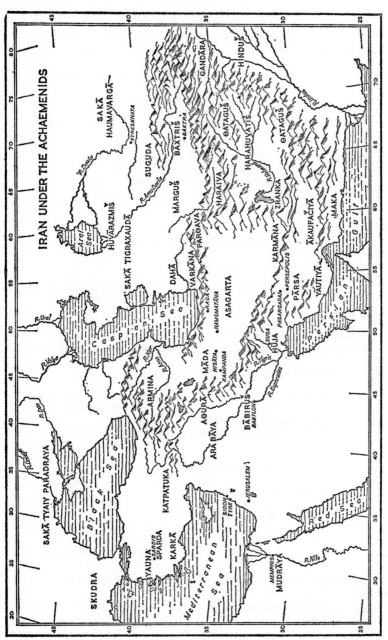

IRAN UNDER THE ACHAEMENIDS

By courtesy of Professor Richard N. Frye, *The Heritage of Persia*, Weidenfeld and Nicolson, 1966

TENTATIVE GENEALOGICAL TABLE OF
THE ARSACID KINGS

Arsaces I (*'ršk*) 247-? - - - - - Tiridates (*tyrdt*) *ca.* ?-211 BC
                                     Artabanus I (*'rtpn*) *ca.* 211-191 BC

                             Priapatius (*prypt*) *ca.* 191-176 BC

Mithradates I (*mtrdt*) - - - - -Phraates I (*prdh* or *prdty*) *ca.* 176-171 BC
ca. 171-138 BC

Phraates II *ca.* 138-128 BC - - - ?   Sinatrukes (*sntrwk*) *ca.* 80-69 BC
                                Gotarzes I (*gwtrz*) *ca.* 91-87? BC
                                Orodes I (*wrwd*) *ca.* ?-77 BC

Artabanus II *ca.* 128-123 BC   Phraates III *ca.* 69-57 BC

Mithradates II *ca.* 123-87 BC
               Orodes II *ca.* 57-37 BC - - - - -Mithradates III *ca.* 57-55 BC

Tiridates II   Phraates IV *ca.* 38-2 BC
ca. 30-25 BC
               Phraataces (*prdtk*) *ca.* 2 BC-AD 4 - - - Vonones I (*whwnm*?) *ca.*
                                                        AD 7-12

Orodes III *ca.* AD 4-7

Artabanus III *ca.* AD 12-38   Tiridates III *ca.* AD 36
Vardanes (*wrt'n*) *ca.* AD 39-47 - - - - Gotarzes II (*gwtrz*) *ca.* AD 38-51

Vonones II *ca.* AD 51

Vologeses I (*wlgš*) *ca.* AD 51-80   Pakores (*pkwr*?) *ca.* AD 79-115
                                               Oroses *ca.* AD 109-128

Artabanus IV *ca.* AD 80-81
Vologeses II *ca.* AD 105-147   Mithradates IV *ca.* AD
                                              128-147?

Vologeses III *ca.* AD 148-192

Vologeses IV *ca.* AD 191-207

Vologeses V *ca.* AD 207-227 (?)
                         - - - - Artabanus V *ca.* 213-224
                                      Artavasdes (*'rtwzd*) *ca.* 226-
                                      227?

Vertical lines mean father to son succession while horizontal lines mean blood or adopted brothers.

By courtesy of Professor Richard N. Frye, *The Heritage of Persia*, Weidenfeld and Nicolson, 1966.

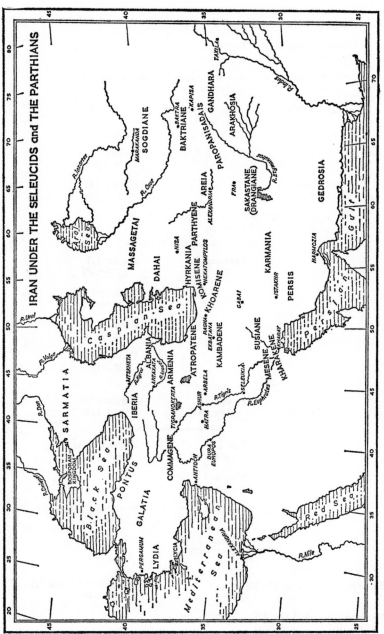

By courtesy of Professor Richard N. Frye, *The Heritage of Persia*, Weidenfeld and Nicolson, 1966

THE DYNASTY OF THE SASSANIANS*

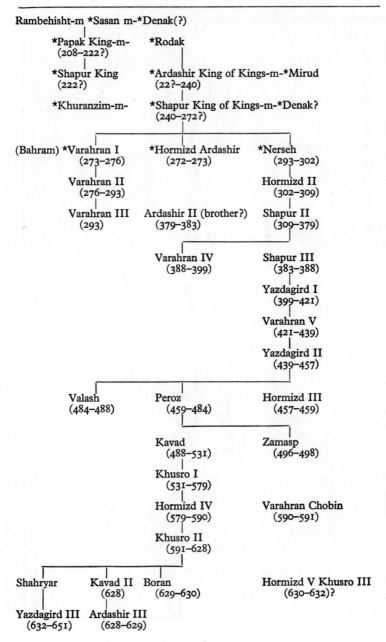

Rambehisht-m *Sasan m-*Denak(?)

*Papak King-m-   *Rodak
(208–222?)

*Shapur King   *Ardashir King of Kings-m-*Mirud
(222?)   (22?–240)

*Khuranzim-m-   *Shapur King of Kings-m-*Denak?
(240–272?)

(Bahram) *Varahran I   *Hormizd Ardashir   *Nerseh
(273–276)   (272–273)   (293–302)

Varahran II   Hormizd II
(276–293)   (302–309)

Varahran III   Ardashir II (brother?)   Shapur II
(293)   (379–383)   (309–379)

Varahran IV   Shapur III
(388–399)   (383–388)

Yazdagird I
(399–421)

Varahran V
(421–439)

Yazdagird II
(439–457)

Valash   Peroz   Hormizd III
(484–488)   (459–484)   (457–459)

Kavad   Zamasp
(488–531)   (496–498)

Khusro I
(531–579)

Hormizd IV   Varahran Chobin
(579–590)   (590–591)

Khusro II
(591–628)

Shahryar   Kavad II   Boran   Hormizd V Khusro III
           (628)   (629–630)   (630–632)?

Yazdagird III   Ardashir III
(632–651)   (628–629)

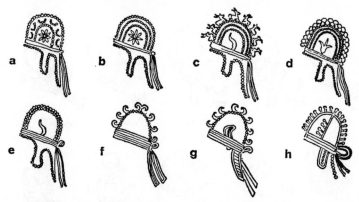

Fig. 44. SOME PARTHIAN (ARSACID) CROWNS. a. Mithradates II; b. Sinatrukes.
(Orodes I); c. Phraates III. (Sinatrukes and Phraates III); d. Unidentified king. (Phraates III); e. Mithradates III. (Darius); f. Volo-
gases II. (Vologases III); g. Vologases III. (Vologases IV); h. Vologases
V. Artavasdes. (Vologases VI, Artavasdes).
(*By courtesy of Dr. Hubertus von Gall,* 'Arsakidisches Diadem und
Parthische Bildkunst', Istanbuler Mitteilungen, Band 19/20. Berlin
1969–70.)
Identification by Warwick Wroth, 'A Catalogue of the Greek Coins in
the British Museum; Parthia', Bologna, 1964. Later identification in
brackets from David Sellwood, 'An Introduction to the Coinage o f
Parthia', London, 1971.

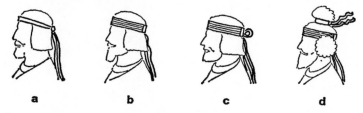

Fig. 45. PARTHIAN DIADEMS. a. Simple Hellenistic textile band (Tiridates I,
Orodes I); b. Ribbed band (Pakoros I. Phraates V); c. Ribbed band
with loops (Vonones I, Artabanos V); d. Diadem with band for hair
buff (Osroes and Vologases IV, V).
(*By courtesy of Dr. Hubertus von Gall.* 'Arsakidisches Diadem und
Parthische Bildkunst', Istanbuler Mitteilungen, Band 19/20. Berlin
1969–70)

Footnote to 'Dynasty of the Sassanians'
★ Names preceded by an asterisk are found in KZ, and -m- means married.
Rodak might be the name in the Shahname (Calcutta ed. 1.1365) where *rūdyāb*
is given as the patronymic of Papak unless a common noun meaning 'seized
liver' i.e. 'troubled' or 'agitated' is meant. (KZ=ka'aba-i Zardusht.)

By courtesy of Professor Richard N. Frye, *The Heritage of Persia,* Weidenfeld
and Nicolson, 1966.

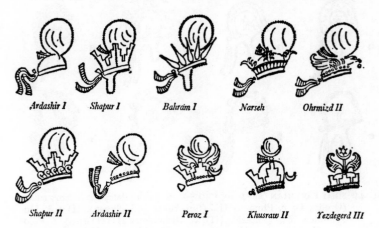

Ardashir I *Shapur I* *Bahram I* *Narseh* *Ohrmizd II*

Shapur II *Ardashir II* *Peroz I* *Khusraw II* *Yezdegerd III*

Fig. 46. STYLES OF SASSANIAN CROWNS (after Erdmann).
From *Ancient Iran,* Edith Porada.
(*By courtesy of the editors of* Ars Orientalis)

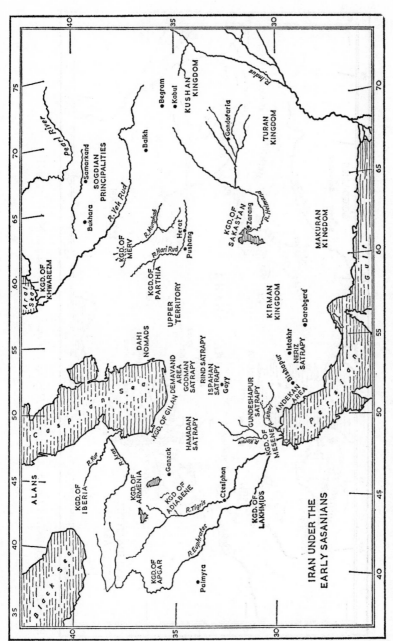

By courtesy of Professor Richard N. Frye, *The Heritage of Persia*, Weidenfeld and Nicolson, 1966

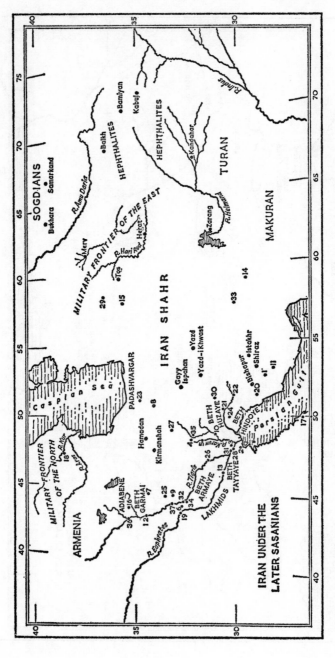

IRAN UNDER THE
LATER SASANIANS

By courtesy of Professor Richard N. Frye, *The Heritage of Persia*, Weidenfeld and Nicolson, 1966

THE spellings of names on the maps may vary slightly from the usually simplified forms in the text.

On map one, the locations of Thatagush- and Akaufachiya are uncertain. The locations of the following areas on map three are uncertain: Godman satrapy, Rind satrapy, Andekan area.

LIST OF CITIES UNDER THE LATER SASSANIANS

1 Ardashir Khwarreh or Gor (Firuzabad).
2 Astarabad Ardashir, or Wahishtabad Ardashir or Karka da Maishan (in Mesene).
3 Awaz Kawad or Izad Kawad or Nehargur (Madhar) near Ahwaz.
4 Eran Asan Kart Kawad or Karka da Redan (Ivan-e Karkha).
5 Eran Khwarreh Shahpuhr (Susa under Shahpuhr II).
6 Eran Khwarreh Khusro (near Ctesiphon?).
7 Eran Shad Kawad (near Khaniqin).
8 Eran Winart Kawad (Qumm).
9 Dastagerd-e Khusro or Dastagerd-e Malik (Eski Baghdad).
10 Hormizd Ardashir (Ahwaz).
11 Kawad Khwarreh (south of Gor, Karezin?).
12 Karkha da Peroz (north of Samarra).
13 Khusro Shad Hormizd (Uruk?).
14 New Hormizd Ardashir or Narmashir (in Kirman east of Bam).
15 New Shahpuhr or Abrshahr (Nishapur).
16 Nod Ardashir (near Arbela).
17 Panyat or Pasa Ardashir (Khatt or al-Qatif).
18 Peroz Kawad (Bardha or Perozapat in Armenian).
19 Peroz Shahpuhr or Faishabur (al-Anbar).
20 Ram Ardashir or Ramishn Ardashir (Tawwaj?).
21 Ram Hormizd (Ardashir) (Ramuz in Khuzistan).
22 Vam Kawad, also called Weh Amid Kawad (Arrajan).
23 Ram Peroz (near Rayy).
24 Rew Ardashir (Rishahr in Khuzistan or al-Rumiyya).
25 Roshan Kawad or Roshan Khusro, or Khusro Roshan Kawad (Zengabad on the Diyala River).
26 Roshan Peroz (in the Kashkar district of Iraq).
27 Shahpuhr Khwast (south of Khurramabad in Luristan?).

28 Shad Shahpuhr or Rema ('Ubulla).
29 Shahr Ram Peroz (near Abiward).
30 Wahisht Hormizd (near Malamir in Khuzistan).
31 Wahuman Ardashir (near Basra).
32 Weh Ardashir (Seleukia on the Tigris).
33 Weh Ardashir or Bardashir (Kirman).
34 Weh Antiok Khusro or Rumagan or Rumiyan (near Ctesiphon).
35 Weh Antiok Shahpuhr or Gundeshapur.
36 Weh Hormizd Kawad (Mosul), the same as Weh Kawad on Tigris?
37 Wuzurg Shahpuhr ('Ukbara).

Other sites include Kam Peroz between Kazerun and Firuzabad and Mihragan Katak in Media between Hamadan and Hulwan.

Appendix 3 : Godin Project Chronology

Estimate Date	Godin Project Period Name	Godin Tepe Deep Sounding	Seh Gabi
A.D. 1800– present	Recent	I	Mounds C? and D?
750–550 B.C.	Median	II	....
1300–1000 B.C.	Iron I	(2 graves south Outer Town flat)	Mound D?
2400–1300	Godin	III	....
2950–2400	Yanik	IV	Scattered sherds
3200–3000	BRB (Bevel Rim Bowl)	V	Flat between Mounds A and E
3500–3200	Cheshmeh Nush	VI	Upper Mound E, Mound F and G
3700–3500	Hosseinabad	VII	Lower Mound E, Mound A and F?
3850–3700	Taherabad	VIII	....
4100–3850	Seh Gabi	IX	Upper Mound B and Mound G?
4600–4100	Dalma	X	Lower Mound B
5000?–4600	Kucheh	XI	....
6000?–5500?	Shahnabad	....	Mound C

325

Bibliography

(Numbers apply to publications referred to in the text.)

(1) ADAMS, Robert Mc. C. and Donald P. HANSEN. 'Archaeological Reconnaissance and Soundings in Jundi Shahpur', *Ars Orientalis*, Chicago, Ann Arbor, 1968.

(2) AMIET, Pierre. *Elam*, Paris, 1966.

(3) ARNE, T. J. *Excavations at Shah Tepe, Iran*, Stockholm, 1945.

(4) ASLANAPA, O. and R. NAUMANN (eds.), *Forschungen zur Kunst Asiens*, (in memoriam Kurt Erdmann), Istanbul, 1969.

(5) ATARASHI, Kikuo, and Kiyoharu HORIUCHI. *Excavations at Tepe Suruvan in 1959—Report 4*, Tokyo, 1960.

(6) AZARPAY, Guitty. *Urartian Art and Artifacts—A Chronological Study*, Berkeley, 1967.

(7) BEAZLEY, Elisabeth, and Samuel STERN, 'The Castle of Khan Lanjan', *Iran*, Vol. IX, London, 1971.

(8) BIVAR, A. D. H. and S. SHAKED. 'The Inscriptions at Shimbar', *Bulletin of the School of Oriental and African Studies*, Vol. XXVII, Part 2, London, 1964.

(9) BIVAR, A. D. H. and G. FEHERVARI. 'The Walls of Tammisha', *Iran*, Vol. IV, London, 1966.

(10) BIVAR, A. D. H. 'A Hoard of Ingot-Currency of the Median Period from Nush-i Jan', *Iran*, Vol. IX, London, 1971.

(11) BOYCE, Mary. 'The Legend of Bibi Shahrbanu', *Bulletin of The School of Oriental and African Studies*, Vol. XXX, Part I, London, 1967.

(12) BRAIDWOOD, Robert J. 'First Steps Towards a Food-Producing Way of Life in Late Prehistoric Iran, *Archaeologia Viva*, Vol. I, No. 1, Paris, 1968.

(13) BURNEY, Charles A. 'The Excavations at Yanik Tepe, Azerbaijan, 1962: Third Preliminary Report', *Iraq*, XXVI, London, 1964.

(14) BURNEY, Charles A. 'Excavations at Haftavan Tepe 1973: Fourth Preliminary Report', *Iran*, Vol. XIII, London, 1975.

(15) BURTON BROWN, T. *Excavations in Azarbaijan, 1948*, London, 1951.

(16) BURTON BROWN, T. 'Excavations in Shahriyar, Iran', *Archaeology*, Vol. 15, No. 1, New York, 1962.

(17) CALDWELL, Joseph and C. C. LAMBERG-KARLOVSKY. 'Recent

Trends in the Archaeology of Southeastern Iran', *Asia Bulletin* (Journal of the Asia Institute, Pahlavi University, Shiraz), A. U. Pope Memorial Volume, 1971.

(18) CALDWELL, Joseph R. et al. *Investigations at Tal-i Iblis*, Illinois State Museum Preliminary Report No. 9, Springfield, Illinois, 1967.

(19) CAMERON, George. *Persepolis Treasury Tablets*, Oriental Institute Publications, LXV, Chicago, 1948.

(20) CLEVENGER, W. M. 'Some Minor Monuments in Khurasan', *Iran* VI, London, 1968.

(21) COLLEDGE, Malcolm A. R. *The Parthians*, London, 1967.

(22) CONTENAU, George and Roman GHIRSHMAN. *Fouilles du Tépé Giyan, près de Néhavand, 1931 et 1932*, Paris, 1935.

(23) COON, Carleton S. *Cave Explorations in Iran, 1949*, Philadelphia, 1951.

(24) COON, Carleton S. *Seven Caves*, New York and London, 1957.

(25) CRAWFORD, Vaughn E. 'Beside the Kara Su', *Bulletin of the Metropolitan Museum of Art*, April 1963, New York.

(26) CRAWFORD, Vaughn E. 'Excavations in Iraq and Iran', *Archaeology*, Vol. 16, New York, 1963.

(27) DALTON, O. M. *The Treasure of the Oxus*, 3rd edition, London, 1964.

(28) DE CARDI, Beatrice. 'The Bampur Sequence in the third millennium B.C.', *Antiquity*, Vol. XLI, Cambridge, 1967.

(29) DE CARDI, Beatrice. 'Bampur, a Third Millennium Site in Persian Baluchistan', *Archaeologia Viva*, Vol. I, No. 1, Paris, 1968.

(30) DE CARDI, Beatrice. 'Excavations at Bampur. A Third Millennium Settlement in Persian Baluchistan, 1966.' *Anthropological Papers of the American Museum of Natural History*, New York, 1970–71.

(31) DELOUGAZ, Pinhas and Helene J. KANTOR, 'New Light on the Emergence of Civilization in the Near East', *Courier*, Vol. I, No. 4, (UNESCO), Paris, 1969, & 'Chogha Mish', *Iran*, Vol. XIII, London, 1975.

(32) DESHAYES, Jean. 'Céramiques Peintes de Tureng Tépé', *Iran*, Vol. V, London, 1967.

(33) DESHAYES, Jean. 'Tureng Tepe and the Plain of Gorgan in the Bronze Age', *Archaeologia Viva*, Vol. I, No. 1, Paris, 1968.

(34) DESHAYES, Jean. 'New Evidence for the Indo-Europeans from Tureng Tepe', *Archaeology*, Vol. 22, No. 1, New York, 1969.

(35) DESHAYES, Jean. 'Tureng Tepe: 10th Campaign', *Iran*, Vol. XII, London, 1974.

(36) DIEULAFOY, Marcel. *L'Art Antique de la Perse*, Vols. I–V, Paris, 1884–85.

(37) DIEZ, Ernst. *Churasanische Baudenkmäler*, Berlin, 1918.

(38) DYSON, Robert H., Jr. 'Death of a City', *Expedition*, Pennsylvania, 1960.

(39) DYSON, Robert H., Jr. 'Problems of Protohistoric Iran as seen from Hasanlu', *Journal of Near Eastern Studies*, Vol. XXIV, No. 3, Chicago, 1965, & 'Hasanlu Excavations', report, *Iran* XI, 1973.

(40) DYSON, Robert H. 'The Burned Building of Tepe Hissar IIIB; a Re-statement', *Bastan Chenassi va Honar-e Iran*, No. 9–10, Tehran, Dec. 1972.

(41) DYSON, Robert H., Jr. 'The Archaeological Evidence of the Second Millennium B.C. on the Persian Plateau', *Cambridge Ancient History*, Fasc. No. 66, Cambridge, 1968.

(42) DYSON, Robert H., Jr. 'Hasanlu and the Solduz and Ushnu Valleys', *Archaeologia Viva*, Vol. I, No. 1, Paris, 1968.

(43) DYSON, Robert H., Jr. 'Annotations and Corrections of the Relative Chronology of Iran, 1968', *American Journal of Archaeology*, Vol. 72, 1969.

(44) EGAMI, Namio and Seiichi MASUDA. *Marv Dasht I, Excavations at Tall-i-Bakun, 1956*, Tokyo, 1962.

(45) EGAMI, Namio and Toshihiko SONO. *Marv Dasht II, the Excavations at Tall-i-Gap, 1959*, Tokyo, 1962.

(46) EGAMI, Namio, Shinji FUKAI and Seiichi MASUDA. *Dailaman I: Excavations at Ghalekuti and Lasulkan in 1960*, Tokyo, 1965.

(47) EGAMI, Namio, Shinji FUKAI and Seiichi MASUDA. *Dailaman II: Excavations at Noruzmahale and Khoramrud, 1960*, Tokyo, 1966.

(48) EHRICH, Robert W. (ed.). *Chronologies in Old World Archaeology*, Chicago and London, 1965.

(49) ERDMANN, Kurt. 'Das Iranische Feuerheiligtum', *Sendschriften der Deutschen Orient-Gesellschaft* 11, Leipzig, 1941.

(50) ERDMANN, Kurt. *Die Kunst Irans zur zeit Der Sasaniden*, Berlin, 1943 (reprinted 1969).

(51) FAIRSERVIS, Walter A., Jr. 'Archaeological Studies in the Seistan Basin of Southwestern Afghanistan and Eastern Iran', *Anthropological Papers of the American Museum of Natural History*, Vol. XLVIII, Part 1, New York, 1961.

(52) FLANDIN, E. and P. COSTE. *Voyage en Perse Ancienne* (6 vols.), Paris, 1843–54.

(53) FRYE, Richard N. *The Heritage of Persia*, Cleveland, 1963.

(54) GALL, H. Von. 'Zu den "Medischen" Felsgräbern in Nordwest-Iran und Iraqi Kurdistan', *Archaeologischer Anzeiger*, Berlin, 1966.

(55) GHIRSHMAN, Roman. *Fouilles de Sialk, près de Kashan* (2 vols.), Paris, 1938–39.

(56) GHIRSHMAN, Roman. *Bichâpour II, Les Mosaïques Sassanides*, Paris, 1956.

(57) GHIRSHMAN, Roman. *The Island of Kharg*, Tehran, 1965.

(58) GHIRSHMAN, Roman. *Iran from the Earliest Times to the Islamic Conquest*, Harmondsworth, 1954.

(59) GHIRSHMAN, Roman. *Persian Art: the Parthians and Sassanians*, London and New York, 1962.

(60) GHIRSHMAN, Roman. *Ancient Persia: from its Origins to the Time of Alexander the Great*, London and New York, 1964.

(61) GHIRSHMAN, Roman. 'Bard-e Nishandeh', *Illustrated London News*, June 26, London, 1965.

(62) GHIRSHMAN, Roman. *Tchogha Zanbil*, Vols. I–IV, Tome XXXIX, M.D.P., Paris, 1966.

(63) GHIRSHMAN, Roman. *La Terrasse Sacrée de Masjid-i Solaiman*, Paris, January, 1970.

(64) GHIRSHMAN, Roman. 'Masjid-i Solaiman', *Iran*, Vol. X, London, 1972.

(65) GNOLI, Gherard D. 'Richerche Storiche sul Sistan Antico' (English summary), Istituto Italiano per il Medio ed Estremo Oriente, Rome, 1967.

(66a) GODARD, André. 'Les Tombeaux de Maragha', *Athar-e Iran*, Tome I, Fasc. I, Paris, 1936.

(66b) GODARD, André. 'Abarquh', *Athar-e Iran*, Tome I, Fasc. I, Paris, 1936.

(66c) GODARD, André. 'Les Tours de Ladjim et de Resget', *Athar-e Iran*, Tome I, Fasc. I, Paris, 1936.

(67a) GODARD, André. 'Les Anciennes Mosquées de l'Iran', *Athar-e Iran*, Tome II, Fasc. I, Paris, 1937.

(67b) GODARD, André. 'Ardistan et Zaware', *Athar-e Iran*, Tome II, Fasc. I, Paris, 1937.

(67c) GODARD, André. 'Isfahan', *Athar-e Iran*, Tome II, Fasc. I, Paris, 1937.

(68) GODARD, André. 'Les Monuments du Feu', *Athar-e Iran*, Vol. III, Fasc. 1, Paris, 1938.

(69) GODARD, André. 'Badr-e Neshandé', *Athar-e Iran*, Vol. III, Fasc. 2, Paris, 1938.

(70) GODARD, André. *Le Trésor de Ziwiye*, Tehran, 1950.

(71) GODARD, André. *The Art of Iran*, London, 1965.

(72) GOFF, Clare. 'Excavations at Tall-i Nakhodi, 1963', *Iran*, Vol. II, London, 1964.

(73) GOFF, Clare. 'Excavations at Baba Jan, 1968: Third Preliminary Report', *Iran*, Vol. VIII, London, 1970.

(74) GRABAR, Oleg. Article on Sarvistan in *Forschungen zur Kunst Asiens* (in memoriam Kurt Erdmann), Istanbul, 1970.

(75) GROPP, G. 'Die Sassanidische Inschrift von Mishkinshahr in

Azarbaidjan', *Archaeologische Mitteilungen aus Iran*, Vol. I, Berlin, 1968.

(76) GULLINI, G. 'Architettura Iranica dagli Achemenidi ai Sasanidi', Turin, 1964.

(77) HAKEMI, Ali. 'Kaluraz and the Civilization of the Mardes', *Archaeologia Viva*, Vol. I, No. 1, Paris, 1968.

(78) HAKEMI, Ali. 'Shahdad', *Iran*, Vol. XI, London, 1973.

(79) HALLOCK, R. T. 'Persepolis Fortification Tablets', *Oriental Institute Publications*, Vol. XCII, Chicago, 1970.

(80) HANSMAN, John and David STRONACH. 'Excavations at Shahr-i Qumis, 1967', *Journal of the Royal Asiatic Society*, Part I, London, 1970.

(81) HANSMAN, John and David STRONACH. 'A Sassanian Repository at Shahr-i Qumis', *Journal of the Royal Asiatic Society*, Part II, London, 1970.

(82) HAUSER, W., J. M. UPTON, and C. K. WILKINSON. Reports on Nishapur. *Bulletin of the Metropolitan Museum of Art*, Vol. 37, New York, 1942.

(83) HENNING, W. B. 'The Monuments and Inscriptions of Tang-i Sarvak', *Asia Major*, N.S. II, 2, London, 1952.

(84) HENNING, W. B. (ed.). 'The Inscription of Sar-Mashad', *Corpus Inscriptionum Iranicarum*, Part III, Vol. III, Portfolio 1, London, 1955.

(85) HENNING, W. R. (ed.). 'The Inscription of Naqš-i Rustam', *Corpus Inscriptionum Iranicarum*, Part III, Vol. II, Portfolio II, London, 1957.

(86) HERRMANN, Georgina. 'The Darabgird Relief—Ardashir or Shahpur ?', *Iran*, Vol. VII, London, 1969.

(87) HERZFELD, Ernst. *Iranische Felsreliefs*, Berlin, 1910.

(88) HERZFELD, E. 'Die Gumbadh-i Alwiyyan und die Baukunst der Ilkhane in Iran', *Oriental Studies Presented to E. G. Browne*, Cambridge, 1922.

(89) HERZFELD, E. *Archaeological History of Iran*, London, 1935.

(90) HERZFELD, Ernst. *Iran in the Ancient East*, London, 1941.

(91) HILL, Derek and Oleg GRABAR. *Islamic Architecture and its Decoration, A.D. 800–1500* (2nd edition), London, 1967.

(92) HILLENBRAND, Robert. 'Islamic Monuments in Northern Iran', *Iran, VIII*, London, 1970, & 'Pir-e Takestan', *Iran*, Vol. X, London, 1972.

(93) HINZ, Walther. *Altiranische Funde und Forschungen*, Berlin, 1969.

(94) HOLE, Frank, Kent V. FLANNERY and James A. NEELY. 'Prehistory and Human Ecology of the Deh Luran Plain', *Memoirs of the Museum of Anthropology*, University of Michigan, No. 1, Ann Arbor, 1969.

(95) HOLE, Frank, Kent V. FLANNERY and James A. NEELY. *Excavations in the Deh Luran Plain*, Ann Arbor, 1970.

(96) HUFF, Dietrich. 'Takht-i Suleiman', *Iran*, Vols. VII–XII, London, 1969–74.

(97) HUTT, Antony. 'Islamic Monuments in Kirman and Khurasan Provinces', *Iran*, VIII, London, 1970.

(98) JONES, Rhys. 'Mammalian Remains from the Great Cave of Moghan', *Iran*, Vol. IV, London, 1966.

(99) KENT, R. G. *Old Persian Grammar: Text and Lexicon*, New Haven, 1953.

(100) KLEISS, Wolfram. 'Urartäische Plätze in Iranisch–Azerbaidjan', *Istanbuler Mitteilungen*, Band 18, Berlin, 1968.

(101) KLEISS, Wolfram. 'Das Armenische Kloster des Heiligen Stephanos in Iranische-Azerbaijan', *Istanbuler Mitteilungen*, Band 18, Berlin, 1968.

(102) KLEISS, Wolfram. 'Bericht über Erkundungsfahrten in Iran im Jahre 1971', *Archaeologische Mitteilungen aus Iran*, Neue Folge Band 5, Berlin, 1972.

(103) LAMBERG-KARLOVSKY, C. C. 'The Cairn Burials of South East Iran', *East and West*, Vol. 18, Nos. 3 and 4, Rome, 1968.

(104) LAMBERG-KARLOVSKY, C. C. 'Tepe Yahya', *Iran*, Vols. VIII–XII, London, 1971–4.

(105) LAMBERG-KARLOVSKY, C. C. and Maurizio TOSI. 'Shahr-i Sokhta and Tepe Yahya: Tracks on the Earliest History of the Iranian Plateau', *East and West*, Vol. 2, Nos. 1–2, Rome, 1973.

(106) LANE, Arthur. *Early Islamic Pottery*, London, 1947.

(107) LANGSDORFF, Alexander and Donald E. McCOWN. 'Tall-i Bakun A, Season of 1932', *Oriental Institute Publications*, Vol. LIX, Chicago, 1942.

(108) LAYARD, Henry. *Early Adventures in Persia, Susiana and Babylonia*, Vol. I, London, 1887.

(109) LE STRANGE, Guy. *Lands of the Eastern Caliphate* (2nd edition), London, 1930.

(110) LEWIS, Bernard. *The Assassins*, London, 1967.

(111) LOCKHART, L. *Persian Cities*, London, 1960.

(112a) LUSCHEY, H. 'Der Löwe von Ekbatana', *Deutsche Archaeologische Mitteilungen aus Iran*, N.S. Vol. I, Berlin, 1968.

(112b) LUSCHEY, H. 'Bisitun, Geschichte und Forschungsge-Schichte', *Archaeologische Anzeiger*, Berlin, 1974.

(112c) LUSCHEY, H. 'Zur Datierung der sasanidischen Kapitelle aus Bisitun und des Monuments von Taq-i-Bostan', *Deutsche Archaeologische Mitteilungen aus Iran*, Vol. I, N.S., Berlin, 1968.

(113) MALEKI, Yolande. 'Abstract Art and Animal Motifs', *Archaeoogia Viva*, Vol. I, Paris, 1968.

(114) McBURNEY, C. B. M. 'The Cave of Ali Tappeh', *Proceedings of the Prehistoric Society*, Vol. 34, Liverpool, 1968.

(115) MELDGAARD, Jørgen, Peder MORTENSEN, and Henrik THRANE. 'Excavations at Tepe Guran, Luristan', *Acta Archaeologica*, Vol. 34, Copenhagen, 1964.

(116) *Mémoires de la Délégation en Perse*. Tome I–XIII, Paris, 1900–12. *Mémoires de la Mission Archéologique de Susiane*. Tome XIV, Paris, 1913. *La Mission Archéologique de Perse*. Tome XV, Paris, 1914. *Mémoires de la Mission Archéologique de Perse, Mission de Susiane*. Tome XVI–XXVIII, Paris, 1921–39. *Mémoires de la Mission Archéologique en Iran, Mission de Susiane*. Tome XXIX–XXXVI, Paris, 1943–54. Tome XXXVIII, Paris, 1965. Tome XXXIX, Paris, 1966. Tome XL, Paris, 1968.

(117) MOGHADAM, Selma. *Suse et Tchoga Zanbil*, Tehran, 1963.

(118) MORIER, James. *A Journey Through Persia*, London, 1818.

(119) MOSTAFAVI, Seyed Mohamed Taqi. *Persian Architecture at a Glance*, Tehran, 1967.

(120) MUSCARELLA, Oscar White. 'The Iron Age at Dinkha Tepe, Iran', *Metropolitan Museum of Art Journal*, Vol. 9, New York, 1974.

(121) MUSCARELLA, Oscar White. 'The Tumuli at Se Girdan', *Bulletin of the Metropolitan Museum of Art*, Vol. II, New York, 1969.

(122) NEELY, James A. 'The Deh Luran Region', *Iran*, Vol. VIII, London, 1970.

(123) NEGAHBAN, Ezat O. *A Preliminary Report on Marlik Excavation 1961–1962*, Tehran, 1964.

(124) NICOL, Murray B. 'Darvazeh Tepe', *Iran*, Vol. IX, London, 1971.

(125) NYLANDER, C. 'Clamps and Chronology', *Iranica Antiqua*, Vol. VI, Leiden, 1966.

(126) OSTEN, H. H. von der and R. NAUMANN. 'Takht-i Suleiman, Vorläufiger Bericht über die Ausgrabungen, 1959', *Teheraner Forschungen*, Vol. I, Berlin, 1961.

(127) OSTEN, H. H. von der. *Die Welt der Perser*, Stuttgart, 1965.

(128) POPE, Arthur Upham (ed.). *A Survey of Persian Art from Prehistoric Times to the Present*, 6 volumes, 1938–39, London, New York (re-issued in 1967 in 13 volumes).

(129) POPE, Arthur Upham. *Persian Architecture*, London, 1965.

(130) PORADA, Edith. *Ancient Iran, The Art of Pre-Islamic Times*, London, 1965.

(131) ROGERS, J. M. 'The 11th Century—a Turning point in the Architecture of the *Mashriq*?', in *Islamic Civilisation 950–1150*, ed. D. S. Richards, Cassirer, Oxford, 1973.

(132) SAMI, Ali. *Pasargadae*, Shiraz, 1956.

(133) SAMI, Ali. *Persepolis* (*Takht-e Jamshid*), Shiraz, 1967.

(134) SARRE, Friedrich and Ernst HERZFELD. *Iranische Felsreliefs, Aufnahmen und Untersuchungen von Denkmälern aus Alt- und Mittel- Persischer Zeit*, Berlin, 1910.

(135) SCERRATO, Umberto. 'Excavations at Dahan-i Ghulaman (Seistan Iran), First Preliminary Report (1962–63)', *East and West*, N.S., Vol. 16, Nos. 1–2, Rome, 1966.

(136) SCHIPPMANN, Klaus. 'Hinweise und Anmerkungen zu einigen Sasanidischen Monumenten', *Iran*, Vol. VII, London, 1969.

(137) SCHIPPMANN, Klaus. 'Eine Erkundungsreise in den Bach- tiaribergen', *Archaeologische Mitteilungen aus Iran*, Vol. III, Berlin, 1970.

(138) SCHIPPMANN, Klaus. *Die Iranischen Feuerheiligtümer*, Berlin, 1971.

(139) SCHMIDT, Erich F. *Excavations at Tepe Hissar, Damghan 1931–1933*, Philadelphia, 1937.

(140) SCHMIDT, Erich F. *Flights Over Ancient Cities of Iran*, Chicago, 1940.

(141) SCHMIDT, Erich F. *Persepolis I. Structures, Reliefs, Inscriptions*, Chicago, 1953.

(142) SCHMIDT, Erich F. *Persepolis II. Contents of the Treasury and other Discoveries*, Chicago, 1957.

(143) SCHMIDT, Erich F. *Persepolis III*, Chicago, 1970.

(144a) SIROUX, Maxime. 'Petit Monument Sasanide près de Kazerun', *Athar-e Iran*, Vol. III, Fasc. I, Paris, 1938.

(144b) SIROUX, Maxime. 'Takht-e Rustam et Takht-e Kaikaus', *Athar-e Iran*, Vol. III, Fasc. I, Paris, 1938.

(144c) SIROUX, Maxime. 'Le Kale Dukhtar de Shahrestanek', *Athar-e Iran*, Vol. III, Fasc. I, Paris, 1938.

(144d) SIROUX, Maxime. 'Le Temple Zoroastrien de Sharifabad', *Athar-e Iran*, Vol. III, Fasc. I, Paris, 1938.

(145) SIROUX, Maxime. 'Ateshgah près d'Isfahan', *Iranica Antiqua*, Vol. V, Fasc. I, Leiden, 1966.

(146) SIROUX, Maxime, 'Le Site d'Atesh-kouh près de Delijan', *Syria*, Vol. XLIV, Fascs. I and II, Paris, 1967.

(147) SIROUX, Maxime. 'Trois Monuments Inconnus de l'Iran Ancien', *Iranica Antiqua*, Vol. VII, Leiden, 1967.

(148) SMITH, Myron B. 'The Manars of Isfahan', *Athar-e Iran*, Vol. II, Fasc. 2, Paris, 1937.

(149) SMITH, Phillip E. L. 'Ghar-i Khar and Ganj-i Dareh', *Iran*, Vol. V, London, 1967.

(150) SMITH, Phillip E. L. 'Ganj-i Dareh Tepe', *Iran*, Vol. XIII, London, 1975.

(151) SONO, Toshihiko and Shinji FUKAI (ed.). *Dailaman III: Excavations at Hassani Mahale and Ghalekuti, 1964,* Tokyo, 1968.

(152) STARK, Freya. *The Valleys of the Assassins,* London, 1934.

(153) STEIN, Sir Aurel. *Innermost Asia,* Vol. II, Oxford, 1916 (second edition), 1928.

(154) STEIN, Sir Aurel. 'An Archaeological Tour in the Ancient Persis', *Iraq,* Vol. III, London, 1936.

(155) STEIN, Sir Aurel. *Archaeological Reconnaissances in North-Western India and South-Eastern Iran,* London, 1937.

(156) STEIN, Sir Aurel. *Old Routes of Western Iran,* London, 1940, reprint New York, 1969.

(157) STERN, S. M. 'The Inscriptions of the Kharraqan Mausoleums', *Iran,* Vol. IV, London, 1966.

(158) STEVENS, Sir Roger. *The Land of the Great Sophy,* London, 2nd edition, 1971.

(159) STRONACH, David. 'Excavations at Pasargadae, Third Preliminary Report', *Iran,* Vol. III, London, 1965.

(160) STRONACH, David. 'The Kuh-i Shahrak Fire Altar', *Journal of Near Eastern Studies,* Chicago, October, 1966.

(161) STRONACH, David. 'Excavations at Ras al 'Amiya', *Iraq,* Vol. 23, Part II, London, 1966.

(162) STRONACH, David and T. Cuyler YOUNG, Jr. 'Three Octagonal Seljuq Tomb Towers from Iran', *Iran,* Vol. IV, London, 1966.

(163) STRONACH, David. 'Urartian and Achaemenian Tower Temples', *Journal of Near Eastern Studies,* Chicago, October, 1967.

(164) STRONACH, David. 'Tepe Nush-i Jan, a Mound in Media', *The Bulletin of the Metropolitan Museum of Art,* Vol. XXVII, New York, 1968.

(165) STRONACH, David. 'Tepe Nush-i Jan', *Iran,* Vol. XIII, London, 1975, and with Michael ROAF, *Iran,* Vol. XII, London, 1974.

(166) SYKES, Sir Percy M. *10,000 Miles in Persia or Eight Years in Iran,* London, 1902.

(167) THRANE, Henrik. 'Archaeological Investigations in Western Luristan', *Acta Archaeologica,* Vol. XXXV, Copenhagen, 1964.

(168) THRANE, Henrik. 'Tepe Guran and the Luristan Bronzes', *Archaeology,* New York, Jan., 1970.

(169) TILIA, Ann Britt. 'Studies and Restorations at Persepolis and other sites of Fars', *Reports and Memoirs,* Vol. XVI, IsMEO, Rome, 1972.

(170) TILIA, Ann Britt. 'Reconstruction of the Parapet on the Terrace Wall at Persepolis, South and West of Palace H.', *East and West,* N.S., Vol. 19, Nos. 1–2, Rome, 1969.

(171) TOSI, Maurizio. 'Excavations at Shahr-i Sokhta, a Chalcolithic

Settlement in the Iranian Sistan. Preliminary Report on the First
Campaign, October-December, 1967', *East and West*, N.S., Vol. 18,
Nos. 1–2, Rome, 1968.

(172) VANDEN BERGHE, Louis. *Archéologie de L'Iran Ancien* (includes 'Bibliographie par Régions et par Sites'), Leiden, 1959.

(173) VANDEN BERGHE, L. 'Récentes Découvertes de Monuments
Sassanides dans le Fars', *Iranica Antiqua I*, Leiden, 1961.

(174) VANDEN BERGHE, L. (a) 'Les Reliefs Elamites de Malamir',
Iranica Antiqua, Vol. III, Leiden, 1963. (b) 'Les Reliefs de Hung-i
Nauruzi', *Iranica Antiqua*, Vol. III, Leiden, 1963.

(175) VANDEN BERGHE, L. *La Nécropole de Khurvin*, Istanbul, 1964.

(176) VANDEN BERGHE, L. 'Nouvelles Découvertes de Monuments du
Feu d'Epoque Sassanide', *Iranica Antiqua*, Vol. V, Fasc 2, Leiden,
1965.

(177) VANDEN BERGHE, L. 'On the Track of the Civilizations of
Ancient Iran', *Memo From Belgium*, No. 104–105, Brussels, 1968.

(178) VANDEN BERGHE, L. 'Luristan, from Bani Surmah to War
Kabud', *Archaeologia Viva I*, Paris, Sept., 1968.

(179) VANDEN BERGHE, L. 'La Nécropole de Kulleh Nisar', *Archeologia*, Paris, Jan.–Feb., 1970.

(180) WHITEHOUSE, David, and Andrew WILLIAMSON. 'Sassanian
Maritime Trade', *Iran*, Vol. XI, London, 1973, and 'Siraf', *Iran*,
Vols. VIII–XIII, London, 1970–5.

(181) WILBER, Donald N. *Persepolis: the Archaeology of Parsa, Seat
of the Persian Kings*, London, 1969.

(182) WILBER, Donald N. *Architecture of Islamic Iran: the Il-Khanid
Period*, Holloway, 1969.

(183a) WILLEY, Peter. *The Castles of the Assassins*, London, 1963.

(183b) WILLEY, Peter. *The Assassins of Central Asia*, London, 1971.

(184) WILKINSON, Charles K. 'The Achaemenian Remains at Qasr-i
Abu Nasr', *Journal of Near Eastern Studies*, Vol. XXIV, Chicago,
October, 1965.

(185) WILLIAMS, E. Crawshay. *Across Persia*, London, 1907.

(186) WULSIN, F. R. 'Excavations at Tureng Tepe, Near Asterabad',
supplement to *The Bulletin of the American Institute for Persian Art and
Archaeology*, New York, 1932.

(187) YOUNG, T. Cuyler, Jr., and P. E. L. SMITH, 'Research in the Prehistory of Central Western Iran', *Science*, Vol. 153, Washington, 1966.

(188) YOUNG, T. Cuyler, Jr., and Louis D. LEVINE. 'Excavations of the
Godin Project: 2nd Progress Report,' *Royal Ontario Museum Art &
Archaeology Occasional Paper 26*, R. O. M., 1974, and *Iran*, Vol. XII,
London, 1974.

Additional Recommended Reading

AMIET, Pierre. 'La Civilisation du Désert de Lut', *Archeologia*, No. 60, Paris, July 1973.

ARBERRY, A. J. (ed.) *The Legacy of Persia*, Oxford, 1953.

Archaeologia Iranica, Vol. VII *Miscellanea in Honorem R. Ghirshman*, Leiden, 1970.

Archaeologische Mitteilungen aus Iran, (A.M.I.) Neue Folge Band 6, Berlin, 1973.

BAUSONI, A. *The Persians*, London, 1971.

BIVAR, A. D. H., *Catalogue of the Western Asiatic Seals in the British Museum. Stamp Seals, II, the Sassanian Dynasty*, London, 1969.

BIVAR, A. D. H. and G. Fehervari. 'Ghubayra', *Iran*, Vol. XIII, London, 1975.

BLUNT, W. *Isfahan, Pearl of Persia*, London, 1966.

BULGARELLI, Grazia Maria. 'Tepe Hissar', *Iran*, Vol. XI, London, 1973.

CALMEYER, Peter. *Datierbare Bronzen aus Luristan und Kirmanshah*, Berlin, 1965.

CALMEYER, Peter. 'Reliefbronzen in Babylonischen Stil', *Bayerische Akademie der Wissenschaften*, Munich, 1973.

CAMERON, George G. *History of Early Iran*, Chicago and London, 1936.

CASAL, Jean-Marie. 'Fouilles de Mundigak', Vols. I and II, *Mémoires de la Délégation Archéologique Française en Afghanistan*, Tome XVII, Paris, 1961.

CHRISTENSEN, A. *L'Iran Sous les Sassanides*, (2nd edition), Copenhagen, 1944.

CULICAN, William. *The Medes and Persians*, London, 1965.

CULICAN, William. *Imperial Cities of Persia. Persepolis, Susa and Pasargadae*, London, 1970.

CURZON, G. *Persia and the Persian Question*, (2 vols.), London, 1892.

DE WAELE, Eric. 'Les Reliefs Rupestres d'Izeh, Malamir', *Archeologia*, No. 60, Paris, July 1973.

ERDMANN, Kurt. 'Die Entwicklung der Sasanidischen Krone', *Ars Islamica*, Vols. XV–XVI, Ann Arbor, 1951.

FARD, Kambakhsh. 'Fouilles Archéologiques à Kangavar. Le Temple d'Anahita', *Bastan Chenassi va Honar-e Iran*, Nos. 9–10, Tehran, December 1972.

FRANKFORT, Henri. *The Art and Architecture of the Ancient Orient*, London, 1954.

FRYE, Richard Nelson (ed.). *Bulletin of the Asia Institute*, Shiraz.

GABRIEL, A. *Die Erforschung Persiens*, Vienna, 1952.

GALDIERI, Eugenio. *Isfahān: Masǧid-i Ǧumʿa*, 2. *The Al-i Būyid Period*, IsMEO, Rome, 1973.

GOFF, Clare L. 'Neglected Aspects of Luristan Art', *Persica*, Vol. V, The Hague, 1970–1.

GOFF, Clare L. 'Luristan before the Iron Age', *Iran*, Vol. IX, London, 1971.

GOLOMBEK, Lisa. 'The chronology of Turbat-i Shaikh Jam', *Iran*, Vol. IX, London, 1971.

HAMLIN, Carol. 'The Early Second Millennium Ceramic Assemblage of Dinkha Tepe', *Iran*, Vol. XII, London, 1974, and 'Dalma Tepe', *Iran*, Vol. XIII, London, 1975.

HANSMAN, John. 'Elamites, Achaemenians and Anshan', *Iran*, Vol. X, London, 1972.

HAWKER, C. L. (ed.) *Simple Colloquial Persian*, London (2nd edition), 1941. Reprinted 1961.

HERODOTUS. *The Histories* (translated by A. de Selincourt), Harmondsworth, 1955.

HINZ, Walther. 'Persia, c. 2400–1800', *Cambridge Ancient History*, Fasc. 19, Cambridge, 1963.

HINZ, Walther. 'Persia, c. 1800–1550 B.C.', *Cambridge Ancient History*, Fasc. 21, Cambridge, 1964.

HINZ, Walther. *Das Reich Elam*, Stuttgart, 1964.

HOUT, Jean-Louis. *Persia. Vol. I, From its Origins to the Achaemenids*, London, 1965.

HUFF, Dietrich. 'Firuzabad', *Istanbuler Mitteilungen*, Band 19/20, Berlin, 1969–70.

HUFF, Dietrich. 'Der Takht-i Nishin in Firuzabad', *Archaeologischer Anzeiger*, Heft 3, Berlin, 1972.

HUFF, Dietrich. 'Das Felsengrab von Fakhrikah', *Istanbuler Mitteilungen*, Band 21, Berlin, 1971.

HUFF, Dietrich. 'Qal'a-ye Dukhtar bei Firuzabad', *Archaeologische Mitteilungen aus Iran*, Neue Folge Band 4, Berlin, 1971.

HUFF, Dietrich. 'Firuzabad' report, *Iran*, Vol. XI, London, 1973.

Iran, Les Guides Nagel, Geneva, 1973.

JACKSON, A. V. W. *Persia, Past and Present*, Norwood, Massachusetts, 1906.

KEALL, E. J. 'Qal'eh-i Yazdigird', *Iran*, Vol. V, London, 1967.

KLEISS, Wolfram. Reports on Qurveh and Takestan. *Archaeologische Mitteilungen aus Iran*, Neue Folge Band 4, Berlin, 1971.

KLEISS, Wolfram. Reports on Bastam, Leilan, Kale Zohak, etc. *Archaeologische Mitteilungen aus Iran*, Neue Folge Band 6, Berlin, 1973.

LABAT, René. 'Elam and Western Persia, *c.* 12–1000 B.C.', *Cambridge Ancient History*, Fasc. 23, Cambridge, 1964.

LE BRETON, Louis. 'The Early Periods at Susa, Mesopotamian Relations', *Iraq*, Vol. XIX, London, 1957.

LUKONIN, W. G. *Persia, II. From the Seleucids to the Sassanians*, London, 1971.

MALLOWAN, M. E. L. *Early Mesopotamia and Iran*, London, 1965.

MASUDA, Seiichi. 'Excavation at Tappe Sang-e Čaxamaq'. *Proceedings of 1st Annual Symposium of Archaeological Research in Iran*, Iran Bastan Museum, Tehran, November 1972, and report in *Iran*, Vol. XII, London, 1974.

Memorial Volume (I) of the Vth International Congress of Iranian Art and Archaeology, 1968. Tehran, 1972.

MIDDLE EAST, The. Hachette World Guides, Paris, 1966.

MORRIS, James, Roger WOOD and Denis WRIGHT. *Persia*, London, 1969 (and Tehran, 1969, title *Iran*).

MORTENSEN, Peder. 'The Hulailan Survey', *Iran*, Vol. XIII, 1975.

MUSCARELLA, Oscar White. 'Excavations at Agrab Tepe, Iran', *Metropolitan Museum of Art Journal*, Vol. 8, New York, 1974.

NAUMANN, Rudolf. 'Takht-i Sulaiman', *Iran*, Vol. XIII, London, 1975.

NEYSARI, Salim. *English-Persian Phrase Book*, (2nd edition), Tehran, 1962.

OLMSTEAD, T. *History of the Persian Empire*, Chicago, 1948.

POPE, Arthur Upham. *Introducing Persian Architecture*, Shiraz, 1969.

RYPKA, J. *Persische Literaturgeschichte*, Leipzig, 1959.

SEHERR-THOSS, Sonia P. and Hans C. *Design and Colour in Islamic Architecture*, Washington, 1968.

SELLWOOD, David. *An Introduction to the Coinage of Parthia*, London, 1971.

SIROUX, Maxime. 'Anciennes Voies et Monuments Routiers de la Région d'Ispahan', *L'Institut Français d'Archéologie Oriental du Caire*, Vol. LXXXII, Cairo, 1971.

STRONACH, David. 'A Case for Building Rites in 7th/6th century B.C. Media?', *Proceedings of the 2nd Annual Symposium of Archaeological Research in Iran*, Iran Bastam Museum, Tehran, November 1973.

STRONACH, David. 'Description and Comment. Une Statue de Darius Découverte à Suse', *Journal Asiatique*, Paris, 1972.

SUMNER, W. M. 'Excavations at Tal-i Malyan, 1971–72', *Iran*, Vol. XII, London, 1974, and 'Malyan' (1974), *Iran*, Vol. XIII, London, 1975.

SYKES, Sir Percy M. *A History of Persia*, London, 1915 (reprint, 1963).

VANDEN BERGHE, L. 'La Signification Iconographique du Relief Rupestre Sassanide de Sarab-i Qandil (Iran)', *Paleis der Academien*, Brussels, 1973.

VANDEN BERGHE, L. 'Cinquième Campagne: 1969. Prospections dans le Pusht-i Kuh Central', *Iranica Antiqua*, Vol. IX, Leiden, 1972.

VANDEN BERGHE, L. 'Prospections Archéologiques dans le Pusht-i Kuh Central, VII (1971) et VIII (1972) campagnes', *Archeologia*, No. 63, Paris, 1973.

VANDEN BERGHE, L. 'La Necropole de Dum Gar, IX campagne (1973)', *Archeologia* No. 79, Paris, 1975.

VANDEN BERGHE, L. 'La Necropole de Hakalan, VII (1971) et VIII (1972) campagnes', *Archeologia*, No. 57, Paris, 1973.

VANDEN BERGHE, L. 'La Necropole de Kutal-i Gulgul. VII (1971) et VIII (1972) campagnes', *Archaeologia*, No. 65, Paris, 1973.

VON GALL, Hubertus. 'Arsacid Diadems', *Istanbuler Mitteilungen*, Band 19/20, Berlin, 1969/70.

WARD, Philip. *Touring Iran*, London, 1971.

WEISS, Harvey, and T. Cuyler YOUNG, Jr. 'The Merchants of Susa; Godin V and Plateau-Lowland Relations in the Late Fourth Millennium B.C.' *Iran*, Vol. XIII, London, 1975.

WHEELER, Sir Mortimer. *Flames Over Persepolis*, London, 1968.

WIDENGREN, G. *Die Religionen Irans*, Stuttgart, 1965.

WRIGHT, H. T., J. A. NEELY, G. A. JOHNSON and John SPETH, 'Early Fourth Millennium Developments in South-western Iran'. *Iran*, Vol. XIII, London, 1975.

ZAEHNER, R. C. *The Dawn and Twilight of Zoroastrianism*, London, 1961.

New Hotels and Restaurants

New hotels, tourist camps and restaurants seem to appear almost overnight now in all parts of Iran, just as roads and other forms of communication are improving so rapidly that a Guide such as this can only give an indication of conditions which must be checked with the appropriate Government organization for the latest information. The Tourist Organization in particular has been constructing much new tourist bungalow, hotel and camping accommodation along the Caspian and elsewhere in Iran.

Some of the newer restaurants and hotels noted during 1975 are listed below, excluding Tehran which would need a volume to itself: * indicates de luxe prices.

HOTELS:

Abadan: *Caravanserai; Abadan Persian Hotel (under construction 1975).

Ahwaz: *Royal Astoria.

Baluchistan: Khash, 40–bed Government Hotel planned (1975); Zahidan, 20–room Tourist Inn.

Caspian: *Hyatt Regency (under construction 1975), nr. Chalus; *Motel Sahara, Nowshara.

Isfahan: *Ali Qapu and *Dariush International, in Chahar Bagh; *Kurosh International on Julfa Bank. New Julfa Hotel near Armenian Cathedral (moderate prices).

Kerman: 60–room hotel under construction 1975.

Mashad: *Hyatt Omar Khayyam (and several variously priced under construction 1975).

Persepolis: *Darius Intercontinental.

Shiraz: *Cyrus Intercontinental; Court, Kh. Lotfullah Khan (very moderate prices).

RESTAURANTS:

Isfahan: Hazar-o Yek Shab (1001 Nights), 'Safavid' atmosphere, Chahar Bagh; Long Branch Saloon (American style food and drink), Apadana Avenue; Maharaja (Indian food), Chahar Bagh; Pamchal (Armenian bistro-style), Kurosh Boulevard near Pol-e Marnun; Pizza Palace (no alcohol), in Julfa near Cathedral, Luigi's (Italian, Mexican), Kurosh Boulevard.

Shiraz: Chen Chene (take-away and drive-in food), two branches, Bagh-e Nari and Ghasrodasht; '103', Kh. Anvari off Karim Khan Zand (pleasant 'traditional Persian' atmosphere); Pizza Shor, Karim Khan Zand.

Index

354 INDEX

Safavids–*continued*
  252; Shah Ismail, 26, 186, **296**;
  Shah Tahmasp, 55–6; Sheikh Safi
  al-Din, 71, 78, 184; arts, architec-
  ture, 26, 182–3; occupation, 26,
  182–3, 210, 264; tombs, 78, 169
Saffarids: dynasty, Taj al-Din the
  Elder, Malik Taj al-Din Harab, 283
Sahneh, tombs, 125
St. Bartholomew, 81
St. James, 86
St. Mary's, Rezaiyeh, 90; Tabriz, 79
St. Stephanos, 80
St. Thaddeus (*see* Tadios)
Sakavand (*see* Eshaqvand)
Saljuqs: dynasty, 25; Alp Arslan, 183,
  187; Mahmud, 187; Malik Shah,
  55, 69, 174, 183, 186–7, 188, 199;
  Sanjar, 98, 151, 206, **288–9**; Tughril
  Beg, 48, 183, 199; ministers, Nizam
  al-Mulk, 183, 185–6, 199; Taj al-
  Mulk, 185; art, architecture, 25–6,
  44–5, 47–8, 51, 55, 61, 66, 69–70,
  72, 78, 80, 90, 97, 99, 104, 107, 109,
  111, 115, 119, 151, 156, 167, 169,
  172–4, 179–87, 188–92, 192, 194–6,
  198–200, 203, 205–6, 260, 263–7,
  279, **288–9**, **295**, **296**, **298**, **299**;
  battles, occupation, 69, 109, 131,
  135, 271–2, 279; trade centre, 173;
  library, hospital, 198
Salles, G. A., 238
Salmas (*see* Sarmas)
Salzmann, W., 128
Samanids, 62
Sami, Ali, 216, 219, 226
Samiran (Darband), castles, tomb-
  towers, 58
Sanandaj (Sisar, Sinneh), 105–6
Sangan-i Pa'in, 205, **298–9**
Sangar, Urartian fortress, 82
Sangbast: tomb-tower of Arslan
  Jadhib, 62, 200–1; minaret, 200–1;
Sang-i Dukhtar, canal-head, 212
Sang-i Sanduk, fire altar, 213
Sang-i Siah, 245, **302**
Sanjar, Sultan (*see* Saljuqs)
Saqqiz, near Ziwiye citadel site, 96
Sarab Bahram bas-relief, 242
Sarab-i Qandil, bas-relief, 237–8
Sarakhs: Gonbad-i Sheikh Luqman,
  204

Sarbaz Kalat, castles, 274, 277
Sarfaraz, Ali Akbar, 14, 138, 162,
  237–41, 249, **302**
Sargon II (*see* Assyrians)
Sar-i Masjid (*see* Masjid-i Sulaiman)
Sar-i Pul-i Zuhab (Holvan), bas-
  reliefs, 135–6, **294**
Sarmas (Savus, Salmas), bas-relief,
  89
Sar Mashad, bas-relief, 256
Sarre, Friedrich, 221
Sarvistan (Khavristan): Imamzadeh
  Pol, 258; Palace of Bahram V, 51,
  137, 257, 258–9
Sassanians: dynasty, 24, 318; Ardashir
  I, 24–5, 89, 140, 221–2, 224, 253–4,
  261, 264, 266; his queen, 132, 222;
  Ardashir II, 130; Bahram I, 242;
  Bahram II, 50, 111, 212, 224–5,
  241–2, 256; Bahram IV, 131, 225;
  Bahram V Gur, 50, 111, 256, 259;
  Queen Boran, 281; Hormizd I,
  222; Hormizd II, 225, 246;
  Hormizd IV, 194; Kavad I, 197;
  Khusraw I, Anushirvan, 66–7, 157;
  Khusraw II, 128, 131, 137–8, 197;
  Narseh, 225, 242; Peroz, 131;
  Shahpur I, the Great, 25, 53, 89,
  119–20, 140, 149, 152, 156–7, 159,
  199, 220, 222–3, 225, 238–42, 254,
  261; Shahpur II, 130, 149, 152,
  157, 199, 202, 225, 231, 242,
  249; Shahpur III, 130–1; Queen
  Shireen, 137; Queen Shushan-
  Dukht, 111; Yazdigird I, 111, 182,
  256; Yazdigird II, 199; Yazdigird
  III, 25, 49, 115; Mehr Narseh,
  Minister, 256, 259; arts and
  architecture, 25, 42, 46, 50–1, 55,
  60–1, 66–70, 78, 89, 100, 102–4,
  119–20, 127–8, 136–8, 140, 150,
  152–4, 159–62, 172–3, 175–6, 179,
  181, 183, 185, 190, 195, 201, 205,
  211, 213, 221, 238–41, 243–62,
  266–7, 274, 278–9, 281–3, **289**, **296**,
  302; battles, occupation, 24–5, 47–
  50, 64, 77–8, 88, 96, 106, 109, 115,
  132, 139–40, 149, 154, 156, 169,
  175, 177, 182, 188, 191, 194, 197,
  199, 208, 210, 219, 221, 248, 264,
  268, 272, 278; bas-reliefs, inscriptions, 89, 211–12, 214, 220,